X Window System
Administrator's Guide

Volume Eight

X Window System
Administrator's Guide

---

for X Version 11

By Linda Mui and Eric Pearce

O'Reilly & Associates, Inc.

X Window System Administrator's Guide

Editor: Tim O'Reilly

Printing History:

October 1992:	First Edition.
February 1993:	Minor corrections.
July 1993:	Minor corrections.

Book Alone: ISBN 0-937175-83-8

Table of Contents

Chapter 3 The X Display Manager 43

Chapter 4 Security 73

Chapter 5 Font Management 101

Chapter 8 Building the X Window System 185

Appendix A Useful Things to Know 233

Appendix B Compiling Public Domain Software 247

Appendix G Error Messages 315

Figures

Tables

Preface

This preface outlines who should be reading this book, and what readers should expect from it.

In The Preface:

Preface

UNIX machines can be difficult to maintain. Traditionally, UNIX administration has meant juggling dozens of configuration files and supporting end users who may not understand how the system actually works. Because it is infinitely flexible, UNIX can be a power-user's paradise and a beginner's nightmare, with the administrator sandwiched somewhere in between.

This book is designed to bridge that gap. It provides detailed information and procedures for setting up a system that gives users access to the full power of X, without the headaches.

How to Use this Book

This book has been written to be useful to as many types of X Window System administrators as possible. Some readers are full-time system administrators at large academic sites who are well-versed in UNIX and X, but are always looking for new tips. Other readers are part-time administrators at smaller sites who know a good amount about UNIX and X but are tired of always having to reinvent the wheel. Still other readers are workstation owners who are forced to do their own administration, interested only in getting their system running smoothly.

Since this book is aimed at such a wide audience, not all readers will be interested in every chapter. If we tell you about platforms you don't use, issues that aren't relevant to you, or describe basic concepts with more detail than you need, we hope that you'll be patient and just skim through to find what you need to know.

Chapter 1, *An Introduction to X Administration*, briefly introduces the design of X, with emphasis on the administrative issues that arise out of that design. Beginners to X and X administration should read this chapter.

Chapter 2, *The X User Environment*, describes issues for configuring the X user environment. Readers who need to set up new users should read this chapter. This chapter is also a good place for readers who are new to X and need to learn more about how it works from the user's point of view.

Chapter 3, *The X Display Manager*, describes the X Display Manager (*xdm*) and how to configure it. Readers who are interested in running *xdm* should read this chapter.

Chapter 4, *Security*, describes security issues for X. We recommend that managers of all networked X environments study this chapter.

Chapter 5,   *Font Management*, describes issues with using and adding fonts, both under the standard methods and through the X11 Release 5 font server. Readers who are interested in adding fonts to their system or using a networked font server should read this chapter.

Chapter 6,   *Color*, describes how color works in X, and how to add new colors in both the RGB and Xcms color databases. Readers who have color displays may want to read this chapter to learn more about how color works and how it can be manipulated.

Chapter 7,   *X Terminals*, describes the different types of X terminals, how to set up the network for new X terminals, how to install fonts on the host, and how to reconfigure the host machine to support more processes. If you use or intend to use X terminals at your site, you should read this chapter.

Chapter 8,   *Building the X Window System*, describes the issues involved with building X from source. Readers who must build X from source, or who are interested in understanding more about the basic structure of the X software should read this chapter.

Appendix A,   *Useful Things to Know*, documents various "miscellaneous" procedures and odds-and-ends that many users will already be familiar with, but which we want to include for the benefit of those users who are not. This appendix shows how to *ftp* files, how to export NFS directories, how to add a hostname to your name server, etc. Browse through this chapter at least once to see if there's anything new in there; throughout the book, we refer to sections of this chapter when applicable.

Appendix B,   *Compiling Public Domain Software*, a tutorial, describes how to find and compile public domain software. Readers who aren't familiar with this process should read this appendix.

Appendix C,   *X Servers on Non-UNIX Platforms*, briefly describes issues with using X11 servers on DOS-based PC and Apple Macintosh machines. Readers who are interested in running X on these platforms should read this appendix.

Appendix D,   *Resources and Keysym Mappings*, provides a more thorough description of resources and keysym mappings. You can't work with X without needing to understand these topics at least a little bit, so we include some background here. Some of this material duplicates what you'll find in Volume Three, *X Window System User's Guide*, but we also give some useful tips and advanced information for administrators. So even if you are familiar with how to use resources, you may want to scan this appendix.

Appendix E,   *The Components of X Products*, lists the directory structure of MIT X11 and various vendors' implementations. Use this appendix as needed.

Appendix F,   *Getting X11*, lists sites that have made the X11 source code available. Reprinted from the *comp.windows.x* newsgroup Frequently Asked Questions list. Use this appendix if you need to obtain the X11 source code.

Appendix G,   *Error Messages*, lists some of the error messages users may encounter. Refer to this appendix when troubleshooting.

Assumptions

To get the most out of this book, you should be familiar with UNIX and with general principles of system and network administration. If you have never administered a UNIX system or a TCP/IP network, see the Nutshell Handbooks *Essential System Administration* by Æleen Frisch (O'Reilly & Associates, 1991) and *TCP/IP Network Administration* by Craig Hunt (O'Reilly & Associates, 1992).

A firm understanding of X is helpful. If you have never used X, you should have a copy of Volume Three, *X Window System User's Guide*, close at hand. However, we have included a lot of background information on X for the benefit of readers who have not had a formal introduction to X.

Readers are not expected to have any C programming experience, although UNIX shell programming experience may come in handy for understanding some of the examples.

Readers are assumed to have the X manpages available, or to be able to obtain them easily. (These pages are reprinted in the *X Window System User's Guide* and are also available online with many X distributions.) This book does not attempt to replace the X manpages.

Related Documents

The following Nutshell Handbooks published by O'Reilly & Associates, Inc. may also be helpful:

> *Managing Projects with make*, by Andy Oram and Steve Talbott
> *Managing NFS and NIS*, by Hal Stern
> *Practical UNIX Security*, by Simson Garfinkel and Gene Spafford
> *System Performance Tuning*, by Mike Loukides
> *DNS and BIND*, by Cricket Liu and Paul Albitz
> *The Whole Internet User's Guide and Catalog*, by Ed Krol
> *TCP/IP Network Administration*, by Craig Hunt

Several other books and a journal on the X Window System are available from O'Reilly & Associates, Inc.:

> Volume Zero — *X Protocol Reference Manual*
> Volume One — *Xlib Programming Manual*
> Volume Two — *Xlib Reference Manual*
> Volume Three — *X Window System User's Guide*, Motif and Standard editions
> Volume Four — *X Toolkit Intrinsics Programming Manual*, Motif
>   and Standard editions
> Volume Five — *X Toolkit Intrinsics Reference Manual*
> Volume Six — *Motif Programming Manual*
> Volume Seven — *XView Programming Manual*

PHIGS Programming Manual
PHIGS Reference Manual
Quick Reference — *The X Window System in a Nutshell*
The X Resource

In addition, each chapter ends with its own topical list of related documentation.

Font Conventions Used in This Book

Italics are used for:

- UNIX pathnames, hostnames, domain names, client and UNIX command names, and command-line options

- New terms where they are defined

- Emphasis

Typewriter Font is used for:

- Output in an example, i.e., prompts and messages from commands

- The contents of configuration files

- Flags used to build X

- Display names

- IP addresses

- Resource names

Bold Typewriter Font is used for:

- Input in an example, i.e., what the user types on a command line

- Highlighting lines of code

Helvetica Italics are used for:

- Titles of figures and tables

Helvetica Bold is used for:

- Chapter and section headings

We'd Like to Hear From You

We have tested and verified all of the information in this book to the best of our ability, but you may find that features have changed (or even that we have made mistakes!). Please let us know about any errors you find, as well as your suggestions for future editions, by writing:

```
O'Reilly & Associates, Inc.
103 Morris Street, Suite A
Sebastopol, CA 95472
1-800-998-9938 (in the US or Canada)
1-707-829-0515 (international/local)
1-707-829-0104 (FAX)
```

You can also send us messages electronically. To be put on the mailing list or request a catalog, send email to:

```
info@ora.com        (via the Internet)
uunet!ora!info      (via UUCP)
```

To ask technical questions or comment on the book, send email to:

```
bookquestions@ora.com   (via the Internet)
```

Bulk Sales Information

For information on volume discounts for bulk purchase, call O'Reilly & Associates, Inc. at 800-998-9938, or send e-mail to linda@ora.com (uunet!ora.com!linda).

For companies requiring extensive customization of the book, source licensing terms are also available.

Acknowledgments

Though it might seem a logical addition to our X Window System series, we didn't think up this book on our own. It was a customer call that set the project in motion. Scott Hunter of Oracle called up to ask if we had anything on X administration in the works. We said we didn't, but that we thought it was a great idea. Scott and his co-worker Mike Riggs outlined for us the kinds of problems they were facing that made such a book a necessity. We would like to thank Scott and Mike for their initial efforts in conceiving the book, as well as Mary Beth Hagan and Marilyn Grady, who did some of the initial research and writing before it fell into our laps.

We would also like to thank the technical reviewers for the first edition of this book. They were David Lewis; Jeffrey Vogel; Mike Braca of Visual Technology; Stephen Gildea of the X Consortium; Liam Quin and Ian Darwin of Softquad, Inc.; Doug Klein, Dave Lemke, and the staff at Network Computing Devices; Dave Curry of Purdue University; Dinah McNutt of Tivoli Systems; Miles O'Neal of Pencom; Jim Frost of CenterLine Software; Jon Werner of International Business Machines; Spencer Murray of Silicon Graphics, Inc.; Joe Ilacqua;

Valerie Quercia, David Flanagan and Adrian Nye of O'Reilly & Associates; Al Tabayoyan of North Valley Research; and Upesh Patel of The Santa Cruz Operation.

Our thanks to each of these reviewers for taking the time to make this book useful and complete. Additional thanks to David Tolman of Human Designed Systems and R. Lee Rainey of Tektronix for supplying information on their company's X terminals, and to Garry Paxinos of MetroLink, Inc. and Greg Mudge of PhoeniX Software Solutions for helping to clear up some details about running X on PC hardware. Also, thanks to Dave Curry, Chris Calabrese of AT&T Bell Labs, Joe Ilacqua, and David Lewis for supplying random number generation methods for use with the discussion of MIT-MAGIC-COOKIE-1 in Chapter 4. David Lewis was also kind enough to allow us to reprint the material in Appendix F from the *comp.windows.x* Frequently Asked Questions list that he maintains.

Several vendors were kind enough to lend us software or hardware for testing purposes. These were Silicon Graphics, Visual Technology, Human Designed Systems, Unipress Software, White Pine Software, Network Computing Devices, Locus Computing Corporation, Unipress Software, VisionWare Ltd., Quarterdeck Office Systems, FTP Software, Hummingbird Communications Ltd., and Starnet Communications.

We would also like to thank those who worked on the production of the book. At O'Reilly & Associates, we would like to thank Gigi Estabrook for her initial copy-edit, Chris Reilley for the figures, Ellie Cutler for indexing, and Rosanne Wagger and Mike Sierra for production of the final copy. We would also like to thank Lenny Muellner for tools support and for allowing us to disrupt his life whenever we had the urge to make screendumps.

Finally, we would like to thank our editor, Tim O'Reilly, for his initial trust in us and for his patience during the countless months it took us to put the book together.

Of course, we alone take responsibility for any errors or omissions that remain.

1

An Introduction to X Administration

This chapter provides an introduction to X and to X administration.

In This Chapter:

1
An Introduction to X Administration

Administrators make things work. On the surface, the X Window System is just one more software package that the administrator needs to install, maintain and support for users. X runs on any architecture, so there are fewer differences between systems than with most software. What makes X different from other packages, however, is that it provides a great deal of configurability. It's relatively easy to get X to run on your site with its default settings, but it requires a bit more homework to take advantage of its flexibility and create a secure, centrally-maintained environment for users. This book does the homework for you.

Administrators need to know how X works before they can figure out how to make it work for them. This chapter provides an introduction both to X and to X administration.

1.1 The Design of X11

The X Window System, called X or X11 for short, is a network-based graphics window system that was developed at the Massachusetts Institute of Technology. X is based on the *client/server model*, in which the application program (the *client*) does not directly access the display, but communicates with an intermediary display program (the *server*).

One important feature of the client/server model is that the client and server programs can communicate over a network. They do not need to run on the same machine, or even in the same building. This means that an X display is an ideal front end for a distributed computing environment. A system administrator might open windows on each of a dozen machines she is maintaining; a financial analyst at a Wall Street firm might have a spreadsheet in one window, Quotron data "off the wire" in another, and a custom mainframe-based analysis program in another.

The client and server communicate using the *X Protocol*, which can run on top of UNIX domain sockets, TCP/IP, or DECnet. Technically, the X Protocol is the true definition of X. However, when we refer to X, we often mean not only the protocol but also the widely available implementation of clients, servers and libraries that use that protocol.

Since the client and server can run on different machines, the local display machine can get away with running a server program and nothing else. X servers can run on single-tasking DOS-based PCs, which connect across the network to multi-user systems capable of running multiple graphical applications. More importantly, this feature has led to the development of low-cost *X terminals*, designed specifically for running X servers. Using X terminals, a company can give multiple users the ability to run graphics-intensive programs, without having to buy each user a machine powerful enough to execute the graphics programs themselves.

X has great commercial potential because X can be ported to any architecture, operating system, or display type. Servers have been written for all sorts of architectures, under all sorts of operating systems, for all types of displays. The only requirement is that there be a keyboard, a graphic display, and an input pointer (such as a mouse). And because the server handles the hardware and operating-system dependencies, client programs can be almost completely portable.

Currently, most client programs run on some flavor of the UNIX operating system, but they have also long been available under many other operating systems (such as VMS), and recent products now run X clients (as well as servers) on DOS and Macintosh machines. Furthermore, clients have been written to be heavily dependent on programming libraries. This means that once the libraries are ported to another operating system, clients using those libraries should be easily ported as well.

X was developed at the Massachusetts Institute of Technology and is maintained by a non-profit consortium of vendors and universities. The source code to X11 is free. As a result, X has led to an explosion of free software not seen since the heyday of Berkeley UNIX development.

The fact that X was developed by a consortium and had to meet the sometimes conflicting needs of many different vendors, does, however, lead to a few complications. At times, it seems that the developers have gone overboard to make X flexible, configurable and extensible, so that it could be adapted to the needs of whatever platform and environment it is ported to. However, in the end, it is hard to fault the bias towards flexibility. The almost universal adoption of X is a tribute to just how insightful those design decisions were.

One very concrete expression of X's political heritage is that X itself is a no-frills window system. Rather than choose between competing graphical user interfaces (GUIs), the X designers chose to articulate "mechanism not policy." That is, they provided base technology for manipulating windows, but didn't insist on a particular "look and feel." X keeps the GUI distinctly separate from the window system itself. Several GUIs (notably those based on the OSF/Motif and OPEN LOOK specifications) have already been built upon X11. What's more, because X doesn't have a GUI to get in the way, it has been integrated with other window systems such as Microsoft Windows and the Macintosh Finder. In such implementations, X windows exist side-by-side with the native windows of that GUI.

1.1.1 Display Servers

Client-server terminology often seems "backwards" to people who are new to X. Since the X display runs on a local machine on the user's desk, you might think that the X display should run the X *client* program. People are used to thinking of servers as something they access across the network (such as file or print server).

If you think about it more carefully, though, you realize that the terminology is exactly right. The X server is a *display server*. It makes your display and keyboard available to applications running on other machines across the network. The fact that you can and often do run clients locally doesn't make the display server any less a server. Clients must still connect to it to make use of the services (display and keyboard) it manages.

The X display server accepts connections from any number of X application clients. These clients might run on any machine on the network, as shown in Figure 1-1.

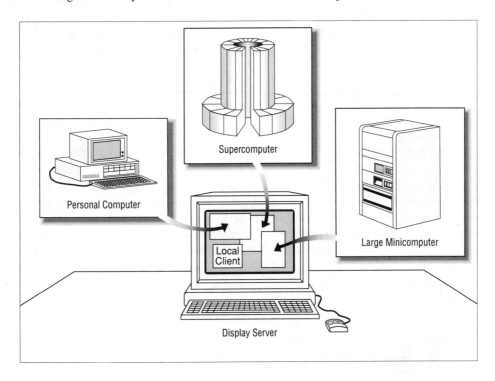

Figure 1-1. An X server with clients from multiple hosts

An X server can be written for any sort of graphic display. These displays, each consisting of a pointing device, a keyboard and at least one monitor, can differ in several ways.

- Monitors have different screen sizes and different resolutions. Some monitors have color support. A server might support anywhere from 1 to 24 bits of color per pixel.

- The pointing device might be a mouse, a touchscreen, or a pen. Most displays use a mouse as a pointing device, but the mouse might have 1, 2, or 3 buttons.

- Different keyboards have different layouts, and each key generates different control sequences. You can depend on alphanumeric keys on U.S. or European keyboards, but you can't depend on there being function keys, an ALT key, or a numeric keypad.

On other window systems, you might be able to configure this information directly into the application at installation time, since there's only one display that the program can access. X clients, however, need to be able to run with all possible servers. The X server therefore needs to mediate between clients and the specifics of the display.

For the output device—i.e., the monitor—the server not only needs to know how to draw to the display as specified by the client, it also needs to be able to tell the client the screen dimensions or whether color is supported. If a user has more than one monitor, each monitor can be used as a separate *screen* of the display.

Input devices (the mouse and keyboard) can also differ. In order to insulate clients from these differences, the server maintains a mapping between physical buttons and keys and corresponding logical identifiers. For example, the code generated by each key is assigned a symbol, called a *keysym*. Clients refer only to keysyms, and the server performs the actual translation between keysyms and the actual keycodes generated by a particular keyboard. (For more information on keysyms, see Section D.2.)

1.1.2 Clients and Resources

Because X applications, or *clients*, can display on any X server on the network that allows the connection, X applications must be configurable. However portable the X client-server model makes an application, there are going to be dependencies and preferences that the user needs to be able to express. A font that looks good on one display might be too small on another; a key that is easily reached on one keyboard might be a stretch on another.

On another window system, such as that on a Macintosh or on a PC running DOS, all application preferences can be set at the application level. This makes sense, because the Macintosh OS and DOS are single-user operating systems with only one display to connect to. All preferences might as well be stored in the same place.

By necessity, X needs to deal with application resources more robustly. X generally runs on multi-user systems, so clients need to be configurable by each individual user. (Character-based UNIX programs already do that using "dot" files in the user's home directory, such as *.exrc*, *.newsrc* and *.mailrc*.) X clients can display on any server on the network, and each server may require its own preferences; so X clients also need to be configured for each individual server. And because binaries are often shared among several different hosts, each X client executable might be run on any number of systems, so system-specific defaults are needed.

X applications need to be configurable at each of these levels. X applications are configured primarily via *resources*. Resources are variables that are used by X clients and that can be set at the user level, system level, server level, and client level.

It is essential that a system administrator thoroughly understand the resource mechanism. Resources are discussed in detail in Volume Three, *X Window System User's Guide*. In addition, Appendix D provides a summary of the most important points of syntax and usage.

1.1.3 Toolkits and GUIs

X clients are built using a number of programming libraries that progressively insulate the programmer from the details of the X protocol. The lowest layer is Xlib, which maps fairly directly to the protocol, and requires the programmer to do a great deal of "handwork." Each event generated by mouse movement, key presses, or graphics exposure must be handled explicitly. Writing a graphical user interface with Xlib would be a bit like starting out with logs when you want to build a house. For this reason, in most X clients, Xlib is used chiefly for drawing, or in cases where the programmer needs more direct control of the dialog with the server.

The X Toolkit Intrinsics (Xt) are built on top of Xlib. They simplify the job of building a graphical user interface by creating support for objects called *widgets*. Widgets are prototypes for common user interface elements such as scrollbars, menus, and so forth, plus other objects that can be used to glue these elements together into a complete application window.

But Xt itself does not provide a GUI. This is the job of additional libraries that are layered on top of Xt in turn. The three most common GUIs are provided by the Athena widgets and the OSF/Motif and OPEN LOOK specifications. What's more, even a widget set provides only part of the GUI's look and feel. The basic framework for moving, resizing, and managing windows is handed over to a separate program called a *window manager*.

Athena is a bare-bones widget set originally developed by MIT as a "proof of concept" for Xt. Athena is not terribly pretty, but is widespread because most of the original MIT client programs were written with the Athena widgets. The corresponding window manager is usually *twm*.

OSF/Motif is a GUI that was developed by the Open Software Foundation and is sold by various licensed resellers. (Motif source can be purchased directly from OSF.) OSF/Motif consists of a set of Motif libraries and widgets, a style guide, several demo clients, and the Motif window manager (*mwm*).

OPEN LOOK is a GUI specification with multiple implementations. The OLIT toolkit is an Xt-based toolkit developed by AT&T. The XView toolkit was developed by Sun directly on top of Xlib, with an API similar to its native SunView user interface, which predated X. XView is available in the *contrib/* part of the MIT distribution. OpenWindows is a complete windowing environment distributed by Sun Microsystems that is compatible with the OPEN LOOK specification, and which includes a window manager client called *olwm*.

To further complicate the picture, clients can be written using one set of widgets, yet work with the window manager of a competing GUI. This is most common with MIT clients written with the Athena widgets, which are often used with *mwm* or *olwm*. Fortunately, there is a set of conventions (called the Inter-Client Communication Conventions) that ensure interoperability of clients and window managers from different X-based GUIs.

1.2 X Administration

One of the philosophies that X is built on is that it provides "mechanism, not policy." This is good for developers, since it allows them to decide how X should be used. But until a single standard emerges, it leaves users (and administrators) without much guidance. This book hopes to come to the rescue.

One complication for users and administrators is that there are so many different flavors of X. There's "standard" X—that is, the client, server and library distribution maintained by the X Consortium at MIT. Then there are the various vendor-configured versions that are derived from MIT X11 but then configured for a vendor's operating system and proprietary "look and feel." There's OpenWindows, which runs on Sun workstations. There's Open Desktop, which runs on PCs running SCO UNIX. There's DECWindows, which runs on DEC workstations, and AIXWindows, which runs on IBM workstations running AIX. And many more.

This means that X may not look the same on different platforms. A user who thinks he or she has learned X may find that they're totally lost in a co-worker's environment across the hallway. Furthermore, an administrator might have several different platforms to maintain. This book concentrates on "standard" X11 as distributed by MIT, but also covers conflicts with vendor distributions of X, as well as conflicts between different releases of X11.

Another complication is that while the X Consortium provides only "mechanism" and relies on vendors to decide how to use it, there are some gaps where no robust, universally-accepted way of dealing with the mechanism has come to light. For example, resources have the potential to be a very powerful tool, but are currently difficult to understand, manipulate, and debug. You need to know what's "under the hood" before you can use resources properly.

This is one of the most difficult things about X administration: you may need to know an awful lot about how things work before you can do what you really want. This book tries to make it easier to configure X for your site by describing procedures step-by-step. At the same time, we try to provide background information for readers who continue to have problems or are interested in knowing more.

The X sources provide ample documentation, but it's often difficult to weed through the documentation tree to find what you want to know. For example, to learn how to use security features of X11, you need to read the *xauth*, *Xsecurity*, *xhost* and *xdm* manpages before you can begin to get an idea of how it works. This book attempts to group together everything you need to know to get X working on your site.

1.2.1 Installing X

You can get X from your operating system vendor, or you can use the standard MIT X11. Which you choose to do depends on what you plan to do with it.

If you plan to run specific clients, you may have no choice: a client might run only with a vendor's distribution of X (such as OpenWindows), or it might run only with X11R5 (which at this writing is unavailable from OS vendors).

If technical support matters a lot to you, you might prefer to stick with your vendor's distribution of X11. If having the "latest and greatest" is more important to you, you probably want to build MIT X11 with all the latest patches.

If you plan to develop your own X applications, you may want several different X distributions installed, so you can test (or port) your applications on multiple platforms. In addition to the X distribution itself, you will probably also need other toolkits installed, such as OSF/Motif, OLIT or XView.

Chapter 8 describes how to build X11 from source.

In addition to the X distribution of clients, libraries and a local server, administrators need to provide X servers for users. X terminals are available from many different vendors. X servers that run on top of PC and Macintosh environments are also available. Chapter 7 discusses the issues of choosing and installing an X terminal, and Appendix C discusses X servers that run on PCs, on Macintosh computers, and on NeXT computers.

1.2.2 Supporting Users

Your users might all be self-sufficient power users, or they might need their hands held with every step. You probably have both types on your site, as well as every gradation in between. You will need to set up default environments for the users on your site, and be prepared to help them debug their environment when things go wrong. Remember that the more time you spend on setting up templates for users, the faster users will be able to be productive, and the less time you'll spend later on debugging their environments. Chapter 2 covers some of the issues that you will need to address when setting up a user's environment.

If you have any X terminals at your site, you should run the X Display Manager (*xdm*) to provide an easy way for those users to log on and start their X sessions. You might also want to set up *xdm* to control X servers running on workstations as well, since among other things, *xdm* provides a way to configure user environments in a central place. Chapter 3 describes how to set up *xdm* for your site.

Unless everyone at your site trusts everyone else, you should probably look into using security for X servers on your site. If you are on the Internet, you should *definitely* use security. If someone's determined to snoop on you, they can probably get through, but there are a few things you can do to trip up the more casual attacker. Chapter 4 describes security issues for X11.

1.2.3 Maintaining Software

After you have everything running smoothly on your site, you'll find that most of your time as administrator will involve getting and installing new software, and upgrading existing software. In addition to commercial software, sources to many X programs are available in the public domain. Appendix B is a tutorial on how to find and build public domain software.

New clients often call for new fonts. These fonts have to be made available to all servers that might run the client. Chapter 5 describes how to install new fonts and how to convert fonts from other formats.

1.2.4 Maintaining Multiple Machines

The whole idea of X is to have many machines networked together: PCs, workstations, X terminals, minicomputers, supercomputers, you name it. This can become a lot of work for administrators, since that means multiple machines to configure and maintain consistently. One useful tool is to keep up-to-date documentation on how each machine is configured. This is especially helpful on a large site, particularly on one with more than one administrator.

But maintaining many different machines can be made much easier if you configure machines centrally when you can. This book describes the various mechanisms X provides for doing so. The X Display Manager can be used to maintain all X sessions centrally. Many X terminals can be configured remotely from a host machine. The font server, new with X11R5, provides a way to supply fonts to multiple servers.

1.2.5 A "Philosophy" of X Administration

If we had to come up with a "philosophy" of X administration, it would be that X is made to fit the needs of its users. As the administrator, you have the responsibility to determine your users' needs and configure X accordingly.

X is installed in all sorts of environments, from universities with hundreds of student users, to home offices with a single standalone machine. For that reason, almost everything in X is configurable at multiple levels. Application resources can be set in several different places. You can create new fonts and define new colors. The X Display Manager can be configured to meet practically any need. Even the source code to X is available for programmers who want to create their own workarounds if none already exist. The fundamental idea is that if you don't like the way something works, change it.

From the onset, you'll see that this book is less about making X work than it is about getting X to work for you.

2

The X User Environment

Administrators need to configure X environments for their users. This chapter describes the issues involved in making an X environment work properly.

In This Chapter:

2
The X User Environment

2.1 The Configured X Session

We set up an X environment for a new employee, Joan, whose job involves internal project management. Joan is new to both UNIX and X. We've set up her environment so that when she logs in via the X Display Manager, *xdm*, she gets an environment resembling that in Figure 2-1.*

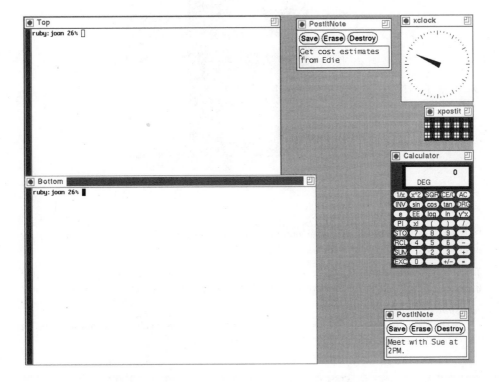

Figure 2-1. A configured X session

---

*If you aren't already running *xdm*, see Section 3.3 for information on how to set it up the first time.

- Joan gets two terminal emulator windows. The top one is labeled "Top" and the bottom one is labeled "Bottom."

- Joan has a clock in the upper-right corner of the screen.

- Joan wants to have a calculator available all the time, since her job involves juggling numbers.

- The rest of the windows are from a public domain application called *xpostit*, which Joan can use to keep notes and reminders on her desktop.

The *root window* is the screen background behind the X client windows. If Joan presses her first mouse button while the pointer is in the root window, she gets a *root menu* resembling that in Figure 2-2. We've configured her root menu so she can start new clients easily:

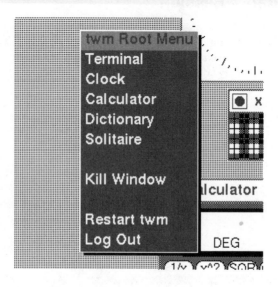

Figure 2-2. A root menu

By pressing down her first mouse button and then selecting the "Dictionary" option, for example, Joan can bring up a dictionary application.

To create this environment, we needed to set up three X configuration files in Joan's home directory, in addition to the "standard" UNIX shell startup files. The X configuration files are:

.xsession

> The *.xsession* file is the shell script that actually starts each of the applications in Joan's startup environment. The *.xsession* script reads:

```
#!/bin/sh

# Add /usr/local/bin to the path for this script:
PATH=$PATH:/usr/local/bin
export PATH

# Set up a pattern for the root window:
```

```
xsetroot -bitmap /usr/include/X11/bitmaps/dimple1

# Merge in user resources:
xrdb -merge $HOME/.Xresources

# Start some applications:
xterm -title Top -g 70x35+1+1 &
xterm -title Bottom -g +1-0 &
xclock -g -0+0 &
xcalc -g -0+298 &
xpostit -sv -g 110x50-0+200 &

# Start a window manager in the foreground:
twm
```

.Xresources

The *.Xresources* file contains resource definitions. These resources define Joan's client preferences. Currently, Joan's resources are used to set some preferences for her *xterm* terminal emulator windows. We set her up to use a font that we think she would prefer over the default, we turned on a scroll bar, and we set the number of lines to be saved for scrolling to be 200. The *.Xresources* file reads:

```
! Resource definition file.

! XTerm definitions:
XTerm*font:-misc-fixed-bold-r-normal--15-140-75-75-c-90-iso8859-1
XTerm*scrollBar:true
XTerm*saveLines:200
```

.twmrc

The *.twmrc* file is a configuration file for Joan's window manager, *twm*. A window manager is a special client that controls how windows are moved and resized. In addition, the window manager defines the root menu shown in Figure 2-2. The *.twmrc* file is long, but we can show you the part that defines the root menu:

```
menu "rootmenu"
{
"twm Root Menu" f.title
"Terminal"      f.exec "xterm &"
"Clock"         f.exec "xclock &"
"Calculator"    f.exec "xcalc &"
"Dictionary"    f.exec "xwebster &"
"Solitaire"     f.exec "spider &"
""              f.nop
"Kill Window"   f.destroy
""              f.nop
"Restart twm"   f.restart
"Log Out"       f.quit
}
```

Together, these files define Joan's X user environment. They are defined in addition to the shell startup files that she needs to define her UNIX shell environment.

Now, imagine that you're Joan, new to both UNIX and X, and you're faced with these startup files. Each file has its own peculiar syntax that she might be able to follow, but will probably have trouble duplicating. Where did we get that arcane font name? Why do some of the commands in *.xsession* end in ampersands (&) while others don't?

2.1.1 The Twilight Zone

One day Joan logs in at a workstation. The X server isn't running on the workstation console, so Joan tries to start her X session by typing *X*. What she gets is a blank screen with an "×" representing her pointer. She is unable to start applications and after several minutes decides to start over.

After rebooting the machine, Joan learns that she should use the *xinit* command, not *X*. When she does this, she gets a single *xterm* terminal emulation window with a very small font, and no window manager, as shown in Figure 2-3.

Figure 2-3. An unconfigured X session

(Unknown to Joan, this has happened because the *.xsession* file is the one primarily responsible for configuring Joan's user environment under *xdm*. Under *xinit*, she needs an *.xinitrc* file. See Section 2.4 for more information on starting the X session using *xinit*.)

Joan tries to start a clock using the *xclock* command, shown in Figure 2-4.

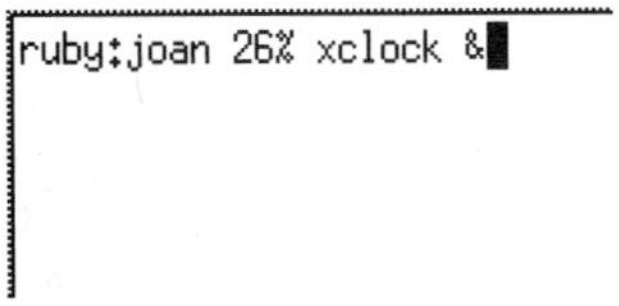

```
ruby:joan 26% xclock &█
```

Figure 2-4. Starting a new client

What happens is that the clock appears on top of the *xterm* window, obscuring her prompt, as shown in Figure 2-5.

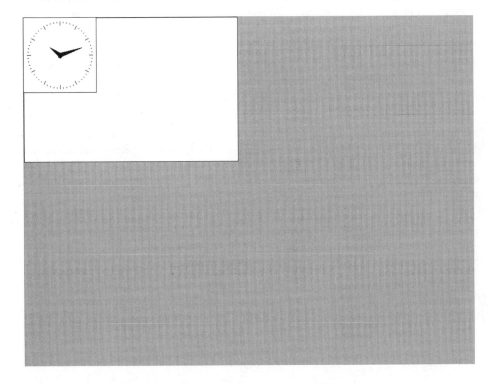

Figure 2-5. xclock window over xterm window

Since there is no window manager running, Joan can't move the new *xclock* window from on top of the *xterm* window. She needs to place her pointer on the *xterm* window and type RETURN a few times before her prompt peeks out from underneath the clock window.

What Joan has stumbled onto is X in its unconfigured state.

Joan types "XYZZY". Nothing happens.

2.2 Components of the X Environment

Joan's adventures are meant to show the world of difference between X in its raw state, and X when it has been configured. You might think of it as the difference between an unfurnished apartment and a home.

Like someone's home, the X user environment is made up of many components. You can't just bring in furniture and expect the house to look lived-in; similarly, you can't just start a window manager and expect the X environment to be complete.

Some users would prefer to configure their own environments. Other users won't have the slightest idea of where to begin. As an administrator, you have to decide whether you want to set up an environment with reasonable defaults for new users, or whether you'd rather just give users a bare-bones environment and let them figure it out on their own.

Our opinion is that it's always better to take the time to set up a decent environment for your users. "Power" users can always rip apart what you set up and start again from scratch; but users who are just interested in getting their jobs done will appreciate having something workable to begin with.

One approach to creating a useful default environment is to alter the system-wide files. For example, if a user has no *.twmrc* file, they will use the file */usr/lib/X11/twm/system.twmrc*. If a user has no *.xsession* file, they will use commands specified in the */usr/lib/X11/xdm/Xsession* file. As shipped in the MIT distribution, the defaults in these files are fairly basic. But you can configure these defaults system-wide to better accommodate your users.

The preferable approach is the "template" approach, as we set up earlier for the user named Joan. We gave Joan a set of configuration files that had been tried and tested and *liked* by other users. The advantage to using templates is that when users are ready to edit their environment, it's much easier if the configuration files are already set up locally.

Either way, the administrator needs to take a strong hand in setting up the user environment. The administrator is all that stands between a user and the abyss of the default X environment.

There are an endless number of factors that can influence a user's X environment, but the simplest user environment (like Joan's) consists of a window manager, a little client customization, and a startup script to bring it all together.

2.2.1 Window Managers

As we mentioned earlier, window managers are special clients that allow you to move, resize, and iconify windows. The window manager provided in the X source distribution is *twm*, the Tab Window Manager. Window managers are generally started in the user's startup script, but like other clients, they can be started on the command line as well, as shown in the following figure.

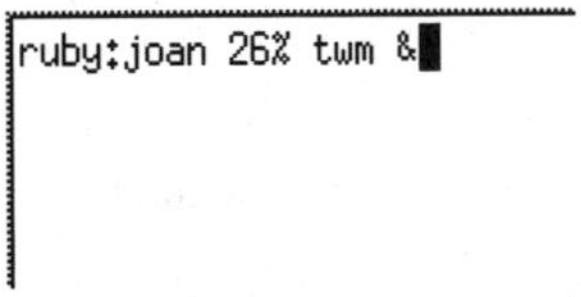

```
ruby:joan 26% twm &▮
```

Figure 2-6. Starting the window manager

If a window manager were already running, the command would fail with a message resembling:

```
twm:   another window manager is already running on screen 0?
twm:   unable to find any unmanaged screens
```

The window manager gives each window its own borders and titlebar. By pressing the pointer on the titlebar (i.e., holding down the first mouse button while the pointer is on the titlebar), you can move the window. By pressing the icon at the upper right corner of the titlebar, you can resize the window. By pressing the icon at the upper left corner of the titlebar, the window is iconified.

Once the window manager is started, you can use it to move windows on the screen. You can also use it to start new applications on the root menu, as shown in Figure 2-2.

When a new window appears, *twm* allows you to place the window by displaying an outline of the window with the upper left corner at your current pointer position. When you press the first mouse button, the window will be placed at that position.

The behavior of *twm* can be configured by editing a file called *.twmrc* in your home directory. Alternatively, the default behavior of *twm* on a system can be changed by editing the *system.twmrc* file, usually in the */usr/lib/X11/twm* directory. For information on how to configure *twm*, see either the *twm* manual page or *The X Window System User's Guide, Standard Edition* (O'Reilly & Associates, 1990).

twm is the only window manager supplied with the MIT X distribution, but there are many other window managers distributed by vendors. One of the most popular window managers is *mwm*, the Motif Window Manager. *mwm* is a window manager which implements the OSF/Motif "look and feel." Another popular window manager is *olwm*, a window manager for OPEN LOOK. Other window managers are *swm* (the Solbourne window manager, which can simulate both *olwm* and *mwm* in separate "modes"); *gwm* (a public domain window manager that uses LISP-like syntax in its configuration, and can simulate *mwm*); and *tvtwm* and *olvwm*, which are versions of *twm* and *olwm* (respectively) that support a "virtual" root window. A virtual root window is a root window that is larger than the portion visible on your display. It can be scrolled around to move different sections into view. This simulates having a much larger display and gives more room to display clients.

See *The X Window System User's Guide, Motif Edition* (O'Reilly & Associates, 1992) for more information on *mwm* and Motif. For more information on *olwm* and OPEN LOOK, see the upcoming *X Window System User's Guide, OPEN LOOK Edition* (O'Reilly & Associates, 1993).

2.2.2 Customizing Clients

There are two ways to customize clients: with command-line options, and with resources.

The use of command-line options to modify the behavior of a program should be familiar to any UNIX user, but even so, it's worth reviewing a few of the most commonly-used X options—those for specifying fonts, window size and placement, and colors. This discussion will also serve to introduce the treatment of resources, which provide a convenient way to set "global" options.

2.2.2.1 The -fn Command-line Option

For specifying a font, the *xterm* client provides a *–fn* command line option. Font names in X are a bit unwieldy, but you can use the *xlsfonts* command to get a list of fonts available for your X server. For example:

```
% xlsfonts
-adobe-courier-bold-o-normal--10-100-75-75-m-60-iso8859-1
-adobe-courier-bold-o-normal--11-80-100-100-m-60-iso8859-1
-adobe-courier-bold-o-normal--12-120-75-75-m-70-iso8859-1
   ...
-misc-fixed-bold-r-normal--15-140-75-75-c-90-iso8859-1
   ...
```

(You might also try the *xfontsel* client, which can be used to display fonts available to your server.)

See Chapter 6 for a description of each of the fields in a font name. For now, let's use the fixed font that we showed in the output of *xlsfonts*. Use the *–fn* option:

```
% xterm -fn -misc-fixed-bold-r-normal--15-140-75-75-c-90-iso8859-1 &
```

This command line gives you a window resembling that in Figure 2-7.

2.2.2.2 The -geometry Command-line Option

The *-geometry* or *–g* command-line option can be used to specify two things: where the client window initially appears and what size it should initially be. To have an *xterm* window that's 92 characters across and 40 lines long (instead of the default 80×24), enter:

```
ruby:joan % xterm -geometry 92x40 &
```

To have an *xterm* window appear at position (324,190) on the screen, enter:

```
ruby:joan % xterm -geometry +324+190 &
```

You can combine the two requests into one argument:

```
ruby:joan % xterm -geometry 92x40+324+190 &
```

You see a window resembling that in Figure 2-8.

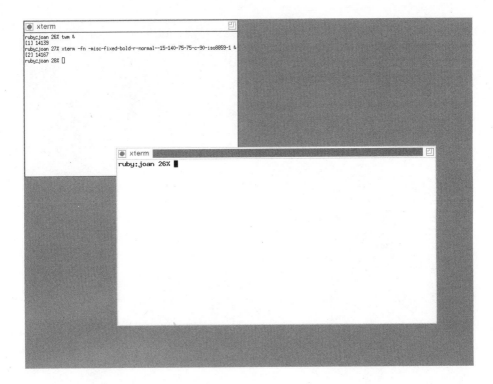

Figure 2-7. xterm window with new font

The position (0,0) is the upper left corner of the root window. The numbers following the plus signs (+) signify the offset (in number of pixels) from (0,0). The top left corner of window is placed at these coordinates when the offset is positive. It is also possible to specify a negative offset using minus signs (−):

```
ruby:joan % xterm -geometry 85x40-50-150 &
```

The bottom right corner of the window is offset 50 pixels from the right border and 150 pixels up from the bottom of the screen. Since displays differ in the number of pixels, a window may be placed differently depending on the size and resolution of your display. Using a negative offset will guarantee that the window is always a certain distance from the right side and bottom, regardless of the size. This is handy if you often move from one type of display to another, as your windows will always remain within the screen borders. In the *.xsession* file we showed earlier, we had set up some windows to position themselves at particular positions, using the *−g* shorthand for *−geometry*:

```
xterm -title Top -g 70x35+1+1 &
xterm -title Bottom -g +1-0 &
xclock -g -0+0 &
xcalc -g -0+298 &
xpostit -sv -g 110x50-0+200 &
```

Figure 2-8. A window with a specified geometry

- The top *xterm* window appears at the upper left corner of the screen, and is resized to be 70×35.

- The bottom *xterm* appears flush to the bottom left corner of the screen.

- The *xclock* window appears flush to the upper right corner of the screen.

- The *xcalc* and *xpostit* windows appear flush to the right edge of the screen. The *xpostit* control box is also resized a little to look nice.

Without a specified geometry, the placement of windows is controlled by the window manager, appearing at (0,0) if no window manager is running.

The size of the *xterm* window is given in character widths and heights. For most other X clients, however, the unit of measurement used for window size is generally the number of pixels. See the client manpage for information on what units are used for size specification.

2.2.2.3 Specifying Colors

If you have a color monitor, you might want to use some colors in your display. You can specify a new foreground and background color using the *–fg* and *–bg* command-line options. For example, for a window with a powder blue background and hot pink foreground, enter:

```
ruby:joan % xterm -bg powderblue -fg hotpink &
```

Use the *showrgb* command for a list of colors available on your system for color displays.

On a monochrome display, you can get a black background and white foreground with:

```
ruby:joan % xterm -bg black -fg white &
```

Or get the same results by calling *xterm* with the special *–rv* option, for reverse video:

```
ruby:joan % xterm -rv &
```

Either command line will give you a window resembling that in Figure 2-9.

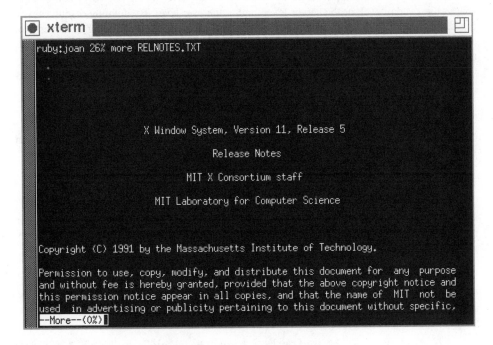

Figure 2-9. An xterm window in reverse video, decorated by twm

See Chapter 6 for a complete discussion of color.

2.2.2.4 Using Resources

Command-line options are the quick and dirty way of customizing a client. Before we go on, however, we should tell you a little about the alternative, using *resources*.

There are a few disadvantages to using command-line options. One is that you can end up with some awfully long command lines. For example, if you want to specify a different geometry, new font, and different background and foreground colors, your command line might look like this:

```
% xterm -fn -misc-fixed-bold-r-normal--15-140-75-75-c-90-iso8859-1 \
-geometry 90x40 -bg yellow -fg navyblue &
```

If you don't want to type this out every time you start up a new *xterm* window, you could set up your window manager to run the entire command from your root menu. But the better solution is to use resources to set up your client preferences.

Resources are variables that are used by X clients. They have the advantage of being definable at the system level, at the server level, and at the user level. By defining resources, you can change the default behavior of clients for your account or for a particular X server. For example, you can set the following resources in a file called *.Xresources* in your home directory:

```
XTerm*font: -misc-fixed-bold-r-normal--15-140-75-75-c-90-iso8859-1
XTerm*Background:     yellow
XTerm*Foreground:     navyblue
XTerm*VT100.geometry:  90x40
```

(The string VT100 used in the geometry specification is the name of a *widget* used within *xterm*.)

To load these resources into the server, where all clients can access them, type:

```
ruby:joan % xrdb -merge .Xresources
```

After these resources are loaded into the server, all subsequent *xterm* windows will appear the way you want them. You can just type:

```
ruby:joan % xterm &
```

We have described only a small subset of the things that can be set using resources. A client may provide resources to redefine almost any variable it uses. For example, in the *.Xresources* file we showed earlier, we set the scrollBar resource, and specified the number of lines to be saved for scrolling:

```
XTerm*font:          -misc-fixed-bold-r-normal--15-140-75-75-c-90-iso8859-1
XTerm*scrollBar:     true
XTerm*saveLines:     200
```

Resources might be used for anything that the program wants to leave configurable by the user or administrator. For example, an *ftp* client may use resources to set the default *ftp* server to connect to; the *xcalc* client uses resources to define all of its buttons and the functions they call; and the *xdm* client uses resources to point to its configuration files. For a listing of the resources used by a particular client, refer to the manpage provided with that client. For more information on resources, see Appendix D.

2.2.3 The Startup Script

The startup script is what brings a user's entire X environment together. If you use *xdm* to start your X sessions, this script is called *$HOME/.xsession*. If you use *xinit*, the script is called *$HOME/.xinitrc*.* We'll show the simple startup script that we used earlier:

```
#!/bin/sh

# Add /usr/local/bin to the path for this script:
PATH=$PATH:/usr/local/bin
export PATH

# Set up a pattern for the root window:
xsetroot -bitmap /usr/include/X11/bitmaps/dimple1

# Merge in user resources:
xrdb -merge $HOME/.Xresources

# Start some applications:
xterm -title Top -g 70x35+1+1 &
xterm -title Bottom -g +1-0 &
xclock -g -0+0 &
xcalc -g -0+298 &
xpostit -sv -g 110x50-0+200 &

# Start a window manager in the foreground:
twm
```

The first thing that this startup script does is set the path to be used for commands for that script. By default, *:/bin:/usr/bin:/usr/bin/X11:/usr/ucb* is used as the search path for the startup shell. Since the *xpostit* command resides in */usr/local/bin*, it needs to be called with its full pathname, or */usr/local/bin* needs to be appended to the search path. This path is then exported, so that it will also be used by other clients such as *twm*.

The startup script uses *xsetroot* to give the user a nicer background than the default root window background.

Next, the startup script calls the *xrdb* client. It is this command that reads the resources defined in the *.Xresources* file. The *xrdb* client loads resources directly into the X server. There are alternate ways of reading resources (as described in Section D.1.2), but if you load the resources directly into the server, you guarantee that all clients displaying to that server will be able to access them. *xrdb* should be run before any applications are run, since you want to make sure that the resources are loaded before you start any applications that use them; and it should be called in the foreground, to guarantee that the resources are fully loaded before the script continues.

The applications are then started. We described how the *–g* options are being used in Section 2.2.2.2. Note that each of these command lines are placed in the background.

Finally, the *twm* window manager is started. When *twm* starts up, it is configured by the *.twmrc* file.

---

*See Section 2.4 for more information on using *xinit*. See Chapter 3 for more information on using *xdm*.

2.2.3.1 The Foreground Process

As shown in the sample startup script, clients such as *xrdb* and *xsetroot* are not run in the background. *xrdb* and *xsetroot* are non-interactive clients that exit as soon as they are completed.

On the other hand, clients like *xterm* and *xcalc* need to be put in the background, or the script will hang until they are completed (or killed). What the user will see is that the top *xterm* window appears, but nothing else; after the user exits *xterm*, the bottom *xterm* window appears; the second *xterm* window has to be killed before the *xclock* window pops up; and so on.

There is one exception: the last interactive client is always left in the foreground. Otherwise (like any shell script), the startup script exits immediately, and the X server resets (killing all clients). What the user will see is that all windows appear and then instantly disappear.

The last interactive client therefore keeps the X session alive. When it is exited (or killed), the entire X session exits as well. For that reason, the last process is also frequently called the *controlling process*.

The sample script makes the *twm* window manager the foreground process. The root menu option to exit *twm* is labeled "Log Out" to make it clear that exiting *twm* will log you out of your X session. In real life, you can make any interactive client your foreground process.

In general, users make their foreground process either an *xterm* client or their window manager. If you use the window manager, exiting the window manager exits the entire X session, which is an intuitive way to exit but means that you can't change window managers without editing your startup file and restarting X. If you use an *xterm* window, you may want to run the window with the *–iconic* option, in the hope that if the window is iconified, then the user is less likely to exit accidentally. Users with console *xterm -C* or *xconsole* clients often use the console window as the controlling process.

Another possibility is to use the built-in shell command *wait* at the end of the startup script, in which case you will have to exit each X client individually before your X session exits.

If you use an *xterm* window for your controlling process, beware of the "autologout" feature available for some shells. With the "autologout" feature, you can set it up so that your shell is killed when it is idle for a certain amount of time, e.g., 60 minutes. You can be working frantically in another X window, but if you have `autologout` set for your controlling *xterm* shell, then your whole X session will be killed after 60 minutes of idle time in the controlling shell.

2.3 The Shell Environment

Now we've talked a little about the X environment, we have to discuss how it relates to the UNIX shell. Although the shell is external to the X environment, X clients running on UNIX systems necessarily depend on the shell being set up properly. This means making sure that environment variables are set up properly and that the search path is correct. For remote clients, you have to deal with the shell environment on the remote machine as well.

2.3.1 Setting the DISPLAY Variable

The most important shell environment variable for X clients is DISPLAY. When a user logs in at an X terminal, the DISPLAY environment variable in each *xterm* window is set to her X terminal's hostname followed by :0.0.

```
ruby:joan % echo $DISPLAY
ncd15.ora.com:0.0
```

When the same user logs in at the console of the workstation named *sapphire*, the DISPLAY environment variable is defined as just :0.0:

```
sapphire:joan % echo $DISPLAY
:0.0
```

(Before X11 Release 5, the DISPLAY variable might appear as unix:0.0.)

The DISPLAY environment variable is used by all X clients to determine what X server to display on. Since any X client can connect to any X server that allows it, all X clients need to know what display to connect to upon startup. If DISPLAY is not properly set, the client cannot execute:

```
sapphire:joan % setenv DISPLAY foo:0
sapphire:joan % xterm
Error: Can't Open display
```

You can override the value of DISPLAY by using the *–display* command-line option. For example:

```
sapphire:joan % xterm -display sapphire:0.0 &
```

The first part of the display name (up to and including the colon) identifies the type of connection to use and the host that the server is running on. The second part (in most cases, the string 0.0) identifies a *server number* and an optional *screen number*. In most cases, the server and screen numbers will both be 0. You can actually omit the screen number name if the default (screen 0) is correct.

Note that we used both ":0.0" and "sapphire:0.0" to access the local console display of the workstation named *sapphire*. Although both these names will work, they imply different ways of connecting to the X server.

1. The ":" character without an initial hostname specifies that the client should connect using UNIX domain sockets (IPC).

   Instead of specifying :0.0, you can also prepend the word "unix" for an IPC connection:

   ```
   sapphire:joan % setenv DISPLAY unix:0.0
   ```

   (This is used in pre-R5 releases of X11.)

   Since processes can communicate via IPC only if they are running on the same host, you can use a leading colon or the unix keyword in a display name only if both the client and server are running on the same host—that is, for local clients displaying to the local console display of a workstation.

2. Using the hostname followed by a colon (e.g., sapphire:) specifies that the client should connect using Internet domain sockets (TCP/IP). You can use TCP/IP connections for displaying clients on any X server on the TCP/IP network, as long as the client has permission to access that server (see Section 2.3.4 for information on running remote clients). You can also use the hostname form for displaying clients on the local server, although many people argue that it's preferable to use unix:0.0 for any local clients. (It's faster, and there's no danger of a misconfigured name server getting in the way).

3. There is one other way of connecting: on a DECnet network, the syntax is the same as for TCP/IP except that two colons are used instead of one. To connect to an X server running on a host named *oravax* on a DECnet network, you might use the string oravax::0.0.

2.3.1.1 Complications with Display Names

Occasionally, especially when testing a new server, you may find that you can't open a particular display. When confronted with such a situation, we recommend trying the following:

- Make sure that you are using the proper name of the display, especially if you are running a client from a foreign host. A common mistake is to use :0 or unix:0, forgetting that different hosts have different ideas of what these display names refer to.

- Make sure that TCP/IP is properly configured by confirming that other connections work, using (for example) *rlogin* or *telnet*.

  If you suspect the problem is with your name server, substitute the IP address of the display for the hostname:

  ```
  ruby:joan % xterm -display 140.186.65.35:0
  ```

- Make sure that access control isn't the problem by temporarily allowing access to all hosts on the server machine. (Remember to undo this after the experiment!)

  ```
  sapphire:joan % xhost +
  ```

  If this turns out to be the problem, see Chapter 4 for more information on how to configure server access control more robustly.

- Some versions of TCP/IP, particularly on PCs, restrict the number of allowed connections. Find out whether the machine running the server program is restricted to a certain number of TCP/IP connections and increase it as needed. (How you actually do this is dependent on the TCP/IP vendor.)

Note that like all other environment variables set in your shell environment, the DISPLAY environment variable will propagate to all processes you start from that shell.

When you run clients from remote machines, some additional problems with the DISPLAY environment variable need to be addressed. See Section 2.3.4 for more information on running remote clients.

2.3.2 Redefining the Search Path

The command search path needs to include the directories containing X executables. This search path should live in the user's startup shell script (*.cshrc* or *.profile*). Assuming that the X executables are in */usr/bin/X11* and */usr/local/bin/X11*, here's a simple adapted entry for a *.profile* file (Bourne shell):

```
PATH=/usr/ucb:/bin:/usr/bin:/usr/bin/X11:/usr/local/bin/X11:.
export PATH
```

And here's one for a *.cshrc* file (C shell):

```
set path = (/usr/ucb /bin /usr/bin /usr/bin/X11 /usr/local/bin/X11 .)
```

(For security reasons, you may want to omit the current directory (.) from your path.)

If the path is not set properly, you will get the notorious "Command not found." error message for all X clients.

Unless specified otherwise, the *.xsession* startup script has the search path set to */:/bin:/usr/bin:/usr/bin/X11:/usr/ucb*. If you run clients in your startup script that reside in a different directory, you may need to reset the search path within the startup script. You may need to do this if you generally use the C shell, but your *.xsession* is a Bourne shell script. For example:

```
#!/bin/sh
PATH=$PATH:/usr/local/bin/X11:$HOME/bin
export PATH
    ...
```

Alternatively, you can write your *.xsession* as a C shell script, in which case it will automatically run your *.cshrc* file and inherit the search path set in that file.

2.3.2.1 Setting the Search Path for OpenWindows Support

If you are running OpenWindows, you need to add the following directories to your search path along with your vanilla X11 binary directories:

```
set path = ($path /usr/openwin/{bin,demo} )
```

(In OpenWindows 3.0, the */bin/xview* directory is now linked to *bin*.)

In addition, you need to set the shared library path to */usr/openwin/lib*:

```
setenv LD_LIBRARY_PATH /usr/openwin/lib:/usr/lib
```

If the OpenWindows distribution is elsewhere on your system, you can set the OPENWINHOME environment variable and use it in place of */usr/openwin*. For example, if the OpenWindows distribution is in */usr/local/openwin*, C shell users can enter in their *.cshrc* files:

```
setenv OPENWINHOME /usr/local/openwin
set path = ($path $OPENWINHOME/{bin,demo} )
setenv LD_LIBRARY_PATH $OPENWINHOME/lib:/usr/lib
```

In Bourne shell syntax, this might read:

```
OPENWINHOME=/usr/local/openwin
PATH=$PATH:$OPENWINHOME/bin:$OPENWINHOME/demo
LD_LIBRARY_PATH=$OPENWINHOME/lib:/usr/lib
export OPENWINHOME PATH LD_LIBRARY_PATH
```

2.3.2.2 Setting the Search Path for Mixed Environments

If you are running multiple releases of X11 on your system, you need to set your search path appropriately according to which executables you want to run. One situation in which you might want to run multiple releases is if you are testing a new release of X11 before setting it loose on your users. For example, suppose that you have X11R4 installed and running in */usr/lib/X11* and */usr/bin/X11*, and have just compiled and installed X11R5 into */usr/X11R5/lib* and */usr/X11R5/bin*. For testing your new environment, enter the */usr/X11R5/bin* directory into your command search path before */usr/bin/X11*:

```
set path = ( /usr/X11R5/bin $path )
```

On SunOS, you also need to enter */usr/X11R5/lib* into your LD_LIBRARY_PATH:

```
setenv LD_LIBRARY_PATH /usr/X11R5/lib
```

Another possibility is to set the LD_LIBRARY_PATH environment variable for each command:

```
% (setenv LD_LIBRARY_PATH /usr/X11R5/lib ; /usr/X11R5/bin/xterm)&
```

2.3.3 xterm Issues

The *xterm* client, which starts up a terminal shell, has its own particular issues. *xterm* has to have its **termcap** or **terminfo** entries installed, and since *xterm* windows can be resized, it needs to be able to adjust those entries dynamically for different dimensions.

2.3.3.1 xterm and Terminal Emulation

Among other common functions, shell startup scripts such as *.login* and *.profile* generally deal with setting the terminal type for that shell. This might be as simple as setting the TERM environment variable, or something more elaborate using *tset*.

Setting the terminal type, however, is not required for *xterm* terminal windows. The *xterm* client has its own way of dealing with terminal types. Several terminal entries work with standard-sized (80×24) *xterm* windows, including "xterm," "vt102," "vt100," and "ansi." The *xterm* client automatically searches the terminal database for these entries (in order) and sets the TERM environment variable according to which entry it finds first.

Since *xterm* takes care of setting terminal emulations by itself, you may want to remove any lines in startup files that set the terminal type, or have them default to "xterm."

There are two types of terminal databases available on UNIX systems: **termcap**, usually associated with BSD-based systems, and **terminfo**, associated with System V-based systems. The *xterm* source directory contains files called *termcap* and *terminfo* that contain the **termcap** and **terminfo** definitions for *xterm*. The *termcap* file for *xterm* should be entered as one of the first entries in your */etc/termcap* file. The *terminfo* file is meant to be compiled with *tic*, the TermInfo Compiler. For more information on **termcap** and **terminfo**, see the Nutshell Handbook, *termcap and terminfo* (O'Reilly & Associates, 1991).

Your vendor may supply its own version of *xterm* with its own terminal emulation and other enhancements (e.g., *hpterm*, *aixterm*, or *scoterm*). See your vendor's documentation for more details.

2.3.3.2 The resize Client

When the *xterm* client is called, it not only sets the TERM environment variable, but it also adjusts the terminal definition for the size of the window that is being created. The size of *xterm* windows, however, can be changed later on by using the window manager. If the window is resized, then the user's shell may need to be passed the new size information as well, or programs that use **termcap** and **terminfo** won't work correctly. The *resize* client is provided for redefining the number of lines and columns for the terminal database that is used in an *xterm* window. Note that *resize* cannot be used for terminal emulators other than *xterm*, since it depends on *xterm*'s escape sequences.

Some systems can send a "window size changed" signal (SIGWINCH) to programs and do not require *resize* to be run for a resized *xterm* window. We recommend using *resize* only if terminal-based programs start to have problems with your window size. A typical terminal-based program that is having problems with the window size is shown in Figure 2-10.

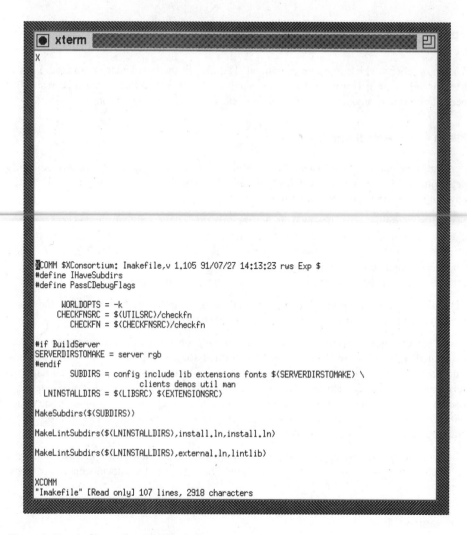

```
█COMM $XConsortium: Imakefile,v 1.105 91/07/27 14:13:23 rws Exp $
#define IHaveSubdirs
#define PassCDebugFlags

     WORLDOPTS = -k
   CHECKFNSRC = $(UTILSRC)/checkfn
      CHECKFN = $(CHECKFNSRC)/checkfn

#if BuildServer
SERVERDIRSTOMAKE = server rgb
#endif
      SUBDIRS = config include lib extensions fonts $(SERVERDIRSTOMAKE) \
                  clients demos util man
  LNINSTALLDIRS = $(LIBSRC) $(EXTENSIONSRC)

MakeSubdirs($(SUBDIRS))

MakeLintSubdirs($(LNINSTALLDIRS),install.ln,install.ln)

MakeLintSubdirs($(LNINSTALLDIRS),external.ln,lintlib)

XCOMM
"Imakefile" [Read only] 107 lines, 2918 characters
```

Figure 2-10. vi using only part of a window

The *resize* client is typically used immediately after the dimensions of an *xterm* window are changed. A peculiarity of the *resize* client is that it does not access the shell itself, but simply returns the shell commands that would be needed; to have those commands read by the shell, you have to either save its output in a file and source it in with the "." command (Bourne shell) or *source* (C shell) commands, or call it using the shell command *eval*. For example, after resizing a window you would type in that shell:

```
% eval `resize`
```

When you call the *resize* command under a **termcap** system, it produces the commands for resetting the TERMCAP environment variable with the *li#* and *co#* capabilities reflecting the current dimensions. When you call the *resize* command under a **terminfo** system, it produces the commands for resetting the LINES and COLUMNS environment variables.

The *resize* command consults the value of your SHELL environment variable and generates the commands for setting variables within that shell. If you are using a non-standard shell, *resize* may still recognize your shell; as of R5, *resize* recognizes *tcsh*, *jcsh*, *ksh*, *bash*, and *jsh*. But if *resize* does not recognize your shell, try using the –*c* or –*u* options to force *resize* to use C Shell or Bourne Shell syntax (respectively), depending on which syntax is appropriate for your shell.

2.3.3.3 xterm and the Login Shell (C Shell)

Most people who use the C shell know that the *.cshrc* file is read for every *csh* command run, and the *.login* file is read only once, at the beginning of each "login shell." One thing that X does is to effectively redefine the meaning of the "login shell."

Before X, you could assume that a user had a single interactive shell per login. Since the *.login* file would therefore be read only once, at the beginning of the login session, you could use it as a "batch" file to run some daily commands. For example, you might have it show the "message of the day" and start *mail* for you first thing in the morning:

```
cat /etc/motd
mail
```

Since X gives you the ability to run multiple *xterm* windows, however, the usage of the *.login* file becomes more confused. You probably don't want to read your mail and see the "message of the day" every time you call up a new *xterm* window. It makes more sense for these functions to be taken up by your X startup script, and to run X clients rather than text-based applications. For example, if you log in via *xdm*, your *.xsession* might contain the lines:

```
# Show the message of the day:
xmessage -file /etc/motd &

# Start a mail application:
zmail -gui &
```

Here, we use the *contrib* client *xmessage* to show the message of the day, and we call up an X-based commercial mail application, *zmail*.

What does that leave for terminal emulator windows like *xterm*? Well, by default, *xterm* shells are not login shells—that is, *xterm* shells don't run *.login*, but just the shell startup file *.cshrc*. You can call up a login shell *xterm* by starting *xterm* clients with the –*ls* option. (Alternatively, you can set up all *xterm*s to run login shells by setting the XTerm*loginShell resource to true.)

Whether you want to set up *xterm* as login shells depends on what you use *.login* for. However, you might want to start thinking of the *.login* file as the startup file for ASCII-based user sessions only. Some of the functions of the *.login* script don't make sense for *xterm* shells (such as setting the terminal type, which *xterm* is smart enough to do on its own). But those functions are still useful for when you log in at an ASCII terminal, which you undoubtedly still do on occasion (for example, when dialing in on a modem line).

The *.cshrc* file therefore takes on a lot more responsibility for your shell environment, since it needs to make the *xterm* shell environment complete on its own. Since it's also used for C shell scripts, you can write it so it tests for a prompt and provides interactive-shell startup commands for interactive shells only:

```
# Make default file mode -rw-rw-r--.
umask 002

set path=(/usr/local/bin /usr/ucb /usr/bin /usr/bin/X11 .)

# Fix "dirs" and "$cwd" not to be fooled by symbolic links:
set hardpaths

# ALIASES AND OTHER INTERACTIVE COMMANDS GO BETWEEN HERE AND endif:
if ($?prompt) then
        set history=50 savehist=25
        set host=`hostname`
        set mail=(300 /usr/spool/mail/$user)
        set prompt="${host}:$user \!% "
        alias h history
        alias ls "ls -F"
        alias rm "rm -i"
        stty erase '^h'
        setenv PRINTER dodo_ps
endif
```

In this example, the part between "if ($?prompt)" and "endif" are only executed for the primary interactive shell.

Note that if you use *xinit* to start your X session, then your *.login* file is executed when you first log in prior to starting the X server. If you use *xdm* to start your X session, the *.login* file is never executed at all unless you run *xterm* with the *–ls* option.

2.3.4 Starting Remote Clients

One of the advantages of a window system like X is that you can run applications remotely and view them on the local display. You can try this easily enough by just doing a *rlogin* to the remote host, setting the DISPLAY environment variable, and starting up a client. In the following example, we start up a new *xterm* client running on the host *ruby*:

```
sapphire:joan % rlogin ruby
Password:
Last login: Tue May 12 16:27:23 from sapphire.ora.com
SunOS Release 4.1.2 (RUBY+COALM+PPP) #1: Tue Mar 3 23:29:52 EST 1992
You have mail.
TERM = (vt100) xterm

ruby:joan % setenv DISPLAY sapphire:0
ruby:joan % xterm &
```

(You must, of course, have an account on the remote system.)

The first thing that might go wrong is that you may run into server access control. If you see the following error:

```
Xlib:  connection to "sapphire:0" refused by server
Xlib:  Client is not authorized to connect to Server
Error: Can't open display: sapphire:0
```

you can probably fix it by typing "xhost +ruby" in a *sapphire* window, and running the command again on *ruby*.* Or, if you use user-based access control on the local host, use the *xauth* command to propagate the access code to the remote machine. See Chapter 4 for more information on server access control.

(Other possible problems may be with your host database, with Yellow Pages (NIS), or with the Domain Name Service. See Section 2.3.1.1 for more information on conflicts with display names.)

Once you have networking and access control issues solved, you should be able to display clients from the remote machine. The next issue is how to run remote clients *easily*.

2.3.4.1 Starting a Remote Client with rsh

The preferable way to start a remote client is the same way you'd start any remote command: using the *rsh* command:

```
sapphire:joan % rsh ruby -n xterm -display sapphire:0
```

There are a few issues to be ironed out first, though.

In order to run *rsh* successfully, you need to make sure that you have permission to run remote shells on the remote machine. This means that the local machine must be listed either in the remote machine's */etc/hosts.equiv* file, or in your personal *$HOME/.rhosts* file on the remote machine. For example, an *.rhosts* file might read:

```
sapphire.ora.com
harry.ora.com
```

If the host is properly set up on the remote machine, then *rsh* will execute properly and *rlogin* will no longer ask for a password when you try to connect to the remote machine. If it is not set up properly, then *rlogin* will prompt for a password, and *rsh* will fail with the message "Permission denied."

Using *.rhosts* or */etc/hosts.equiv* for this purpose might be considered a breach of security, since it means if someone breaks into your account on one machine, they can break into your account on all other machines as well. Clearly, you want to be careful what hosts you list in *.rhosts*. For that reason, it's better to use the fully qualified domain name (i.e., *harry.ora.com* instead of just *harry*).

There are a few more rules:

- The *.rhosts* file will be ignored if it is publically writable, for security reasons. Make sure that the *.rhosts* file is writable only by you.

- Make sure you are running the correct *rsh* command. Some systems have a "restricted" shell, also named *rsh*. If you get the following error:

```
ruby: ruby: No such file or directory
```

---

*The security-conscious may prefer to use the fully qualified domain name on the *xhost* command line (such as xhost +ruby.ora.com).

or:

```
ruby: ruby: cannot open
```

where *ruby* is the name of the system that you wanted to run the remote shell on, the problem is probably that are using the wrong *rsh* command. Use the *which* or *whereis* command to track down which *rsh* you are using:

```
sapphire:joan % which rsh
/bin/rsh
sapphire:joan % echo $path
/bin /usr/bin /usr/bin/X11 /usr/bsd
```

On some System V-derived systems such as IRIX, the restricted shell *rsh* might live in */bin*, while the remote shell *rsh* (the one you want) resides in */usr/bsd*. */bin* often shows up in search paths earlier than */usr/bsd*, so on those systems you need to explicitly redefine your path so that */usr/bsd* is searched before */bin*.

- You may need to use the *–n* option to *rsh* to avoid a "Stopped" error message on some machines.

- You need to be sure that the directory containing X binaries is defined in your search path in either *.cshrc* or *.profile* on the remote system.

- If you are using host-based access control, you need to execute the *xhost* client to extend access to the remote host before the *rsh* command is run. Otherwise, clients from the remote host will not have permission to access your display. If you are using user-based access control, you may need to run the *xauth* command to copy your access code to the remote machine. See Chapter 4 for more information on server access control.

- You have to use the *-display* option in calling a remote shell, or the "Can't Open display" error will be returned. (Alternatively, you can have your DISPLAY environment variable hard-coded into your *.cshrc* or *.profile* on the remote machine, but this is a Very Bad Idea.) See Section 2.3.1 for more information on setting your display.

- Be careful not to use unix:0.0 or :0.0 as the display name! Otherwise, the client will display the window on the local display of the remote host. If this succeeds, the user on that display could either become very annoyed, or could take advantage of the sudden access to your account to read personal files and send nasty mail to your boss. You would have no warning; all you would know is that your window didn't appear. (See Section 2.3.1 for more information on the DISPLAY environment variable.)

  A common situation is to start *rsh* commands as follows:

  ```
  sapphire:joan % rsh ruby -n xterm -display $DISPLAY
  ```

  This works great if your DISPLAY variable is set to something like sapphire:0.0, but if it's set to unix:0.0 or :0.0 (as is the default for X sessions begun on the console display), then the wrong display name will be sent to the remote machine.

The X11R5 distribution contains a shell script called *xrsh* in the *contrib/clients* area. This script sets the DISPLAY variable for the remote client and handles authentication according to the value of an XRSH_AUTH_TYPE environment variable. See the manpage on *xrsh* for more information.

2.4 Startup Methods

The X Display Manager, *xdm*, is the method of choice for starting your X session. The main reason for this is that *xdm* is the only elegant way of starting an X session on an X terminal or other remote "passive" X server. However, for local X servers, you can use the *xinit* or *startx* command to start both the X server and your X session in a single step. If you are running a vendor-configured version of X, there might also be another command for starting the X server, such as *openwin* for Sun OpenWindows; see your vendor's documentation for details.

On an X server controlled by *xdm*, the X server is always running, and users start their individual X sessions by logging in via a login box window.

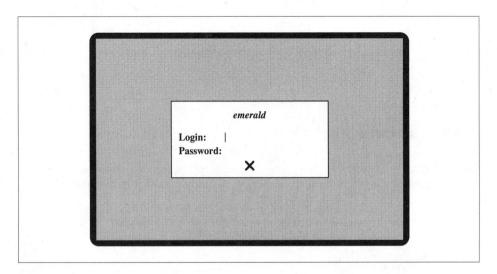

Figure 2-11. Logging in with xdm

When you log in, your window manager and other X clients are automatically started, as specified in your *.xsession* startup script. Chapter 3 discusses *xdm* in detail.

On a local console display server that does not already have the X server running (i.e., is not controlled by *xdm*), you log in as usual on the console (using *getty*) and type *xinit* to start both the X server and the X clients specified in your *.xinitrc* script.

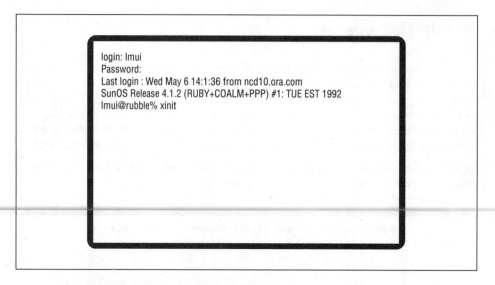

```
login: lmui
Password:
Last login : Wed May 6 14:1:36 from ncd10.ora.com
SunOS Release 4.1.2 (RUBY+COALM+PPP) #1: TUE EST 1992
lmui@rubble% xinit
```

Figure 2-12. Starting the X server with xinit

2.4.1 xinit and startx

The *xinit* program first starts up the X server for the local display. By default, it starts the X server by running the program called */usr/bin/X11/X*. *X* is usually a link to another server program, for example, *Xsun* on a Sun workstation.

You can override the server command by entering another command in a file called *$HOME/.xserverrc*. For example, it could contain:

```
/usr/bin/X11/XsunMono
```

You may want to set up a new command in *$HOME/.xserverrc* if you are testing a new server for your display, or if you prefer to start up your server with particular command-line options.

If you want to test an option to the X server, follow the *xinit* command with two dash characters (– –) and it will pass any following command-line options onto the server. For example:

```
% xinit -- -dev /dev/cgthree0
```

After starting the server, *xinit* looks for a shell script called *$HOME/.xinitrc*. As we saw in Section 2.1.1, if *$HOME/.xinitrc* does not exist, a single *xterm* window is sent to the local display to get you started.

The *startx* script is a front end to *xinit* provided in X11R4 and X11R5. Like *xinit*, it looks for an *.xinitrc* file in your home directory; however, if you don't have an *.xinitrc*, it then uses a system-wide default file in */usr/lib/X11/xinit* called *xinitrc*. This file can also be used as a template for *.xinitrc* files. *startx* also uses a file called *xserverrc* in the same directory for users who don't have an *.xserverrc* file in their home directory.

The X Window System Administrator's Guide

2.4.2 Differences Between .xinitrc and .xsession

All of the rules about configuring *.xinitrc* files also apply to *.xsession* files. For that reason, many users simply link their *.xinitrc* files to their *.xsession* files. However, there are three points to consider:

1. The *.xsession* file is generally a shell script, but it can actually be any executable file, such as a session manager or desktop manager. *.xinitrc* must be a Bourne shell script.

2. The *.xsession* file *must* be an executable file. If you get bounced back to your *xdm* login box, you might have to do the following:

   ```
   % chmod +x .xsession
   ```

   The *.xinitrc* file does not have to be executable.

3. The *.xsession* script does not inherit the user's login shell environment. The *.xinitrc* script inherits the environment from the shell from which it was run.

2.5 Related Documentation

For more information, see the *X Window System User's Guide*, by Valerie Quercia and Tim O'Reilly, published by O'Reilly & Associates, Inc.

The following X manual pages may be of interest: *X*, *xrdb*, *xinit*, *xset*, *xterm*, *twm*, *mwm*, *olwm*, *xlsfonts*, *showrgb*, and *resize*.

The following UNIX manual pages may be of interest: *rsh*, *csh*, and *sh*.

3

The X Display Manager

The X Display Manager provides a way for users to log on and start initial clients, regardless of which X server they use. This chapter shows how to get xdm *going and how to configure it to the needs of your site.*

In This Chapter:

3
The X Display Manager

The X Display Manager, *xdm*, runs as a daemon on a host machine. It provides a way for users to log on and start initial clients, regardless of what X server they use.

Not all sites use *xdm* to control X sessions. Many workstation users still prefer to log on as usual on the console and use the *xinit* program to start the X server and any preferred clients. *xinit*, however, is considered obsolete by the X Consortium, with all new functionality being built into *xdm*. And on a site that includes X terminals, *xdm* is an essential tool for providing a standard way for users to log on across the network.

xdm also provides a way for administrators to configure environments system-wide. So if you don't already use *xdm* to control X sessions for users on your site, we encourage you to give it a try.

---

xdm and Vendor Environments

If you're running a vendor-distributed version of X that's greatly modified from the MIT version, your mileage may vary with this chapter. For example, the OpenWindows 2.*x* server doesn't work very well with *xdm* at all. The OpenWindows 3.*x* distribution, meanwhile, supplies its own version of *xdm* which is somewhat modified from the version documented here.

SCO Open Desktop has its own version of *xdm*, called *scologin*, which must be used for all logins. *scologin* is enhanced in that it has SCO's session manager *scosession* built-in as the controlling process for the X session, and it checks for expired passwords. *scologin* also provides a front end (*/etc/scologin*) to facilitate some administrative responsibilities.

In addition, many vendor-supplied X environments already have *xdm* pre-configured when X is installed.

3.1 xdm Concepts

The *xdm* program is simply an X client that manages the first and last points of connection, control, and coordination of the user session. If you need a conceptual feel for what the X Display Manager is, think of *xdm* as working for network-connected X servers the way *init*, *getty*, and *login* work for serial-connected ASCII terminals. This is only a loose comparison, but it will serve our purposes in conveying the general function of *xdm*.

Like *init*, *xdm* keeps track of which X servers are available to be connected. When *init* has determined that an ASCII terminal is available to be managed, it spawns the *getty* program, which puts up a login prompt. Similarly, when *xdm* is given management of an X server, it sends a login box to the server display.

When a user types a name and password on a serial ASCII terminal, that information is sent to the *login* program, which authenticates the password and then starts up whatever program is specified in the user's */etc/passwd*, almost always an interactive shell. When the shell begins, user-configurable batch files are executed, *$HOME/.profile* for the Bourne/Korn shell or *$HOME/.cshrc* and *$HOME/.login* for the C shell. The user is then deposited in the selected shell environment, ready to run UNIX commands.

For a user who logs in with an *xdm* login box, the name and password are also authenticated, using the same mechanism as the *login* program. However, this is where the functions of *login* and *xdm* diverge. As shown in Figure 3-1, instead of running an interactive shell, *xdm* runs a series of shell scripts. These scripts normally start all your desired X clients, including

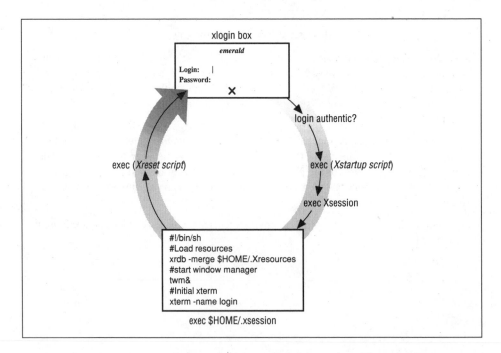

Figure 3-1. xdm flow chart

one or more terminal emulators, each of which will contain an interactive shell. In the default *xdm* configuration, *Xsession* is one of the shell scripts that are executed. *Xsession* then calls another script called *$HOME/.xsession* (if it exists).

When a user logs out on a character-based terminal, control of the terminal returns to *getty*, sending another login prompt to the terminal. Consistent with that model, when a user logs out of an X session (i.e., when the "controlling" process of the X session has been terminated), *xdm* closes all connections and resets the terminal to a "ready for log on" state, displaying a new login box, ready for another user session.

As you can see, *xdm* is a very ambitious program. It can be configured to control logins on multiple X servers connected to the same machine, creating customized sessions, and offering some basic network security features.

The conclusion is that *xdm*, when set up properly, enables users to walk up to a display and log in by typing their usernames and passwords, the same as they would on an ASCII terminal. *xdm* then runs their startup scripts automatically, setting up customized environments and enabling users to begin productive work immediately. When users finish their X sessions, *xdm* resets each display for the next user. With the X session startup process incorporated into the login process, users need to know relatively little about X11 to start working—given, of course, that *xdm* and users' individual environments are configured appropriately.

History of xdm and XDMCP

xdm was introduced with X11R3, to support the X terminals that were just coming to the market. That first version of *xdm* had several problems, which were solved in X11R4 by the introduction of the XDM Control Protocol (XDMCP).

The most urgent problem that XDMCP addressed was the problem of X terminals that are turned off and on again. Prior to XDMCP, the only way *xdm* knew to control an X terminal was to look for its entry in the *Xservers* file (see Section 3.5.2 for more information). Since *Xservers* is consulted only when *xdm* is first started, this caused problems when X terminals were turned off temporarily, or when new X terminals were attached. It meant that every time a user turned an X terminal off and on, the system administrator needed to send a *SIGHUP* to *xdm*. XDMCP provides a solution to this problem.

XDMCP, introduced in X11R4, is a protocol shared by the *xdm* client and X servers throughout the network. Using XDMCP, the X server has the responsibility of actively requesting an *xdm* connection from the host. If an X server uses XDMCP, therefore, it no longer requires an entry in *Xservers* since the host no longer has the burden of initiating the connection.

Almost all X terminals sold today are XDMCP-compatible. R4 and R5 servers running on local console displays are also XDMCP-compatible, but XDMCP queries are not enabled by default.

3.2 xdm Configuration Files

xdm is configured through a set of editable ASCII files for some of the mechanisms you would expect—a list of servers to be explicitly controlled by *xdm*, resources to be used by *xdm*, error messages, whether to use security, etc.—but it also provides ASCII files for setting up an initial default session and setting resources to be loaded by the server itself. The files used for *xdm* configuration in */usr/lib/X11/xdm* are listed here (and shown in Figure 3-2), to be discussed in detail later in the chapter:

xdm-config Resources specified for *xdm*. Note that the location of all other files listed below can be redefined with resources specified in *xdm-config*. (The location of the *xdm-config* file itself can be reassigned using the *–config* option to *xdm* when it is started.)

Xservers A list of servers to be explicitly managed by *xdm*. The local display server usually needs to be listed here.

Xsession The initial startup script used by each individual X session.

Xresources Resources to be loaded via *xrdb* by servers managed by *xdm*.

xdm-pid A file containing the process ID of *xdm*. (This file is not designed to be edited by administrators, but is for informational purposes only.) (X11R4 and later only.)

xdm-errors The error log file for *xdm*. (This file is not designed to be edited by administrators, but is for informational purposes only.)

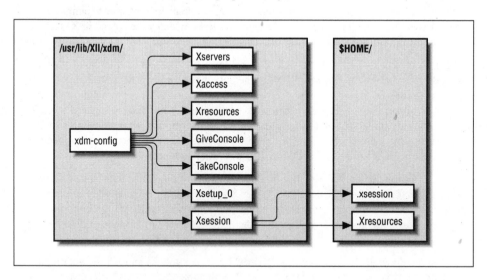

Figure 3-2. Default xdm configuration files

Xaccess   A file for configuring access control for XDMCP, specifying different behavior according to the sort of query used. This configuration file is new to X11R5.

GiveConsole

     A shell script that changes the ownership of the console to the user. This file is new to X11R5. See Section 4.6.2 for information on how the *GiveConsole* script is used.

TakeConsole

     A shell script that changes the ownership of the console back to root. This file is new to X11R5. See Section 4.6.2 for information on how the *TakeConsole* script is used.

Xsetup_0   A shell script used for display setup specific to the local console server. This file is new to X11R5.

In users' home directories, the following files are used by *xdm* in its default configuration:

$HOME/.xsession

     User-specific startup script executed by the systemwide *Xsession* script.

$HOME/.Xresources

     User-specific resources read by the systemwide *Xsession* script if *$HOME/.xsession* does not exist. (If *$HOME/.xsession* does exist, then the *.xsession* script is responsible for loading user-specific resources from *.Xresources* or any other resource file.) See Appendix D for information on setting resources.

$HOME/.xsession-errors

     Errors specific to a user's X session (R5 only). This file is not designed to be edited.

$HOME/.Xauthority

     Machine-readable authorization codes for the user's server. This file is not designed to be edited by hand. See Chapter 4 for information on how the *.Xauthority* file is used.

Note that the user-configurable *.xsession* file is available only because it is *exec*'d by the *Xsession* shell script. If you don't understand yet why this is important, consider that any administrator can remove that functionality, or can add any other clients or resources to be used by all X user sessions. So *xdm* configuration is unusual in that you can do just minimal configuration (just set things up so it runs and then leave it alone) or you can go wild setting up a global user environment.

We'll talk about all these files in detail later in the chapter. First, though, we'll give a quick and dirty procedure to get a minimal setup running.

3.3 xdm the Easy Way

For those of you that are interested in just getting *xdm* working for the first time, you can follow the steps below to set up *xdm* on a standalone workstation. These steps assume that you are using the MIT-distributed version of *xdm*, and that the *xdm* configuration files have not been changed from the defaults distributed by MIT.

1. Edit the *Xservers* file in */usr/lib/X11/xdm* as needed. If you want *xdm* to control the local display server, the *Xservers* file should contain the line:

    ```
    :0 local /usr/bin/X11/X
    ```

    If you don't want *xdm* to control the local display server, this line should be omitted. In all likelihood, the default *Xservers* file will work just fine.

2. If you're currently running the X server on the local console display, you should exit it. It's also a good idea to have an alternate way to log in to the workstation (such as a remote login across the network, or an ASCII terminal connected to a serial port), since if something goes wrong, your console may become unusable.

3. Start *xdm* as **root**:

    ```
    # /usr/bin/X11/xdm
    ```

The X server will take over your display and you should see a login box resembling that in Figure 3-3.

Figure 3-3. xdm login box

The X Window System Administrator's Guide

Now log in. You should get an *xterm* window and a *twm* window manager, as shown in Figure 3-4.

Figure 3-4. Default xdm environment

You can configure this environment by creating a shell script in your home directory called *.xsession* and making it executable. If written as a Bourne shell script, the rules for writing the *.xsession* file are similar to those for the *.xinitrc* file used for *xinit*. Unlike *.xinitrc*, however, *.xsession* does not have to be a Bourne shell script, it can be any executable. For information on configuring individual X sessions at the user level, see Chapter 2.

See Section 3.7 for information on how to install *xdm* to start at boot time.

3.4 Troubleshooting xdm

Problems with logging in via *xdm* might be traced using *xdm* error messages. Many errors are placed in the file */usr/lib/X11/xdm/xdm-errors*, but if you are using R5 *xdm*, the first place to look is in the file *$HOME/.xsession-errors*. *$HOME/.xsession-errors* contains errors generated only under your user account. In addition, some of the more common situations are listed here:

- *If the server doesn't start or if you don't get the login box*, there is probably something wrong with your *xdm* configuration files. Kill *xdm* from the alternate login we recommended in Step 2, and look in the file */usr/lib/X11/xdm/xdm-errors* for hints. Good candidates for mistakes of this magnitude are the *Xservers*, *xdm-config*, and *Xaccess* files. If you'd rather not deal with it, try to restore the files to the MIT defaults (or to the versions originally distributed by your vendor) and try again.

- *If you get the "Login incorrect" error*, guess what, you typed your login name or password wrong. Try again. *xdm* uses the same login authentication as the *login* program does, so if you can log on at the console or at any other terminal window, then you can log on using *xdm*.

- *If you log on and the login box returns instantly*, something's wrong with your environment. Either the */usr/lib/X11/xdm/xdm-errors* file or *$HOME/.xsession-errors* (under R5) will contain error messages that can help you track the problem.

  - One possibility is that your *.xsession* file isn't executable. Try pressing F1 (or in R5, CTRL-RETURN) after your password instead of the RETURN key to access the "failsafe" session. This will bypass your *.xsession* and give you a single *xterm* window, sufficient to edit your environment. If your problem is that your *.xsession* isn't executable, the error message in *.xsession-errors* (or *xdm-errors* in R3 and R4) will read something like:

    ```
    /usr/lib/X11/xdm/Xsession: /home/judy/.xsession: Permission denied
    ```

    If this is your problem, simply do:

    ```
    % chmod +x .xsession
    ```

    This might need to be done if you've just created your *.xsession* file, or if you've just copied it from another machine using *ftp*.

  - Under some early distributions of R5, another possibility is that there is a problem writing to your *$HOME/.xsession-errors* file. One reason this might happen is if your home directory isn't properly NFS-mounted from another host. The "failsafe" session won't help in this case; instead, if you're on the console display server, press CTRL-R at the login box to disable both the *xdm* connection and the X server on that display. The error message in *xdm-errors* will read:

    ```
    /usr/lib/X11/xdm/Xsession: /home/tim/.xsession-errors: Permission denied
    ```

    Either your home directory doesn't exist, or your home directory isn't writable by you, or your *.xsession-errors* file isn't writable by you ... track down the problem, correct it, and try again.

- *If you log on, windows flicker on your screen, and then the login box reappears*, you probably put all your clients in the background in your *.xsession* script. Press F1 after your password to access the "failsafe" session and edit your *.xsession*. You need to put the last interactive client in the foreground by omitting the trailing "&." See Section 2.2.3.1 for more information.

  (Note that if this is your problem, *xdm* will not generate an error message since as far as *xdm* is concerned, everything was executed successfully.)

Now that you have *xdm* working for your local display, it's trivial for it to control other X servers at your site. If you have X terminals that are XDMCP-compatible, you should be able to just set them up to query your host for an *xdm* connection. See Section 7.5.1 for more information on setting up X terminals for use with *xdm*.

Some readers will want to stop reading this chapter right here. However, if you're interested in refining your *xdm* configuration or you just want to know more about how *xdm* works, please read on.

3.5 Customizing xdm

Now that we've told you the general idea of *xdm* and how to get it going, it's time to talk about the gory details.

The following sections describe the xdm configuration files in detail.

3.5.1 The Master Configuration File (xdm-config)

All of the configuration files used by *xdm* are specified in the *xdm-config* file (with the notable exception of *xdm-config* itself), so it's worth your while to become very familiar with its contents. You can consider it to be the starting point of your *xdm* configuration.

The *xdm-config* file is really just a resource file for the *xdm* client. For that reason, the syntax for *xdm-config* follows standard resource specification syntax. See Appendix D for more information on resource syntax (although you might be able to get through this chapter without it).

The following is the sample *xdm-config* file as it comes from MIT in Release 5 of X11:

```
DisplayManager.errorLogFile:      /usr/lib/X11/xdm/xdm-errors
DisplayManager.pidFile:           /usr/lib/X11/xdm/xdm-pid
DisplayManager.keyFile:           /usr/lib/X11/xdm/xdm-keys
DisplayManager.servers:           /usr/lib/X11/xdm/Xservers
DisplayManager.accessFile:        /usr/lib/X11/xdm/Xaccess
DisplayManager._0.authorize:      true
DisplayManager._0.setup:          /usr/lib/X11/xdm/Xsetup_0
DisplayManager._0.startup:        /usr/lib/X11/xdm/GiveConsole
DisplayManager._0.reset:          /usr/lib/X11/xdm/TakeConsole
DisplayManager*resources:         /usr/lib/X11/xdm/Xresources
DisplayManager*session:           /usr/lib/X11/xdm/Xsession
DisplayManager*authComplain:      false
```

The keyword `DisplayManager` starting each resource name is the internal "class name" for *xdm*. *xdm* uses some resources for configuring *xdm* itself, and other resources for configuring its behavior once individual X display servers have connected to it. In particular, resource specification in *xdm-config* follows one of the following forms:

```
DisplayManager.variable:          value
        or
DisplayManager.DISPLAY.variable:  value
        or
DisplayManager*variable:          value
```

- In the first form, the `DisplayManager` keyword is separated from the variable name by a single period, meaning that this is a resource that makes sense only when applied to *xdm* proper. An example of a resource like this is `DisplayManager.servers`, for specifying which file should be used for listing the X servers to be managed by *xdm*. You can think of this sort of resource name as applying to *xdm*'s behavior independent of its connection to any particular X server: which servers to connect to, where to copy its process ID, where to put error messages, etc.

- The second form is used to specify a resource that should apply to a single display server only. Here's where the tricky part to resource naming rules for *xdm* comes into play: since the colon (`:`) has special meaning in resource specification syntax, the underscore (`_`) is used where these would normally occur in a display name. For example, the display name `bigbird:0` becomes `bigbird_0` if it appears in a resource name. Without an underscore to specify that a particular server is being referred to, the name is taken to represent a group of X servers, called a *display class*. See Section 3.5.6 for more information on display classes.

  The server for which you'd most want to define a specific resource is the local console display (`:0`, specified as `_0` in resource specifications). An example of one of these is the `DisplayManager._0.authorize` resource—you usually want to enable access control on the local server, but you may not want it enabled on X terminals if they don't support that functionality.

- The third form of an *xdm* resource specification is really just a generalization of the second form. By putting an asterisk between the `DisplayManager` keyword and the variable name, where a display name would normally be, you can define this value for all servers not specifically defined otherwise. As a common example, you could use the following lines:

  ```
  DisplayManager*authorize:      false
  DisplayManager._0.authorize:   true
  ```

  and only the local display server will use access control.

In resource lingo, these are called "loose" and "tight" bindings. We discuss resource bindings in detail in Appendix D.

See your *xdm* manpage for a description of other resources that can be specified in the *xdm-config* file.

For testing purposes, you can use the *-config* option to *xdm* to test new configuration files. For example, to start *xdm* with a customized configuration file, enter:

```
# /usr/bin/X11/xdm -config ./my.xdm-config
```

The `DisplayManager.autoRescan` resource controls whether *xdm* automatically rereads the configuration files after they have been changed. If set to `true` (the default), *xdm* will reread the *xdm-config* file the next time a server connects to *xdm*. If set to `false`, then if you edit the *xdm-config* file while *xdm* is still running, you have to send *xdm* a *SIGHUP* signal before it will be reread. See Sections 3.6.2 and 3.6.3 for more information on sending a *SIGHUP* to *xdm*.

3.5.2 Listing X Servers (the Xservers File)

The *Xservers* file was originally designed in X11R3 to list all X servers to be managed by *xdm*. The XDM Control Protocol, introduced in R4, changes the function of the *Xservers* file significantly.

Under X11R3, all X servers managed by *xdm* required entries in *Xservers*. The only way *xdm* would know to connect to a server is if it appeared in the *Xservers* file at startup. In that way, *Xservers* acted somewhat like an *inittab* for *xdm*.

With X11R4 and XDMCP, the X terminal takes responsibility for querying the host for an *xdm* connection. For that reason, any X terminal that supports XDMCP should have its entry removed from *Xservers* on a host running X11R4 or later.

The *Xservers* file is not yet obsolete, however. It is still used to start the X session on the local console display, which does not normally use XDMCP queries. It is also used to tell *xdm* how to start up the X server on the local machine.

3.5.2.1 Xservers Syntax

The syntax for each line in the *Xservers* file varies on whether it's for a server that runs on the local machine, and whether a display class is specified in *Xservers* for that machine. The only X servers that you need to enter into the *Xservers* file are those that do not use XDMCP to request a connection. For the most part, the only X server that needs to be specified in *Xservers* is the console display server. If your console display server is R4- or R5-compatible, it probably supports XDMCP queries but does not have them enabled by default. So you need to enter the local server into the *Xservers* file if you want it to be managed by *xdm*:

```
:0 local /usr/bin/X11/X
```

The console display name, `:0`, is followed by the word `local` to tell *xdm* that it's an X server running on the local machine, and then by the command used to start the X server. This command, */usr/bin/X11/X*, is executed when *xdm* is started up. */usr/bin/X11/X* is usually a symbolic link to another server program.*

Since X terminals run their server on another machine, they have a slightly different syntax in *Xservers*. You only need to enter X terminals in *Xservers* if they don't support XDMCP or if you're running R3 *xdm* on the host. The following are examples of *Xservers* entries for X terminals:

```
ncd1:0 foreign NCD xterminal
visual1:0 VISUAL-X19TURBO foreign Visual xterminal
bigbird:0 XNCD19r foreign Eileen's xterminal
```

---

*An example of when this would be useful is for a '386 workstation, on which any number of third-party monitors might be installed, requiring multiple servers to support them all. Among the steps required to install a new monitor may be to link *X* to a different server program.

Managing Another Workstation's Display

It's common to use *xdm* on a given host to manage X terminals, but what if you want it to manage the display server on another workstation? This can be done, it just needs a little coordination between the two hosts. For example, if you want to set up a host *rock* to manage the display of the workstation *scribe*, you have to do the following:

1. First of all, make sure *xdm* isn't being run on the workstation *scribe*, since you probably don't want it running. If for some bizarre reason you *do* want it running, make sure that the local server isn't listed in the *Xservers* file on *scribe*—that is, if *xdm* is running, make sure the following is commented out in *Xservers*:

   ```
   #:0 local /usr/bin/X11/X
   ```

2. You have to decide which end you want to start the *xdm* connection on.

   a. If you want to start the connection on the server side, have the X server started with an active XDMCP query.

   ```
   % /usr/bin/X11/X -query rock.west.ora.com
   ```

   If you want to set it up permanently, put this command in */etc/rc.local*.

   The *-query* option tells the X server to place a Direct XDMCP query to the specified host. Use the *-indirect* option in place of *-query* for an Indirect query to the specified host—for example, to get a *chooser* box from R5 *xdm* (see Section 3.5.3.2 for more information on the *chooser* client). You can also use the *-broadcast* option for a Broadcast query, in which case the first *xdm* host who replies to the query gets control of the server. The *-broadcast* option is not followed by a hostname.

   b. If you want to start the connection on the host side, put in the *Xservers* file on the host running *xdm* (*rock* in this example):

   ```
   scribe:0   foreign   X server on workstation "scribe"
   ```

   And have the X server on *scribe* started "passively", such as:

   ```
   % /usr/bin/X11/X
   ```

   (Again, to set it up permanently, put this command in */etc/rc.local*.)

As a policy, it's probably better to have the connection started via an XDMCP query and avoid explicitly listing hosts in *Xservers*. A disadvantage to listing hosts in *Xservers* is that you have to make sure that you don't end up having the same server listed in two *Xservers* files on two different hosts. If you see the following error in the */usr/lib/X11/xdm/xdm-errors* file:

```
error (pid n): WARNING: keyboard on display ... could not be secured
```

what might have happened is that another host has the server listed in its *Xservers* file and is currently running *xdm* on the same X server.

As with the entry for the local server, each of these entries starts with the display name. In the first of these, the display name, `ncd1:0`, is followed by the word `foreign` to signify that it's an X server running on another machine.* The other entries are examples of entries for X terminals with *display classes* specified. If the name of a display is followed by something other than `local` or `foreign`, it's taken as a display class. (See Section 3.5.6 for more information on display classes.) In the example, the display classes used are VISUAL-X19TURBO and XNCD19r. The name of the display class is then followed by `foreign`.

The rest of the line is ignored, and can be used for a comment. In R3, beware that although the rest of the line is ignored, it must consist of at least one word.

Note that like the *xdm-config* file, the `DisplayManager.autoRescan` resource controls whether *xdm* automatically rereads the *Xservers* file if it has been changed, or requires a *SIGHUP* signal before it rereads configuration files. By default, any configuration files that have been changed are automatically reread when the next server connects to *xdm*. See Sections 3.6.2 and 3.6.3 for more information on sending a *SIGHUP* to *xdm*.

3.5.3 xdm Host Access Control: the Xaccess File (R5 Only)

In X11R5, the *Xaccess* file is introduced to allow administrators to control how *xdm* responds to different types of XDMCP queries. It's important to note that the *Xaccess* file is not related to server access control, which is controlled by the `DisplayManager*authorize` resource. See Chapter 4 for information on server access control. All the *Xaccess* file controls is what servers can get a login window; users still need to supply their user name and password when they actually log in.

As mentioned earlier, there are three types of queries defined for X terminals using XDMCP: Direct, Indirect, and Broadcast. If an X terminal is set up to use "Direct," it means that it will ask a particular host for a connection. If it is set up to use "Broadcast," it means that it will send out a general query throughout the network, for any host running *xdm* to answer—for most X servers, the first host that answers is the one that gets control of the terminal.

"Indirect" queries are for hosts that might forward the connection to another host, but hosts that could actually do this were few and far between before R5 *xdm*. Ideally, you would want a user to have a choice among multiple hosts to connect to. Some X servers have this functionality built in, using either "Indirect" or "Broadcast" queries. But to control those X terminals that did not have it built in, administrators had to resort to hacking *xdm* to support it. This has changed with X11R5.

With R5, the *Xaccess* file starts to put all this in place. Among other things, it provides a way of using the *chooser* client, which allows the user to choose among multiple other hosts. Indirect, Direct, and Broadcast queries are shown in Figure 3-5.

---

*In R3 *xdm*, the display type `transient` was used for some foreign displays. "Transient" is no longer a valid display type.

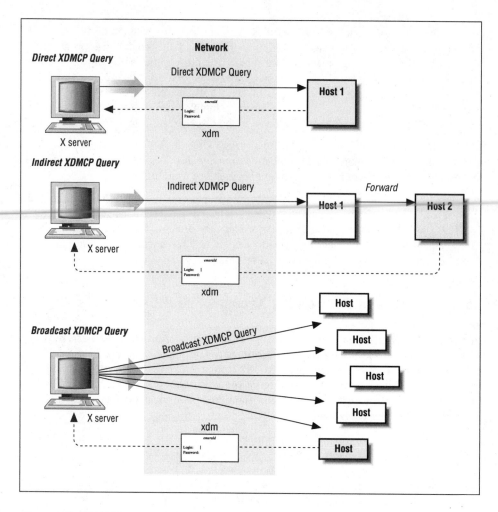

Figure 3-5. XDMCP Direct, Indirect, and Broadcast queries

3.5.3.1 Direct and Broadcast Access

In its simplest form, the *Xaccess* file can be used to restrict access to particular X servers who request access via Direct and Broadcast queries. You can just list the addresses of X servers that you want to allow connections from, using standard UNIX wildcards (? to match a single character, * to match any number of characters). To omit a particular X server from the list of those allowed, start the name with an exclamation point (!). For example, to restrict access to servers in the *ora.com* domain, you might do:

```
*.ora.com
```

To allow connections from all X servers in the *ora.com* domain except for a workstation named *harry*, do:

```
!harry.ora.com
*.ora.com
```

In its MIT-distributed form, the *Xaccess* file is configured to allow Direct and Broadcast connections from all X servers:

```
*                    #any host can get a login window
```

3.5.3.2 Indirect Access and the Chooser

Until R5, the distinction between Direct and Indirect queries was poorly defined—there didn't seem to be any difference between connecting via a Direct query or an Indirect query to a particular host. The R5 *Xaccess* file changes that.

An Indirect query basically allows *xdm* on the host to determine what to do with the query. If *xdm* encounters a Broadcast or Direct query, it either pops up a login box or it doesn't (depending on whether the node is allowed access in the *Xaccess* file, as described above). Responding to an Indirect query, however, the *Xaccess* file gives the administrator a chance to configure whether to respond directly, whether to pass the query on to another host, or whether to give the user a choice between multiple hosts.

For example, to configure *xdm* to transfer an Indirect query from any NCD X terminals (named *ncd1*, *ncd2*, etc.) directly to the host *ruby.ora.com*, you might enter in *Xaccess*:

```
ncd*.ora.com    ruby.ora.com
```

Alternatively, you can set up *xdm* to respond to Indirect queries with a *chooser box*. This gives the user the opportunity to choose between several hosts, as shown in Figure 3-6. The *chooser* client, implemented via the CHOOSER keyword in the *Xaccess* file, is a big plus in R5. To allow the NCD X terminals to choose from *harry.ora.com*, *ruby.ora.com*, and *rock.west.ora.com*, enter into *Xaccess*:

```
ncd*.ora.com    CHOOSER harry.ora.com ruby.ora.com rock.west.ora.com
```

The *chooser* box would resemble the box in Figure 3-7.

The *chooser* client itself resides in */usr/lib/X11/xdm*, with everything else. Note that unlike the other files in that directory, it is not a readable ASCII file, but a compiled executable.

Yet another possibility might be to set up the *chooser* client so it just does a broadcast among all hosts on the network and allows the user to choose among them. To do this, just use the keyword BROADCAST following the CHOOSER keyword.

```
ncd*.ora.com    CHOOSER BROADCAST
```

To customize the appearance of the *chooser* client, use the *Xresources* file. The default *Xresources* file defines the following resources used by the *chooser* client:

```
Chooser*geometry:            700x500+300+200
Chooser*allowShellResize:    false
Chooser*viewport.forceBars:  true
Chooser*label.font:          *-new century schoolbook-bold-i-normal-*-240-*
Chooser*label.label:         XDMCP Host Menu  from CLIENTHOST
Chooser*list.font:           -*-*-medium-r-normal-*-*-230-*-*-c-*-iso8859-1
Chooser*Command.font:        *-new century schoolbook-bold-r-normal-*-180-*
```

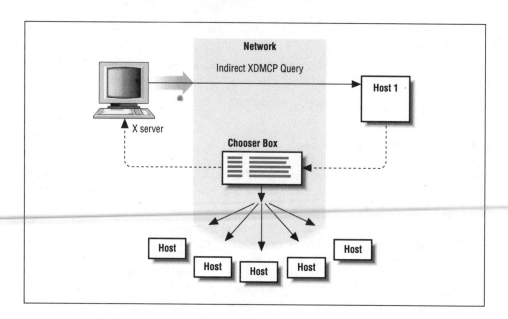

Figure 3-6. The chooser

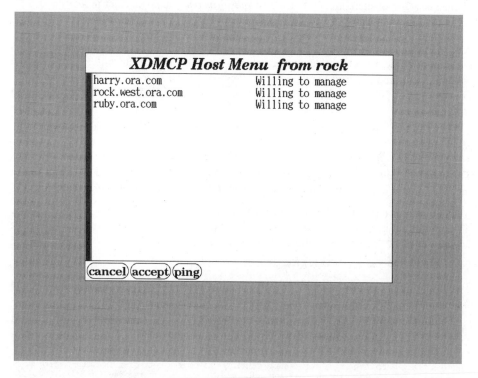

Figure 3-7. An example chooser box

The X Window System Administrator's Guide

3.5.3.3 Using Macros

The *Xaccess* file allows you to define *macros* to group together a set of hosts. A macro definition starts with a percent character (%), followed by the macro name, followed by a list of hostnames (with a backslash at the end of the line signifying that the definition continues onto the next line). The macro is then called later on, preceded by the %. An alternative way of allowing X terminals to choose among *harry*, *ruby* and *rock* might be:

```
%NCDHOSTS       harry.ora.com ruby.ora.com rock.west.ora.com

ncd*.ora.com    CHOOSER %NCDHOSTS
```

3.5.3.4 Advantages and Disadvantages of the Chooser

The big advantage that the *Xaccess* file provides is that it can make it much easier to maintain and control X terminals on a network. Without the chooser, the host to query is configured directly on the setup menu of an X terminal using XDMCP. If you want to move the management of some X terminals to another host, it may involve personally visiting each terminal and editing their setup menus manually, step-by-step. However, using the *Xaccess* file, you can simply set up a single host as the primary *xdm* server, designed to accept Indirect queries and determine where they should be transferred. Using this scheme, switching *xdm* management from one host to another is a matter of editing a single file.

In our bicoastal environment, we use the *chooser* to allow East Coast employees to access their environments from the West Coast without having to do contortions: they simply choose the East Coast *xdm* host and they are greeted by the same friendly login box they're used to at home.

A problem with the *chooser* functionality is that due to a bug in R4 *xdm*, it can be used only to transfer *xdm* control to another host running R5. For example, if you had in your *Xaccess* file:

```
%R5HOSTS  harry.ora.com ruby.ora.com rock.west.ora.com
%R4HOSTS  opal.ora.com

*       CHOOSER %R5HOSTS %R4HOSTS
```

with *opal* running R4 *xdm*, the chooser box would look like the one in Figure 3-8.

Note that only the R5 hosts (*harry*, *ruby* and *rock*) are reported as "Willing to manage." If you select one of the R5 hosts you'll get the *xlogin* box as expected; but although the R4 host is listed, if you select *opal* you'll be temporarily "hung" and then you will be returned to the *chooser* box without a chance to log on.

Note that like the *xdm-config* file, the `DisplayManager.autoRescan` resource controls whether *xdm* automatically rereads the *Xaccess* file if it has been changed, or requires a *SIGHUP* signal before it rereads configuration files. By default, any configuration files that have been changed are automatically reread when the next server connects to *xdm*. A message appears in the *xdm-errors* file:

```
info (pid 1564): Rereading access file /usr/lib/X11/xdm/Xaccess
```

See Sections 3.6.2 and 3.6.3 for more information on sending a *SIGHUP* to *xdm*.

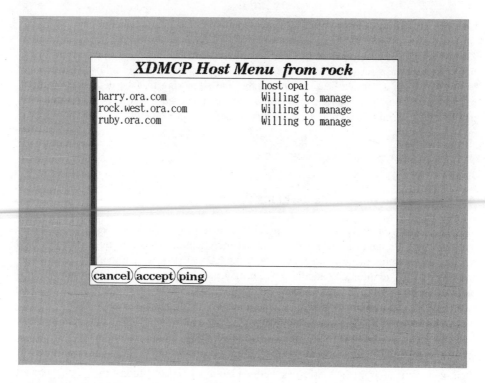

Figure 3-8. Chooser box with an R4 host

3.5.4 The Xresources File

The *Xresources* file is loaded into each individual X server as it is connected to *xdm*. The most important function of the *Xresources* file is to set resources for clients or widgets that are run before the user actually logs in. In particular, the *xlogin* widget's resources need to be loaded into the server by *xdm* itself, since it is (by necessity) run before the user logs in. In R5, the *chooser* and *xconsole* clients may also be run before the user logs in, so those clients need their resources specified in *Xresources* as well.

As each X server connects to *xdm*, the resources in the *Xresources* file are loaded by the server via the *xrdb* client. See Section D.1.3 for more information on *xrdb*.

3.5.4.1 Configuring the Login Box

The login box displayed on an X server controlled by *xdm* can be configured using the *Xresources* file. In its default configuration, that file contains the following lines:

```
xlogin*login.translations: #override\
    Ctrl<Key>R:  abort-display()\n\
    <Key>F1:  set-session-argument(failsafe) finish-field()\n\
    Ctrl<Key>Return:  set-session-argument(failsafe) finish-field()\n\
    <Key>Return:  set-session-argument() finish-field()
xlogin*borderWidth:  3
```

```
xlogin*greeting: CLIENTHOST
xlogin*namePrompt: login:\
xlogin*fail: Login incorrect
#ifdef COLOR
xlogin*greetColor: CadetBlue
xlogin*failColor: red
*Foreground: black
*Background: #fffff0
#else
xlogin*Foreground: black
xlogin*Background: white
#endif
```

The resources starting with the string xlogin are used by the *xlogin* widget. *xlogin* sends the box to the display, prompting the user for a name and password. The *xlogin* box typically resembles Figure 3-3.

Note that the first resource for *xlogin* is a translation table, used for defining how special keystrokes might be used within the client. (See Section D.1.4 for more information on translation tables.) This translation table is particularly important. What it does is to allow you to log in without running your *.xsession* file, by pressing F1 after your password instead of RETURN.*

Instead of running your *.xsession*, pressing F1 tells *xdm* to run a "failsafe" X session, defined as a single *xterm* window. (You can actually change this in the *Xsession* file. See Section 3.5.5 for more information on the *Xsession* file.) This is important, since otherwise you may have no way of logging in if your *.xsession* is corrupted.

The other important translation listed here is that you can use CTRL-R to stop *xdm* from managing your display entirely. This feature, new to R5, is useful for the local console display, where you might want to return to the console to start another windowing system or load a different X server image. Note that this only works if the X server isn't initiating XDMCP queries; otherwise, CTRL-R will abort the current *xdm* connection, but a new one will instantly replace it.

The remainder of the resources set for *xlogin* are fairly straightforward, used largely to specify the messages used for prompts and error messages. Note that since this resource file is loaded into the server via *xrdb*, *cpp* pre-processor commands (particularly #ifdef, #else, and #endif) can be used. In the R5 default shown above, the pre-processor commands are used to specify how the *xlogin* box should appear, depending on whether the display has color support. COLOR is one of the variables that are pre-defined in R5 *xrdb*; see Section D.1.3 for more information on *xrdb* pre-defined variables.

One resource you may want to change is the greeting in the *xlogin* box. In previous releases of X11, this box said "Welcome to the X Window System" by default; in R5, it simply gives the hostname, as shown in Figure 3-3. If you want to change this greeting, edit the resource definition:

```
xlogin*greeting: CLIENTHOST
```

---

* Alternatively, in R5 you could also enter CTRL-RETURN, for those users who don't have an F1 key.

to something like:

```
xlogin*greeting:  CLIENTHOST's House Party
```

The resulting login box will look like the one in Figure 3-9.

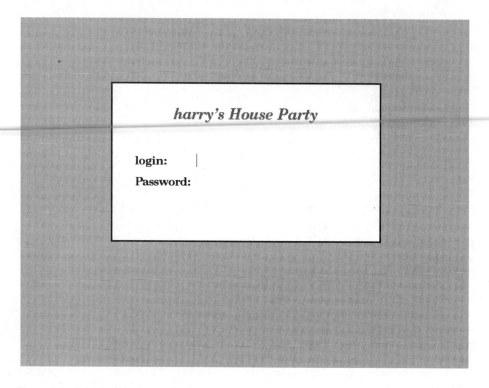

Figure 3-9. Adapted xlogin greeting

See the *xdm* manpage for more information on *xlogin* resources, including the default translation table.

3.5.4.2 The xconsole Client

As of R5, the `DisplayManager._0.setup` resource is used to point to a script to be run when the *xdm* connection to the local display server is initialized. The script, *Xsetup_0*, simply runs the *xconsole* client:

```
#!/bin/sh
xconsole -geometry 480x130-0-0 -daemon -notify -verbose -fn fixed -exitOnFail
```

This ensures that console messages are sent to a window in between console logins, rather than spewing across the screen and disrupting the display. The resources for *xconsole* are set in *Xresources*:

```
XConsole.text.geometry:     480x130
XConsole.verbose:     true
XConsole*iconic:      true
XConsole*font:        fixed
```

See the manual page for *xconsole* for more information.

3.5.5 Starting Up Individual X Sessions (the Xsession File)

Now that you have a picture of how *xdm* starts up and finds out how to respond to individual display servers on the network, it's time to discuss the part where the user actually logs in.

What happens now is completely up to the administrator. All *xdm* knows about is that it executes the file pointed to by the `session` resource for that display. In the distribution of R5, that file reads:

```
#!/bin/sh

exec > $HOME/.xsession-errors 2>&1

case $# in
1)
        case $1 in
        failsafe)
                exec xterm -geometry 80x24-0-0
                ;;
        esac
esac

startup=$HOME/.xsession
resources=$HOME/.Xresources

if [ -f $startup ]; then
        exec $startup
else
        if [ -f $resources ]; then
                xrdb -load $resources
        fi
        twm &
        exec xterm -geometry 80x24+10+10 -ls
fi
```

See Section 2.2.3 for more information on configuring the *.xsession* file.

- The first thing that happens is that all subsequent error messages are sent to a file in the user's home directory called *.xsession-errors*. In R4 and earlier, users' error messages were mixed in with all other errors in the file pointed to by the `Display-Manager.errorFile` resource, usually *xdm-errors*.

- Next, if the script has been called with the `failsafe` argument, a single *xterm* window is sent to the display and the script exits. Where does this argument come from? Well, remember in the *Xresources* file, under the *xlogin* translation table:

```
<Key>F1:  set-session-argument(failsafe) finish-field()\n\
Ctrl<Key>Return:  set-session-argument(failsafe) finish-field()\n\
```

We told you that this key translation set things up so if you typed F1 or CTRL-RETURN after your password instead of RETURN, you would avoid running your *.xsession* script and would get a lone *xterm* instead. Now you know how that gets implemented. Administrators can use this as a model to write translations that pass other arguments for *Xsession* to interpret.

- Next, the script looks for a script in the user's home directory called *.xsession*. If it exists, it *execs* it.

- If the *.xsession* script doesn't exist, the *Xsession* script creates a workable X session by first looking for a resource file called *.Xresources*, and if that file exists, loading it with *xrdb*; regardless, it then starts the *twm* window manager and a single *xterm* window.

This is actually a fairly simple script, when you consider that it controls every X server connecting to *xdm*. It also gives the administrator an unusual amount of power over each X session. At the most innocuous, an administrator could use the *Xsession* file to add some functionality that all users may need—for example, to add a local font directory into font paths using the *xset* client. At a slightly more intrusive level, the administrator could use it to set up a message-of-the-day client for users to see when they first log in. But there are really no limits—an administrator could set up a network so that users have no control at all over their own X sessions (by removing the line that executes *.xsession*), and in fact don't have *xterm* windows to start new clients (presuming that all they'd want to do is run a mail client and a word processor).

Note that the *Xsession* script is defined as a loose binding, `DisplayManager*session`. You could therefore set up a separate X session file for particular X servers. For example, you might want to set up an X session file called *Xsession_0*:

```
DisplayManager._0.session:      Xsession_0
```

The only difference in *Xsession_0* might be that the *xterm* called in the failsafe situation would be called with –*C*, so that console messages will be diverted to this *xterm* window:

```
exec xterm -geometry 80x24+10+10 -ls -C
```

(See Sections 4.6.1 and 4.6.2 for more information on the *xterm* console window.)

You can also use display classes to group several X terminals together. See Section 3.5.6 for more information on display classes.

3.5.5.1 No Home Directory? (R5)

The redirection of error messages to *$HOME/.xsession-errors* is a nice addition to R5—it means that if users are having problems, they don't need to weed through the systemwide *xdm-errors* file, but can start looking for problems locally. This makes life easier for users and administrators alike. However, it does present a problem under some versions of R5 if for some reason you don't have a home directory on the host.

Since *Xsession* is executed as a Bourne shell script, the line:

```
exec > $HOME/.xsession-errors 2>&1
```

produces a fatal error if it cannot be completed. One reason that may happen is if you don't have a home directory, either because it's a new machine or because there is a problem with your NFS link. The shell tries to create a file in a directory that does not exist and when it can't, the script aborts. The effect is that the user logs in and is immediately bumped out, with no sign of what happened except in *xdm-errors*:

```
error (pid 2547): can't lock authorization file /home/lmui/.Xauthority or
backup /usr/lib/X11/xdm/.Xautha02547
error (pid 2547): No home directory /home/lmui for user lmui, using /
/usr/lib/X11/xdm/Xsession: /home/lmui/.xsession-errors: No such file or
directory
error (pid 2549): fatal IO error 32 (Broken pipe)
```

To remedy this situation, you might change the line in *Xsession* to read:

```
if [ -d $HOME -a -w $HOME ]; then
    exec > $HOME/.xsession-errors 2>&1
fi
```

(Patch 20 of X11R5 has rewritten the *Xsession* script to fix this problem.)

3.5.6 Display Classes

Display classes provide a way to group together several X servers connecting to the same host. The display class is built into the X server, and is presented to *xdm* when the X server connects via XDMCP. To find out the display class for a given X terminal, you can look it up in the documentation or ask the manufacturer; or, if it won't disturb any users, kill *xdm* and then restart it at a high "debug" level:

```
# /usr/lib/X11/xdm -debug 9
```

Running *xdm* at this level of debugging is likely to give you far more information than you really want. Among this stream of messages, however, is information about any X server that connects to *xdm*, including its display class:

```
Starting display visual5.ora.com:0,VISUAL-X19TURBO
```

This tells us that the Visual X terminal we're experimenting with is in the display class VISUAL-X19TURBO.*

Display classes come in useful in allowing you to fine-tune your *xdm* configuration differently according to the display type. Thus far, almost all our examples of display-specific resources have been about the local display server, _0. However, because of hardware peculiarities, there are situations when you would want to set resources for individual X servers or for a group of X servers.

For example, the Visual X19TURBO terminal has 2-bit gray scale support. This is nice, except that it confuses FrameMaker into thinking it has color support. FrameMaker therefore tries to show menus with its color defaults of black text on blue background; the X terminal

---

*In X11R3, XDMCP was not available, so the *Xservers* file was used to explicitly list the display class used by an X server; see Section 3.5.2.1 for more information.

tries to display that blue and comes up with a dark gray; and all menus are subsequently unreadable.

One solution was just to change the resource files for each user that encountered this problem. That is, we'd add the following line to the user's *.Xresources* file:

```
Maker*Background:        white
```

But this resource really shouldn't be tied to the user. If the user logs on at a color display, the menus won't look the way Frame intended them to; and if someone else logs on at the gray-scale display, the new user will need the same resource set for his account as well. This resource should be set at the server level.

Using display classes, we can set up a separate *Xsession* file to be used only for the Visual X19TURBO by editing the *xdm-config* file:

```
DisplayManager*session:              /usr/lib/X11/xdm/Xsession
DisplayManager.VISUAL-X19TURBO.session: /usr/lib/X11/xdm/X19TURBOsession
```

And then edit the new *X19TURBOsession* file to include the required resource:

```
     . . .
if [ -f $startup ]; then
        echo "Maker*Background:        white" | xrdb -merge -
        exec $startup
else
        if [ -f $resources ]; then
                xrdb -load $resources
        fi
        echo "Maker*Background:        white" | xrdb -merge -
        twm &
        exec xterm -geometry 80x24+10+10 -ls
fi
     . . .
```

This will force the *X19TURBOsession* script to be run only by users logging on the X19TURBO X terminals, while users on all other X servers will continue to run the default *Xsession* script. The X19TURBO users become the only ones to have the new resource loaded into their servers.

(Note that this example depends on users using *xrdb –merge* in their own *.xsession* scripts, or the Maker*Background resource will be lost.)

3.6 Testing Your xdm Setup

After you modify the *xdm* files to reflect your system, take it out for a test drive. Beware that testing *xdm* on a system others are using is likely to be extremely disruptive. For that reason, it's wise to find out if anybody else is running *xdm* already on your network. In case your console gets hung in a weird state (not unusual), it's a good idea to have an alternate way to log into the system, either over the network (e.g., via *telnet*), or from a terminal attached to a serial port on the system. On a PC UNIX machine, you can simply use one of the alternate consoles available by holding down the CTRL and ALT keys while pressing one of the function keys.

You can test *xdm* by starting it from the command line:

```
# /usr/bin/X11/xdm
```

If you are doing this on the console display and the console is set up to be managed by *xdm*, beware that your current login will become unusable once *xdm* is running. If you want to make small changes to the configuration files without restarting *xdm*, it might reread the configuration files on its own (if the `DisplayManager.autoRescan` resource is set to `true`), or you can tell it to reread the files by sending it the *SIGHUP* signal. (See Sections 3.6.2 and 3.6.3 for more information.)

Remember that you can use the *–config* option to *xdm* to specify a configuration file other than *xdm-config*. It's generally a good idea to use this feature while testing; that way, you leave the default configuration intact while you edit your own files. For example, you might create a new file called *xdm-testconfig*, containing:

```
DisplayManager.errorLogFile:    /usr/lib/X11/xdm/testxdm-errors
DisplayManager.pidFile:         /usr/lib/X11/xdm/testxdm-pid
DisplayManager.keyFile:         /usr/lib/X11/xdm/testxdm-keys
DisplayManager.servers:         /usr/lib/X11/xdm/testXservers
DisplayManager.accessFile:      /usr/lib/X11/xdm/testXaccess
DisplayManager._0.authorize:    true
DisplayManager._0.setup:        /usr/lib/X11/xdm/testXsetup_0
DisplayManager._0.startup:      /usr/lib/X11/xdm/testGiveConsole
DisplayManager._0.reset:        /usr/lib/X11/xdm/testTakeConsole
DisplayManager*resources:       /usr/lib/X11/xdm/testXresources
DisplayManager*session:         /usr/lib/X11/xdm/testXsession
DisplayManager*authComplain:    false
```

And call *xdm* with the command line:

```
# /usr/lib/X11/xdm -config xdm-testconfig
```

3.6.1 Resetting the Keyboard

On Sun workstations, the abnormal termination of the X server may leave the keyboard in a weird state. (If you don't know what we mean by this, believe us, when you see it you'll know it.) MIT provides the command */usr/bin/X11/kbd_mode* to restore the keyboard on a Sun workstation. Since your keyboard is unusable, you'll have to use the alternate login we recommended earlier.

```
# /usr/bin/X11/kbd_mode -a > /dev/console
```

If you manage to render the system totally unusable and cannot recover, you can always reboot. Since you haven't yet added the *xdm* daemon to the system boot process, you will get your system back to a usable state after a reboot.

3.6.2 Restarting xdm Using xdm-pid (R4 and Later)

In R4 and R5, the *xdm* process ID is stored in whatever file is pointed to by the `Display-Manager.pidFile` resource, *xdm-pid* in the default configuration. If you are running R4 or R5, you can use the *xdm-pid* file to send a signal to *xdm*. This file contains the process ID of *xdm*.

```
# cat /usr/lib/X11/xdm/xdm-pid
28683
```

You can send *xdm* the *SIGHUP* signal by using the *cat* output directly:

```
# kill -HUP `cat /usr/lib/X11/xdm/xdm-pid`
```

The *xdm* process should now reflect the current configuration files for any new sessions.

If *xdm* becomes unusable and you are not able to fix it by editing the configuration files, you can kill it for real. (You'll have to use a more severe signal (*SIGTERM*) to tell it you are serious.)

```
# kill -TERM `cat /usr/lib/X11/xdm/xdm-pid`
```

Beware that all active sessions managed by *xdm* will be killed if you use *SIGTERM*.

3.6.3 Rereading xdm Configuration Files (R3)

To force *xdm* to reread its configuration files on an R3 system, you need to find the process ID of *xdm* manually in order to kill it.

First find the process ID of the parent *xdm* process using the *ps* command. Then send the *SIGHUP* signal to the process.

```
% ps agx|grep xdm
 2547 ? IW 0:30 -xterm1:0 (xdm)
13511 ? IW 0:56 -xterm2:0 (xdm)
13757 ? IW 0:58 -xterm4:0 (xdm)
15199 ? IW 1:08 -xterm5:0 (xdm)
19175 ? S 1:51 -xterm7:0 (xdm)
19466 ? IW 2:08 -xterm3:0 (xdm)
28683 ? IW 0:09 /usr/bin/X11/xdm
28685 ? S 2:07 -xterm9:0 (xdm)
28743 ? IW 0:00 /bin/sh /usr/lib/X11/xdm/Xsession
17796 p0 S 0:00 grep xdm
```

The parent *xdm* stands out, since the *xdm* processes associated with a particular display change their names to the name of the display. (The arguments to the *ps* command, as well as its output, will vary according to the flavor of UNIX you are running.) If you send signals to the wrong *xdm* process, only the display being controlled by that *xdm* process will be affected.

Controlling scologin

scologin (the version of *xdm* on Open Desktop, which runs on SCO UNIX machines) has its own ways of starting and restarting the display manager. The *scologin* daemon has a front end, */etc/scologin*, which takes the following options:

start　Starts the *scologin* process; if *scologin* is already running, the *start* command will cause *scologin* to reread the configuration files *Xconfig*, *Xservers* and *Xresources*.

reread　If *scologin* is already running, the *reread* command will cause *scologin* to reread the configuration files *Xconfig*, *Xservers* and *Xresources*.

stop　Stops *scologin*. All X sessions currently managed by *scologin* will be halted.

query　Returns the current status of *scologin*.

disable　Stops *scologin* and disables it from restarting when the system reboots.

enable　Starts *scologin* if not already running, and ensures that it will start automatically at the next reboot.

init　If *scologin* is enabled, the *getty* processes on terminals configured for *scologin* are disabled. This option should be run only by *init* at boot time.

For example, to have your configuration files reread, enter:

```
# /etc/scologin reread
```

3.7 Permanent Installation of xdm

When you are happy with your *xdm* setup, it is time to install it so it will start automatically when the system boots. The way you do this is system dependent, but it is the same procedure as adding any other kind of daemon. In a typical BSD system, you would modify the */etc/rc.local* script. Under System V, edit */etc/inittab*. (Remember to keep backup copies of any system files you modify!)

Here are a few examples of installing *xdm* on various platforms:

Installing *xdm* on SunOS 4.1.1

Add *xdm* to */etc/rc.local*:

```
if [ -f /usr/bin/X11/xdm ]; then
     /usr/bin/X11/xdm; echo -n "XDM"
fi
```

Then reboot the system.

Installing *xdm* on Ultrix 4.2

Add *xdm* to */etc/rc.local*:

```
[ -f /usr/bin/X11/xdm ] && {
        /usr/bin/X11/xdm & echo -n `xdm ` > /dev/console
}
```

Then reboot the system.

Installing *xdm* on a System V Machine (IRIX 4.0)

(Your system may already be set up for running *xdm* as shipped. Check before continuing.)

Add *xdm* to */etc/inittab*:

```
xw:23:respawn:/usr/bin/X11/xdm -nodaemon
```

Then reboot the system.

Installing *xdm* on AIX 3.1

Add *xdm* to */etc/rc.tcpip*:

```
start /usr/bin/X11/xdm "$src_running"
```

Then reboot the system.

3.8 Related Documentation

For more detailed information on *xdm* and its resources, see the *xdm* manual page.

For documentation on XDMCP, look in the X source distribution, in *mit/hardcopy/XDMCP/xdmcp.PS.Z*.

"The X Administrator: Taming the X Display Manager," by Miles O'Neal, published in *The X Resource, Issue 4*, O'Reilly & Associates, Inc., Fall 1992.

4

Security

Because X runs in a networked environment, it's particularly important that administrators be aware of its security lapses and how to reduce the risks of running X. This chapter discusses security issues as they relate to X.

In This Chapter:

4
Security

X runs in a networked environment. Because of X's design, your workstation is no longer your private preserve but hypothetically can be accessed by any other host on the network. If you are on the Internet, your display may be accessible world-wide. This is the true meaning of the server concept: your display can serve clients on any system, and clients on your system can display on any other screen.

The possibilities for abuse are considerable. When our office was introduced to X11, one of the first things we learned how to do was to play pranks on one another. Call it a "learning experience"— we became familiar with X by sending prank clients to remote servers: *xmelt* to make someone's screen melt away, *xsetroot* to put a giant bitmap picture of our boss on someone else's root window, etc. When we got a hold of anything "neat" (e.g., kaleidoscope, a GIF file of Bart Simpson, a bitmap of Bill the Cat), we fired it off to a friend's display to amuse him, and then ran down to his office to see his reaction.

If this scares you, it should. Within our office, among our friends, we had no intention of hurting anyone, and if anyone seemed busy or grouchy we left them alone. But if good intentions were enough, none of us would have passwords for our accounts. Having unlimited access to someone's display leaves a lot of potential for serious damage. Our pranks involved clients that the user could see, be amused (or annoyed) by, and then promptly kill. However, if you can run one client on a display then you can run any other client on that display.

The X Window System design allows any client that successfully connects to the X server to exercise *complete control* over the display. This means that clients can take over the mouse or the keyboard, send keystrokes to other applications, or even kill the windows associated with other clients.

It is difficult to make X completely secure. However, there are four access control mechanisms, one host-based and three user-based. The host-based scheme involve a system file (*/etc/Xn.hosts*) and can be controlled using the *xhost* client. The user-based schemes involve authorization capabilities provided by the *xauth* program and by the X Display Manager Control Protocol (XDMCP). There is also a "secure keyboard" feature in the *xterm* terminal emulator that can provide protection against some problems.

4.1 Host-based Access Control

One way of protecting against unauthorized clients is to use host-based access control, shown in Figure 4-1. The way this works for workstations is that, by default, the server running on the local workstation only accepts clients that are running on that workstation. For example, the local display `sapphire:0`, which runs on the console of the host *sapphire*, would only accept clients started on *sapphire*.

For the local display server of a workstation, the list of hosts that can send clients to display on *sapphire:0* can be supplemented by adding a hostname to the */etc/Xn.hosts* file (where *n* is the number of the display), or by using the *xhost* client. Many X terminals also support host-based access control (sometimes called "TCP/IP access control"), with the list of hosts specified on the setup menu or uploaded via remote configuration from the host.

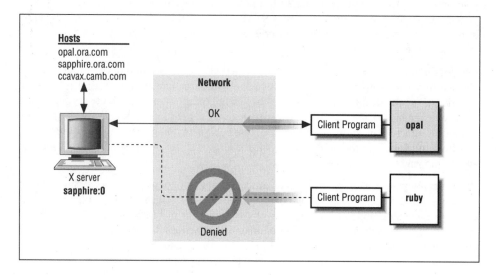

Figure 4-1. Host-based access control

4.1.1 The /etc/Xn.hosts File

The */etc/Xn.hosts* file contains a list of systems that are allowed to access local server *n*. On most workstations, only one server runs at a time, so */etc/X0.hosts* is the only file you need to be concerned with. This list of hosts is read by the server at startup time. The */etc/X0.hosts* file can be edited so that it contains the list of systems you want to allow access to your server on a regular basis. For example, the file */etc/X0.hosts* on the host *sapphire* might contain the following:

```
opal.ora.com
sapphire.ora.com
ccavax.camb.com
```

(The *letc/X0.hosts* file is not included in any default configurations of X11, but needs to be created by the system administrator.)

In this example, the local server `sapphire:0` can be accessed by the hosts named *opal* and *sapphire* in the *ora.com* domain, and *ccavax* in the *camb.com* domain. (Hosts in the current domain do not require the domain name suffix, but it's a good practice to always use fully-qualified domain names, to prevent a machine named *opal* in another domain from connecting to the server.) If you try sending a client to the *sapphire* display from a host not on that list, the client will be rejected:

```
lmui@ruby % hostname
ruby
lmui@ruby % xterm -display sapphire:0
Xlib: connection to "sapphire:0.0" refused by server
Xlib: Client is not authorized to connect to Server
Error: Can't Open display
```

Note that hardcoding hosts into *letc/Xn.hosts* makes sense only for workstations used by a single user, since the list of hosts you want to enable access from is likely to be user-specific. If a workstation is in a public area and is used by many different users, then the host access list is likely to change, and only the administrator should be able to edit *letc/Xn.hosts*.

X terminals that support host-based access control have the hostnames manually added to an access control list on the setup menu. See your X terminal's documentation for details.

4.1.2 The xhost Client

To supplement the *letc/Xn.hosts* file, the *xhost* client can be used to give (or deny) systems access to the server interactively. To use the *xhost* client to add *ruby.ora.com* to the list of hosts that can display to `sapphire:0`, you have to run *xhost* in an *xterm* window running on *sapphire*:

```
lmui@sapphire 87% xhost +ruby.ora.com
ruby added to access control list
```

The `sapphire:0` display will now be able to display clients from *ruby* in the domain *ora.com*.

You can only run *xhost* from a window displaying on the server in question. If you try running *xhost* from a remote display, you get the error:

```
xhost:  must be on local machine to add or remove hosts.
```

Specifying a hostname with an optional leading plus sign (+) allows the host to access the server, and specifying a hostname with a leading minus sign (-) prevents a previously allowed host from accessing the server. (Note that removing a host applies only to future requests from clients to the display—it's too late to stop any clients that are already connected.) Multiple hosts can be specified on the same line. Running *xhost* without any arguments prints the current hosts that are allowed access to your display.

To allow access to the local display from *all* hosts, enter:

```
% xhost +
```

Needless to say, we strongly discourage you from doing this.

You can use the *xhost* client to enable access from a specific host only long enough to start up clients from that host, and then disable access immediately. For example, a script might do something like this:

```
xhost +sapphire
rsh sapphire xterm -display reno:0
sleep 15
xhost -sapphire
```

You can also use the remote host's IP address instead of the hostname.

```
% xhost +140.186.65.13
```

The IP address is useful when the remote hostname isn't known to the name server. (The name server translates domain names into IP addresses.) Also, in the rare case when a host is on two different networks and has two different IP addresses, *xhost* may get confused. You might have to explicitly specify the IP address the host uses on the current network. (The better solution is to fix the problem for good, by re-linking X with updated resolver libraries; but in the interim, using the direct IP address may do the trick.)

If the above description left you in the dark—if you don't know name servers from X servers, and IP addresses are greek to you—consult the Nutshell Handbook *TCP/IP Network Administration* by Craig Hunt (O'Reilly & Associates, 1992).

4.1.3 Problems with Host-based Access Control

Host-based access control is better than nothing, but it has some basic conceptual problems that make it insufficient for true security. One problem is that, while the primary reason for denying a remote system access to your display is to prevent a person working on the remote system from displaying on your server, this also prevents you from running clients from that remote system on your display. So you have to deny yourself functionality in order to deny it to others.

The main problem with host-based access control, however, is that it's easy to get around. It's a great idea if workstations are really single-user machines, where only the person who actually uses a given host has an account on it. But on today's UNIX networks, you are probably running yellow pages (NIS) to simplify account allocation and file permission issues. On these networks, as long as a prankster has an account on one of the hosts you do allow access from, *xhost* provides no protection. Any user with an account on your machine (or any other host your server allows access to) can access your display.

On an X terminal, host-based access control makes even less sense. X terminals are dependent on a host to run almost all of its clients. That host is often a compute server used to support several other X terminals as well. So X terminals that support host-based access control generally need to list a host with many other users on it, meaning that all those users can access each others' displays. This is still better than nothing, but definitely not secure.

If you're running Secure RPC, you can use the SUN-DES-1 method of security and use *xhost* to give access to a particular user in a given domain, such as "xhost +dave@ora.com." This is really the best way to control access to a server, since it is entirely user-based. Not all machines support Secure RPC, however. See Section 4.4 for more information on SUN-DES-1.

4.2 Access Control with MIT-MAGIC-COOKIE-1

With Release 4 of X11, a user-based access control mechanism can be used to supplement or replace host-based access control. User-based access control is built into the XDM Control Protocol (XDMCP), but it can be used independently of *xdm*. In Section 4.2.3, we show how you can use it with *xinit*. In addition, it is automatically enabled when the *openwin* server is started under OpenWindows.

The most common method of user-based access control (and the only one available under R4) is a mechanism known as MIT-MAGIC-COOKIE-1. This scheme might be called permission-based rather than user-based, since it depends on UNIX file permission more than anything.

If both the host and the X server are configured to use MIT-MAGIC-COOKIE-1, then when you log in using *xdm*, a machine-readable code is put in a file called *.Xauthority* in your home directory, belonging to you. This is shown in Figure 4-2. This code, called a *magic cookie*, is also told to the server. The magic cookie code can be thought of as a password known only to the server and to the user who logs in using *xdm*. Users don't have to actually type the code at any point, they just need to be able to run the programs that manipulate it.

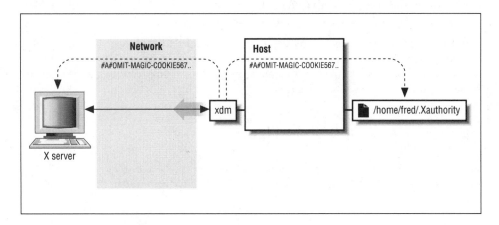

Figure 4-2. XDMCP and the access code

Once the code is established for that X session, a client must present the code before it is allowed to connect to the server. The client gets the code by reading the *.Xauthority* file in the user's home directory. This file has the permissions "-rw------", meaning that it can be read and written only by the owner. The MIT-MAGIC-COOKIE-1 mechanism therefore takes advantage of the fact that all processes started by a user inherit that user's permissions. Figure 4-3 shows a user who does not have access to the code being rejected.

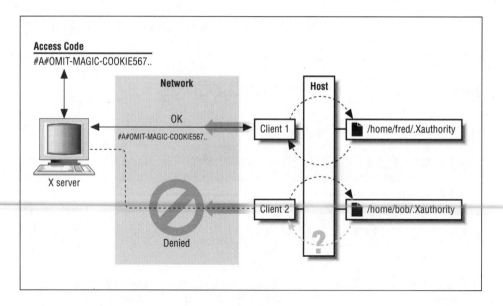

Figure 4-3. User-based access control

Since this type of access control is based entirely on UNIX file permissions, it is only as secure as the user's account—if you don't have a password, for example, it's totally useless since anyone can log in as you and then do whatever they want to your server.

User-based access control is clearly more secure than host-based access control, but it depends on the server being programmed to take advantage of it. Not all X terminals are capable of using the magic cookie. Furthermore, magic cookie-type access control is tightly bound to the operating system, which is not in the spirit of X.

4.2.1 Using MIT-MAGIC-COOKIE-1 with xdm

In Chapter 3, we discussed the resources for *xdm* specified in the *xdm-config* file. In addition to pointers to several special files, the *xdm-config* file contains these resource specifications:

```
DisplayManager._0.authorize:    true
DisplayManager*authorize:       false
```

The first resource specification turns on authorization for the local display. The second one turns the scheme off on all other displays. To turn authorization on for any other servers that are connected to the host, change the second resource definition:

```
DisplayManager*authorize:       true
```

xdm is probably configured to reread the configuration file on its own (by setting the `DisplayManager.autoRescan` resource, which is on by default), but if not, you can send *xdm* a SIGHUP so it will reread its configuration file:

```
root# kill -HUP `cat /usr/lib/X11/xdm/xdm-pid`
```

In addition to this, some X terminals need to be explicitly configured to use MIT-MAGIC-COOKIE-1. See your X terminal's documentation for more information.

4.2.2 The xauth Program

A problem with user-based access control is that it relies on all your clients having access to the magic cookie. This is reasonable to expect if you run all your clients on the same host or if your home directory is shared (for example, using NFS or AFS) across all the hosts you run clients on. Since all the necessary information is in your *$HOME/.Xauthority* file, you can access your server from all hosts with the same shared home directory. But what about the situation when you want to run clients from a host that does not have a shared home directory?

The solution is a program called *xauth*, used to propagate the magic cookie from one host to another. The most common use for *xauth* is to extract a user's authorization information for the current display, copy it to another machine, and merge it into the *$HOME/.Xauthority* file on the remote machine, as shown in Figure 4-4. From a host where the user already has the magic cookie listed, this can be accomplished with the following command line:

    % xauth extract - $DISPLAY | rsh remotehost xauth merge -

For example, to share the authorization information for the reno:0 display with your user account on the host *ruby*, type:

    % xauth extract - reno:0 | rsh ruby xauth merge -

The *extract* function takes the magic cookie from the *.Xauthority* file in your home directory on *reno*. Since you may be logged on at several different displays at once, you need to specify which display you want to extract the magic cookie for. In the example above, we want to extract the magic cookie for the local display server, reno:0. By using a dash (-), the magic cookie is written to standard output.

The xrsh Command

If you run remote clients using the *xrsh* shell script provided in the R5 *contrib/clients/xrsh* directory, *xauth* is automatically run to propagate the magic cookie code to the remote machine before the remote client is started. For example:

    % xrsh -auth xauth ruby xterm

starts up *xterm* on the host *ruby* after first using *xauth* to transfer the cookie.

If you use host-based access control, *xrsh* can also give the remote host access to the server. This is the default behavior:

    % xrsh -auth xhost ruby xterm

You can also set the XRSH_AUTH_TYPE environment variable to specify which type of authorization you need enabled for the remote host. The default behavior is for *xhost* authorization.

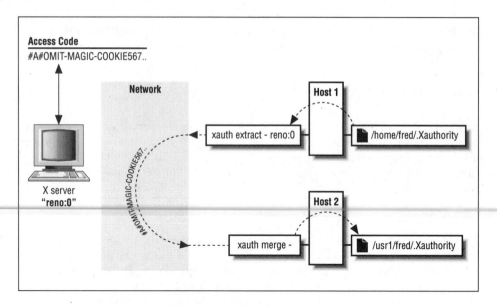

Figure 4-4. Propagating the magic cookie between two hosts

The *xauth merge* function accepts magic cookie codes from the specified file—in this case, from standard input. It then merges that information into the *$HOME/.Xauthority* file on that system.

Since only you have access to the magic cookie for your server, only you can successfully run *xauth* to send that code to another host.

Particularly picky readers might point out that technically, *xauth* is not a client program since it never contacts the X server itself, but is simply used to manipulate the *.Xauthority* file.

Our examples so far have only shown how to use *xauth* to extract the magic cookie code from a local machine and merge it into a remote one. But it's just as easy to do it the other way around. In the following example, we *rlogin* to a machine called *rock*, try to run an *xterm* window, and when we are rejected we simply copy the magic cookie and try again. Note that as far as the shell is concerned, *reno* is now the remote machine and *rock* is the local one, so *rsh* needs to be called on the *xauth extract* command.

```
lmui@reno 79% rlogin rock
Last login: Fri Sep 18 07:27:17 from ruby.ora.com
SunOS Release 4.1.2 (ROCK) #1: Fri Sep 11 17:56:56 PDT 1992
lmui@rock % xterm -display reno:0
Xlib:  connection to "reno:0.0" refused by server
Xlib:  Client is not authorized to connect to Server
Error: Can't open display: reno:0
lmui@rock % rsh reno xauth extract - reno:0 | xauth merge -
lmui@rock % xterm -display reno:0 &
      (client runs successfully)
```

It's also possible to copy a code from one host to another from an uninvolved third host, but it's hard to come up with a circumstance in which you'd need to do that.

Note that since *xauth* depends on using *rsh*, it requires that you have set up either *$HOME/.rhosts* or */etc/hosts.equiv* on the remote machine to permit the remote shell command. If you get a "Permission denied." error, it's because your account on the remote system isn't configured to allow remote commands from the local system, not because of any problem with X. See Section 2.3.4.1 for more information.

4.2.3 Using MIT-MAGIC-COOKIE-1 with xinit

Although MIT-MAGIC-COOKIE-1 is designed to be used with XDMCP, you can use the *xauth* program directly to use the magic cookie with an X session started with *xinit*.

You have to do some extra work in order to use user-based access control with *xinit*, however. When using security on the console display server, *xdm* is nice enough to generate a unique magic cookie code for you, put it in *$HOME/.Xauthority*, and then start up the X server with the *–auth $HOME/.Xauthority* option. This tells a R4- or R5-compatible server to look in *$HOME/.Xauthority* for the magic cookie code that *xdm* just put there. If you're starting X with *xinit*, you have to do this work yourself.

The first thing you need to do is to generate a magic cookie code and place it in *.Xauthority*. To create the magic cookie code, you need to generate a "random" number (or at least one that's hard to guess). If you have *perl* installed on your system, you can use *perl*'s random number generator, as in the following:

```
randomkey=`perl -e 'srand; printf int(rand(10000000000000000))'`
```

or (for a more robust script):

```
randomkey=`perl -e 'for (1..10) {
        srand(time+$$+$seed);
        printf("%4.4lx", ($seed = int(rand(65536))));
}
print "\n";'`
```

The Korn shell (*ksh*) also has a built-in random number generator, so you can do something like:

```
randomkey=`ksh -c 'echo $(( $RANDOM * $RANDOM * 2 ))'`
```

Using standard UNIX tools, you can start with some number that will be different every time (such as the process ID of the *.xserverrc* shell, or the output of the *date* command), and then convert it into something unrecognizable. Just using *date* (if your *date* command supports this syntax), you might do something like:

```
randomkey=`date +"%y%m%d%H%M%S"`
```

Using the process ID, you might disguise it by passing it through the *bc* command:

```
randomkey=`echo "{obase=16;$$^3}" | bc`
```

Whichever method you use, apply the key to *xauth* to add it to the *.Xauthority* file:

```
randomkey=`your favorite random number generation scheme here`
xauth add ${HOST}/unix:0 . $randomkey
xauth add ${HOST}:0 . $randomkey
```

The *add* keyword to *xauth* tells it to add the given code for the given server into the *.Xauthority* file. Note that you need two entries: the first adds the key for the server under the IPC name of `unix:0`, and the second adds the key for the server under the TCP/IP name `hostname:0`. If you access your server as `localhost:0`, you might want to add an entry for that too. (See Section 2.3.1 for information on display names.) Note that the screen number that is often found in display names is omitted, since access control for a given server covers all screens for that server.

The lone period (.) in the *xauth* command line signifies that the default protocol, MIT-MAGIC-COOKIE-1, should be used.

Once you have added the new code to *$HOME/.Xauthority*, you need to start up the X server using the code. For example:

```
% xinit -- /usr/bin/X11/X -auth $HOME/.Xauthority
```

If you'd like *xinit* to do all of this automatically, you can combine the steps into your *.xserverrc* file:

```
#!/bin/sh

# Get hostname
HOST=`hostname`

# Create new magic cookie key
randomkey=`perl -e 'srand; printf int(rand(100000000000000000))'`

# Add new magic cookie key into .Xauthority
xauth add ${HOST}/unix:0 . $randomkey
xauth add ${HOST}:0 . $randomkey

# Start the X server with authorization turned on
exec /usr/bin/X11/X -auth $HOME/.Xauthority
```

4.2.4 xauth vs. xhost

User-based access control is overridden by host-based access control. For example, if you add the host *ruby* to the list of hosts that are allowed access to your server, every user on *ruby* will be able to access your server regardless of whether you use user-based access control as well. For that reason, you generally want to make sure that no hosts are listed on your access control list. If you enable *xauth*-type user-based access control, you should confirm that host-based access control is set up to restrict access from all hosts.

```
% xhost
access control enabled, only authorized clients can connect
harry.ora.com
ruby.ora.com
opal.ora.com
```

As shown above, three hosts are allowed access to your server. That means that any user-based access control you have enabled is close to pointless. If you have hosts specified in the */etc/X0.hosts* file, you need to remove hosts from that file. You can also remove hosts you have added to the access control list with *xhost +* by using *xhost −*:

```
% xhost -
access control enabled, only authorized clients can connect
```

To verify that all access from all hosts has been disallowed, call *xhost* with no arguments:

```
% xhost
access control enabled, only authorized clients can connect
```

Now, only clients with access to the magic cookie in *$HOME/.Xauthority* can connect to your server.

Some X terminals that support the magic cookie scheme also support host-based access control, and allow you to enable or disable it via the setup menu. This can be confusing. You might think that you want to disable host-based access control (since you'll be using user-based access control). However, disabling host-based access control may effectively allow all hosts access to your server, equivalent to doing an *xhost +*. For these X terminals, you want to enable host-based access control, but make sure that the access control list is empty. To make sure the access control list is empty, you may have to explicitly place an *xhost −* in your *.xsession* script for X terminals supporting both host-based and user-based access control.

Access Control and Commercial X Servers

Most X terminals and PC X servers support XDMCP, but that doesn't necessarily mean that they support MIT-MAGIC-COOKIE-1. You should contact the manufacturer or consult the documentation to determine if the server uses the magic cookie. Many servers running on X terminals and PCs also provide their own access control features, mostly host-based access, although some (like MacX) can be configured so that any client requesting access to the server needs to be approved on the display. How this fits into user-based access control is dependent on the manufacturer.

4.3 The XDM-AUTHORIZATION-1 Mechanism (R5)

X11R5 provides two new schemes for display access control: XDM-AUTHORIZATION-1 and SUN-DES-1. These are designed to be used in place of MIT-MAGIC-COOKIE-1, and are more secure than MIT-MAGIC-COOKIE-1 since they encrypt the authorization code as it is transferred across the network.

The XDM-AUTHORIZATION-1 method of access control is similar to MIT-MAGIC-COOKIE-1. The advantage it gives is that it uses DES (Data Encryption Standard) encryption, so it cannot be "snooped" over the network.

Because of export restrictions, *xdm* is built without the DES encryption code enabled by default, and hence without XDM-AUTHORIZATION-1 support. To be able to support XDM-

AUTHORIZATION-1, you need to build *xdm* with the implementation of DES in *mit/lib/Xdmcp/Wraphelp.c*.* You should also make sure that the `HasXdmAuth` build flag is set to YES. See Section A.2 for information on how to *ftp* a file.

Once you are sure that *xdm* supports XDM-AUTHORIZATION-1, you can enable it on the local display server by simply redefining the `DisplayManager._0.authName` resource in the *xdm-config* file. (By default, the MIT-MAGIC-COOKIE-1 mechanism is used.) The `authorize` resource must also be turned on.

```
DisplayManager*authorize:        true
DisplayManager._0.authName:      XDM-AUTHORIZATION-1
```

Note that we only redefined the `authName` resource for the local display, `:0`. At this writing, no X terminals support this mechanism.† The `authName` resource actually accepts a list of authorization schemes which *xdm* will use in order, so you could also just set the following global resource:

```
DisplayManager*authName:         XDM-AUTHORIZATION-1 MIT-MAGIC-COOKIE-1
```

After the *xdm-config* file is reread by *xdm*, *xdm* will use XDM-AUTHORIZATION-1 for the local display server. As with MIT-MAGIC-COOKIE-1, the server is started with the *–auth* option and the code is placed in the *.Xauthority* file. In this case, however, the code consists of two parts, a 56-bit encryption key and 64 bits of random data.

Once you log in using *xdm* and XDM-AUTHORIZATION-1, check that you're using access control properly with *xauth list*:

```
eap % xauth list
nugget.west.ora.com:0  XDM-AUTHORIZATION-1 bd4dc546c869a81f00979e36956f6c95
nugget/unix:0  XDM-AUTHORIZATION-1  bd4dc546c869a81f00979e36956f6c95
```

Note that XDM-AUTHORIZATION-1 is only available for X sessions that are managed by *xdm*.

4.4 The SUN-DES-1 Mechanism (R5)

The SUN-DES-1 server access control scheme uses the Data Encryption Standard (DES) for encryption of authorization data. This scheme uses Sun's Secure RPC to pass authorization data across the network, and it uses NIS to maintain a database across the network. DES code has export restrictions, so it may not appear on systems outside of the U.S.

Since SUN-DES-1 uses Secure RPC, you need to have Secure RPC installed before you can use it. Secure RPC, in turn, requires NIS (Network Information System).

---

*If this file does not appear in your distribution but you can legally use it, you can get it via *ftp* from *export.lcs.mit.edu*. The procedure is a little convoluted; see the file *pub/R5/xdm-auth/README* for information on how to obtain and incorporate the DES code.

†If the X terminals initiate the connection using XDMCP, they will ignore the `authName` resource anyway. This resource is only used for X servers that are listed in the *Xservers* file. When the XDMCP connection is initiated from the server side, *xdm* uses whatever authorization mechanism the server specifies at initiation.

SUN-DES-1 gives you true user-based access control. Unlike the magic cookie and XDM-AUTHORIZATION schemes, the entire mechanism does not rely on the security of the *.Xauthority* file. You have to explicitly use the *xhost* command to add specific users to the list of users who can access your display. This gives you a degree of specificity that is unavailable under the other schemes.

4.4.1 Public Key Encryption

Before you can set yourself up to use SUN-DES-1, you need to understand a little about how Secure RPC works.

Secure RPC is a system that uses both a public key and a private key. It uses a *principal* to identify an instance of a user. The principal is composed of the word `unix` combined with a user ID and the name of the current NIS domain:

    unix.<uid>@<NIS domain>

If the NIS domain is omitted, the current domain is assumed. If you do not know your user ID, use the *ypmatch* command:

```
% ypmatch eap passwd
eap:z7xoeuD8WpyOG:243:100:Eric Pearce:/home/eap:/bin/tcsh
```

The user ID is the third field of the *passwd* entry. In this example, our user ID is 243. If you need to learn the NIS domain name, use the *domainname* command. Note that although the NIS domain may be the same as the Internet domain, they are not related and do not necessarily correspond.

```
% domainname
west
```

So in this example, the principal for user *eap* in the current domain would be:

    unix.243@west

Or, since the current domain is the default:

    unix.243@

A special case is the principal for **root**. The principal for **root** uses the hostname in place of the user ID. For example, on the machine *nugget*, the principal for **root** is:

    unix.nugget@west

The principal is stored with a *public key* in the public key database. The public key is truly "public"—take a look at the file */etc/publickey*, which is world-readable:

```
#
# Sun Public Key Database
#
# To add an entry to this file, an administrator should use the NIS command
# "newkey" on the Network Information Services master machine.
#
# Users can also insert their own entries into this file using the chkey
# command. Commenting out the "nobody" entry below disallows this feature,
# and chkey will only allow users to change their existing entry, not create
```

```
# a new one.
#
nobody c3d91f44568fbbefada50d336d9bd67b16e7016f987bb607:7675cd9b8753b5db09da
bf12da759c2bd1331c927bb322861fffb54be13f55e9
unix.243@west 348088b7430e213d8a253d2959cecb927b9b26c829c30a43:c6eb324ed85de
e5f47d936f81d4e198504482e9dc415389ebab1848555b38e76
unix.206@west 18ebefb0ee5fdcfa6ea6deab6fef48b0495064ea39f4f86b:6471489f26949
4cabefcc8924f8d26343dd5a89a81bc3e9a6bcfa30cc85604e3
```

This file contains a list of principals and public keys. It is maintained in the NIS map *pub-lickey.byname*. You can look at it on NIS clients using *ypmatch*:

```
% ypmatch unix.243@west publickey.byname
348088b7430e213d8a253d2959cecb927b9b26c829c30a43:c6eb324ed85dee5f47d936f81d4
e198504482e9dc415389ebab1848555b38e76
```

Each user of the public key system has an entry in this file.

The SUN-DES-1 scheme generates a *private key* using the public key and your login pass-word. In order to use the Secure RPC system, you must create a public key at least once. The public key can be created by an unprivileged user using the *chkey* command, or by **root** using the *newkey* command. The private key is generated every time you log in and type your pass-word. If you can log in without typing a password (via *.rhosts* or */etc/hosts.equiv*), you should generate a private key using the *keylogin* command.

4.4.2 Prerequisites for Using SUN-DES-1

Before you can use SUN-DES-1, you have to meet a series of requirements.

- In recent versions of SunOS, the DES code is not included in the base operating system and must be added by the administrator. If you are not sure if you have the encryption software, try looking for the *crypt* command. Systems with Secure RPC should have *crypt* installed:

  ```
  % which crypt
  /bin/crypt
  ```

  Systems without the DES software do not have *crypt* installed:

  ```
  % which crypt
  crypt: Command not found.
  ```

  If you do not have DES installed, order the "Encryption Kit" from your OS vendor.

- You need to have built the X distribution with the HasSecureRPC flag set to YES. This is the default for the *mit/config/sun.cf* file:

  ```
  #define HasSecureRPC      YES
  ```

- NIS must be installed and running. If you are not sure if NIS is running, try an NIS com-mand. Systems running NIS should return a hostname from the *ypwhich* command:

  ```
  % ypwhich
  ruby
  ```

Systems not running NIS will complain that *ypbind* isn't running:

```
% ypwhich
ypwhich: bigbird is not running ypbind
```

For information on NIS, see *Managing NFS and NIS* by Hal Stern (O'Reilly & Associates, 1991).

- The private key server, *keyserv*, must be running. This is usually started at system startup in */etc/rc* or */etc/rc.local*. Use the *ps* command to confirm that it is running:

```
% ps agx | grep keyserv | grep -v grep
   74 ?  IW   0:01 keyserv
```

- Each user of the Secure RPC system should have a unique public key entry. You can have each user to do this on their own using *chkey*:

```
% chkey
Generating new key for unix.243@west.
Password:
Sending key change request to nugget...
Done.
```

or the system administrator can create public keys for users with the *newkey* command:

```
# newkey -u eap
Adding new key for unix.243@west.
New password:
Retype password:
Please wait for the database to get updated...
Your new key has been successfully stored away.
```

You can also create a new public key for **root** on a given host using *newkey*:

```
# newkey -h nugget
Adding new key for unix.nugget.west.ora.com@west.
New password:
Retype password:
Please wait for the database to get updated...
Your new key has been successfully stored away.
```

- You must propagate the public key information from NIS clients to the NIS master when you add or change a public key on the client. If you are running the *rpc.ypupdated* daemon, this will be done automatically. To see if the daemon is running:

```
% ps agx | grep rpc.ypupdated | grep -v grep
   70 ?  IW   0:00 /usr/etc/rpc.ypupdated
```

If you do not run *rpc.ypupdated*, *chkey* and *newkey* will not automatically update the public key map on the NIS master. If you have **root** permission on the NIS master machine, you can push the NIS map for *publickey.byname* on the NIS master manually:

```
# cd /var/yp
# make
```

It might be easier, however, to just enable *rpc.ypupdated*. You can make sure it will be enabled at the next reboot by adding it to */etc/rc.local*:

```
if [ -f /usr/etc/rpc.ypupdated -a -d /var/yp/$dname ]; then
        rpc.ypupdated;  echo -n ' ypupdated'
fi
```

Or you can uncomment it from */etc/inetd.conf*:

```
ypupdated/1 stream  rpc/tcp wait root /usr/etc/rpc.ypupdated rpc.ypupdated
```

and *kill –HUP inetd* so it will be enabled right away:

```
# ps agx | grep inetd | grep -v grep
  197 ? IW    2:24 inetd
# kill -HUP 197
```

You can use the SUN-DES-1 scheme only after you have an entry for your principal in the NIS master's public key map. This is also true for anybody else that wants to connect to your X server.

4.4.3 Using SUN-DES-1 with xdm

Once you have confirmed that SUN-DES-1 works on your machine, you can set up *xdm* to use it on the local console display server the same way you set up *xdm* to use XDM-AUTHORIZA-TION-1 as shown in Section 4.3.

Make sure that the `authorize` resource is turned on and then redefine the `Display-Manager._0.authName` resource for the local display only:

```
DisplayManager*authorize:     true
DisplayManager._0.authName:    SUN-DES-1
```

When you next connect, *xdm* will set up the server for SUN-DES-1. After logging in, check using *xhost*:

```
eap % xhost
access control enabled, only authorized clients can connect
eap@ (unix.243@west)
unix.nugget@west
```

Note that not only are you listed under the *xhost* list, but so is the principal for **root** on *nugget*, `unix.nugget@west`. The first line indicates the user with user ID 243 can connect to the server from any host within the NIS domain *west*. The second line indicates that **root** on *nugget* can connect. Don't remove the **root** principal from the *xhost* listing, since you'll need it if you want to run any *setuid* clients, such as *xterm*. See Section 4.4.6 for more information.

If you do an *xauth list*, you'll see this special **root** principal listed again:

```
eap % xauth list
nugget.west.ora.com:0  SUN-DES-1  unix.nugget@west
nugget/unix:0  SUN-DES-1  unix.nugget@west
```

xdm is run as **root**, and *xdm* is responsible for starting the server. Since the server is started as **root**, **root** is considered the "owner" of the server.

4.4.4 Using SUN-DES-1 with xinit

As with MIT-MAGIC-COOKIE-1, you need to do a little of the dirty work yourself if you want to use SUN-DES-1 with *xinit*. First we'll show the procedure by hand, and then we'll show how to automate it using *.xinitrc*. This example is on a machine with a local display named *nugget*. User **eap** has a user ID of 243, and the NIS domain name is *west*.

1. Start with a clean *.Xauthority* file:

   ```
   nugget% rm -f .Xauthority
   ```

2. Create an entry for each type of connection from your host to your server. Use *xauth* with SUN-DES-1, with the syntax:

   ```
   xauth add <display> SUN-DES-1 unix.<uid>@<domain>
   ```

   Give yourself permission to the machine using both its TCP/IP address and its IPC address:

   ```
   nugget% xauth add nugget:0 SUN-DES-1 unix.243@west
   xauth:  creating new authority file /home/eap/.Xauthority
   nugget% xauth add nugget/unix:0 SUN-DES-1 unix.243@west
   nugget% xauth list
   nugget.west.ora.com:0  SUN-DES-1  unix.243@west
   nugget/unix:0  SUN-DES-1  unix.243@west
   ```

3. Start the server with the *.Xauthority* file just created:

   ```
   nugget% xinit -- -auth ~/.Xauthority
   ```

When the server is up and running, check who has access by using the *xhost* command:

```
nugget% xhost
access control enabled, only authorized clients can connect
nugget.west.ora.com
localhost
```

The hosts list has the local machine listed by default, both by its hostname and by *localhost*. Using the *xhost* command, you need to give yourself permission to your server. If you want to be able to run *xterm* clients (or any other *setuid* clients) from the local host, you also have to give permission to **root** (see Section 4.4.6 for an explanation of why **root** needs to be on your access control list). You then need to remove the other entries. The syntax for giving a user permission is:

```
xhost +username@domain
```

The *domain* field can be left empty if it is the current NIS domain. Give both yourself and **root** permission to access the server. Note that when giving permission to **root**, you have to use the **root** principal for that machine (unix.*hostname@domain*), not **root@**.

```
nugget% xhost +eap@ +unix.nugget@west
eap@ (unix.243@west) being added to access control list
unix.nugget@west being added to access control list
```

Then remove permission from the entire host:

```
nugget% xhost -nugget.west.ora.com -localhost
nugget.west.ora.com being removed from access control list
localhost being removed from access control list
```

This ensures that only user **eap** in the current NIS domain and **root** on the host named *nugget* can connect to your server.

Note that since the *.Xauthority* file only contains information about the principal that started the server, the SUN-DES-1 security method does not depend on the security of the *.Xauthority* file. Unlike the MIT-MAGIC-COOKIE-1 and XDM-AUTHORIZATION-1 methods, if other users gain read access to your *.Xauthority* file, they still can't access your server unless you explicitly grant them access with *xhost*.

To automate this process, you need to edit your *.xinitrc* script.

```
#!/bin/sh

# Get user ID:
uid=`ypmatch ${USER} passwd.byname | awk -F: '{print $3}'`

# Get hostname:
host=`hostname`
domain=`domainname`

# Get principal:
principal=unix.${uid}@${domain}

# Add entries to .Xauthority file:
xauth add ${host}:0 SUN-DES-1 ${principal}
xauth add ${host}/unix:0 SUN-DES-1 ${principal}

# Add permission to self, remove permission from entire host:
xhost +${USER}@ +unix.${host}@${domain} -${host} -localhost

# Start some clients:
twm &
xterm &
    ...
```

When you start the server with *xinit*, this will set up your workstation display and prepare it for SUN-DES-1 use.

Note that a private key is automatically generated only when you log in with your password. If you log in without typing your password, you need to run the *keylogin* command to generate a new private key:

```
% keylogin
Password:
```

You might need to do this if you can remotely log into a machine because of entries in *$HOME/.rhosts* or */etc/hosts.equiv*.

4.4.5 Adding Another User with SUN-DES-1

To allow another user to connect to your host using SUN-DES-1 security, you have to run *xhost* to give the remote user access, and the remote user also has to run *xauth* to place an entry for that server in their *.Xauthority* file.

For this example, user **cathyr** on the host *rock* in the NIS domain *west* wants to connect to the host *nugget* in the same NIS domain, where user **eap** is currently running a server.

1. User **eap** has to give **cathyr** permission to access the server using *xhost*:

   ```
   nugget% xhost +cathyr@
   cathyr@ (unix.206@west) being added to access control list
   nugget% xhost
   cathyr@ (unix.206@west)
   eap@ (unix.243@west).
   unix.nugget@west
   ```

2. User **cathyr** has to create an *.Xauthority* file entry with the server she wants to connect to (*nugget*) and the principal of the user running the server:

   ```
   rock% xauth add nugget:0 SUN-DES-1 unix.nugget@west
   ```

   Note that this means that **cathyr** needs to know which user is running the server, and she needs to know that user's principal. In this case, the server was started using *xdm*, so it belongs to **root**. **cathyr** therefore needs to add **root**'s principal, not **eap**'s.

3. **cathyr** should now be able to connect to *nugget*'s X server:

   ```
   ruby% xroach -display nugget.west.ora.com:0 &
   ```

   Something went wrong if **cathyr** gets the following error:

   ```
   Xlib:  connection to "nugget:0.0" refused by server
   Xlib:  Client is not authorized to connect to Server
   Error: Can't open display: nugget:0
   ```

You might want to run X clients from a host in another NIS domain. The first complication is that if you're in another NIS domain, it's harder to find out what principal to use in the *xauth* command line. If the server was started with *xdm*, then you can use **root**'s principal; but if the server was started with *xinit* then you have to do some research.

If **cathyr** is in the same NIS domain (as in the example above), she can figure out what principal to use with only a little bit of detective work. She can just see who owns */dev/console*, and use *ypmatch* and *domainname* to figure out that user's principal. If *cathyr* were in a remote domain, however, she would have to be able to run a remote shell to the local host to get that information:

```
ruby% rsh nugget ls -l /dev/console
crw--w--w- 1 eap      0,  0 Sep 3 15:56 /dev/console
ruby% rsh nugget ypmatch eap passwd
eap:XZ7OEUd8wjYgo:243:100:Eric Pearce:/home/eap:/bin/tcsh
ruby% rsh nugget domainname
west
```

or she would be dependent on **eap** to tell her that information.

If you have accounts on machines in different NIS domains, you may want to display clients running on the remote machine to your local server. You need to run *xauth* (using the local principal) on the host you want to run client on, and you need to add yourself to the *xhost* list again, using the remote domain name. On the remote machine:

```
ruby% xauth add nugget:0 SUN-DES-1 unix.nugget@west
```

And on the local machine running the server:

```
nugget% xhost +eap@east
eap@east being added to access control list
```

Note that when you add a user for a remote domain, *xhost* doesn't know that user's ID and doesn't repeat it.

4.4.6 xterm and SUN-DES-1

A known problem with using the SUN-DES-1 mechanism and *setuid* clients (such as *xterm*) is that *setuid* clients use the wrong principal. Clients like *xterm* that are *setuid* to **root** try to connect with the **root** principal:

```
unix.nugget@west
```

instead of with the user's principal:

```
unix.243@
```

If you start your X session using *xdm*, the **root** principal is given access automatically, so an *xterm* will be able connect to the server. If you start your X session using *xinit*, however, you need to explicitly add **root** to your *xhost* list or you won't be able to run any *xterm* clients.

Note that this means that if you can run an *xterm* to your server, so can anyone else on the same host as long as you have the **root** principal listed in the *xhost* access list. This also means that if you want to run an *xterm* client from a remote host, you have to add the **root** principal for that machine to your *xhost* list as well.

```
% xhost +unix.rock@ +unix.ruby@ora.com
```

4.4.7 Troubleshooting SUN-DES-1

The SUN-DES-1 scheme is pretty complicated compared to the other security schemes. There's lots of potential for user errors, especially when creating entries with *xauth*. The daemons used in the process will also cause problems if they are not set up correctly. Some errors you may encounter are listed here with suggestions on what may have caused them:

- If you use an incorrect password for the user ID:

```
% keylogin
Generating new key for unix.243@west.
Password:
Invalid password.
```

- If NIS is not running on the host (in this case, the host is *rock*):

  ```
  Sending key change request to rock...
  chkey: unable to update NIS database (11): can't communicate with ypserv
  rock is down or not running rpc.ypupdated
  ```

- If */usr/etc/keyserv* is not running, you might get any of the following errors:

  ```
  Sending key change request to rock...
  chkey: unable to update NIS database(7): local resource allocation failure
  I couldn't generate a secure RPC authenticator to rock
  The keyserver /usr/etc/keyserv must be running.
  You may have to keylogin before doing a before doing a chkey.
  If you do not have a key, you may need to get a system
  administrator to create an initial key for you with newkey.
  The system could be loaded, so you might try this again.
  ```

  or:

  ```
  auth_create: Bad file number
  Error: Can't open display: nugget:0.0
  ```

  or:

  ```
  Could not set unix.243@west's secret key
  Maybe the keyserver is down?
  ```

- If you are running a (pre-R5) version of *xauth* that does not know about SUN-DES-1:

  ```
  xauth: (argv):1:  key contains odd number of or non-hex characters
  ```

- If you are running a (pre-R5) version of *xhost* that does not know about SUN-DES-1:

  ```
  access control enabled (only the following hosts are allowed)
  <unknown address in family 254>
  ```

If you run a mixed environment with R4 programs as well as R5 programs, make sure you have the R5 versions of *xauth* and *xhost* in your path before the R4 versions. This applies not only to MIT X11R4 but also any commercial X distributions that are not yet updated to R5.

4.5 xterm and Secure Keyboard

The *xterm* client has a *Secure Keyboard* option that you can enable on the *xterm* Main Menu. (You can access the Main Menu by holding down the CTRL key while pressing the second mouse button.) This feature can be used to prevent others from reading what you type in that window.

By enabling *Secure Keyboard*, *xterm* performs a *GrabKeyboard()* protocol request. Only one client can grab the keyboard at a time, so the *Secure Keyboard* feature can be enabled only temporarily; however, if you are typing a sensitive document or entering a password in that *xterm* window, enabling *Secure Keyboard* ensures that only *xterm* is receiving input directly from the keyboard. By using *Secure Keyboard*, you can be sure that no other client can be snooping on what you type.

When you enable *Secure Keyboard*, the *xterm* window should reverse its colors. If the colors do not reverse, then *xterm* was unable to grab the keyboard, and it is very possible that your display is being snooped.

The *Secure Keyboard* feature provides some protection against a particular kind of snooping, but it has many drawbacks. One drawback, of course, is that it is available only using *xterm*. Another is that it's a security feature that requires the user's intervention to be enabled—like a seatbelt, it's only as effective as its users make it. Since it grabs the keyboard, it's annoying to use—you have to disable it every time you want to type in another client window. And it doesn't protect against taking screendumps of a display, just against people snooping on keyboard input itself. The big thing it buys you is protection on passwords, since passwords are not copied on the display. But the rest of your display is still up for grabs.

4.6 Other Security Issues

Thus far we've only discussed security issues as far as server access control is concerned. X has many more security issues, which we discuss briefly here.

4.6.1 The Console xterm (R4 and Earlier)

The *–C* option to *xterm* gives the user a console window for the host running the *xterm* client. Prior to X11R5, any user can run an *xterm -C* regardless of whether they are logged on to the console.* Furthermore, multiple users can each run *xterm –C*, and the console messages will simply display on whichever console window was opened last. This means that the person on the console display won't receive console messages, and will have no indication that messages are not being shown.

On some systems, a console window which has been diverted to a foreign server may also prevent new login sessions on the console display. When an X server started with *xinit* shuts down on the console, the login prompt may be diverted to the console *xterm* window instead of to the console itself.

There is also a possibility that if root is logged in on the console, users running *xterm –C* can get root permission.

For all these reasons, many systems do not support the *-C* option to *xterm*. As an alternative, some systems (such as SCO Open Desktop) have each error message appear in a separate pop-up window on the console. For getting a diverted console window back, the following C program may be of use:

```
/* This will redirect console input and
   output back to /dev/console.
 */
#include <fcntl.h>
```

---

*For SunOS, you may wish to look at patch 100188-01 that addresses this issue.

```
#include <sys/termios.h>
main()
{
    int fd;
    if ((fd = open("/dev/console", O_RDWR, 0)) >= 0)
        ioctl (fd, TIOCCONS, 0);
    close(fd);
}
```

If you suspect that the console has been redirected, try compiling this program and running it as root.

```
% cc -o console console.c
% su
# ./console
```

4.6.2 The Console and xdm (R5)

With Release 5 of X11, many of the concerns about console ownership have been solved. In R5, *xterm* has been adjusted to allow only the owner of */dev/console* to start up a console window. Other users are able to run the –C option without receiving an error message, but no console messages will appear in their window. The R5 solution, however, requires a bit of fiddling for workstations configured to use *xdm* on the console display.

When you start X using *xinit*, you have to first log into the console using *getty* and *login*, so you necessarily own */dev/console*. When you log in using *xdm*, however, you bypass the *getty/login* mechanisms, so you have to be given ownership of */dev/console* explicitly. For that purpose, the default *xdm* configuration is altered in R5 to define scripts that are run when a user logs in on the console and when the user logs out again. The *xdm-config* file specifies:

```
DisplayManager._0.startup:      /usr/lib/X11/xdm/GiveConsole
DisplayManager._0.reset:        /usr/lib/X11/xdm/TakeConsole
```

(The _0 means that this resource is used only for *xdm* sessions on the display named : 0, i.e., the console display. See Chapter 3 for more information on configuring *xdm*.)

Both the *GiveConsole* and *TakeConsole* scripts are specified as display-specific resources for the local console display. The *GiveConsole* script is specified with the `Display-Manager._0.startup` resource, which defines a program that is run when the user has first logged in, but before any other clients are executed. The *TakeConsole* script is specified with the `DisplayManager._0.reset` resource, defining a program run after the user logs out but before a new connection is established. Both scripts are executed as **root**. Although all three files are currently shell scripts, they can be any executable file. (Note that since these scripts are run as **root**, you should be *extremely* careful should you choose to edit them.)

The *GiveConsole* script in the R5 distribution does a simple *chown* to give the user ownership of */dev/console* so that the user might get console messages:

```
#!/bin/sh
# Assign ownership of the console to the invoking user
#
# By convention, both xconsole and xterm -C check that the
```

```
# console is owned by the invoking user and is readable before attaching
# the console output.  This way a random user can invoke xterm -C without
# causing serious grief.
#
chown $USER /dev/console
```

Similarly, the *TakeConsole* script returns ownership of */dev/console* to **root**:

```
#!/bin/sh
# Reassign ownership of the console to root, this should disallow
# assignment of console output to any random users's xterm
#
chmod 622 /dev/console
chown root /dev/console
```

Together, *GiveConsole* and *TakeConsole* ensure that the user running *xdm* on the local display server can receive console messages.

4.6.3 Hanging the Server Remotely (R3)

In X11 Release 3, there's a bug where the server looks for a small packet from the client before it determines whether or not the client is in the *xhost* list. The server halts operation until this packet is sent. You can find out if your X server has this problem by running:

```
% telnet localhost 6000
```

(6000 is the TCP/IP port used by server 0 on the local host.)

If your X server freezes, then your workstation has this problem. Some servers will time out after 30 seconds, but others will remain blocked until the *telnet* connection is closed. Note that since this freezes your server, it's better not to try this from a window on your local display!

4.6.4 Reading the Framebuffer (Sun Workstations)

Sun workstations have a special device called a *framebuffer*, represented by the file */dev/fb*. The framebuffer contains the current image on the console. Sun workstations supply commands, called *screendump* and *screenload*, for copying the framebuffer to a file and displaying that file, respectively. If someone can log onto your Sun workstation, they can usually read your framebuffer regardless of any X security you have in place. To view the screen on one Sun workstation from another, try:

```
% rsh host screendump | screenload
```

From any X server, you can use the public domain *xloadimage* client:

```
% rsh host screendump | xloadimage
```

To prevent this, you could try changing the permissions on the framebuffer (i.e., chmod 600 /dev/fb), but this might break other programs and interfere with the functionality of your workstation. Another possibility might be to make the framebuffer readable by only a special group and have all commands that access it *setgid* to that group, similar to how permission to */dev/kmem* is restricted to the **kmem** group.

The best solution is to use the file */etc/fbtab* to control access to the frame buffer. Uncomment the line that lists the frame buffer:

```
/dev/console   0600   /dev/fb:/dev/bwone0:/dev/bwtwo0
```

and log out completely from the system and then log back in. The frame buffer device will now be owned and only readable by you, preventing another user from reading it. As long your account remains secure, your frame buffer should also. See the manual page for *fbtab* for more information.

4.6.5 Removing Files in /tmp

Another trick for disrupting the server on a workstation is to remove the files in */tmp/.X11-unix*. This directory contains a UNIX socket file for each X server running on that workstation.

```
% ls -l /tmp/.X11-unix
srwxrwxrwx  1 lmui              0 Apr 27 09:46 X0
```

This file is the socket descriptor used by X to connect to local server :0 via IPC. And by default, everyone has write permission (and thus delete permission) to */tmp/.X11-unix*. So another trick for perverse users is to delete the *X0* file on someone else's workstation.

```
% rsh harry rm /tmp/.X11-unix/X0
```

The workstation will subsequently be unable to use IPC to start local X clients anymore. That is, clients will not be able to connect using the display name unix:0.0 or :0.0, but only via TCP/IP or DECnet.

To protect against the *X0* file being deleted, turn on the sticky bit for the */tmp/.X11-unix* directory on systems that support that functionality:

```
root# chmod 1777 /tmp/.X11-unix
```

This will prevent users from deleting files that belong to other users in that directory.

While you're there, you might want to make sure the sticky bit is set for */tmp* itself. But note that setting the sticky bit for */tmp* does not set it recursively—you need to explicitly set it for */tmp/.X11-unix* as well.

On some versions of SunOS, *cron* automatically removes files in */tmp*, including the *.X11-unix/* subdirectory. On those systems, change the *cron* job to exclude sockets by adding "! -type s" to the *find* command line.

4.6.6 The Network Design

Despite all the work in keeping others from interfering with your server or snooping on your work, the basic security problem is in the very design of X11: if the client and server are running on different machines, then they necessarily communicate over the network. This means that anyone who knows the X protocol and who knows how to snoop over TCP/IP can follow everything you do over the network, and none of the security mechanisms described in this chapter can prevent them from doing that. The X protocol itself can be encrypted, but not without a substantial loss in efficiency.

Since new clients are started all the time, the magic cookie code itself is being sent over the network repeatedly—so even that can be captured, and the snoop will then have direct access to your display. X11R5 makes DES (Data Encryption Standard) available with both XDM-AUTHORITY-1 and SUN-DES-1, so that the magic cookie is encrypted across the network; but commercial servers are slow to incorporate DES code, and there are export restrictions on DES that make it unavailable outside of the United States.

Several X vendors have implemented the U.S. Government specification on Compartmented Mode Workstations (CMW), which allows the X workstation to run as a standalone trusted system. On a CMW, for example, each window has its own security label. (See the Nutshell Handbook *Computer Security Basics* by Deborah Russell (O'Reilly & Associates, 1991) for more information on security labels and trusted systems.) As you would imagine, however, all bets are off on a networked environment. There are trusted networking specifications being worked on (such as MaxSix), but X still has a long way to go before it can be considered secure.

4.7 Related Documentation

"Issues in Building Trusted X Window Systems," by Jeremy Epstein and Jeffrey Picciotto, published in *The X Resource, Issue 0*, O'Reilly & Associates, Inc., Fall 1991.

The *Xsecurity*, *xauth*, *xhost*, *xterm*, *fbtab*, and *xdm* manual pages.

"Framework Generic Requirements for X Window System Security, Issue 1," by Maria Cangelosi and Charles Blauner, published by Bell Communications Research, Inc. (Bellcore), document number FA-STS-001324, July 1992.

For more information on Secure RPC, see *Managing NFS and NIS* by Hal Stern (O'Reilly & Associates, 1991).

5

Font Management

The fonts *used by an application need to be available to every server that might display it. This chapter discusses the issues with using fonts, installing new fonts, and converting fonts from other formats. It also discusses the X11R5 font server.*

In This Chapter:

☞

5
Font Management

The number of fonts available under X11 is enormous, and there's no limit to adding more. Each size and orientation is treated as a different font. Furthermore, fonts are stored in several different formats, so the same font might be stored five different ways.

The administrator's role is to ensure that each server can access the fonts it needs for a given application. In Release 3 and Release 4, fonts for servers needed to be available locally—usually stored on a local disk drive or made to appear local via a NFS or AFS filesystem. In Release 5, fonts can be obtained either locally or through a *font server*, which allows access to fonts on more than one host on the network.

5.1 Fonts on the X Window System

In general, a client has default fonts chosen by the programmer, but administrators or users may want to change them to their own preference. The default fonts may be too small to read, unavailable for a given server, or just plain ugly. For example, the default font for *xterm* is usually the font *fixed*, a 13-pixel semi-condensed font that tends to be quite small on high-resolution monitors.

Before we discuss the administrative issues of fonts, let's talk about how fonts are designated on the X Window System. An example of a font name and its components is shown in Figure 5-1.

The field names have the following meanings:

Foundry   This is a registered name for the font "foundry" (usually a company name) that supplied the font to the X Consortium ("Adobe," "Bitstream," etc).

Family   The "family" or typographic style of the font ("Courier," "Lucida," etc).

Weight   The typographic weight or "blackness" of the font ("medium," "bold," etc).

Slant   The "posture" of the typeface ("Roman" is upright, "Italic" is slanted, etc).

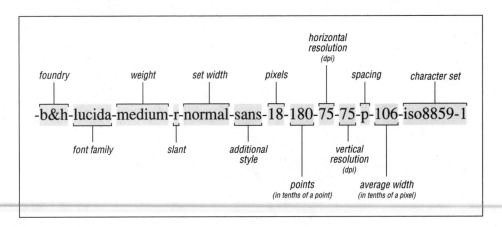

Figure 5-1. Components of a font name

Set Width   The horizontal width of the font ("Normal," "Narrow," etc).

Additional Style   An additional style that expresses information not present in the other fields
                   ("sans," or not specified).

Pixel Size   A height measurement in pixels at a certain point size and resolution.

Point Size   The size of the font in typographic "points" (1/72 of an inch).

Horizontal and Vertical Resolution
                   The horizontal and vertical resolution in dots per inch (dpi) from when the
                   font was originally designed.

Spacing   The description of how the width affects placement of adjacent characters.
                   A proportional ("p") font's characters vary in width, so some characters
                   may appear closer to each other. This is usually desirable for hardcopy,
                   such as book, but is inappropriate for terminal displays (such as for *xterm*).
                   A monospaced ("m") font's characters each have the same width. A char-
                   acter cell ("c") font treats each character as a little box of the same dimen-
                   sions as all the other characters. Although both "m" and "c" fonts can be
                   used for *xterm* windows, you should use character cell fonts for *xterm* since
                   monospaced fonts are not well-contained and may leave garbage "pixels"
                   on the screen.

Average Width   The average width of the font in tenths of a pixel.

Character Set and Encoding
                   The encoding standard to which the font conforms to (ISO is the Interna-
                   tional Standards Organization) and the particular character set.

The fields that are usually the most important to the X administrator are:

• The size and resolution (for controlling the size of the font on the screen).

• The spacing (for use with terminal emulators).

Fonts are specified to a client either as a resource or with the *–fn* option. For example, a user can put the following line in a resource file:

```
xterm*font: -misc-fixed-bold-r-normal--15-140-75-75-c-90-iso8859-1
```

or invoke *xterm* with the following command line:

```
% xterm -fn -misc-fixed-bold-r-normal--15-140-75-75-c-90-iso8859-1
```

The default resources for most clients are specified in their *application defaults* file. See Section D.1.2 for more information on where resources are defined.

There are several clients that deal directly with fonts. These can be used to find and list all the fonts available from the X server.

5.1.1 xlsfonts

To see all the fonts a X server knows about, run the *xlsfonts* command. *xlsfonts* accepts wildcards within the font specification and will list all the matching names. For example:

```
% xlsfonts -fn '-dec-*-*-*-*--*-*-*-*-*-*-*'
-dec-terminal-bold-r-normal--14-140-75-75-c-80-dec-dectech
-dec-terminal-bold-r-normal--14-140-75-75-c-80-iso8859-1
-dec-terminal-medium-r-normal--14-140-75-75-c-80-dec-dectech
-dec-terminal-medium-r-normal--14-140-75-75-c-80-iso8859-1
```

Note that only a small subset of the available fonts is appropriate for the *xterm* client. Only character cell fonts (with -c- in the 11th field) are recommended for use in *xterm* windows. Although mono-spaced -m- fonts like Courier and Lucida Typewriter can be used for *xterm* most of the time, some "garbage" characters may occasionally appear if you use those fonts, since mono-spaced fonts can extend outside of the character cell.

5.1.2 xfd

The *xfd* client will display all the characters of a particular font. It can be used as a quick test to make sure a font exists and looks okay. For example, the command line:

```
% xfd -fn -adobe-courier-bold-r-normal--14-140-75-75-m-90-iso8859-1
```

would yield the window shown in Figure 5-2.

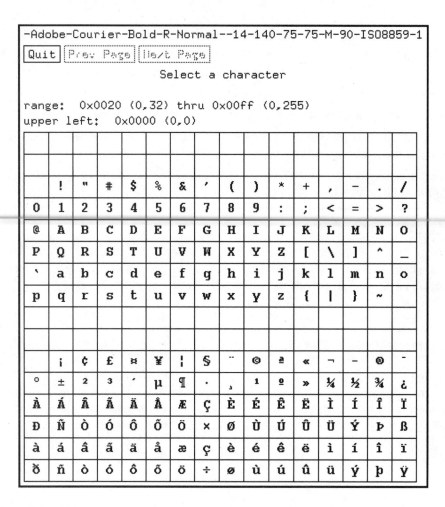

Figure 5-2. xfd

5.1.3 xfontsel

The *xfontsel* client (which was new in R4) allows browsing through all the available fonts and seeing each one in turn. When you find a font that you are happy with, click on the "select" button and the selection can be pasted into a file or command line without having to type it by hand.

The X Window System Administrator's Guide

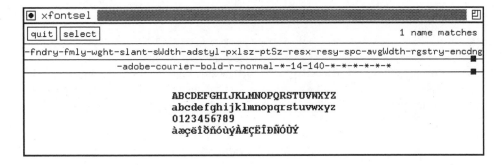

Figure 5-3. xfontsel

Consult the manual pages for *xlsfonts*, *xfd*, and *xfontsel* for more information.

5.1.4 The Font Path

The *font path* is a list of directories in which the server looks for fonts. On the X Window System, fonts are usually stored in a subdirectory of */usr/lib/X11/fonts*. The MIT Release 4 distribution of X contains three subdirectories in */usr/lib/X11/fonts*: *75dpi*, *100dpi* and *misc*. The *dpi* suffix refers to the dots-per-inch or screen resolution of the display that the server is going to use; the *misc* directory contains random useful fonts for the display.

The default font path for a given server is usually set when the server is built from source code. The typical MIT-derived local display server will come with the *75dpi*, *100dpi*, and *misc* directories in its font path by default. You can check the current font path at any time with the *–q* (query) option to the *xset* client. For a typical R4 server:

```
% xset -q
FontPath:
/usr/lib/X11/fonts/misc/,/usr/lib/X11/fonts/75dpi/,/usr/lib/X11/fonts/100dpi/
```

Release 5 includes the *Speedo* font directory of scalable fonts as well. (See Section 5.2.1 for more information on Speedo fonts.)

```
% xset -q
Font Path:
/usr/lib/X11/fonts/misc/,/usr/lib/X11/fonts/Speedo/,/usr/lib/X11/fonts/75dpi/,
/usr/lib/X11/fonts/100dpi/
```

Each of these directories is searched in order for a specified font. The server will use the first match it finds when there is more than one font with the same name. Users can change the default font path with the *fp* option to the *xset* command. For example, to add a font directory to the font path, you might type:

```
% xset +fp /usr/lib/X11/fonts/local
```

This command adds the directory */usr/lib/X11/fonts/local* to the current font path. The "*+fp*" option prepends a directory to the font path, while "*fp+*" appends it.

```
% xset -q
Font Path:
/usr/lib/X11/fonts/local,/usr/lib/X11/fonts/misc/,/usr/lib/X11/fonts/75dpi/,
/usr/lib/X11/fonts/100dpi/
```

The *local* directory is now searched before the regular directories. If you want to redefine one of the default fonts, you can install a new one in the *local* directory and the server will access the new one instead.

Rehashing the Font Path

Each time the font path is changed, the server reads the *fonts.dir* and *fonts.alias* files in each directory listed in the new font path. The server then maintains a list of valid font names in memory instead of searching for a font in the filesystem every time it is requested. If a new font is added to one of the font directories and the *fonts.dir* or *fonts.alias* files are changed, you need to update the list of fonts known to your server with the command:

```
% xset fp rehash
```

The *rehash* command tells the server that something has changed and it should rebuild this internal list.

The *xset* client controls many server features. See the manual page for *xset* for more information.

The font path can also be specified when the server is first started. For example, on the command line:

```
% xinit -- -fp /usr/lib/X11/fonts/local,/usr/lib/X11/fonts/misc/,\
/usr/lib/X11/fonts/75dpi/,/usr/lib/X11/fonts/100dpi/
```

or in the *Xservers* file:

```
:0 local /usr/bin/X11/X -fp /usr/lib/X11/fonts/local,/usr/lib/X11/fonts/misc/,\
/usr/lib/X11/fonts/75dpi/,/usr/lib/X11/fonts/100dpi/
```

5.1.5 The Font Directory File

When a client requests a specified font, the server searches in each of the directories in its font path for a file called *fonts.dir*, as in */usr/lib/X11/fonts/75dpi/fonts.dir*. The *fonts.dir* file maps the name of the requested font to the filename of the font as it is stored in the filesystem. If there is no match, the client reverts to its own defaults (e.g., *xterm* reverts to "*fixed*").

The *fonts.dir* file is needed because some operating systems have restrictions on filenames. For example, MS-DOS, VMS, and UNIX all have restrictions on filename length or on the characters used within filenames. When installing a new font, you should choose a filename for the new font that conforms to the semantics of your operating system. The *fonts.dir* file contains the mapping of the font filename to the name of the font itself.

The *fonts.dir* file's presence is required for the server to access any fonts within a directory. It is created by the *mkfontdir* command. You have to run *mkfontdir* every time you add or delete a font from a directory to keep the *fonts.dir* file in sync with the actual contents of the font area. (See Section 5.3.1 for an example of how to use *mkfontdir*.) The *fonts.dir* file has a simple format—the first several lines of a sample R4 file resemble the following:

```
200
courBO10.snf -adobe-courier-bold-o-normal--10-100-75-75-m-60-iso8859-1
courBO12.snf -adobe-courier-bold-o-normal--12-120-75-75-m-70-iso8859-1
courBO14.snf -adobe-courier-bold-o-normal--14-140-75-75-m-90-iso8859-1
courBO18.snf -adobe-courier-bold-o-normal--18-180-75-75-m-110-iso8859-1
courBO24.snf -adobe-courier-bold-o-normal--24-240-75-75-m-150-iso8859-1
    .
    .
    .
```

The number at the top is the number of fonts in the directory. The remaining lines are pairs of filenames and font names. The *.snf* extension to filenames in this example indicates the format that the font is stored in—in this case, the Server Natural Format. (See Section 5.2.2 for more information on font formats.) The files may also have a *.Z* extension, if the server supports compressed fonts.

OpenWindows-specific Features

Sun's OpenWindows has a different system for fonts (scalable *F3* format), but most of the font administration utilities parallel the MIT ones in function. The OpenWindows file *Families.list* is similar in function to the *fonts.dir* file. It is created by the *bldfamily* command, which should be run any time the contents of the font directory are changed, in the same manner as *mkfontdir*.

5.1.6 The fonts.scale File (R5 only)

In R5, the outline or scalable fonts (as described in Section 5.2.1) introduce a problem with creating the *fonts.dir* file. It is difficult for *mkfontdir* to determine the values in the font name fields for a scalable font. If there are scalable fonts within a font directory, a *fonts.scale* file should be created by hand. When *mkfontdir* is run, it will create entries in *fonts.dir* for each bitmap font it finds and will then append the contents of the *fonts.scale* file.

The Speedo fonts distributed with R5 come with a *fonts.scale* file that is installed along with the fonts in */usr/lib/X11/fonts/Speedo*. It contains an entry for each scalable font:

```
8
font0648.spd -bitstream-charter-medium-r-normal--0-0-0-0-p-0-iso8859-1
font0649.spd -bitstream-charter-medium-i-normal--0-0-0-0-p-0-iso8859-1
font0709.spd -bitstream-charter-bold-r-normal--0-0-0-0-p-0-iso8859-1
font0710.spd -bitstream-charter-bold-i-normal--0-0-0-0-p-0-iso8859-1
font0419.spd -bitstream-courier-medium-r-normal--0-0-0-0-m-0-iso8859-1
```

```
font0582.spd -bitstream-courier-medium-i-normal--0-0-0-0-m-0-iso8859-1
font0583.spd -bitstream-courier-bold-r-normal--0-0-0-0-m-0-iso8859-1
font0611.spd -bitstream-courier-bold-i-normal--0-0-0-0-m-0-iso8859-1
```

As there are no other fonts in the Speedo directory, the contents of the *fonts.scale* file and the resulting *fonts.dir* file are identical.

5.1.7 Wildcards

As shown in our *xlsfonts* example earlier, users don't have to use the full names of a font when specifying them. *Wildcards* can be used to limit the amount of typing required and provide flexibility.

Users can use asterisks ("*") in the font specification, such as:

```
% xterm -fn '-fixed-*-*-*-*--15-140-*-*-*-*-*-*'
```

The asterisks will match any of the possible values for a given field in the font specification.

Notice that a font name using an asterisk as a wildcard needs to be single-quoted on the command line. This is to protect the asterisks from being interpreted by the shell.

The first font found in the font path that matches the pattern is the one that is used. If you supply the pattern to *xlsfonts*, you can see which fonts in your font path match the pattern:

```
% xlsfonts -fn '-fixed-*-*-*-*--15-140-*-*-*-*-*-*'
-misc-fixed-bold-r-normal--15-140-75-75-c-90-iso8859-1
-misc-fixed-medium-r-normal--15-140-75-75-c-90-iso8859-1
```

Although *xlsfonts* may report more than one font name, only the first font listed will be used by a client when supplied a font name using the same wildcards. If you run *xfd* with the same font pattern, the name of the first matching font is displayed at the top of the window:

```
-misc-fixed-bold-r-normal--15-140-75-75-c-90-iso8859-1
```

Using wildcards could have a surprising effect, especially when a new font is installed: if an administrator adds a new font that is similar in name to an already existing font, users may end up matching the new one instead of the one they thought they were requesting. Other surprises could occur when a new version of X11 is installed, as each release has had more fonts than the previous release, leading to new matches to a wildcard.

Using wildcards can make an application more flexible, as it may still find a usable font if the intended one is missing, whereas a complete font specification may cause a failure if not matched exactly.

5.1.8 Aliases

A font subdirectory can contain a file called *fonts.alias*, which contains aliases for font names. An example of an alias is the default *fixed* font, which is defined in *fonts.alias* in the MIT distribution of X as:

```
fixed -misc-fixed-medium-r-semicondensed--13-120-75-75-c-60-iso8859-1
```

An administrator can make it easier for users to specify fonts by defining aliases for frequently used fixed-width fonts. For example, if the administrator enters the following line into the *fonts.alias* file:

```
fb15 -misc-fixed-bold-r-normal--15-140-75-75-c-90-iso8859-1
```

Users can then call the 15-point fixed bold font with the command line:

```
% xterm -fn fb15
```

Font aliases can be used in resource files as well, as follows:

```
xterm*font: fb15
```

You could argue that this is a bad idea, as non-standard aliases would likely fail if you used your resource files on another server.

Aliases also add flexibility to applications, as they can be assigned to more than one font. For example, the name *lucidasans-10* is aliased in */usr/lib/X11/fonts/75dpi/fonts.alias* as:

```
lucidasans-10 -b&h-lucida-medium-r-normal-sans-10-100-75-75-p-58-iso8859-1
```

and in */usr/lib/X11/fonts/100dpi/fonts.alias* as:

```
lucidasans-10 -b&h-lucida-medium-r-normal-sans-14-100-100-100-p-80-iso8859-1
```

Which one is used depends on which directory occurs first in the font path. In this example, the alias creates flexibility in the resolution of the display.

Another reason to alias a file is that the font name may be inconvenient to use on the command line. The "b&h" fonts shown above contain the "&" character in the font name, which will confuse the shell.

Under OpenWindows, the files *Compat.list* and *Synonyms.list* provide the alias mechanism.

5.1.8.1 The FILE_NAMES_ALIAS Alias

The "magic" alias "FILE_NAMES_ALIASES" indicates that the actual filenames of the font files, with the suffixes removed, can be used as aliases for the fonts. For example, the DECWindows fonts all have filenames that are also valid aliases when you remove the extension. If the *fonts.dir* file has the following entry:

```
terminal_wide14.snf -dec-terminal-medium-r-wide--14-140-75-75-c-120-iso8859-1
```

The name *terminal_wide14* would be a valid alias for this font if "FILE_NAMES_ALIASES" is present in the *fonts.alias* file.

This method of aliasing is being downplayed by the X Consortium, as its use encourages nonstandard font names. You should not rely on this mechanism in the future.

5.2 All About Fonts

There are many different font formats in use and each vendor has made changes on its own. The first step in resolving the problems caused by this is to identify what type of font is being used. The next step is to find the right tool to make the font available to your application.

5.2.1 Bitmap Versus Outline Fonts

For MIT servers prior to R5, a separate font was required for each size of the font. For example, to display the font *-b&h-lucida-bold-i-normal-sans* at the point sizes of 11, 14, 17, 20, and 34, you needed a font for each:

```
-b&h-lucida-bold-i-normal-sans-11-80-100-100-p-69-iso8859-1
-b&h-lucida-bold-i-normal-sans-14-100-100-100-p-90-iso8859-1
-b&h-lucida-bold-i-normal-sans-17-120-100-100-p-108-iso8859-1
-b&h-lucida-bold-i-normal-sans-20-140-100-100-p-127-iso8859-1
-b&h-lucida-bold-i-normal-sans-34-240-100-100-p-215-iso8859-1
```

This is simply because the fonts are *bitmaps* and are stored as such. In R5, *outline* or "scalable" fonts are also available. These are stored as a description of the outline of the font and can be scaled by the server to any point size. Scalable fonts have been available in NeWS servers (Sun OpenWindows and SGI X/NeWS/GL) only prior to R5. The Speedo fonts in R5 are of the outline type. Outline fonts can be recognized by 0 values for the size fields in the font name:

```
-bitstream-charter-bold-r-normal--0-0-0-0-p-0-iso8859-1
-bitstream-charter-bold-i-normal--0-0-0-0-p-0-iso8859-1
-bitstream-courier-bold-r-normal--0-0-0-0-m-0-iso8859-1
-bitstream-courier-bold-i-normal--0-0-0-0-m-0-iso8859-1
```

When the font is requested, the size fields are filled in with the desired value:

```
% xlsfonts -fn '-bitstream-charter-bold-r-normal--12-*-*-*-*-*-*'
-bitstream-charter-bold-r-normal--12-120-75-75-p-75-iso8859-1
```

Some advantages to outline fonts are:

- They need only one font file per font, vastly simplifying administration and conserving disk space.

- They are more flexible, as it may be impossible to predict all sizes that might be requested by users or required by different displays.

Some advantages to bitmap fonts are:

- They usually look better than scaled fonts, as they are *tuned* for each size.

- They may be faster to request, as there is no scaling overhead before the font can be used.

You can convert specific sizes of an outline font into a bitmap font using the font conversion tools described in Section 5.2.3. Some vendors provide bitmap versions of outline fonts at several common sizes to boost performance.

5.2.2 Font Formats

If you are building an X11 distribution from MIT source, the fonts arrive with a *.bdf* suffix, indicating that they are in BDF format (*Bitmap Distribution Format*). BDF format has been the default format since the early releases of X. When the standard X11 distribution is built, BDF font files are converted into a format suitable for your server.

If you are not building X11 from source, the fonts are usually sent with the individual server (for example, on a font tape sent with an X terminal). The fonts will have another suffix, probably *.snf*, indicating that they are in SNF format (*Server Natural Format*). In R5, fonts default to PCF format (Portable Compiled Font), with *.pcf* suffixes.

Following are some common extensions and what they indicate about the font:

.bdf   *Bitmap Distribution Format*. This is the form most fonts will arrive in if the final destination is unknown. BDF files can be converted to most of the final formats that would be used by a server. If you want to supply someone else with a font, use the BDF format for interchange. They are ASCII files and can be edited with a normal text editor. The MIT server is able to read BDF files directly, but it is not the optimal format for storage.

.snf   *Server Natural Format*. This format is used by most MIT servers in Releases 2 through 4. Fonts are stored in a binary file and are host byte order dependent. This means you cannot share fonts between a *big endian* and *little endian* machine in most cases. Some vendors have servers that are smart enough to detect this and convert the font "on-the-fly." See 7.4.1 for more information on SNF fonts and byte order dependencies.

.pcf   *Portable Compiled Font*. The PCF format was designed by DEC for use with DECWindows. It offers some advantages over SNF, in that it is host byte order independent. This means hosts of different byte orders can share the same font. DEC has made this format available to the X Consortium, and it is now the default for MIT Release 5. It is also used by recent versions of IRIX on the Silicon Graphics platform.

.spd   *Speedo-Bitstream*. These are commercial-quality outline fonts donated to the X Consortium by Bitstream Inc. They are included in MIT Release 5. They can be distinguished by the fact that they all have point sizes of 0, as they are scaled to a particular point size when they are requested.

.f3b, .fb   *X11/NeWS*. These formats are used by Sun Microsystem's X11/NeWS Server and older versions of the Silicon Graphics X11/NeWS/GL Server. The *.f3b* files are scalable F3 (formerly named "Folio") format fonts. The *.fb* files are F3 format fonts scaled to certain point sizes. Some of their administration tools parallel the MIT ones and will be mentioned in context.

.ps   *PostScript Type 3*. Several of these fonts come with the Sun OpenWindows distribution. They can be loaded into the X11/NeWS server with the *ldf* program.

.Z   *Compressed* file. This extension indicates that the *compress* program has been run on the font file. This should reduce the size of the file on disk. Some servers (such as those from MIT) can read compressed fonts directly, but this is not true for all implementations.

5.2.3 Format Conversion Tools

There are several commands for converting from one format to another, as illustrated in Figure 5-4. The following are some common examples. See the manual pages for these commands for more information.

bdftosnf   Converts BDF to SNF. This command should come with any server that uses SNF, such as the stock MIT server Releases 2 through 4. Example usage:

```
# bdftosnf myfont.bdf > myfont.snf
```

bdftopcf   Converts BDF to PCF. This command should come with any server that uses PCF, such as DECWindows and MIT Release 5. Example usage:

```
# bdftopcf -o myfont.pcf myfont.bdf
```

dxfc   Converts BDF to PCF. This command is distributed with DECWindows. Example usage:

```
# dxfc myfont.bdf > myfont.pcf
```

snftobdf   Converts SNF back to BDF. This program can be found on various anonymous *ftp* sites and X source archives.* Example usage:

```
# snftobdf myfont.snf > myfont.bdf
```

convertfont   Converts BDF to several X11/NeWS formats and back. This command comes with Sun OpenWindows. Example usage:

```
# convertfont -f 32 myfont.bdf
```

                 See Section 5.3.6.3 for an example using *convertfont*.

fstobdf   Dumps the BDF version of any font available to the font server. See Section 5.5 for more information on the font server.

```
# fstobdf -s tcp/harry.ora.com:7000 -fn fixed > fixed.bdf
```

getbdf   Dumps the BDF version of any font available to the X server. See Sections 5.3.4.2 and 5.3.5 for examples of using *getbdf*.

```
# getbdf -font 9x15 > 9x15.bdf
```

---

* One *ftp* site is *export.lcs.mit.edu* in *contrib/snftobdf.tar.Z*.

makeafb   Converts F3 fonts into Adobe Bitmap Format. This is an intermediate format used when converting X11/NeWS fonts.

```
# makeafb -16 LucidaSans-Bold.f3b
```

Note that font files can be read by some servers in a compressed format, so administrators may be able to save space by compressing font files on their systems. Compression may cause some performance loss, as the fonts will have to be uncompressed by the server when they are read. The space savings is desirable, as you are likely to accumulate hundreds of fonts once you get the hang of it. The fonts may turn out to be the single largest consumer of disk space of all the X components.

Be aware that converting a font from one vendor's machine for use on another may be illegal, attractive as the idea might be. There may also be restrictions on how the fonts are to be used—for example, they may be licensed for screen use, but not for hardcopy. Check the copyright notices before proceeding.

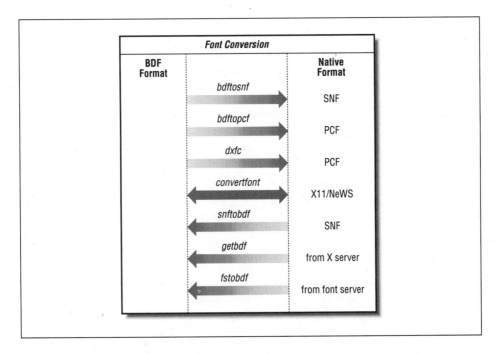

Figure 5-4. Font conversion utilities

5.3 Adding New Fonts

There are lots of reasons to expand the numbers of fonts available. Some applications, especially desktop publishing packages, provide new fonts as part of their installation. Clients that support languages other than English are becoming commonplace and are widely available on the Internet—these clients require large numbers of new fonts to be added.

It is possible to access fonts in your home directory by adding paths to existing font paths with the *fp* option to the *xset* command. This is useful for testing. It also means that you can have users install the fonts they want in their own home directories if you don't think everyone will want to use them.

5.3.1 Adding a Single Font

Let's step through the procedure for adding a new font in a stock MIT R3 or R4 environment. (For an R5 environment running a font server, the font may already exist on another system and you can just tell the font server where it is. See Section 5.5 for more information.)

You may come across an application that requires some non-standard fonts, say a *Kanji* font for the OSF/Motif demo program *hellomotif*.* This font is distributed in BDF format.

1. Convert it to SNF (or whatever is appropriate for your server) with the *bdftosnf* command:

   ```
   # bdftosnf -t k14-1.bdf > k14-1.snf
   # bdftosnf -t rkana14.bdf > rkana14.snf
   ```

   The *–t* flag indicates that these fonts are going to be displayed on a "terminal" (such as *xterm*) and each character should be same size.

2. Copy the SNF files into one of the font directories. For this example, the *misc* directory is a good candidate:

   ```
   # cp k14-1.snf /usr/lib/X11/fonts/misc
   # cp rkana14.snf /usr/lib/X11/fonts/misc
   ```

3. Rebuild the *fonts.dir* file with the *mkfontdir* command:

   ```
   # mkfontdir /usr/lib/X11/fonts/misc
   ```

   This command will increment by 2 the number of fonts listed on the first line of the *fonts.dir* file, and add two pairs of entries: the filename and the font name.

   ```
   k14-1.snf   -k14-screen-medium-r-normal--14-140-75-75-m-140-jisx0208.1983-1
   rkana14.snf -romankana14-screen-medium-r-normal--14-140-75-75-m-70-jisx0201.
   1976-0
   ```

   The next step would be to add aliases to *fonts.alias* for convenience. In the *hellomotif* case, the application requests the font by its full name, not by an alias—so unless you intend to access the font from other applications, it probably isn't worth aliasing.

---

*OSF/Motif source can be purchased from the Open Software Foundation.

4. Before the server can know about the new font, the font path needs to be *rehashed*. Otherwise, an error will be returned. For example, if you try to display the new font immediately with the *xfd* client, using the font name in the second column of the *fonts.dir* file:

```
% xfd -fn -k14-screen-medium-r-normal--14-140-75-75-m-140-jisx0208\
.1983-1
```

you will get an error such as:

```
Warning: Cannot convert string "-k14-screen-medium-r-normal--14-140-75-75
-m-140-jisx0208.1983-1" to type FontStruct
```

For the modified *fonts.dir* file to be reread without restarting the server, you must run the *xset* command:

```
% xset fp rehash
```

Try *xfd* again to verify that it worked. If *xfd* can display the font, it is likely to be available for any client that requests it from your server.

Your server may cache a font, so don't expect a font to disappear immediately even if you delete the file that contains it on disk.

5.3.2 Adding Multiple Fonts

Some applications may require that a large number of fonts be added to your local font area. One example of this is the public domain *TeX dvi* file previewer *xtex*.* *TeX* is a popular typesetting program that runs on most systems that are around today. A *dvi* file is the device-independent output of the TeX program. The term *previewer* refers to a program that displays something on your screen to preview what it would look like on the final output, which is usually done on a laser printer or typesetter.

The *xtex* program expects a separate X11 font to exist for each size (*magsteps*, for you TeX font weenies) of each TeX font requested by a *dvi* file.† In a situation like this, it is probably worth creating a new directory in your font area for easier administration.

There are a few advantages to breaking up the font area into subdirectories:

- By separating the "stock" or "vanilla" environment from the "local" areas, administration is easier. You can save a lot of time when upgrading, as you don't have to worry about trashing all your hard work if you have distinct areas that won't be overwritten by a software upgrade. This concept can be applied to other areas of X, where it may be desirable to keep files that you install in an area separate from the vendor-supplied files.

- Multiple subdirectories give you, the administrator, control over whether or not to export the font areas in a networked filesystem. You may want to give the font areas different permissions, or to give a group of users and programs permission to add new fonts

---

* xtex can be *ftp*'d from *foobar.colorado.edu*. It is part of a larger package called *SeeTeX*.

† The *xdvi* program also previews TeX dvi files, but is able to read TeX fonts directly without converting them to an X11 format. *xdvi* is available via *ftp* from *export.lcs.mit.edu* in */contrib*.

without intervention of the system administrator. TeX programs are an example of this, as some are able to create fonts "on-the-fly" and want to add the newly created font to a font area so it will be there the next time it is requested.

- By breaking fonts up into multiple directories, you also make it easier to view the directory contents. The TeX example alone has several hundred entries.

The disadvantages to this approach include the fact that special knowledge is required by the end users if they want to access a font in a nonstandard directory (you could alleviate this problem by providing new users with start-up files that include these special paths).

5.3.2.1 Multiple Font Example

For the *xtex* example, let's create a subdirectory in the font area called *tex*. The *xtex* package describes how to create the SNF files from the BDF files in the distribution.

1. Once the SNF files are created, copy the SNF files to the new directory and rebuild the *fonts.dir* file:

```
# cp *.snf /usr/lib/X11/fonts/tex
# cd /usr/lib/X11/fonts/tex
# mkfontdir
```

If you get an error such as:

```
Duplicate font names cmr10
        cmr10.snf goof.snf
mkfontdir: failed to create directory in .
```

then there is more than one font with the same name. In this rigged example, two *.snf* files for the same font exist in a common directory. The solution would be to delete the one you do not want from this directory.*

2. Since you are adding a new area to the font search path, you will need to tell the server where to look with the *xset* command.

```
% xset fp+ /usr/lib/X11/fonts/tex
```

You probably made a typo or specified an invalid pathname if you get an error such as:

```
X Error of failed request: BadValue (integer parameter out of range
for operation)
          Major opcode of failed request: 51 (X_SetFontPath)
          Minor opcode of failed request: 0
          Resource id in failed request: 0x4
          Serial number of failed request: 5
          Current serial number in output stream: 8
```

---

* You could also change the name of the font in the BDF file before converting it into SNF, but something is probably wrong if you are having a name conflict.

The X Window System Administrator's Guide

3. Verify your current font path using the *xset* command:

```
% xset -q
Font Path:
/usr/lib/X11/fonts/misc/,/usr/lib/X11/fonts/75dpi/,
    /usr/lib/X11/fonts/100dpi/,/usr/lib/X11/fonts/tex
```

Note that, in order to access the new fonts, users have to run the *xset fp+* command specified above every time they start their server. Their *.xsession* or *.xinitrc* files would be an appropriate place for the command. For sites that start their X sessions from *xdm*, you can add local changes like this one to the *xdm* startup files. This will add the font path for all users who start their X sessions using *xdm*.

Rather than creating multiple font directories to be added to the font path of each server, you could just put all non-standard fonts into one directory, for example, */usr/lib/X11/fonts/local*. Some vendor implementations (such as DECWindows) provide a "local" directory structure just for this purpose. The path is already known to the server, so you can add fonts and they will be available without further changes.

You could also define this path within the default search path when you build the X11 distribution from source (using the `DefaultFontPath` build flag) or supply a font path when starting the X server. See Section 8.5 for information on how to change your build flags when building X11 from source. To supply a new font path when starting the X server, most servers accept a *–fp* option on the command line.

5.3.3 Problems with Running Vendor-specific Clients

The fonts available to a server vary from one vendor to another. If a client requests a font from the server and it is not recognized, this may render an application unusable or just make it look strange.

Let's say you are on a Sun running an MIT Release 4 server and wish to run the DECWindows desk calendar *dxcalendar* off a remote Ultrix host. *dxcalendar* looks for specific fonts that are not available on the Sun, and the program will complain about the missing fonts:

```
scud% dxcalendar
X Toolkit Warning: Cannot convert string "-*-MENU-MEDIUM-R-Normal
-*-120-*-*-P-*-ISO8859-1" to type FontList, using fixed font
X Toolkit Warning: Cannot convert string "-*-Menu-Medium-R-Normal
-*-100-*-*-P-*-ISO8859-1" to type FontList, using fixed font
X Toolkit Warning: Cannot convert string "-*-Menu-Medium-R-Normal
-*-120-*-*-P-*-ISO8859-1" to type FontList, using fixed font
```

The application in this example will still run, but it doesn't look as good as it should.

The *InfoExplorer* utility in AIXWindows also has its own set of fonts. While *InfoExplorer* will run without its fonts, you can improve its appearance on a non-AIXWindows server by making these fonts available to it.

The OpenWindows *cm* (calendar manager) is a highly desirable program, but it, like most OpenWindows applications, will look terrible running under the MIT R4 server if you don't make its special fonts available. It will also complain about missing fonts:

```
h-street% cm
XView warning: Cannot load font '-b&h-lucida-medium-r-normal-sans-*
-90-*-*-*-*-*-*' (Font package)
XView warning: Cannot load font '-b&h-lucida-bold-r-normal-sans*-9
0-*-*-*-*-*-*' (Font package)
```

For all these examples, the solution is to make the font available to the local server. (This may cause some confusion for people new to X, as the fonts might appear to be available along with the clients on a remote host.)

Sometimes the solution to supplying a missing font may be as simple as creating an alias to it from an existing font. It is also possible to convert fonts required by a special client into a format that is recognized by your server, but this may involve some work. The *getbdf* program is one such font converter that may work.* *getbdf* can query the server for a font and dump it out in the *bdf* form, which can then be converted into the local font format.

In most cases, you should do the conversion from *bdf* to your local format on the machine where the fonts are going to reside. This should avoid any problems with byte order when the conversion takes place.

The *font server* introduced in MIT R5 will probably eliminate these problems, but it will take some time before the font server is available for all X servers. In the meantime, the techniques introduced here should suffice.

These examples may not match the exact problem you are having. Think of them as "case studies" that show problem solving techniques. The purpose of this section is to demonstrate that it is possible for the administrator to compensate for differences between vendor implementations.

5.3.4 DECWindows Examples

The DECWindows software contains fonts in the directory */usr/lib/X11/fonts/decwin* that do not exist in the MIT X11R4 release. There are two ways to get around this problem: alias the DECWindows fonts to existing MIT fonts, or you can convert the DECWindows PCF fonts into SNF fonts that can be used by the MIT R4 server.

For an example problem, the *dxcalendar* program does not look quite right without the DECWindows fonts.

---

* *getbdf* is available via anonymous *ftp* to *larry.mcrcim.mcgill.edu* as *X/getbdf.c*.

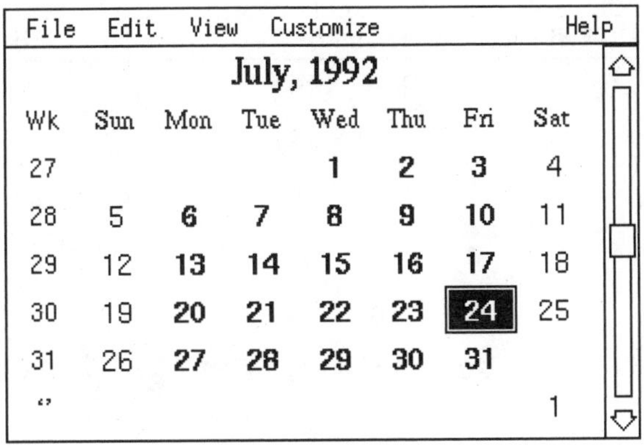

```
┌──────────────────────────────────────────────────┐
│  File  Edit  View  Customize            Help      │
│ ┌───────────────────────────────────────────┐ △  │
│          July, 1992                         │    │
│   Wk  Sun  Mon  Tue  Wed  Thu  Fri  Sat     │    │
│   27              1    2    3    4           │    │
│   28   5    6    7    8    9   10   11       │    │
│   29  12   13   14   15   16   17   18       │    │
│   30  19   20   21   22   23  [24]  25       │    │
│   31  26   27   28   29   30   31            │    │
│   ‹›                            1            │ ▽  │
└──────────────────────────────────────────────────┘
```

Figure 5-5. dxcalendar with the wrong fonts

5.3.4.1 Aliasing

In recent versions of DECWindows documentation (UWS Release Notes), DEC supplies a *fonts.alias* file that maps the DEC font names to reasonable MIT equivalents. The top of the file looks like this:

```
-Adobe-"ITC Avant Garde Gothic"-Book-R-Normal--10-100-75-75-P-59-ISO8859-1
  -Adobe-Helvetica-Medium-R-Normal--10-100-75-75-P-56-ISO8859-1
-Adobe-"ITC Avant Garde Gothic"-Book-R-Normal--12-120-75-75-P-70-ISO8859-1
  -Adobe-Helvetica-Medium-R-Normal--12-120-75-75-P-67-ISO8859-1
-Adobe-"ITC Avant Garde Gothic"-Book-R-Normal--14-140-75-75-P-80-ISO8859-1
  -Adobe-Helvetica-Medium-R-Normal--14-140-75-75-P-77-ISO8859-1
```

The file is rather long. It also exists on various *ftp* sites, if you don't want to type it in.* You can append it to an existing *fonts.alias* in the *75dpi* or *misc* directory on the host where you run the server from:

1. In this example, the aliases are added to the *misc* directory:

   ```
   # cd /usr/lib/X11/fonts/misc
   ```

2. Make a backup copy of the original *fonts.alias* file:

   ```
   # cp fonts.alias fonts.alias.orig
   ```

3. Append the new aliases:

   ```
   # cat DECwindows_on_X11R4_font.aliases >> fonts.alias
   ```

4. Tell the server about the new fonts and try it out:

   ```
   % xset fp rehash
   % dxcalendar &
   ```

---

*One such *ftp* site is *export.lcs.mit.edu*, in *contrib/DECwindows_on_X11R4_font.aliases*.

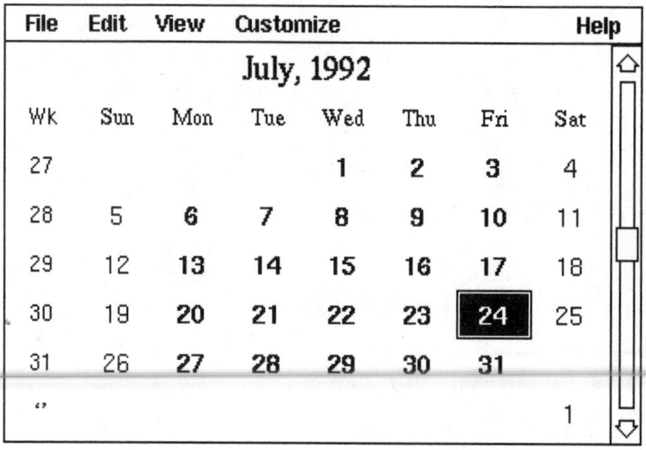

Figure 5-6. dxcalendar with aliases

5.3.4.2 DECWindows Conversion

Another option is to use a program that extracts fonts from the server and outputs them in BDF format. You can then convert them into SNF or whatever your local server requires. Once they are in your local format, you can add them to your font directory.

1. Compile the *getbdf* program on the Ultrix host:

```
% cc -o getbdf getbdf.c -lX11
```

2. On the Ultrix host, run the *getbdf* program to dump out the fonts into BDF format. Since *fonts.alias* contains the keyword FILE_NAME_ALIASES, you know that the filename of the font is also a valid name for the font. You can use this fact to automate the conversion process. If you are using *csh*, the following commands will convert each font in the directory:

```
# cd /usr/lib/X11/fonts/decwin/75dpi
# foreach goo (*.pcf)
? set foo=`basename $goo .pcf`
? getbdf $foo > $foo.bdf
? end
```

The *sh* equivalent would be:

```
# cd /usr/lib/X11/fonts/decwin/75dpi
# for goo in *.pcf
> do
> foo=`basename $goo .pcf`
> getbdf $foo > $foo.bdf
> done
```

The X Window System Administrator's Guide

3. Make a directory on the target machine for the new fonts:

```
# mkdir /usr/lib/X11/fonts/decwin
```

4. Copy all the BDF files to the new directory on the target machine or access them via NFS. On the target machine, convert the BDF fonts to local format (SNF in this example) for your server. This example also uses *csh*:

```
# foreach goo (*.bdf)
? bdftosnf $goo > `basename $goo .bdf`.snf
? end
```

The *sh* equivalent would be:

```
# for goo in *.bdf
> do
> bdftosnf $goo > `basename $goo .bdf`.snf
> done
```

5. Create the *fonts.alias* file:

```
# echo FILE_NAMES_ALIASES > fonts.alias
```

6. Create the *fonts.dir* file:

```
# mkfontdir
```

7. Add the new directory to your font path:

```
% xset fp+ /usr/lib/X11/fonts/decwin
```

8. Try out a program that needs DECWindows fonts:

```
% dxcalendar &
```

5.3.5 AIXWindows Example

The *InfoExplorer* utility on the IBM RS/6000 running AIX also has its own set of fonts. The *InfoExplorer* fonts are in the directory */usr/lpp/info/X11fonts*. As in the Ultrix example, you need to convert the fonts into BDF format and then into the native format of your server. You can use the same font conversion trick here that we used in the DECWindows conversion. In this example, the target server uses the SNF format.

1. Compile the *getbdf* program on the AIX host:

```
% cc -o getbdf getbdf.c -1X11
```

2. Use the *getbdf* program to dump the fonts into BDF format. Since the *fonts.alias* file contains the keyword FILE_NAME_ALIASES, you know that the filename of the font is also a valid name for the font. You can use this fact to automate the conversion process. This example is using csh:

```
# cd /usr/lpp/info/X11fonts
# foreach goo (*.snf)
? set foo=`basename $goo .snf`
? getbdf $foo > $foo.bdf
? end
```

The *sh* equivalent would be:

```
# cd /usr/lpp/info/X11fonts
# for goo in *.snf
> do
> foo=`basename $goo .snf`
> getbdf $foo > $foo.bdf
> done
```

3. Make a new directory on the target machine for the new fonts:

```
# mkdir /usr/lib/X11/fonts/aixwin
```

4. Copy all the BDF files to the new directory on the target machine or access them via NFS. You will also need the *fonts.alias* file from the AIX machine:

```
% cp /usr/lpp/info/X11fonts/fonts.alias aixwin.alias
```

5. On the target machine, convert the BDF fonts to SNF format for your server. If you are using *csh*, the following commands will convert each font in the directory:

```
# foreach goo (*.bdf)
? bdftosnf $goo > `basename $goo .bdf`.snf
? end
```

The *sh* equivalent would be:

```
# for goo in *.bdf
> do
> bdftosnf $goo > `basename $goo .bdf`.snf
> done
```

6. Copy in the *fonts.alias* file:

```
# cp aixwin.alias fonts.alias
```

7. Create the *fonts.dir* file:

```
# mkfontdir
```

8. Add the new directory to your font path:

```
% xset fp+ /usr/lib/X11/fonts/aixwin
```

5.3.6 OpenWindows Example

The *cm* desktop calendar program in the Sun OpenWindows 2.0 distribution does not work properly under MIT R4 without the fonts it needs. To demonstrate the problem, try running the *cm* program without the aliases.

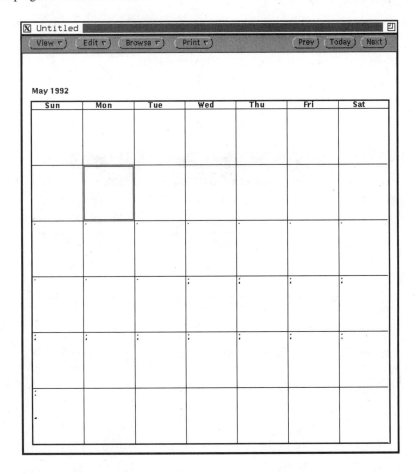

Figure 5-7. cm without aliases

The dates on the calendar are missing, because the necessary fonts are missing.

5.3.6.1 Aliasing

Most of these types of font problems can be handled by a few aliases. Aliases can be added to an existing *fonts.alias* file, such as the one in */usr/lib/X11/fonts/75dpi/*. This example adds the necessary fonts to the *fonts.alias* file so you can run *cm* under an MIT R4 server. Simply append the following lines to the *fonts.alias* file:

```
-b&h-lucida-medium-r-normal-sans-9-90-75-75-p-58-iso8859-1 -b&h-lucida-
medium-r-normal-sans-10-100-75-75-p-58-iso8859-1
-b&h-lucida-bold-r-normal-sans-9-90-75-75-p-58-iso8859-1   -b&h-lucida-
bold-r-normal-sans-12-120-75-75-p-79-iso8859-1
```

Next, tell the server about them:

```
% xset fp rehash
```

Now, run *cm* again, this time with the aliases (see Figure 5-8.)

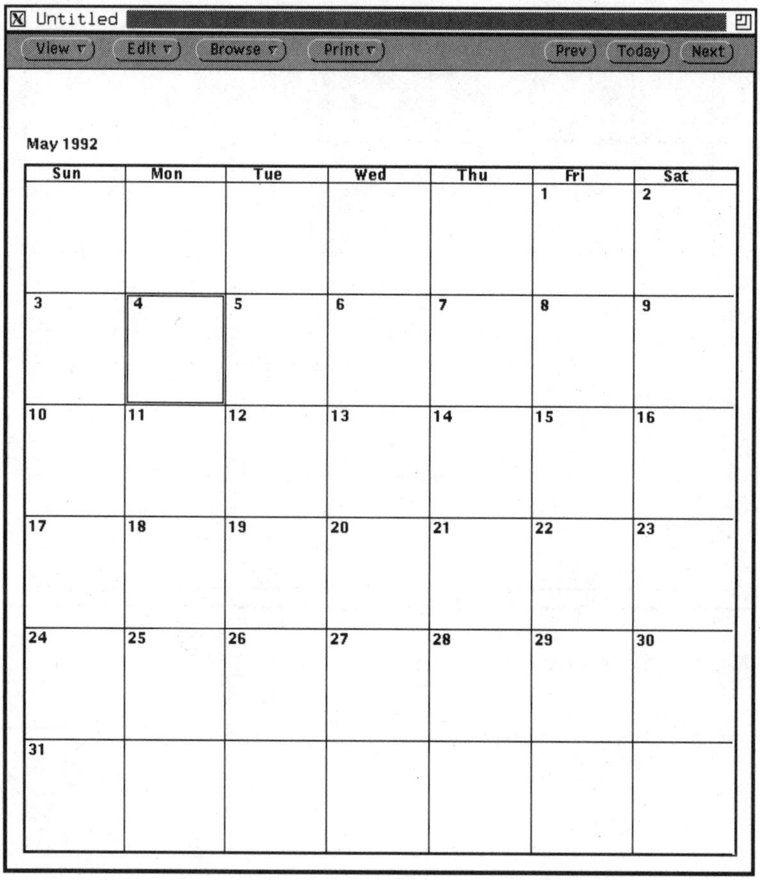

Figure 5-8. cm with aliases

The X Window System Administrator's Guide

5.3.6.2 OpenWindows Conversion

An alternative to aliases would be to convert the OpenWindows X11/NeWS fonts into a form usable by the MIT server.* Since this procedure is unique to OpenWindows, it deserves an explanation.

The X11/NeWS fonts are outline fonts that are scaled to a requested size before rendering. These are stored with the *.f3b* extension. Some examples of the *Lucida* family of fonts are:†

```
LucidaBright-Demi.f3b            LucidaSans-BoldItalic.f3b
LucidaBright-DemiItalic.f3b      LucidaSans-Italic.f3b
LucidaBright-Italic.f3b          LucidaSans-Typewriter.f3b
LucidaBright.f3b                 LucidaSans-TypewriterBold.f3b
LucidaSans-Bold.f3b              LucidaSans.f3b
```

There is some overhead involved in scaling a font. In order to reduce this, some commonly used fonts can be pre-scaled. Pre-scaled fonts have the extension *.fb*. Some examples for the *LucidaSans-Bold* font are:

```
LucidaSans-Bold10.fb    LucidaSans-Bold14.fb    LucidaSans-Bold6.fb
LucidaSans-Bold12.fb    LucidaSans-Bold18.fb    LucidaSans-Bold8.fb
```

These fonts are scaled at the point sizes of 6, 8, 10, 12, 14, and 18.

5.3.6.3 Converting from X11/NeWS to PCF or SNF

It is possible to convert the X11/NeWS format into BDF and then into the local format for your server. As an example, if you need a "Lucida-Sans-Bold" font in 10 point:

1. Find the pre-scaled X11/NeWS version. It will have a *.fb* extension and have the point size as part of the name:

   ```
   # cd /usr/openwin/lib/fonts
   # ls LucidaSans10.fb
   LucidaSans-Bold10.fb
   ```

2. Convert the font into BDF format. The *convertfont* program understands a variety of formats: the *–x* flag tells it to output the font in BDF format. The *–d* flag specifies the directory where the BDF version of the font will be written and the *–s* flag specifies the point size.

   ```
   # convertfont -x -d /tmp -s 10 LucidaSans-Bold10.fb
   LucidaSans-Bold10.fb->/tmp/LucidaSans-Bold10.bdf
   ```

3. Convert the font into the native format of your server (in this example, SNF).

   ```
   # bdftosnf LucidaSans-Bold10.bdf > LucidaSans-Bold10.snf
   ```

---

*If you have a full OpenWindows distribution, BDF versions of the Lucida fonts can be found in the directory */usr/openwin/share/src/fonts/{100dpi,75dpi,misc}*. They can be converted directly to your local server format using *bdftosnf* or *bdftopcf*.

†The pathnames listed in this example are from OpenWindows version 3.0. In OpenWindows 2.0, the font names are abbreviated. For example, *LucidaSans-Bold* in version 3.0 was *LcdS-B* in 2.0.

5.3.6.4 More Conversions

You may want to generate pre-scaled OpenWindows fonts at new point sizes. These can be used under the OpenWindows server or converted for use by the MIT server.

For this example, let's assume you want to generate a 16-point version of *LucidaSans-Bold*. There are several steps needed to do this:

1. Convert the F3 format font (*.f3b*) into an Adobe ASCII format bitmap font (*.afb*) at the size you require (16). The *–M* flag suppresses generation of an Adobe ASCII format metric file (*.afm*):

```
# makeafb -16 -M /usr/openwin/lib/fonts/LucidaSans-Bold.f3b
Creating LucidaSans-Bold16.afb
```

2. Convert Adobe ASCII format bitmap font into X11/NeWS format:

```
# convertfont -b LucidaSans-Bold16.afb
LucidaSans-Bold16.afb->./LucidaSans-Bold16.fb
```

3. In order for the OpenWindows server to be able to use the font, you have to rebuild the *Families.list* file with the *bldfamily* command.

```
# cd /usr/openwin/lib/fonts
# bldfamily
* Terminal-Bold         /usr/openwin/lib/fonts/TerminlB.ff (Encoding: latin)
* Terminal              /usr/openwin/lib/fonts/Terminal.ff (Encoding: latin)
  ...
* nil2                  /usr/openwin/lib/fonts/nil2.ff (Encoding: unknown)
* k14                   /usr/openwin/lib/fonts/k14.ff (Encoding: unknown)
  ...
```

Error messages such as:

```
cat: ./Compat.list: No such file or directory
```

or:

```
* ....                  .....ff (Encoding: unknown)
```

can be ignored. The *Compat.list* and *Synonyms.list* files are optional, much in same manner as *fonts.alias*.

The font is now ready to be used by the OpenWindows server or converted to a MIT format using the method described in Section 5.3.6.3.

5.4 Providing Fonts Over the Network

Diskless workstations and X terminals present a new set of problems for font administration. For an X server to display text on a diskless workstation or X terminal, it has to have access to fonts on a remote host, since X terminals don't have any local permanent storage. X terminals will typically come with a small set of fonts (usually *fixed*, at the minimum) that are stored in ROM, but need to read additional fonts over the network to be useful.

TFTP access is often needed for X terminals to boot off the remote host. When an X terminal is initially powered up or rebooted, it broadcasts a request for boot services over the network and a designated host downloads a kernel or server to the X terminal. See Section 7.4 for more information on fonts and X terminals.

Fonts can also be downloaded using the same mechanism after the X terminal is up and running, but a more flexible approach is to NFS-mount the fonts from a remote host. The server can then add fonts "on-the-fly" after booting. Unfortunately, this also implies all the normal administration problems associated with NFS, such as access control, network loading, and server failures. When using NFS, X terminals become closer to the diskless workstations that they were designed to replace, as they are subject to the same problems. See Section 7.4.3 for more information.

5.5 The R5 Font Server

Previous to Release 5, fonts on the X Window System needed to be available on local disk or provided over the network via TFTP or NFS. Starting with R5, fonts can be requested from a *font server*.

The font server is a program that runs on a host somewhere on the network and provides fonts to your X server. This makes font administration easier, as you can have several sources for a given font, which makes font access more reliable and less dependent on a single host. It also separates font problems from TFTP and NFS problems.

The font server can understand several different font formats. This means that all you have to do to make a font available is to run the font server on the host where the font resides. You no longer have to copy over the font and convert it to a format recognized by your local server. This is great for multi-vendor environments where you have many different font formats, as clients can run under any server and are still able to access special fonts they may require.

There is a host-based security mechanism to limit font access to a group of hosts. This can be used when making licensed fonts available with the font server. The number of simultaneous connections to the font server can be controlled, preventing the font server host from being overloaded. Font requests can also be passed onto other font servers if the current one becomes overloaded.

The font server program supplied in MIT R5 is called *fs* and is usually installed as */usr/bin/X11/fs*. The font server is described in the manual page for *fs*. If you have access to the MIT source code, the file *mit/doc/fontserver/FSlib.doc* describes the font server library functions and *mit/doc/fontserver/design.ms* provides a detailed description of the font server design.

5.5.1 The Configuration File

The font server's operation is controlled by a configuration file, usually named */usr/lib/X11/fs/config*. If you are building R5 from the MIT source code and want to use the font server, you may want to enable the `InstallFSConfig` flag in your *config/site.def* file. Setting the flag to *YES* will copy a sample font server configuration file into */usr/lib/X11/fs/config* when the *make install* is performed. See Section 8.5.1 for more information on configuring X11 at build time.

The syntax of the configuration file is pretty simple. The following is a sample file that contains every option:

```
# font server configuration file (kitchen sink version)
#
cache-size = 2000000
#
alternate-servers = pepper.ora.com:8000,bigbird.ora.com:8001
#
catalogue = /usr/lib/X11/fonts/misc/,/usr/lib/X11/fonts/Speedo/,
/usr/lib/X11/fonts/75dpi/,/usr/lib/X11/fonts/100dpi/
#
client-limit = 10
#
clone-self = on
#
default-point-size = 120
#
default-resolutions = 75,75,100,100
#
error-file = /var/log/fs
#
port = 7000
#
trusted-clients = pepper,bigbird
#
use-syslog = off
#
```

Any line starting with a "#" is treated as a comment and ignored.

The following keywords are defined in the configuration file:

`cache-size`

This is the number of bytes of memory that the font server will allocate in its font *cache*. The cache speeds up font access, as any recently requested font should still be in the cache and immediately available (otherwise, it would have to be read from a file on disk or scaled from an outline font). If the font server is running on a host that has lots of memory, make the cache size larger. The cache size is approximately 2 megabytes in this example.

alternate-servers

> This is a list of alternate font servers for this font server. If the current font server is unable to service the request, it supplies a list of `alternate-servers` to the X server, permitting the X server to try again at one of the alternate font servers. The name of an alternate server is a hostname and port number pair separated by a colon. The alternate servers are referred to as *delegates* in the MIT documentation. The primary server will supply a client with a list of alternate servers that it knows about. This example has two alternate servers, one on the host *pepper* and the other on *bigbird*.

catalogue

> A list of font directories available from this server.* This example lists all the standard MIT R5 font directories. These can be stored in any format recognized by the font server. The font server currently understands the *PCF*, *Speedo*, *SNF*, and *BDF* formats, described in Section 5.2.2. This keyword should not be confused with the *catalogue-list* component of the font server name (see Section 5.5.6 for an explanation).

client-limit

> The number of clients that the font server will allow before cloning itself or rejecting the connection. If the *clone-self* flag is set to *off* and a client attempts a connection, the font server will send back a reply listing other font servers that it knows about. These are specified in the *alternate-servers* list.

clone-self

> Whether the font server should attempt to clone itself or use delegates when it reaches the *client-limit*. In this example, it is set to *on* and the font server would spawn another copy of itself if it received more than 10 (the *client-limit*) connections.

default-point-size

> The default point size (in tenths of a point) for font requests that don't specify this value. These are called *decipoints* in the MIT documentation. The example value of 120 indicates a 12 point size.

default-resolutions

> Default resolutions supported by the server. The numbers are pairs of horizontal and vertical resolutions per inch. Resolutions of 75x75 and 100x100 are specified in the example.

error-file

> The filename of the error log file. You can use this if your system does not support the *syslog()* facility. This file would normally be the first place you would look when debugging the font server configuration file. Leave out this keyword if you have *use-syslog* enabled.

---

*You may notice that the syntax described here differs from the paper "Font Server Implementation Overview," (*mit/doc/fontserver/design.ms*) where a prefix of the font format, such as *pcf* or *Speedo*, is used in front of the font directory list. This feature is not used in the MIT R5 font server.

port
: The TCP port number on which the font server will listen for client connections. Since the font server does not use a privileged port, a user can start up her own font server at any time. As you can choose the port number yourself, you can test the font server without disturbing other servers by selecting a unique port number. The MIT examples all use port 7000. This is a safe distance from port 6000, which is what the X server uses.

use-syslog
: Whether *syslog()* is to be used for error logging. If set to *on*, font server errors will be sent to the *LOG_LOCAL0* syslog facility. You will need to add a line to your */etc/syslog.conf* file to capture the error messages in a file. If you log other messages to the directory */var/log*, the following entry will add logging for the font server:

```
local0.debug                              /var/log/fs
```

This will log errors to the file */var/log/fs*. See the manual page on *syslog.conf(5)* for more information on setting up *syslog*. If you want to use the *error-file* keyword, set *use-syslog* to *off*.

trusted-clients
: The names of hosts the font server will supply fonts to. This can be used to restrict fonts to a certain group of hosts for licensing reasons. An empty list indicates that *any* host can make a connection to the font server.

You probably won't need to specify most of these options for your site. The MIT-supplied configuration file */usr/lib/X11/fs/config* should be good enough to start with:

```
# font server configuration file
# $XConsortium: config.cpp,v 1.7 91/08/22 11:39:59 rws Exp $

clone-self = on
use-syslog = off
catalogue =
/usr/lib/X11/fonts/misc/,/usr/lib/X11/fonts/Speedo/,/usr/lib/X11/fonts/75
dpi/,/usr/lib/X11/fonts/100dpi/
error-file = /usr/lib/X11/fs/fs-errors
# in decipoints
default-point-size = 120
default-resolutions = 75,75,100,100
```

5.5.2 Installing the Font Server

If you wish to have the font server running all the time (as you probably do), you can add it to a system start-up file, such as */etc/rc.local*. However, you probably should not add it to any system files until you are satisfied that it will work correctly. You can test it "by hand" by starting it on the command line.

5.5.2.1 Testing By Hand

The *–config* flag can be used to test a configuration file that is not yet installed or when you do not have write permission to */usr/lib/X11/fs*:

```
# fs -config ./test-config &
```

If the font server dies with the error:

```
Error: Binding TCP socket: Address already in use
Error: Fatal server error!
Error: Cannot establish any listening sockets
```

there is probably another font server (or some other program) running with the same port number. You can specify a number other than 7000 (the default) with the *port* keyword in the configuration file or on the command line with the *–port* flag:

```
# fs -config ./test-config -port 7001 &
```

The *SIGUSR1* signal will cause the server to reread the configuration file. Use this if you have edited the file and wish your changes to take effect without having to kill and restart the font server.

The *SIGUSR2* signal will cause the server to flush the font cache. This may be desirable if you want the server to get a fresh copy of a font instead of using a cached version that may be out-of-date.

The *SIGHUP* signal is used to reset the server, closing all active client connections and rereading the configuration file.

You can kill the font server at any time by sending it the *SIGTERM* signal.

For example, under BSD UNIX:

```
# kill -TERM fs pid
```

Under System V:

```
# killall -TERM fs
```

When you are satisfied with the font server's configuration, it can then be added to the system boot files, which will automatically start it upon the next reboot.

5.5.2.2 Changing BSD Boot Files

In the BSD world, the */etc/rc.local* file is the usual place to add new daemons. You will want to locate the entry for the font server before any other X11-related daemons (such as *xdm*), if they are going to need fonts from the font server.

For SunOS 4.*x*, an example */etc/rc.local* entry would look like this:

```
#
# start up X font server
#
if [ -f /usr/bin/X11/fs ]; then
        /usr/bin/X11/fs &              echo -n ' fs'
fi
#
```

Under Ultrix, it would look like:

```
[ -f /usr/bin/X11/fs ] && {
        /usr/bin/X11/fs ; echo ' fs'     >/dev/console
}
```

Examine your system's startup files and mimic the other daemon entries when adding the font server. The *if* or *[* test syntax is designed to allow the system to continue the boot process without errors if the *fs* executable is missing.

5.5.2.3 Changing System V Boot Files

System V systems usually have a separate file for each daemon that is started when the system boots. Under IRIX (the Silicon Graphics System V derivative), adding the font server would take several steps:

1. Create a shell script to control the font server in */etc/init.d*. Check the current contents of this directory and pick a name for the script that describes it (*fs* is a good choice):

```
# cd /etc/init.d
# ls
MOUNTFSYS   acct       bsdlpr    cron   nck       perf      uucp
README      audio      cdromd.2  lp     netls     savecore  winattr
RMTMPFILES  autoconfig configmsg mail   network   sysetup   xdm
```

The easy way to create a new script is to copy an existing one and modify it:

```
# cp xdm fs
# edit file...
```

This script is copied from *xdm* and modified for the *font server*:

```
#!/bin/sh
#
# Start X Font Server
#
IS_ON=/etc/chkconfig
FS=/usr/X11R5/bin/fs

case "$1" in
  'start')
        if test -x $FS; then
                if $IS_ON fs;
                then
                        $FS &
                fi
        fi
        ;;

  'stop')
        /etc/killall -TERM fs
        ;;

  *)
        echo "usage: /etc/init.d/fs {start|stop}"
        ;;
esac
```

2. Create symbolic links to */etc/init.d/fs* from the */etc/rc0.d* and */etc/rc2.d* directories. The format of the symbolic link name is either a "S" (for *start*) or a "K" (for *kill*), followed by a sequence number that determines the order of the file execution, followed by the name of the file in */etc/init.d*. To determine the sequence number, you need to see what numbers are already in use. Here is a listing from a sample IRIX 4.0 system:

```
% ls /etc/rc2.d
S01MOUNTFSYS    S30network     S50mail         S70uucp       S88configmsg
S20sysetup      S40nck         S58RMTMPFILES   S75cron       S95autoconfig
S21perf         S45netls       S60lp           S78winattr    S97cdromd
S22acct         S48savecore    S61bsdlpr       S83audio      S98xdm
```

The *S98xdm* entry is for the *xdm* daemon. Since *xdm* may require the font server to be running before it starts, you should move it to the next highest number:

```
# mv S98xdm S99xdm
```

And then make a link to the file */etc/init.d/fs* file:

```
# ln -s /etc/init.d/fs S98fs
```

Repeat the process for the */etc/rc0.d* entry:

```
# ls
K15cron    K20mail    K25lp       K30netls   K40network   K90sysetup
K18uucp    K22acct    K26bsdlpr   K35nck     K78winattr
```

In this case, there isn't a sequence number conflict with an existing script:

```
# ln -s /etc/init.d/fs K98fs
```

3. The final step is to add an entry to the */etc/config* directory to enable the script at boot time:

```
# /etc/chkconfig -f fs on
```

5.5.2.4 Changing AIX Boot Files

AIX is a combination of System V and BSD. Starting the font server consists of adding a line to */etc/rc.tcpip*:

```
# Start font server
start /usr/bin/X11/fs ""
#
```

5.5.3 Font Server Name Syntax

Any client wishing to use the font server must be supplied with the name of the host where the font server is running and the port number that the font server is listening on. These two components uniquely identify a particular instance of the font server:

```
transport/hostname:port
```

The following are example font server names:

```
tcp/harry:7000
tcp/ruby.ora.com:7000
tcp/128.197.2.1:7001
tcp/fonts.ora.com:7002
```

The font server name can be specified on the command line with the *–server* option or set with the FONTSERVER environment variable. For example:

```
% setenv FONTSERVER tcp/harry:7000
% fsinfo
```

is equivalent to:

```
% fsinfo -server tcp/harry:7000
```

5.5.4 Debugging the Font Server

The *fsinfo* client gives a quick way to check if the font server is running or not. In this example, the font server is running on port 7000 on the host *harry*:

```
harry% fsinfo -server tcp/harry:7000
name of server: harry:7000
version number: 1
vendor string:  MIT X Consortium
vendor release number:  5000
maximum request size:   16384 longwords (65536 bytes)
number of catalogues:   1
        all
Number of alternate servers: 0
number of extensions:   0
```

The *fsinfo* client will also display any alternate servers known to the current server:

```
   ...
Number of alternate servers: 2
    #0  bigbird:8001
    #1  pepper:8000
   ...
```

If the font server is not running or if you have incorrectly specified the name of the font server, *fsinfo* will fail:

```
harry% fsinfo -server tcp/foo:1234
fsinfo:  unable to open server "tcp/foo:1234"
```

If you have specified the host and port number correctly, make sure the font server program is still running. The *ps* command can be used to check for this.

Under BSD UNIX:

```
% ps agx | grep fs | grep -v grep
 4237 ?  IW    0:01 /usr/bin/X11/fs
```

Under System V UNIX:

```
% ps -ef | grep fs | grep -v grep
root    169     1  0  Jan  2  ?          0:00 /usr/bin/X11/fs
```

If the process doesn't show up, there probably is a serious error in the configuration file or something else is wrong with your system.

If the font server has reached its client limit, a connection to it may fail with:

```
FSlib: connection to "rock:7000" refused by server
FSlib: name of server:  rock:7000
fsinfo:  unable to open server "rock:7000"
```

Turning on the `clone-self` keyword or raising the `client-limit` are possible solutions.

If you have the `error-file` flag specified in the configuration file, all font server error messages will appear in the *usr/lib/X11/fs/fs-errors* file (or the file specified with the `error-file` parameter). If the `use-syslog` flag is enabled, the errors will be logged in the file specified in *etc/syslog.conf* for the *LOG_LOCAL0* facility.

Any error message prefixed with CONFIG: has something to do with the configuration file. A typical error might be:

```
Error: CONFIG: can't open configuration file "/usr/lib/X11/fs/config"
```

usr/lib/X11/fs/config is the default location of the configuration file. Make sure that the file exists and is readable. You can specify another location for the config file with the *–config* option to *fs*. (You might use this option if you are running your own private font server.)

If you get the following error:

```
Error: Can't open error file "/usr/lib/X11/fs/fs-errors"
```

the font server probably does not have write permission to the error file. Any errors will be sent to the controlling terminal or the console. You can specify a different file with the `error-file` keyword in the font server configuration file.

5.5.5 Font Server Clients

Once you have verified the existence of the font server, try requesting a font from it. There are several clients that have names that start with *fs*, indicating that they are for use with the font server.

The *fslsfonts* client is analogous to *xlsfonts* in that it lists the names of all available fonts or just those specified on the command line. It understands the same wildcard syntax you use when specifying fonts elsewhere.

Try a font that you know should be available from the server:

```
harry% fslsfonts -server tcp/harry:7000 -fn "fixed"
fixed
```

If you get an error, such as:

```
fslsfonts: pattern "goof" unmatched
```

the font server configuration file probably has an error in one of the pathnames, or you have specified a non-existent font name.

The *fstobdf* client is used to produce a BDF version of a font requested from a font server. Using the *fixed* font as an example:

```
harry% fstobdf -server tcp/harry:7000 -fn fixed > fixed.bdf
```

This BDF file can then be converted to different formats for use by your server.

As the *fstobdf* client can be used to "steal" fonts from another host, you might want to use the `trusted-clients` parameter to restrict fonts that are licensed to specific hosts.

5.5.6 The Font Path and the Font Server

One or more font servers can be added to your *font path* in the same manner as font directories. These font servers will then be searched in the order they appear in the font path whenever a font is requested. This is the best way to add the font server functionality to clients, as it does not require any changes in the way clients are used.

To add a font server to your font path, just append or prepend it to the font path as you would do for a font directory. The syntax for naming a font server within the font path is simple. For example:

```
% xset fp+ tcp/harry:7000
```

The general syntax for TCP/IP networks is:

tcp/*hostname*:*port-number*[/*catalogue-list*[+*catalogue-list*]]

For DECnet it is:

decnet/*nodename*::font$*objname*[/*catalogue-list*[+*catalogue-list*]]

- The `tcp` or `decnet` string is the network *transport* or protocol used by the font server.

- The *hostname* (or DECnet `nodename`) is the name of machine where the font server is running.

- The *port number* is the port that the font server is listening on.

- The optional *catalogue-list* can specify a subset of the available *catalogues* available from that font server. Catalogue lists are separated by the "+" character. The term *catalogue* has two different meanings in the font server documentation, which may be confusing. The *catalogue* keyword in the font server *config* file specifies a list of directories and the *catalogue-list* in the font server is used to divide up all the available fonts into groups (or *catalogues*). The only *catalogue* currently supported by the font server is *all*. To enable a font server to access all the available catalogues (as you would normally want to do), just omit the catalogue list.

The following example has a font server running on the host *harry*.

First, check the current font path with *xset*:

```
% xset -q
Font Path:
/usr/lib/X11/fonts/misc/,/usr/lib/X11/fonts/75dpi/,/usr/lib/X11/fonts/100dpi/
```

Add the font server entry:

```
% xset fp+ tcp/harry:7000
```

Check the new path:

```
% xset -q
Font Path:
/usr/lib/X11/fonts/misc/,/usr/lib/X11/fonts/75dpi/,/usr/lib/X11/fonts/100dpi/,
tcp/harry:7000
```

If you get the following error from *xset*:

```
X Error of failed request:  BadValue (integer parameter out of range for
operation)
  Major opcode of failed request:  51 (X_SetFontPath)
  Value in failed request:  0x6
  Serial number of failed request:  5
  Current serial number in output stream:  8
```

either you made an error in the font server name, or the font server specified in the font path is no longer running.

Here are some more examples of valid font path entries:

```
tcp/harry:7000
tcp/aixfonts:8000,tcp/decfonts:7000
DECnet/SRVNOD::FONT$DEFAULT
decnet/44.70::font$special/symbols
```

Font path additions can specified anywhere you would normally put them, such as in a user's *.xsession* or *.xinitrc* file:

```
   ...
xset m 2 2
xset b 10 100 10
xset fp+ tcp/decfonts.ora.com:7000
xrdb $HOME/.Xdefaults
xmodmap $HOME/.xmodmaprc
twm &
   ...
```

This example assumes the font server will be running before the user's X session is started. If it is not running, the *xset* command will fail with the BadValue error shown previously.

5.5.7 Hostname Aliases

Using a hostname alias such as *fonts.ora.com* is a clever way to simplify font administration for a group of hosts. The name could be moved to another host without requiring configuration changes to the hosts that are requesting the fonts.

/etc/hosts   On a host using */etc/hosts* just add the alias to */etc/hosts*:

```
140.186.66.2 rock.ora.com rock decfonts decfonts.ora.com
```

NIS   If you are using NIS, the entry will have to be added on the NIS *master* for the NIS domain. Add an entry similar to the one described above and push the NIS hosts map.

DNS   On a host running DNS, add the following alias to the name server database:

```
decfonts            IN      CNAME    rock.ora.com.
```

and tell the name server to reload the database.

You could use a separate font server to supply each group of fonts and have aliases for each of them. For example, a *decfonts* alias could be for DECWindows applications, an *aixfonts* alias could be for AIXWindows applications, and a *texfonts* alias could be used by TeX applications. Users can then select the font server according to the application and its font requirements regardless of what X server they are using.

5.5.8 A Font Server Example

The *xtrek* game provides a good example for using the font server.* It requires a special font, named *xtrek*, that normally has to be installed for every X server that the *xtrek* client is going to be displayed on. For local display servers running on workstations, this means that you have to copy the font into a local directory on each machine and run the *mkfontdir* command on every one of these hosts. A far better solution is to install the font on one host and run a font server that makes the *xtrek* font available to anyone wanting to play.

Let's assume you are on the host *nugget* and you want to start a game on the host *rock*.

You try to run *xtrek*, but it fails, as the font is not found by *nugget*'s server:

```
nugget% xtrek rock
Display: nugget:0.0 Login: eap Name: Dead Meat
Adding player 0 on `nugget:0.0'.
Not all fonts available on nugget:0.0.
```

To fix this problem, let's turn the host *rock* into a server for the *xtrek* font:

1. The *xtrek* font supplied with source code is in the *BDF* format. Convert the font into a format recognized by your X server. In this example, the MIT R5 server expects the PCF format:

---

* *xtrek* is available via anonymous *ftp* as *export.lcs.mit.edu:/contrib/xtrek.tar.Z*.

```
rock% bdftopcf xtrek.bdf > xtrek.pcf
```

2. Copy the font into the font area. In this example, the font will have its own directory, */home/eap/xtrek/fonts*:

```
rock% mkdir /home/eap/xtrek/fonts
rock% cp xtrek.pcf /home/eap/xtrek/fonts
```

3. Create the *fonts.dir* file:

```
rock% mkfontdir /home/eap/xtrek/fonts
```

4. Create a font server configuration file. The easiest way to do this is to copy and then edit the MIT example file */usr/lib/X11/fs/config*:

```
rock% cp /usr/lib/X11/fs/config /home/eap/xtrek/fs-config
rock% edit file...
```

The edited file now contains the following:

```
clone-self = on
use-syslog = off
error-file = /home/eap/xtrek/fs-errors
catalogue = /home/eap/xtrek/fonts
```

5. Start the font server:

```
rock% fs -config /home/eap/xtrek/fs-config &
```

6. Go back to the host *nugget* and add the font server to the font path:

```
nugget% xset +fp tcp/rock:7000
```

7. Now try running *xtrek* again:

```
nugget% xtrek rock
Display: nugget:0.0 Login: eap Name: Dead Meat
Adding player 0 on `nugget:0.0'.
```

game starts successfully ...

Note that this entire procedure can be performed by unprivileged users.

5.6 Related Documentation

The font clients are described in the manpages for *xfd*, *xlsfonts*, and *xfontsel*.

The font server clients are described in the manpages for *fsinfo*, *fslsfonts*, and *fstobdf*.

The OpenWindows font programs are described in the manpages for *convertfont*, *makeafb*, *bldfamily*, and the OpenWindows documentation set.

A technical description of X fonts is in the file *mit/doc/XLFD/xlfd.tbl.ms* (the PostScript version is *mit/hardcopy/XLFD/xlfd.PS.Z*).

For more information on the font server, see the manpage for *fs* and the original design document *mit/doc/fontserver/design.ms*. Beware of differences between this paper and the version of the font server included in the R5 distribution.

The Font Server Protocol is described in the file *mit/doc/fontserver/FSlib.doc* (PostScript version is *mit/hardcopy/FSProtocol/fsproto.PS.Z*).

"The X Administrator: Font Formats and Utilities," by Dinah McNutt and Miles O'Neal, published in *The X Resource, Issue 2*, O'Reilly and Associates, Inc., Spring 1992.

Section 5.5 of this chapter also appeared as an article entitled "The X Administrator: Managing Font Servers," by Eric Pearce, published in *The X Resource, Issue 3*, O'Reilly and Associates, Inc., Summer 1992.

6

Color

This chapter describes the mechanisms used to make color available to X servers that support color. It covers both the RGB and the Xcms methods of color management.

In This Chapter:

6
Color

Color can make a world of difference for a user. Not all X users have servers that support color, but those that do need to be able to assign colors to their applications easily. The X Window System provides a way for colors to be addressed using both familiar names (such as red, blue, yellow) and obscure names (such as papayawhip, pale goldenrod, and dodgerblue). These names are then converted to a numeric representation that the server understands.

Most color monitors are equipped with red, green, and blue electron guns, called "color guns," as shown in Figure 6-1. These color guns can be run at different intensities, producing different colors on the display screen. For example, the color "red" could be displayed by turning the green and blue guns off entirely and turning the red gun on at full capacity. The red, green, and blue gun intensity values are called an *RGB triplet*.

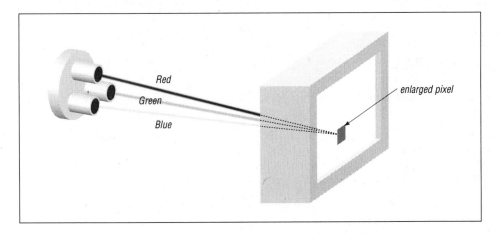

Figure 6-1. Red, green, and blue color guns

Prior to X11R5, there was no built-in mechanism to address the lack of color consistency between displays. The mappings of RGB triplets to color names were hard-coded directly on the host system, using the *RGB System*. This meant that when a user requested "turquoise" on a particular system, he would get the same gun intensities regardless of which X server he was actually using. Since not all monitors are created equal, "turquoise" might look slightly different depending on which display it was being viewed on. R5 addresses this problem with a new device-independent system called the X Color Management System, or *Xcms*. Xcms allows colors to be specified in internationally accepted standards that are in wide use outside of the computer field.

This chapter discusses both the RGB and Xcms systems of color specification.

6.1 Color Specification in Release 4 and Earlier

In Release 4 and earlier, the X Window System uses the RGB system for defining and displaying different colors. MIT X11R4 defines 738 color names by associating names with RGB triplets.

The list of colors available on your system can be retrieved using the *showrgb* client, or by examining the file *rgb.txt*, usually in the directory */usr/lib/X11* or */usr/lib/X11/rgb*. (The contents of the *rgb.txt* file is identical to the output of the *showrgb* client.) If you run the *showrgb* client, be sure to use a pager, as there are screenfuls of output:

```
% showrgb | more
255 239 213 papayawhip
240 255 255 azure
105 105 105 dimgray
176 196 222 lightsteelblue
127 255 212 aquamarine
  0 250 154 mediumspringgreen
238 232 170 pale goldenrod
      . . .
```

Each line contains 4 columns. The first column is the red value, the second column is the green value, and the third column is the blue value. Each value is an integer from 0 and 255, inclusive.

The fourth column is the name assigned on your host system to that particular combination of RGB values.

The color "black" is defined with "0" values for each color gun, and "white" is defined with maximum values for each gun.

```
255 255 255    white
  0   0   0    black
```

For a visual list of colors, try the *contrib* client *xcolors*. It will read the RGB database and display all the colors it finds.

6.1.1 RGB Color Names

You can specify colors for clients by using the *–fg* and *–bg* options on the command line, or by setting the foreground and background resources for the client. For an *xterm* window with an aquamarine background and blue text, for example, you could use the following command line:

```
% xterm -bg aquamarine -fg blue
```

X Window System Administrator's Guide

Alternatively, you could define the following resources:

```
xterm*background: aquamarine
xterm*foreground: blue
```

To become familiar with specifying colors, try picking a few colors and pass them to a client to see the effect. If you get an error such as:

```
Warning: Color name "barfgreen" is not defined in server database
```

you probably chose a non-existent color or spelled a color name incorrectly.

There are several "aliases" provided for a single color—for example, the color "dark slate grey" appears in *rgb.txt* with four different ways to name it:

```
47  79  79    dark slate gray
47  79  79    DarkSlateGray
47  79  79    dark slate grey
47  79  79    DarkSlateGrey
```

All of these names produce the same color.

6.1.2 Numeric Color Values

Clearly, every RGB value cannot have a name associated with it, but you can also specify colors by using the RGB values directly. Any color resource starting with the "#" character is expected to have a number following it. The numbers are expressed in hexadecimal, with one, two, three, or four digits for each value:

```
#RGB
#RRGGBB
#RRRGGGBBB
#RRRRGGGGBBBB
```

where "R","G", and "B" represent red, green, and blue digits. For example, all of the following color specifications represent the same value:

```
XTerm*foreground: #f00
XTerm*foreground: #ff0000
XTerm*foreground: #fff000000
XTerm*foreground: #ffff00000000
XTerm*foreground: red
```

You would usually produce colors with complex hex numbers only if you used a *resource editor* such as OSF/Motif's *mre,* props* in Sun OpenWindows or the *contrib* client *xcoloredit*,† as color names are much easier for humans to deal with.

---

*If you buy OSF/Motif 1.x source code from OSF, the *mre* program is included as "demo" program. There is a *README* file, but no manpage.

†*xcoloredit* is available via anonymous *ftp* from *export.lcs.mit.edu* as */contrib/xcoloredit.tar.Z*.

6.1.3 Adding Your Own Color Names (RGB)

If you come up with your own color, you can add a name for it in the RGB database. The procedure described here requires access to the source code for the X distribution, as the *rgb* program is not normally installed along with the other X programs.

To get a hexadecimal value for the new color, you can use a color editor, such as *mre*, *props*, or *xcoloredit*. When you have selected the color, the program will display the RGB values in hexadecimal or write the value directly into your *.Xdefaults* file.

In the following example, the selected color is a shade of green that comes out as "b7bb6e." The RGB database expects the values to be in a decimal format. An easy way to convert from hex to decimal is to use the UNIX program *bc*:

```
% bc
```

First, set the base of input to 16 (the output defaults to base 10):

```
ibase=16
```

Then enter the numbers to be converted:

```
B7;BB;6E
```

(The *bc* program requires the letters in the hexadecimal numbers to be in uppercase.)

bc then prints out the decimal values for the three colors:

```
183
187
110
```

Type CTRL-D to exit the *bc* program.

Once we know that our RGB triplet is (183,187,110), follow these steps:

1. Add the following line to the *rgb.txt* source file, which is located in the *mit/rgb* directory:*

   ```
   183 187 110 UglyGreen
   ```

2. Run the *rgb* program using the makefile also located in the *mit/rgb* directory. This program converts the text file (*rgb.txt*) into the UNIX *dbm* format (*rgb.dir* and *rgb.pag*), which are the files actually used as the color database:

   ```
   % make
   rm -f rgb.pag rgb.dir
   ./rgb rgb < rgb.txt
   ```

3. Then install the new *rgb* files in */usr/lib/X11*:

   ```
   % make install
   install -c -m 0644 rgb.txt /usr/lib/X11
   install -c -m 0644 rgb.dir /usr/lib/X11
   ```

---

*If you don't have the X11 sources on-line, see Appendix F for information on how to get the MIT source. You only have to build the programs that are necessary for color management, found in the directory *mit/rgb*.

```
install -c -m 0644 rgb.pag /usr/lib/X11
install -c -s  showrgb /usr/bin/X11
install in ./rgb done
```

There are a few alternate color databases that come with the source distribution in *mit/rgb/others*. Examine the *README* file in that directory for details.

6.1.4 Fixing a Corrupted Color Database

If the color name database gets corrupted in some way (e.g., written to accidentally), the server may not be able to find any colors with which to display. On a workstation with a monochrome display, you may get error messages similar to the following:

```
X Toolkit Warning:  Cannot allocate colormap entry for White
X Toolkit Warning:  Cannot allocate colormap entry for Black
X Toolkit Warning:  Cannot allocate colormap entry for white
X Toolkit Warning:  Cannot allocate colormap entry for black
```

If you see errors of this sort, perform Steps 2 and 3 in the procedure described above. This will overwrite the corrupted *rgb* database files.

6.2 Color Specification in Release 5 (Xcms)

Under the RGB triplet system, a color could look quite different due to the type of display, its manufacturer, or the type of machine that is driving it. In Release 5, *Device Independent Color* was introduced in an attempt to standardize the appearance of colors across different platforms.

The X Color Management System (Xcms) was developed by Tektronix, and has been adopted by the X Consortium for Release 5 of X11. Since all RGB functionality is still supported, you can treat the new color system as a superset of the previous RGB system. If you don't want the added functionality, you can pretty much ignore it.

Under Xcms, colors are based upon internationally recognized standards (CIE)* and represent all *visible* colors. This differs from the RGB system, which is based upon display hardware, not human vision. The Xcms system can take color values in several different formats, called *color spaces*. These spaces describe color in a device-independent manner, using terms such as Hue (color family), Value (darkness or lightness), and Chroma (saturation or vividness). Before the values are displayed, they are modified for the particular device they are going to be viewed on. This modification should make the color appear the same regardless of the manufacturer, type, or model of the display. The Xcms system should also make the color appear the same on any other color device, such as a color printer equipped with Post-Script Level 2.

---

*CIE stands for *Commission Internationale de l'Eclairage* or *International Commission on Illumination*.

A complete description of the Xcms color model is beyond the scope of this book, which covers only the aspects of Xcms that affect administrators.

6.2.1 Xcms Color Names

The Xcms color system uses a color database on the client side, whereas the RGB system database is used by the server (see Figure 6-2). All color names are looked up in a Xcms *client database* before being passed onto the server.

Xcms introduces several new ways to specify color and retains all of the old ones. Some examples of colors used in resources are:

```
*Background:            RGBi:1.0/1.0/0.0
*Foreground:            NavyBlue
*Text*Background:       CIElab:0.0/.54/.90
*Text*Foreground:       White
*Text*border:           #ff00fc
```

Under the Xcms system, a color specification is checked as follows:

1. If it begins with the character "#", the rest of the color specification is interpreted as a hexadecimal RGB value:

   ```
   #<red value><green value><blue value>
   ```

   This syntax is still supported, but for only backwards compatibility. You are encouraged to use the newer uniform methods of numeric color specification.

2. If it contains the character ":", the prefix is checked to see if it is a recognized color space and if it is, the rest of the color is taken as a value in that color space:

   ```
   <color space>:<color space specific encoding>
   ```

   The color spaces described here all use the "/" character to delimit the numeric values, as in:

   ```
   <color space>:<value>/<value>/<value>
   ```

   but this method is specific to the particular encoding scheme used.

3. If it contains neither the ":" or "#" character, it is assumed to be a color name that would appear either in the Xcms client database or the RGB server database.

The database is composed of pairs of color names and corresponding numeric color specifications. The prefix on the number indicates the type of color system that is represented by the number. The following is a list of the current *color spaces* and their prefixes in the Xcms database.

Name	Prefixes
Various CIE formats	CIEXYZ, CIEuvY, CIExyY, CIELab, CIELuv
Tektronix HVC	TekHVC
RGB	RGB
RGB intensity	RGBi

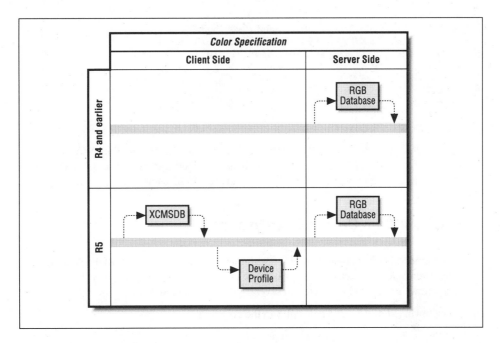

Figure 6-2. Xcms vs. RGB color specification

One problem with the older "#" syntax is that the color value can change depending on how many bits are used to represent the value. For example, the RGB triplet #0f0 uses 8 bits to represent each color. If this was used on a system that expected 24 bits, this would be expanded to #000f00000. The problem with this is that "f" represented a maximum value on a 8 bit system, but is less that a maximum value when you have 24 bits. This could cause a color to appear differently when used on displays of different depth. The newer "RGB:" syntax scales upwardly in a uniform manner, so #0f0 becomes #000fff000 and produces the proper color intensity.

Xcms stores its color database in a file called *Xcms.txt*, usually in */usr/lib/X11*. You can also create your own Xcms database and set the environment variable XCMSDB to it:

```
% setenv XCMSDB /home/eap/mydatabase
```

This will be used instead of the system database.

The database is similar to the *rgb.txt* file in that it maps a color name to a numeric color specification, but differs in that it recognizes all the new color specification formats (*color spaces*) in addition to RGB. It also supports color name aliases, as new names for an existing color can be defined here. The order of the columns is also reversed compared to the RGB database.

Here is a portion of a sample *Xcms.txt* file (anything outside of the lines XCMS_COLORDB_START and XCMS_COLORDB_END is ignored.):

```
XCMS_COLORDB_START 0.1
red          CIEXYZ:0.371298/0.201443/0.059418
```

```
green        CIEXYZ:0.321204/0.660070/0.159833
blue         CIEXYZ:0.279962/0.160195/1.210705
aquamarine   CIEXYZ:0.34672401/0.54832153/0
gray0        TekHVC:0.0/0.0/0.0
gray10       TekHVC:0.0/10.0/0.0
gray20       TekHVC:0.0/20.0/0.0
mygreen      aquamarine
myblack      black
XCMS_COLORDB_END
```

In this example, "red" is described in CIE XYZ space and "gray0" in TekHVC. The name "mygreen" is an alias for "aquamarine," which is described earlier in the same database. "myblack" is an alias for "black," which is in the server's RGB database.

6.2.2 Adding Your Own Color Names in Xcms

Adding a color to the Xcms database is very similar to adding one to the RGB database, but there are several possible ways to describe a color. Tektronix donated a color editor, called *xtici*, that allows a color to be selected in several different color spaces.*

Use the following steps to add a new color to the color database:

1. Start the *xtici* program and select a color.

2. When you find one that you wish to use, click on the "Edit" button.

3. Then click on the "Copy Color ->" button. This will present a menu of three different color spaces, as shown in Figure 6-3.

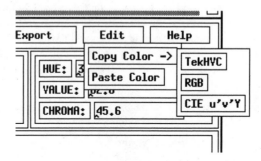

Figure 6-3. xtici Edit menu

4. Select a color space and paste the value into an editor or on the command line using the middle mouse button (or whatever button you have selected for the paste function). The "RGB" button produces the old-style RGB "#" format and you are better off using "Tek-HVC" or "CIE u´v´Y."

---

*The *xtici* program is not part of the normal R5 distribution, but can be obtained via anonymous *ftp* from the host *export.lcs.mit.edu* as */contrib/xtici.tar.Z*. A user manual is included in the *doc* directory in the source code for *xtici*.

For this example, enter these values into the *Xcms.txt* file in between the XCMS_COLORDB_START and XCMS_COLORDB_END lines, along with a prefix of the color space you choose (e.g., TekHVC) and a color name in the left column. *Make sure you use the TAB character between the color name and the beginning of the color specification.* For example, to define the same color we created earlier for the RGB database:

```
UglyGreen      TekHVC:88.00004/72.66564/38.25869
```

5. Unlike the RGB system, you don't have to rebuild the Xcms database into a binary form after you edit it.

6.2.3 Xcms Database Example

To illustrate the use of the client-side database, let's pretend you are a clothing designer for a mail order catalog. The marketing people have suggested that you choose interesting names for the colors of the garments. Let's also assume that you do not want to change any system files, only ones in your home directory.

First, pick some nice colors using a color editor (such as *xtici*) and record the Xcms color specification in a file (maybe called *FallCatalog.txt*). Pick catchy names for each color you design and put them in the Xcms database format described earlier:

```
#
# Ocean's Start Fall Catalog Colors, attempt #1
#
XCMS_COLORDB_START 0.1
Berry          CIEuvY:0.34568/0.45488/0.23013
Port           CIEuvY:0.37875/0.45637/0.05117
Straw          CIEuvY:0.19325/0.53761/0.85767
Paprika        CIEuvY:0.39617/0.51446/0.20947
GrapeFruit     CIEuvY:0.19261/0.52793/0.85069
Pool           CIEuvY:0.15229/0.48240/0.60646
XCMS_COLORDB_END
```

To test out this particular database by yourself, you have to tell Xcms where to look for it:

```
% setenv XCMSDB ~/FallCatalog.txt
```

Let's say your clothing design program is called *autoclad*. You can use the color names listed in the Xcms database as resource specifications:

```
Autoclad*outfit1.pants: Pool
Autoclad*outfit1.tie:   GrapeFruit
Autoclad*outfit1.shirt: Berry
```

You can also specify them on the command line:

```
% autoclad -fg Port -bg Paprika
```

If you want to try another set of colors, you can easily create another database and redefine the XCMSDB environment variable to tell Xcms where to look for the new database.

6.2.4 Device Profiles

An integral part of Xcms is *Device Color Characterization (DCC)*, or a *Device Profile*. This is data that tells Xcms how to modify colors to fit your particular display device so they will look as they should. The data may be specific to the size, brand, model, and the type of screen on which you are displaying the color.

The DCC data is stored in properties on the screen's root window. Some servers are able to automatically load the properties with data appropriate to the attached display(s). For servers that are built from MIT source, you will probably have to load the DCC data by hand. The *xcmsdb* client that comes with the MIT source distribution will load the DCC data from a text file you supply.

There are some sample DCC files in the directory *mit/clients/xcmsdb/datafiles*. Examine the top portion of the file for a description of the monitor. This is from the file *Sparc1-19.dcc*:

```
SCREENDATA_BEGIN        0.3

    NAME                Sun SPARCstation 1 19" color monitor
    PART_NUMBER         3
    MODEL               Hitachi HM-4119-S-AA-0, July 1989
    SCREEN_CLASS        VIDEO_RGB
    REVISION            2.0

    COLORIMETRIC_BEGIN
        XYZtoRGB_MATRIX_BEGIN
            2.898873264142915    -1.405253453722755    -0.401375502033969
           -1.137294035493891     2.090468612762945     0.027097795177010
            0.052401943410025    -0.208571555336254     1.027214718138772
        XYZtoRGB_MATRIX_END
        RGBtoXYZ_MATRIX_BEGIN
            0.473564943660944     0.335917466635681     0.176180053794631
            0.257273262661955     0.659599528857479     0.083127208480565
            0.028079972620921     0.116792496677968     0.981397341912346
        RGBtoXYZ_MATRIX_END
    COLORIMETRIC_END
    INTENSITY_PROFILE_BEGIN 0 3
    INTENSITY_TBL_BEGIN     RED     256
        0x0000 0.000000000000000000
        0x0101 0.000000000000000000
                       .
                       .
                       .
        0xfdfd 0.975557917109458050
        0xfefe 0.980162947219270220
        0xffff 1.000000000000000000
    INTENSITY_TBL_END
    INTENSITY_PROFILE_END

SCREENDATA_END
```

The file contains values that are loaded into the root window properties and then plugged into Xcms functions, converting each device-independent color value into a device-specific value and vice-versa. You can load a DCC file in the same manner as you would load a *.Xdefaults* file with *xrdb*. For example, if you have a Hitachi 19" color monitor on your Sun Sparc-Station 1, use the command:

```
% xcmsdb Sparc1-19.dcc
```

As you would typically want to load the file when your server starts, your *.xinitrc* would be a good place for this command:

```
...
xset m 2 2
xset b 10 100 10
xcmsdb Sparc1-19.dcc
xrdb $HOME/.Xdefaults
xmodmap $HOME/.xmodmaprc
twm &
...
```

If you have the MIT X11R5 *contrib* source code available, there are additional DCC files in *contrib/clients/xcrtca/monitors*:

```
% ls
Apollo19.ca100    NWP-513.ca100      Sparc2-19.ca100  VR290.ca100   VR299.ca100
Apollo19.dcc      NWP-513.dcc        Sparc2-19.dcc    VR290.dcc     VR299.dcc
Apple13.ca100     SGI-PI19.ca100     Sun3-60.ca100    VR297-0.ca100
Apple13.dcc       SGI-PI19.dcc       Sun3-60.dcc      VR297-0.dcc
HP98782A.ca100    Sparc1-19.ca100    Trini19.ca100    VR297-1.ca100
HP98782A.dcc      Sparc1-19.dcc      Trini19.dcc      VR297-1.dcc
```

The *contrib* client *crtca* is used to drive a *colorimeter*. The Tektronix J17 and Minolta CA-100 (with low-luminance option) are colorimeters supported by this program. These devices are used to measure a color displayed on a monitor. The output of the *crtca* program is the *.ca100* files listed above. These are fed into the *xsccd* client which, in turn, produces the device color characterization (*.dcc*) files to be read by the *xcmsdb* client.

There isn't a standard location or naming scheme enforced for DCC files. You may have to investigate to find what you are looking for. Keep in mind that your X display is still usable without loading a DCC file. All you are accomplishing is color correction for your particular display. This is extremely important for some applications, but superfluous for others.

6.3 Related Documentation

See the manpages for *showrgb*, *xcolors*, *props*, *xcoloredit*, and *xtici*.

A detailed user manual comes with the *xtici* source code distribution (in *doc/*).

The file *mit/doc/tutorials/color.tbl.ms* contains a more detailed description of color and X.

Chapter 7 of the *Xlib Programming Manual*, by Adrian Nye (O'Reilly & Associates, 1992).

"A Technical Introduction to the X Color Management System," by Al Tabayoyan, published in *The X Resource, Issue 0*, O'Reilly and Associates, Inc., Fall 1991.

7

X Terminals

X terminals allow you to put X on everyone's desk at relatively little cost. This chapter covers the issues with buying and configuring X terminals on your site.

In This Chapter:

7

X Terminals

Only a few years ago, the average UNIX site was equipped with a few expensive computers, connected to ASCII terminals on every desk. The X terminal is a newcomer in the market of UNIX hardware. Today, the rapidly-growing market of X terminals demonstrates how X11 has changed the landscape of UNIX sites.

An X terminal is as "dumb" as an ASCII terminal, in that without a host computer to connect to, it's nothing but a blank screen with a setup menu. But when properly configured, the X terminal gives the user all the functionality of a workstation without all of its cost and administrative worries.

7.1 Buying an X Terminal: What's What

Today, there are more than two dozen vendors of X terminals. X terminals are sold with a variety of screen sizes, screen depth and resolution, memory configurations, and software. If you are buying an X terminal, you'll probably want to examine recent trade magazines for evaluations of current products. (The market changes so quickly that X terminals tested for this book will undoubtedly be outdated by the time you read this.) But for background of what you're getting into, this section describes some of the areas where X terminals differ and how they should factor in your decision.*

7.1.1 Monitors

The monitor is arguably the single most important part of the X terminal. The size, resolution, and depth of the monitor have a bigger impact on the perceived quality of the terminal than anything else. Accordingly, the type of monitor also has the biggest impact on the *price* of the X terminal as well.

The short story is that, when choosing the monitor for an X terminal, you will end up weighing the user's needs against how much money you have to burn. A user who spends the day in data-entry applications might be satisfied with a monochrome 15-inch monitor, but users

---

*The *comp.windows.x* newsgroup has a quarterly posting on X terminal manufacturers, including pricing information.

who do desktop publishing will probably require a 19-inch grayscale or color monitor for viewing a two-page spread.

7.1.1.1 Screen Size

Common screen sizes for X terminals range from 14 inches to 20 inches, measuring the diagonal. Some users may be made happy with a 14- or 16-inch screen, but real estate will be cramped; if you can afford a 19-inch monitor, go for it. (Beware that the actual image area will be smaller than the screen dimensions imply; that is, a 19-inch screen with approximate dimensions of 15×12 inches may have an image area closer to 13.25×11 inches.)

Some X terminals support a "virtual screen," whereby the screen image is actually *larger* than the screen itself. The portion of the screen that is obscured can be exposed by moving the mouse onto that area. This may be a good compromise for some users, or it may drive them crazy when the screen shifts every time they move the mouse a bit too far.

7.1.1.2 Resolution

The resolution of a screen is usually given with its dimensions in pixels. X terminal displays range from 640×480 pixels to 1280×1024 pixels. A *pixel* is the smallest element of the display that can be addressed. The number of pixels effectively determines how much information can be shown on your screen.

So what does the number of pixels really tell you? If you're a purist, then you're primarily interested in knowing how many dots per inch (dpi) there are. The best way of finding out the dpi is to ask the X terminal manufacturer. You can try to get a reasonable approximation by comparing the number of pixels to the dimensions of the screen image, but you'll have to measure the actual dimensions of the image (since the actual image is smaller than the screen size).

To get an idea of what sort of resolutions should be expected, our monochrome 19-inch NCD terminals have 1280×1024 pixels for approximately 100×100 dots per inch. Our monochrome 14-inch NCD terminals have 1024×1024 pixels for 106×106 dots per inch. The *xdpyinfo* client can be used to learn the dimensions and dots per inch for any server you have network access to. Since *xdpyinfo* requests this information from the server itself, the numbers it reports are only as accurate as the numbers advertised by the vendor.

Beware that for color terminals, you should concern yourself with the *dot pitch* of the monitor as well as the resolution. The dot pitch is the distance between the dots projected by the color guns. If the resolution of the monitor tries to display more pixels than you have dots on the screen, the picture will be fuzzy and cause eye-strain.

Note that the higher the resolution, the more traffic over the network (since higher resolution means more pixels being drawn over the network) and the more memory you'll need for reasonable performance. Low-end color and grayscale displays tend to have lower resolution than monochrome displays, to cut down on required memory (and thus cost).

7.1.1.3 Depth

The *depth* of an X terminal is determined by the number of bits per pixel it supports for color information. A monochrome (a.k.a. static gray) monitor has one bit per pixel: each pixel is either black or white, with no shades of gray. Most grayscale and color monitors have 8 bits per pixel, although some may have as few as 2 or 4, and others may have as many as 12 or 24. A color monitor with 8 bits per pixel can support as many as $2^8 = 256$ simultaneous colors; likewise, a grayscale monitor with 8 bits per pixel can support 256 shades of gray.

If you choose to buy an X terminal with a depth of only 2 or 4 bits per pixel, beware that some X clients are dumber than others. Some of the less robust applications assume that if you have a depth greater than 1, then you must have 8 bits per pixel. (These clients can also cause problems on displays with 12 or 24 bits per pixel.)

Another possible complication is that, if you buy a grayscale monitor, you may find that some applications think you have color. For example, on a 2-bit grayscale display, *FrameMaker* will try to display windows using its color default of a blue background. The best way to deal with this complication is to set up your application resources to use only black and white; see Section 3.5.6 for an example of using *xdm* and display classes to set up different defaults according to the display type.

Although you might be concerned that an X terminal with 8 bits per pixel may produce 8 times as much traffic as one with a monochrome display, this is seldom an issue in practice. Most clients address only 1 bit per pixel, regardless of the depth of the display.

7.1.1.4 Refresh Rate

The *refresh rate* of a monitor is the frequency that the screen is redrawn. If the screen is refreshed too slowly, it may be noticeable to users and quickly cause eye-strain. In general, a refresh rate of less than 70 Hz is considered to be too slow for daily use.

7.1.2 Keyboard and Mouse

There are several different types of keyboards available for X terminals. Since there are few things more frustrating to users than having to use a keyboard they are unaccustomed to, choose the keyboard carefully. DEC users are used to different key configurations than both Sun users and PC users. Users have different ideas of what a "UNIX" keyboard is—some users think it's a Sun3 keyboard, others think it's a Sun4 keyboard, and some think it's a DEC keyboard. (What NCD calls a UNIX keyboard is actually a DEC keyboard.)

Keyboards differ in things like the position of the tilde and escape keys, the position of the Alt key(s), and the positions of the CTRL and CAPS LOCK keys (which are sometimes reversed, to the great frustration of the user). Most X terminal manufacturers also have international keyboards available.

Almost all X terminals come with a 3-button mouse. The only deviations between the mouse distributed with X terminals is whether it's a mechanical mouse or an optical mouse. Optical mice cost a bit more, but many people consider them to be more reliable. Trackballs are also available from many manufacturers at an extra cost.

7.1.3 X Server Software

The X server is essentially the operating system for the X terminal. X terminals differ, however, in where the server program resides, and even where it is run.

- Many older X terminals have the X server built directly into ROM. However, these X terminals tend to be much more expensive, and furthermore they require replacing the ROM at every upgrade.

- Most X terminals are designed to read the X server program from a host on the network at boot time. Upgrades involve replacing a single file on the host. The downside to having the X server software loaded over the network, however, is if you intend to run X over a serial connection—downloading a megabyte of software can take some time over a modem line.

- Some X terminals give you the option of both—they have X server software built in, but can then override it by downloading another server from the network. This method is currently being replaced by another method using FLASH ROM. FLASH ROM is a type of ROM that is updated by being downloaded from a host only once. This means that you don't have to download the entire server image every time you boot the X terminal, but you also don't have to deal with the messiness of opening up each X terminal every time an upgrade comes in. FLASH ROM is expensive, but it's clearly the most efficient way of dealing with X terminal software.

- There are a few low-cost X terminals designed to run over serial lines exclusively.* These X terminals do not actually run the X server, but rely on the host to run the X server as well as the clients. The advantage is that all the traffic between client and server can take place over TCP/IP or IPC, so that the communication over the serial connection can be restricted to keystroke and mouse events and to screen updates. Another great advantage is that, since they need very little memory to run, these serial X terminals tend to be very inexpensive. The disadvantage is that they are still very slow (although faster than many other methods of running X over serial connections).

We strongly recommend that you buy an X terminal with an XDMCP-compliant server (R4 or higher). (Almost all X terminals sold today support XDMCP; see Section 3.1 for more information on XDMCP.) If you run R5 on a host, we also recommend getting an X terminal that supports the R5 font server and (if the X terminal supports color) one that supplies color characterization data for Xcms. (At this printing, X terminals supporting the R5 font server and Xcms are just coming to the market.)

For the purposes of this book, we emphasize setting up X terminals running over TCP/IP with the X server software downloaded over TFTP.

---

*These X terminals are manufactured by Graph-On and Qume. Graph-On terminals are no longer on the market.

7.1.4 Special Features

As the X terminal market has grown, X terminal capabilities have expanded as well.

Local Clients   Some X terminals can run X clients locally. Window managers are the most popular clients to run locally, and can make quite an impact on performance. Note, however, that the more you want your X terminal to do, the more memory you'll need. And remember that the whole idea of X and the X terminal in particular is to have cheap desktop access to remote computing—so don't go wild on local clients unless you have real reasons for keeping network traffic at a minimum. For example, if you're running the X terminal over serial lines, you may want to have a local window manager. In any event, the local window manager will be more responsive, but you have to live with the X terminal vendor's choice of a window manager.

Backing Store   Almost all X terminals are capable of *backing store*. Backing store allows an X server to keep an image of obscured windows in memory so they can be redrawn quickly and without network overhead when exposed. To use this feature, however, terminals need to have some extra memory installed, or they may produce an error message (or crash). Some terminals give the option of using backing store only when there is enough memory available; enable this option if it is provided with your terminal, since it might help performance. Beware, however, that when the X terminal later needs more memory, it may not consider the memory set aside for backing store to be fair game.

Remote Configuration

All X terminals can be configured using a local setup menu. Some X terminals, however, also provide the ability to read their configuration parameters from a file on a remote host at boot time. This becomes a great advantage when you have many X terminals to maintain—it's always easier to edit files on-line than to visit every office on your site after hours. See Section 7.6 for more information on remote configuration.

Peripheral Support

Many X terminals allow you to hang printers off their serial port. In addition, some X terminals made by IBM have a port for connecting a hard drive directly to the X terminal. The hard drive is used for "swapping" large images, reducing memory requirements.

7.1.5 Memory Configuration

X terminals range from 512K of memory to 72MB. As usual, what you should get depends on what you plan to use it for. If you plan to run graphics-intensive applications, you'll want more memory for a reasonable display. Remember that the more pixels on the screen and the greater the depth of your terminal, the more memory you'll need.

In addition, many of the fancier features available for X terminals can be memory-intensive. X terminals that can run clients locally will need more memory to support them. If you want your X terminals to do backing store, that will also require more memory.

Although many X terminals are smart enough to cut down on backing store when memory gets low, beware that some X terminals might crash if they run out of memory. If this happens, it's a good idea to disable backing store completely, if you can.

Some X terminal manufacturers use their own proprietary memory. If you think this may turn into an issue when it becomes time to upgrade the memory, you might prefer to stick to a manufacturer that uses industry-standard SIMMs.

7.1.6 Network Interface

Most X terminals come with built-in Ethernet and TCP/IP support, and most also provide a serial interface. Some X terminals support the IBM Token Ring beneath TCP/IP. DECnet is supported by some X terminals as well.

Most X terminals support SLIP for running X over a modem line. X terminals supporting PPP for modem lines are just now coming to the market. In addition, some X terminal manufacturers have their own serial line protocols that are more efficient than SLIP, such as NCD's *Xremote* and *Serial Xpress* by Tektronix.

X Terminal Alternatives

There are a few alternatives to buying X terminals. If you already have PCs available, there are many X servers that run on PCs. Although PC X servers are slower than X terminals and have inferior resolution, they are often sufficient for "occasional" X users, and can be much cheaper (depending on how "souped-up" your PC is already). See Appendix C for more information on PC X servers.

Another alternative is to use diskless workstations instead of X terminals. New diskless workstations are significantly more expensive than X terminals, and create more administrative overhead. But if they have enough RAM, diskless workstations are generally faster and reduce both network traffic and the load on the central host, since all (or most) X clients can run locally.

You can also turn an older workstation into an X terminal by installing a stripped-down kernel running only the X server. See Section A.10 for more information on how this is done.

7.2 X Terminal Setup

Assuming you now have an X terminal, you probably want to make sure it works before you do any serious configuration. For an X terminal running over TCP/IP, this means you have to perform the following steps. These steps are described in more detail later in this chapter. Please note that X terminals may have different procedures where noted.

1. Configure the local name server to include a new IP address for the new machine. If you aren't already familiar with this procedure, see Section A.6 for more information.

2. Install the fonts on the host machine.

   The X terminal should have arrived with a font tape. Unless both the X terminal and the host support the R5 font server (and to this date, no X terminals do), you need to install the fonts as documented by the X terminal vendor.

   Where you install your fonts depends on how you intend for them to be read. Some X terminals can read fonts via NFS; all X terminals can read fonts via TFTP. Although it may be preferable to read fonts via NFS, it's a bit harder to set up. For easy setup, therefore, install the fonts in */tftpboot/usr/lib/X11/vendor/fonts*. (You can move the fonts elsewhere if and when you switch to NFS.) See Section 7.4 for more information on font management for X terminals. See Section 7.3.3 for more information on TFTP.

   If the X terminal has support for the R5 font server, and you have an R5 machine running the font server, you don't need to install new fonts. You can just set up the X terminal to use the font server, specifying the name of the font server (consisting of transport, host, and port number). Note that some X terminals may use the term "font server" differently—i.e., as the host that the X terminal reads its fonts from, but without actually using the R5 font service protocol.

3. Install the X server.

   If the X server is built into ROM, you can skip this step. Otherwise, the X server software was probably sent on a tape, to be copied onto the host and read by the X terminal at startup via TFTP. Copy the X server program to the proper directory on the host machine (probably */tftpboot*) and make sure that the TFTP daemon is running on the host. (See Section 7.3.3 for more information on TFTP.)

   Next, tell the X terminal where to download the server from. At this point, you need to consult your documentation; however, for an example, our NCD X terminals use a command line similar to the following on their boot monitors:

   ```
   > bt Xncd16 140.186.65.137 140.186.65.25
   ```

   The X terminal will boot using the file */tftpboot/Xncd16* on the host with IP address `140.186.65.25`. The X terminal will use IP address `140.186.65.137`.

   After the X terminal is initially booted, you can configure its setup menu so that it can automatically boot at power up. Alternatively, if the X terminal uses BOOTP, then you can enter this information into */etc/bootptab*; see Section 7.3.2 for more information.

4. Now it's time to connect to a host. If you don't have R4 or R5 *xdm* already running on a host machine, see Section 3.3 for information on how to start it up.*

Once you have *xdm* running on a host machine, some X terminals arrive pre-configured to do a Broadcast query. Those terminals should receive the login box immediately once the X terminal has been supplied a broadcast address. If there's some complication, you can configure the X terminal to query the host running *xdm* directly. See your vendor's documentation to learn how to configure the terminal to use XDMCP.

Connecting with Telnet

If you have trouble connecting using *xdm*, test the connection using *telnet*. Most X terminals are supplied with a *telnet* window for starting an initial client. The *telnet* window may be part of the setup menu, or it may be a local X client. See your vendor's documentation to learn how to access the *telnet* window.

Once you have a *telnet* window, try to connect to a host using its IP address. If you can't connect, there's either a cabling problem or there's something wrong with the network configuration of the X terminal. If you can connect, log in and type "who am i" to confirm that you're resolving to the correct hostname. Then set the DISPLAY environment variable to the hostname, and start an initial *xterm*.

```
lmui@ruby 26% who am i
ruby!lmui ttyp6Aug 20 18:18    (ncd9.ora.com)
lmui@ruby 27% setenv DISPLAY ncd9.ora.com:0
lmui@ruby 28% xterm &
```

If the *telnet* session ran as a local client, the new *xterm* should pop up immediately. If it ran as a subsession of the setup menu, you have to suspend the setup menu to access the *xterm* window.

If an X client can connect to your X terminal this way, then there must be something wrong with your *xdm* configuration. See Chapter 3 for more information.

7.3 Network Setup

Now for the details. To configure the X terminal for the network, you first need to set up the hosts database. If you aren't already familiar with how to do this on your site, see Section A.6 for more information.

The hosts database maps hostnames to IP addresses. The next issue is how the X terminal knows its IP address. Some X terminals can save their IP address in NVRAM (Non-Volatile RAM). Other X terminals, however, have no way of storing their IP addresses. Instead, they have to depend on the host to tell them their IP address at boot time, using RARP (Reverse Address Resolution Protocol) or BOOTP (Bootstrap Protocol).

---

*If you have configured the *Xaccess* file to restrict *xdm* access to specified hosts, you may have to add the X terminal to the list; see Section 7.5.2 for more information.

Another issue, for X terminals that boot over the network, is how the terminal accesses its server binary. The server image for these X terminals resides on a host somewhere on the network, and the X terminal needs to be able to read their boot image using some protocol, generally TFTP (Trivial File Transfer Protocol).

7.3.1 Getting the IP Address Using RARP

The way RARP works is that the host machine keeps a table of Ethernet addresses and the corresponding IP addresses. This table is kept either in */etc/ethers* or in the *ethers* database if the host uses NIS. The *rarpd* daemon waits for broadcast requests from X terminals and other diskless machines. In its broadcast, the X terminal supplies its Ethernet hardware address (which is built into their Ethernet interface). The *rarpd* daemon on the host responds with its IP address on that network.

If you don't run NIS, adding a new RARP entry is just a matter of editing */etc/ethers*. */etc/ethers* has a simple syntax similar to */etc/hosts*. You can get the Ethernet hardware address of the new X terminal from the monitor at boot time. NCD X terminals, for example, print a message similar to the following:

```
Boot Prom  V2.1.0
Testing available memory   3.0 Mbytes
Network controller passed  00:00:A7:10:11:BF
Keyboard controller V2.00
```

To add this terminal as `ncd4`, add the following line to */etc/ethers* (convert the letters in the hex number to lowercase):

```
00:00:a7:10:11:bf    ncd4
```

The RARP daemon uses the *ethers* database along with the *hosts* database to determine the X terminal's IP address. Note that for RARP to work, you must have an entry for the new X terminal in the *hosts* database.

If you run NIS, see Section A.7 for information on how to add an entry to the ethers database.

7.3.2 Getting Information Using BOOTP

BOOTP is similar to RARP, but it gives a bit more information. RARP will tell the X terminal only its IP address. BOOTP can be set up to tell the X terminal its subnet mask, name server host, and what machine and pathname to download the X server from.

The BOOTP daemon *bootpd* uses a file called */etc/bootptab*. The BOOTP protocol has changed over the years, as has the syntax for *bootptab*. Standard BOOTP (RFC951) uses a single-line entry per hardware address, to supply the IP address and the name of the boot file. The first two uncommented lines contain, respectively, the directory in which the boot files reside, and the default boot file. For example:

```
#
# default boot directory
#
```

```
/tftpboot:/

# default bootfile
Xncd19

# bootp clients --
# host htype    haddr           iaddr        bootfile

ncd4 1    00:00:A7:10:11:BF    140.186.65.13  Xncd16
```

The first field is the hostname of the BOOTP client (in this example, ncd4). The second field is the hardware type, with 1=Ethernet. The third and fourth fields represent the hardware and Internet addresses. The fifth field is the name of the boot file to use in the specified directory. (The ": /" following the default boot directory /tftpboot is needed for systems that run TFTP in restricted mode.)

"Extended" BOOTP (RFC1048 with CMU extensions) has syntax similar to that of /etc/termcap and /etc/printcap. A single BOOTP definition is in two parts, a "global" part used for all machines and a part that is particular to the new machine. The "global" part must appear first, and might resemble the following:

```
global:\
    :sm=255.255.255.0:\
    :ht=ethernet:\
    :ds=140.186.65.25:\
    :ns=140.186.65.25:\
    :to=18000:\
    :hn:\
    :vm=rfc1048:
```

The client-specific part might then resemble:

```
ncd4:\
    :hd=/tftpboot:\
    :bf=Xncd16:\
    :tc=global:\
    :ha=0000A71011BF:\
    :ip=140.186.65.13:
```

The two-character capabilities have the following meanings:

bf	Boot file for client machine
ds	IP address of Internet domain name server host
ha	Hardware (Ethernet) address
hd	Home directory for boot files
hn	Host name
ht	Hardware type
ip	Internet address
ns	IP address of UDP name server host
sm	Subnet mask
tc	Append specified entry
to	Time out, in milliseconds
vm	Version number of BOOTP protocol on the host

The hn entry should be set to the hostname of the terminal. For the global entry, hn should be left blank (as shown above).

7.3.3 Trivial File Transfer Protocol (TFTP)

An X terminal needs to use some simple transfer protocol to download its server software. Most X terminals use TFTP as their transfer protocol of choice. Since TFTP does not require a user name or password in order to allow a connection, we strongly recommend running *tftpd* in "restricted" or "secure" mode. Using restricted TFTP, the server code must be copied to the TFTP home directory—usually */tftpboot*—and the X terminal needs to be told which host to boot from. When the X terminal connects to the host via restricted TFTP, the host's TFTP server does a *chroot* to */tftpboot* and reads files relative to the new root.

The TFTP server is usually run from *inetd*, which is started at boot time from */etc/rc* or *rc.local*. *inetd* manages several daemons listed in */etc/inetd.conf*; requests for those services are routed through *inetd*, which then starts up the appropriate daemon.

TFTP is often disabled from *inetd.conf* because it is considered a potential security hole. If you're not sure if TFTP is active, first make sure that *inetd* is running, and if it is, then look in the configuration file for *inetd* (either */etc/inetd.conf* or */etc/servers*) to make sure TFTP is called. In */etc/inetd.conf*, the line starting TFTP should look something like the following:

```
tftp dgram udp wait root /usr/etc/in.tftpd in.tftpd -s /tftpboot
```

In */etc/servers*, it should look like:

```
tftp udp /usr/etc/in.tftpd -s /tftpboot
```

(The *-s* option says to run TFTP in "secure" mode, so that machines connecting via TFTP can read files only in */tftpboot*. On some systems this option appears as *-r*, for "restricted" mode. Since TFTP is such a security hazard, we do not recommend using it except in restricted mode; otherwise, anyone on the network can get any file on your host!)

You can also test if TFTP is running by trying it manually:

```
lmui@reno % tftp ruby
tftp> status
Connected to ruby.ora.com.
Mode: netascii Verbose: off Tracing: off
Rexmt-interval: 5 seconds, Max-timeout: 25 seconds
tftp> get Xncd16
Received 846244 bytes in 8.4 seconds
tftp>
```

(After quitting TFTP and confirming that the file was properly retrieved, you probably want to remove it from the directory it was copied to.)

Test if TFTP is running in restricted mode by requesting a file that isn't in */tftpboot*:

```
tftp> get /etc/motd
Error code 1: File not found
tftp>
```

Another possible error message on some systems is:

```
tftp> get /etc/motd
Transfer timed out.
tftp>
```

If you don't get an error message and TFTP lets you copy */etc/motd* to your current directory, then it isn't running in restricted mode, and you should probably be worried about what other files can be transferred (such as */etc/passwd*!).

If TFTP is not enabled, edit *inetd.conf* or */etc/servers* as appropriate, and send a SIGHUP to *inetd*. This will force *inetd* to reread */etc/inetd.conf*.

```
# vi /etc/inetd.conf
      (restore the TFTP line)
# ps agx | grep inetd
  188 ?  IW    5:06 inetd
 5922 q6 S     0:00 grep inetd
# kill -HUP 188
```

For more information on *inetd*, see the Nutshell Handbook, *TCP/IP Network Administration*, by Craig Hunt (O'Reilly & Associates, 1992).

7.3.4 Setting Up the Network on the X Terminal

If you're using BOOTP, you don't need to do anything on the X terminal end to get the terminal to connect properly to the host with the right IP address and download its boot file. Otherwise, however, you need to do some fiddling on the setup menu.

As far as TCP/IP is concerned, the things you need to tell the X terminal are:

• The X terminal's IP address

• The subnet mask on the network

• The name server address

• The IP address of the host to boot from

• The broadcast address

Each X terminal vendor has its own way of specifying this information in a setup menu. See your vendor's documentation for more information.

One bit of advice about configuring X terminals: remember that many X terminals need to be explicitly told to save current settings in NVRAM, or changes will not take effect after the X terminal is booted.

7.3.5 Debugging Hints

If you think you've done everything right, but the X terminal still can't seem to boot, here are some hints.

7.3.5.1 Error Messages

The X terminal itself may have a diagnostic window for reporting error messages. The diagnostic window is the first place to look for errors. If all the "interesting" information scrolls off the screen too quickly, you may be able to limit the level of diagnostic information by setting a lower error message level via the setup menu; see your vendor's documentation for details.

If the X terminal appears to know its name but is not able to download the boot file, you may also want to look for an error message on the boot host. Errors from *tftpd*, *bootpd*, or *inetd* should be recorded by *syslog* on the host machine. Look in */etc/syslog.conf.* to determine where daemon error messages are being copied to; for example, on our system, */etc/syslog.conf* contains the line:

```
*.err;kern.debug;daemon,auth.notice;mail.crit;user.none   /var/adm/messages
```

All daemon error messages on our system are therefore being copied to */var/adm/messages*.

7.3.5.2 Updating the arp Table

The *arp table* on the boot host has a listing of all hostnames, Ethernet addresses, and IP addresses that the host knows about. You can access this table using the command *arp -a*:

```
% arp -a
ncd4.ora.com (140.186.65.14) at 0:0:a7:10:12:bf
rubble.ora.com (140.186.65.11) at 8:0:20:2:fc:90
rock.west.ora.com (140.186.66.10) at 0:0:c:0:63:4a
cca.camb.com (140.186.64.12) at aa:0:4:0:e2:4
harry.ora.com (140.186.65.17) at 8:0:20:7:c4:d4
  ...
```

Keep in mind that if you replace an X terminal with a new one, you may have to manually delete the cached *arp* entry with the *arp -d* command before the new terminal can be recognized:

```
# arp -d ncd4
```

If you have an old arp entry or have made a mistake in the */etc/ethers* file, you may get the following error:

```
duplicate IP address!! sent from ethernet address: ...
```

7.3.5.3 Name Server Problems

If the X server is running properly but you can't seem to get any clients to open the new display, there may be a problem in the name server. The name server is primarily responsible for looking up a hostname and returning the IP address for that host. You can therefore isolate the problem to the name server by supplying the IP address directly to the client program. For example:

```
lmui@reno % xterm -display 140.186.65.13:0
```

If this command is successful but "*hostname* : 0" was not, then the problem could be with the name server configuration, with the NIS configuration, or with the resolver configuration file (*/etc/resolv.conf*).

7.4 Fonts on X Terminals

Many X terminals have some fonts built into the server, but you usually need to read fonts from the host machine as well. Most X terminal manufacturers supply a "font tape" with their product, with fonts that need to be read on your host system. At minimum, the font tape that comes with the X terminal contains vendor-specific *.snf* or *.pcf* versions of the BDF fonts supplied by the MIT source distribution of X11. Many vendors also supply some additional fonts.

We said earlier that for easy set up, just put the fonts in */tftpboot*. But for real setup, you probably want to think a little harder about where to put the fonts and how they should be read.

7.4.1 Font Formats

Every X server vendor supplies its own font tree for that server. Each font tree takes approximately three to four megabytes of disk space. If you have X terminals manufactured by three different vendors, therefore, you're using up 9 to 12 megabytes just to hold their fonts—not to mention the fonts for running X on the local display of the host machine.

Luckily, you can often get away without keeping multiple fonts on line. For *.snf* fonts, there are four ways that fonts for different servers might deviate: the byte order, the bit order, the scanline unit padding, and the glyph padding. In most cases, the scanline and glyph padding for a server is 1 (the default), so you seldom have to consider those variables for incompatibilities (although if you find that your characters are drawing over one another, you're probably using fonts compiled with a different padding). The byte order and bit order generally go hand-in-hand. So for most cases, you really need to keep at most only two sets of *.snf* fonts on line: one for X terminals that number bytes starting at the high end (*big endian*), and one for X terminals that number bytes starting at the low end (*little endian*).

PCF fonts don't have byte-order incompatibilities, so if all your X terminals support PCF fonts, you might be able to get away with a single set of fonts.

For example, NCD X terminals are *big endian*, so if they are reading fonts from a Sun workstation (a *big endian* machine), chances are that they can read and display the *.snf* fonts compiled for the local server without a hitch. The *bdftosnf* font compiler defaults to the byte order on the host machine, so there should be no problem in font compatibility between Sun and NCD X servers. In this situation, you would not have to keep the NCD fonts on line, but could have the X terminals read the Sun-compiled *.snf* fonts. The easiest way to do this is by linking the standard X11 font directory to the server-specific font directory. For example:

```
# mkdir /usr/lib/X11/ncd
# ln -s /usr/lib/X11/fonts /usr/lib/X11/ncd/fonts
```

(You may still want to use the fonts supplied with the X terminal, since they may be more sophisticated than those on the core MIT distribution, but that's up to you.)

HDS X terminals are *little endian*. This means that the fonts on a Sun are not compatible with those supplied by HDS (although fonts on a VAX are).

There is another hitch. Although each of the factors for font compatibility can be overridden on the *bdftosnf* command line, the options for a different bit or byte order will apply only to the glyph section of the font—the header section will still be in the bit and byte order of the host. So HDS supplies its own font compiler, *bdftohds*, since they cannot rely on the fonts compiled by *bdftosnf* on a *big endian* machine. Many X terminal manufacturers supply their own compiler to convert *.bdf* fonts to their own format.

Some X terminals (e.g., those made by Visual) can read fonts in either byte order. Furthermore, X terminals are beginning to support the *.pcf* font format, which does not have byte-order incompatibilities. Tektronix is one vendor that currently sells X terminals supporting both *.pcf* and *.snf* formats.

7.4.2 The Font Server (R5)

With Release 5 of X11, a lot of the font confusion is cleared up with the font server. R5-compatible X terminals (of which there are currently none) supply a field in the setup menu for the address of the font server. If your X terminal provides this functionality, and you have an R5 host available to run a font server, run (do not walk) to Section 5.5 to learn how to enable the font server on the host. You have been spared a giant headache.

Some X terminal vendors, such as Visual Technology, have their own proprietary font server mechanism. Although they are unlikely to be compatible with the R5 font server, these proprietary font servers are worth looking into if running the R5 font server is not an option.

7.4.3 Choosing TFTP or NFS for Font Access

Assuming that your X terminal does not support the font server introduced with X11R5, you are stuck with either TFTP or NFS. (Some X terminals also support using FTP, but you're probably better off not opening that can of worms.)

7.4.3.1 Reading Fonts Using TFTP

It's easy to install fonts to be transferred with TFTP. But since TFTP doesn't provide any user authentication, you need to decide whether you want to run it in restricted mode or not, and either option has its downside.

If you run TFTP in restricted mode, you have to put the font files in the TFTP home directory tree (usually */tftpboot*). When the X terminal connects to the host using TFTP, it will do a *chroot* to */tftpboot* and then look for the fonts relative to that directory—so, for example, an NCD X terminal will effectively look for its fonts in */tftpboot/usr/lib/X11/ncd/fonts* .

The problem with running TFTP in restricted mode is that it gives you no choice but to install all your fonts in the TFTP home directory. This may mean some creative shuffling, just to put */tftpboot* on a disk large enough to hold all those fonts. Note that the solution that you would like, which is keeping the fonts in */usr/lib/X11/fonts* but creating symbolic links to */tftpboot*, isn't an option—restricted TFTP cannot follow links outside of */tftpboot*.

If you run TFTP in unrestricted mode, you can put the NCD font files where you really want them, in */usr/lib/X11/ncd/fonts*. But you probably don't want to run TFTP in unrestricted mode—after all, do you want anyone over the Internet to be able to read your */etc/passwd* file?

A possibility is to use NFS to mount the fonts from the same machine. That is, you might set up the host *ruby* to export */usr* read-only to itself. On newer NFS implementations, the */etc/exports* would look like:

```
/usr -ro,access=ruby
```

Then have *ruby* mount */usr/lib/X11/**vendor**/fonts* as */tftpboot/usr/lib/X11/**vendor**/fonts*. In */etc/fstab* on the same host:

```
ruby:/usr/lib/X11/ncd/fonts /tftpboot/usr/lib/X11/ncd/fonts nfs ro,bg 0 0
```

This provides you the convenience of TFTP without many of the hassles.

7.4.3.2 Reading Fonts Using NFS

If you are using NFS directly to download fonts, check the */etc/exports* file on the host to confirm that the X terminal has permission to read its font directory, and make sure that directory is exported with the *exportfs* command. See Section A.5 for more information on exporting directories under NFS.

Netgroups are particularly useful for grouping several X terminals together that need the same fonts. See the Nutshell Handbook, *Managing NFS and NIS*, by Hal Stern (O'Reilly & Associates, 1991), for more information.

Using NFS to mount the fonts locally on the X terminal can cause some confusion. The cryptic error message "X Error of failed request: BadValue" means the font can't be read because the specified path doesn't exist. This may happen because the pathname was mistyped; however, it could also be the result of some NFS confusion—the font directory may not be properly exported, or it may be mounted on the local machine under another name. For example, you may mount */export/usr/lib/X11/ncd/fonts* on a fileserver as */usr/lib/X11/ncd/fonts* on the local X terminal. The pathname you specify to *xset* must reflect its pathname on the local machine, i.e., the one running the X server.

Another possible source of confusion is that NFS will not extend permission to any path that is not explicitly exported. That is, if */usr/lib/X11/ncd/fonts* is a symbolic link to */export/usr/lib/X11/ncd/fonts*, exporting */usr* will not grant access to the files that are linked to */export*.

7.5 Configuring for the X Display Manager

If you're using X terminals, you probably want to control them using the X Display Manager (*xdm*). There are other ways of starting sessions, such as logging on via *telnet* and starting clients manually, or using the *rexec* (remote execution) capabilities supported by some X terminals. But if both the host system and the X server support the XDM Control Protocol (R4 or later), then you should definitely use *xdm*.

If you aren't running *xdm* at all, read Section 3.3 for more information to get it started. See Section 3.1 for some background information on XDMCP.

7.5.1 Configuring the X Terminal for xdm

X terminals generally supply three different ways of running XDMCP:

Direct   Calling XDMCP "directly" requires that the name or IP address of the host running *xdm* be supplied. The X terminal will request an *xdm* login box from that host and from that host only.

Indirect   Calling XDMCP "indirectly" requires that the name or IP address of the host be supplied. The host is then expected to pass the XDMCP request to another host or group of hosts. For a host running vanilla X11R4, an "Indirect" query is treated the same as a "Direct" one. For a host running X11R5, it can be configured to respond to an "Indirect" query by forwarding the request to another host or by offering a list of hosts for the user to choose from. See Section 3.5.3 for information on how to configure how "Indirect" queries are treated on an R5 host.

Broadcast   Calling XDMCP in "broadcast" mode does *not* require a hostname or address, but means that the X terminal sends out a general request for an *xdm* login box across the subnet. For most X terminals, the first host that responds is the one that is used. For some smarter X terminals, the X server gathers responses from all hosts on the local network and allows the user to choose one to start up on.

If an X terminal doesn't connect to any host running *xdm* under a Broadcast query, but can connect to hosts via a Direct or Indirect query, then there is probably something wrong with the Broadcast address that you have configured the X terminal to use. See your vendor's documentation for information on how to set the Broadcast address.

Note that Broadcast queries are restricted to the local network or subnet. Unlike Direct and Indirect queries, you cannot use a Broadcast query to access a host through a gateway.

7.5.2 Configuring an R5 Host

If the host is using X11R5, then you need to make sure that the new X terminal is given permission to connect to *xdm* on the host. The */usr/lib/X11/xdm/Xaccess* file controls which X servers can connect to the host. The *Xaccess* file also controls how Indirect queries are dealt with on that host.

For example, to add `ncd4` to the list of X servers that can connect to the host, you can simply add the line:

```
ncd4.ora.com
```

Note that the *Xaccess* file accepts wildcards. So `ncd4` would already have permission to connect to the host if there were a line such as:

```
*.ora.com
```

See Section 3.5.3 for more information on how to configure the *Xaccess* file.

7.5.3 Configuring an R4 Host

If the host is using X11R4, you don't need to make any changes on the host for a XDMCP-compatible X server to use *xdm*—you just need to configure the X terminal to use XDMCP.

7.5.4 Configuring xdm Without XDMCP

If either the X server or the host is *not* XDMCP-compatible (R3 or earlier), then you need to make an entry in the */usr/lib/X11/xdm/Xservers* file in order to manage the X terminal using *xdm*. For example, you can add the line:

```
ncd4.ora.com:0  foreign xxx
```

(The "xxx" is required because although R3 *xdm* ignores the third field in a foreign entry, the field cannot be left empty.)

See Section 3.5.2 for more information on how to configure the *Xservers* file.

The problem with using pre-XDMCP *xdm* is that, should the X terminal be turned off for any reason, *xdm* needs to be restarted before it will know to reconnect to the terminal. If you have no choice but to use an R3 host system, you might be interested in X terminals that offer their own proprietary protocol for controlling *xdm*. X terminals made by Visual, for example, provide XDSXDM for controlling Release 3 *xdm* for their XDS terminals.

7.5.5 Setting Up Server Access Control

As described in Chapter 4, there are two current mechanisms for restricting clients from accessing a particular server: host-based access control and user-based access control.

Host-based access control is controlled entirely by the server. Some X terminals allow you to keep a list of hosts that you want to allow access from, using the setup menu on the X terminal. However, it's better to use user-based access control if you can.

User-based access control is controlled both by the server and by the X Display Manager. Check your X terminal documentation to see if user-based access control is supported. If it is, then check if *xdm* is set up to use user-based access control on X terminals. You can determine this by examining the configuration file for *xdm*, usually */usr/lib/X11/xdm/xdm-config*. The following line:

```
DisplayManager*authorize:          true
```

specifies that authorization is being used for all X servers managed by *xdm* on that host.

Host-based access control overrides user-based access control. This can cause complications when your X terminal supports both types of server access control. Contrary to what your instincts might be, to enable user-based access control you should make sure that host-based access control is also enabled—disabling host-based access control may effectively result in all hosts having access to the server, regardless of any user-based access control in effect. If you want to use user-based access control exclusively, you should make sure host-based access control is enabled but the list of hosts that are allowed access is empty. See Section 4.2.4 for more information.

See Chapter 4 for more information on security issues and X11.

7.6 Remote Configuration of X Terminals

Many X terminals provide a facility called *remote configuration*. Our experience with remote configuration has been very positive, so we recommend that if you have more than one of a single type of terminal, you should consider using remote configuration.

With remote configuration, the parameters in the setup menu can be defined in a file to be downloaded by the X terminal when it boots. What this does for the administrator is that it makes it easy to change a given field—the administrator no longer needs to visit each X terminal on the site after hours and change their setup menus manually, but can simply edit the remote configuration files for each terminal. The next time the terminal is booted, the new values will be read.

Another advantage of remote configuration is ease in troubleshooting. The danger of user-accessible setup menus is that a user might unknowingly change something that disables their terminal. Many terminal manufacturers provide a mechanism for "locking" the current setup menu settings with a password—so that only administrators with the password will be able to make further changes to the X terminal configuration. Using remote configuration, however, the X terminal is configured at boot time from a file residing on a host. If a terminal's set up is corrupted, therefore, the user can restore its settings just by rebooting the X terminal.

Another advantage of using remote configuration is that it can help you get out of a jam if for some reason your current configuration is so corrupted that you cannot even access the setup menu. If you are using remote configuration, you can just edit the file and then reboot the terminal.

Each X terminal vendor has its own syntax for remote configuration. To give you an idea of what they do, here's a description of how remote configuration is handled by various X terminal vendors.

7.6.1 Remote Configuration on NCD Terminals

On NCD X terminals with remote configuration turned on, each X terminal at boot time looks for a configuration file whose name is derived from its IP address, in hexadecimal. For example, an NCD X terminal with IP address 140.186.65.13 would look for a configuration file called *8CBA410D* in the directory */usr/lib/X11/ncd/configs*. (See Section A.9 for information on how to get the hexadecimal equivalent of an IP address.)

If the configuration file for its specific IP address doesn't exist, the X terminal then looks for a configuration file called *ncd_std* in the same directory.

If you are using NFS to read the remote configuration file, the X terminal needs to have read access for the */usr/lib/X11/ncd/configs* directory on the host. If you are using restricted TFTP to read the remote configuration file, the configuration files need to be installed in the */tftpboot/usr/lib/X11/ncd/configs* directory.

The following is a portion of the remote configuration file used by our NCD X terminals:

```
background = white
backing-store = by-request
baud-1 = 9600
boot-at-reset = yes
boot-server = 140.186.65.25
broadcast-address = 140.186.0.0
data-bits-1 = 8
default-cterm-host = 0.0
default-domain = ora.com
    ...
virtual-terminal-at-reset = xdm
xdm-access = direct
    ...
xdm-server = 140.186.65.25
```

Now for the good news: NCD doesn't require you to write it all in by hand. Instead, you can set up a single terminal, make sure it works to your liking, and then download its parameters to a file using the Utilities menu.

The next problem is how to tell the terminal to read the remote configuration file the first time. There's a logistical problem involved: NCD X terminals support NFS only if they're using remote configuration, so if you want to read the actual configuration file over NFS, you need to upload the configuration file initially using TFTP, and then save current values before rebooting.

7.6.2 Remote Configuration on Visual Terminals

On Visual X terminals with remote configuration turned on, the X terminal uses a list of hostnames and optional pathnames to determine which configuration file to use. This list is supplied in the Remote Configuration Menu. The X terminal will search for the configuration files in the order that they are listed. When a specific pathname isn't listed for a given host, the X terminal looks for a configuration file named for its IP address in the */usr/lib/X11/Visual* directory on that host. For example, a Visual X terminal with IP address `140.186.65.13` looks for a configuration file called */usr/lib/X11/Visual/140.186.65.13*. If that file doesn't exist, it then looks for a configuration file called *xds-config* in the same directory.

If you are using NFS to read the remote configuration file, the X terminal needs to have read access for whatever directory the configuration files live in. If you are using restricted TFTP to read the remote configuration file, the files need to be in a subdirectory of */tftpboot*, and the pathname needs to be relative to */tftpboot*.

Visual X terminals use resource syntax for their configuration files. They follow the form:

```
Visual.model.parameter:      value
```

where *model* is the particular model of Visual X terminal, such as `X19`, `X19TURBO`, `X15`, etc. As with standard resource syntax, you can use an asterisk for the *model* field to have a resource apply for all models. The following is a portion of a sample configuration file for Visual X terminals:

```
! --------------------------------
! Ethernet Menu
! --------------------------------
Visual*IpNetworkMask:        255.255.255.0
Visual*IpBroadcastAddress:   140.186.0.0
      ...
! --------------------------------
! X Server Features Menu
! --------------------------------
      ...
Visual*DefaultTextFont:      9x15
Visual.X15.DefaultTextFont:  12x20
```

Note that we've set things up so that the Visual X15 terminal uses the 12×20 font for text, but all other Visual terminals will use the 9×15 font.

7.6.3 Remote Configuration on Tektronix Terminals

For Tektronix X terminals, the syntax for remote configuration files consists of commands followed directly by parameters. Lines starting with "#" are taken as comments. The remote configuration file is read using the same file access method that is used for downloading the server image (i.e., TFTP), so remote configuration is not available for terminals that boot from ROM.

Tektronix remote configuration files need to be thought of somewhat differently, since the terminal executes each line as a command and doesn't just store it as a variable definition. This means that you have to be careful about the sequence of commands. For example, you need to declare a host's address using the *ip_host_table* command before you can use its hostname for the *file_host_name_1* command.

The sample is a portion from a configuration file for Tektronix X terminals:

```
ip_host_table        140.186.65.25 ruby
ip_host_table        140.186.65.35 opal
file_host_name_1     ruby
file_access_1        TFTP
      . . .
```

7.7 Reconfiguring the Host

When you replace an ASCII terminal with an X terminal, you're giving a user a whole new world of functionality. You are also allowing that user to use five to ten times the resources he or she used previously. Whereas a user on an ASCII terminal might run maybe one or two processes in the background (which usually exit on their own), a user on an X terminal can go hog wild, running an *xclock*, *xbiff*, multiple *xterms*, a mail reader, a news reader, etc.—all this before starting actual "work." In addition, *xdm* forks a copy of itself for every display it manages.

In this section, we include an example of how to configure a SunOS system to support more users, processes, pseudo-ttys, and swap space. Refer to your vendor's manual for information on how to reconfigure the kernel on your system.

7.7.1 Increasing the Number of Processes

When you set up a site for running multiple X terminals, you probably want to increase the number of processes that the host can handle at once. If the system runs out of processes, it may give an error:

```
% ls
No more processes
%
```

or commands may fail silently.

To increase the number of processes on SunOS 4.*x*, edit the kernel configuration file. The name of this file follows the form */sys/**arch**/conf/**kernel_name***. For our Sun4, this file is */sys/sun4m/conf/RUBY*. Edit the `maxusers` line as appropriate. For example, change:

```
maxusers        8
```

to:

```
maxusers        48
```

Then rebuild the kernel and reboot:

```
# /etc/config RUBY
# cd ../RUBY
# make
# cp /vmunix /ovmunix
# cp vmunix /
# sync;reboot
```

Be careful to follow the guidelines in vendor OS manuals in increasing `maxusers`. If you increase it beyond the specified upper limit, you run the risk of wasting resources.

7.7.2 Increasing the Number of Pseudo-ttys

Another consideration is the number of pseudo-ttys, or *ptys*, a host can handle. A typical symptom of running out of *ptys* is an immediate logout when trying to open a new connection:

```
% rlogin rock
Password:
SunOS Release 4.1.2 (ORAWEST) #3: Wed Jul 29 12:50:14 PDT 1992
TERM=(xterm)
Connection closed.
```

On SunOS, edit the same kernel config file */sys/**arch**/conf/**kernel_name***. Find the line for *pty* devices.

```
pseudo-device   pty             # pseudo-tty's, also needed for SunView
```

The default entry is for 48 *ptys*. Appending a number suffix changes it accordingly:

```
pseudo-device   pty128          # pseudo-tty's, also needed for SunView
```

We have now set up the system to support 128 *ptys*. (See your documentation to learn what the maximum number of *ptys* on your system is. SunOS 4.1.2 can handle up to 256 *ptys*.)

Next, make more *ptys* in */dev* for each bank of 16 *ptys*. Since we have expanded to 128 *ptys*, this would be 128 ÷ 16 = 8 banks of *ptys* in total. The *pty* banks are numbered from 0, so you'd remake banks 0 through 7:

```
# cd /dev
# MAKEDEV pty0 pty1 pty2 pty3 pty4 pty5 pty6 pty7
# ls pty?? | wc -l
  128
```

Then rebuild the kernel and reboot as shown above.

```
# /etc/config kernel name
```

```
# cd ../kernel name
# make
# cp /vmunix /ovmunix
# cp vmunix /
# sync;reboot
```

There is often a script in /dev for creating new pseudo-ttys. See your vendor's documentation for details.

7.7.3 Increasing the Amount of Swap Space

You may need to increase the amount of swap space when you start to get the dreaded error message:

```
Sorry, pid 3924 (eap) was killed due to lack of swap space
```

There are two ways to deal with swap space under SunOS: either swap to a file or swap to disk partition.*

7.7.3.1 Swapping to a File

To swap to a file, fist create the swap file:

```
# mkfile -v 64m /work/moreswap
/work/moreswap 67108864 bytes
```

Then add an entry in /etc/fstab as follows:

```
/work/moreswap swap swap rw 0 0
```

Finally, enable swapping on the new area:

```
# swapon -a
Adding /work/moreswap as swap device
```

7.7.3.2 Swapping to a Disk

To swap to a disk, add an entry in /etc/fstab to define the new swap partition (in this example, /dev/sd2b):

```
/dev/sd2b  swap       swap rw 0 0
```

Then, before running swapon, check the current size of the swap space:

```
# /etc/pstat -T
163/2758 files
829/1223 inodes
74/778 processes
14488/63972 swap
```

This shows approximately 64 MB of available swap space (with 14 MB already used).

---

*See Essential System Administration, by AEleen Frisch (O'Reilly & Associates, 1991), for more information.

X Window System Administrator's Guide

Finally, run *swapon* and then check the size of the swap space again:

```
# swapon -a
Adding /dev/sd2b as swap device
# /etc/pstat -T
163/2758 files
829/1223 inodes
74/778 processes
14488/127944 swap
```

The swap space has doubled to approximately 128 MB.

7.8 Related Documentation

Articles on X terminals appear frequently in periodicals serving the X and UNIX community. Advertisements (in periodicals that accept them) are also very helpful for keeping track of the latest and greatest X terminal technology.

In addition, a list of X terminal manufacturers is posted quarterly to the *comp.windows.x* newsgroup.

The following Nutshell Handbooks might come in handy: *Managing NFS and NIS* by Hal Stern; *Essential System Administration* by AEleen Frisch; *TCP/IP Network Administration* by Craig Hunt; and *DNS and BIND* by Cricket Liu and Paul Albitz.

8

Building the X Window System

By necessity, you can't do anything with X until it is installed on your system. This chapter tells you how to build and install X.

In This Chapter:

8

Building the X Window System

This chapter tells you how to build and install X. If X is already installed, you can skip this chapter unless you want to learn more about what goes on "under the hood."

If X isn't installed on your system, you have two choices: you can build it yourself or you can purchase pre-built binaries. This chapter begins by telling you what you need to know to make that decision.

If you decide to build X yourself, this chapter tells you how. The amount of work involved in building X depends on the type of installation, the platform you use, and the resources that are available to you (such as disk space, time, tape drive or CD/ROM drive.) You should explore each of these factors before you attempt to build X.

8.1 Installation Issues

First you need to decide what you want to install. This section gives a short description of what types of distributions are available. The easiest installations are described first and without much detail. If your configuration falls under one of these categories, then you can bail out of this chapter early.

If your installation requires more thought (or if you are curious), the remainder of the chapter provides a guide to completing all but the most complicated installations.

8.1.1 Should You Use MIT Source?

The first thing you need to do is to determine whether you want to build X from the MIT sources ("vanilla" or "stock" X11), or whether you'd rather install binaries provided by a vendor.

Using X11 binaries supplied by a vendor has the following advantages:

- X supplied by an OS vendor may be easier to use and may be better integrated with application software than the "stock" MIT X11. Some examples of integrated X distributions would be SGI's IRIX 4.0 environment, SCO Open Desktop and Sun OpenWindows.

- Vendors usually provide a stable release of X. (MIT releases go through many "fixes" before they settle down, because they usually provide new functionality earlier than the vendor-supplied releases.)

- The vendor may add new functionality to the X11 distribution; for example, the vendor may provide support for display PostScript, the Silicon Graphics Graphics Language (GL), special hardware (such as graphics accelerator cards), and multi-processor operating systems.

- Some applications may require vendor-specific features that are unavailable in the stock MIT release of X11. An example of this would be Sun's *AnswerBook* documentation viewer, which runs only under the Sun OpenWindows server.

- You can call technical support (or send e-mail) if you have a question or complaint. (Whether this leads to a resolution of your problem is another topic altogether.)

- Installation of a vendor-supplied X package is usually a breeze, and often requires little technical knowledge.

- MIT may not provide a server that supports all of the vendor's hardware.

Building and configuring the MIT sources has the following advantages:

- Support for the "stock" X11 distribution is pretty good: patches to serious problems are made publicly available quickly. Anyone with a network connection can pick up a patch to the MIT source via *ftp*, or get it via e-mail.

- Vendors are sometimes very slow to update their X product. You are likely to tire of fighting problems with your vendor release if you know the problem is fixed or never existed in a newer MIT release. Other X products that you want to use may work only on releases newer than your vendor's. It can be frustrating to be behind in X development because the version of X that came with your system is holding you up.

- You can standardize the X distribution across several platforms by building the MIT version for each platform. A common X11 distribution would greatly simplify a heterogeneous network environment.

- The MIT source code is free.

8.1.2 Types of Vendor-supplied X Distributions

Vendor-supplied X can be further divided into two groups:

- X that comes from the vendor of your operating system

- X that comes from third-party suppliers

For both of these categories, the documentation that comes with the package is your best resource for information on installing their X11 release. Software installation methods tend to be very system-specific and may change significantly between OS releases.

8.1.2.1 X from Your OS Vendor

Some examples of vendor-supplied X11 are OpenWindows from Sun, DECWindows from DEC, and AIXWindows from IBM. X from your OS vendor is probably the easiest to install. In fact, you may not have to install it at all—more and more UNIX platforms are being shipped with the OS and software packages (such as X) already installed, so you might luck out and have everything in place when your system is delivered. You should be able to tell if X11 is pre-installed by looking in the directory */usr/bin/X11* or the directory that your vendor uses (typically */usr/openwin* for OpenWindows, */usr/lpp/X11* for AIXWindows, etc). If the directory is not empty, you probably have at least some portion of the software already installed. Some systems have tools to tell you what software is installed. For example, *setld –i* on Ultrix and *versions* on IRIX. You could also try starting the window system with *xinit* (or *openwin*) to see what happens.

If you need to install an X distribution provided by your OS vendor, the installation procedure for the X package should be similar to that of any other package that is bundled with the operating system. The X package installation should require whatever tool is normally used for installing software on that platform, i.e., *setld* for Ultrix, *inst* for IRIX, *cdm* or *extract_unbundled* for SunOS, etc.

The vendor may break the X11 package into separate components: an "execution-only" package that allows you to run X servers and clients, and a "development" environment for compiling new X applications. The development environment includes the X libraries, header files and *imake* configuration files. (See Appendix E for more information on the components of the standard X distribution.) If you intend to write your own X programs or compile any of the public domain X applications available on the Internet, you should install a full development environment. See Appendix B for information on installing public domain software.

Be aware that some vendors charge extra for the X11 distribution, and others include it in the cost of the operating system. You should ask the salesperson about this before you order your software configuration.

8.1.2.2 X from a Third Party

There are several third-party vendors who provide pre-compiled X11 distributions for some of the more popular platforms. Some vendors are listed in Appendix F and in the *comp.windows.x* Frequently Asked Questions list.

Third-party X distributions are usually derived from recent MIT releases without adding much functionality. If you are up to the task of building X from the MIT source, you can probably duplicate a third-party distribution for your platform and save some money. However, it may be easier to purchase a third-party X installation than try to figure out what patches, bug fixes, and work-arounds are necessary to build it on your platform. You might also be able to get invaluable technical support from a third-party vendor.

Furthermore, building the MIT distribution is resource-intensive, consuming large amounts of disk space and CPU time. If these resources are in short supply, this may be reason enough to buy a pre-built X distribution.

8.1.3 X Source Code from MIT

A major part of deciding whether to use the MIT source or a pre-built X distribution is how much work it will be to configure the sources and build X yourself. You might say that the amount of work required to build X on your platform falls into one of three categories:

- *Easy*—MIT X11 for your software and hardware platform is one that is well-tested and commonplace. Relax and enjoy the experience: you may be able to build and install X by typing only a few simple commands and get away with not having to understand the building process at all. (This is pretty amazing considering the size and complexity of the software.) You may need some minor adjustments on your system, but they should not be more difficult than any other tasks you face as a system administrator. Platforms on which your build is likely to be trouble-free are a Sun3 or Sun4 running SunOS 4.1.1, a DEC 3100 running Ultrix 4.2, and an RS/6000 running AIX 3.1. Section 8.3 shows an example of a trouble-free build.

- *Some thinking required*—You need to find out what magic flags or little fixes are required to get the MIT source compiled and running on your system. This may require some detective skills and an understanding of how the building process takes place. A typical situation that would fall in this category would be building the MIT source on an operating system that is slighter newer or older than the one described in the MIT documentation. Section 8.5 shows some examples of X builds that may require a little thinking.

- *You are on your own*—Your platform was bought at a garage sale ... the manufacturer went out of business three years ago and you are the only person who bought one ... or your platform is so new that you are the only one who has heard of it. Whichever it is, this chapter addresses only the most minor of the problems you might encounter. This chapter will help you compile the libraries and clients, but your big problem is getting an X server written. Writing an X server on a new machine is quite an undertaking, and is beyond the scope of this book.

Which category do you belong in? Well, the degree to which X from MIT source will work on your system has a lot to do with how popular your platform is. The best way to find out how much work is involved is to read the release notes, which can usually be found in a file called *RELNOTES.TXT* in either the top-most directory of the MIT source or under the *mit/* subdirectory.* In the R5 source tree, a postscript version is available in *RELNOTES.PS*, and *troff* source (using *ms* macros) is in a file called *RELNOTES.ms*.

The release notes in the R5 source tree list the supported platforms under the section entitled "Building the Release":

> 3. Building the Release
>
> The core distribution (code under the mit directory) has been
> built and tested at MIT on the following systems:
>
> AIX 3.1.5, on IBM RS/6000

---

*Appendix F provides some information on where to find the MIT sources, and Section A.2 provides information on how to use *ftp* to get a file.

```
AT&T Unix System V Release 4 V2, on AT&T WGS6386
A/UX 2.0.1
HP-UX 7.0, on HP9000/s300
IRIX 4.0
Mach 2.5 Version 1.13, on OMRON Luna 88k
NEWS-OS 3.3, on Sony NWS-1850
NEWS-OS 5.0U, on Sony NWS-3710
SunOS 4.1.1, on Sun 3, Sparc 1, and Sparc 2
Ultrix-32 4.2, VAX and RISC
UNICOS 5.1
UTek 4.0
VAX 4.3bsd (with unknown local changes)
   ...
```

If your platform is listed in the release notes, then you're probably in good shape. If not, you may still be in good shape: the X distribution is frequently ported to new platforms, with the binary distribution made publicly available. The best way to track the progress of the X distribution on your platform is to watch the appropriate Usenet newsgroup, or post a query to either that newsgroup or to *comp.windows.x.**

Some examples of useful "ports" that appear outside of the official MIT distribution are the XNeXT distribution for NeXT workstations, the X386 server binary for 386-based UNIX machines, and patches for Sun Solaris 2.0.

8.1.4 Complete or Client-only Distribution?

Before buying an X distribution or investing any time in building one from source, you still have a few more decisions to make.

First, you need to decide whether you want a complete distribution or a client-only distribution. A complete distribution includes a server, clients, libraries, header files, fonts and configuration files. A client-only distribution could include only the clients and, if necessary, shared libraries for dynamically linked executables. If you wanted to compile X programs, you would also need libraries and header files.

Client-only installations make sense for hosts that don't have a bitmapped console display, such as a fileserver, compute server, or NFS server. The X clients are expected to display on remote X servers (for example, X terminals) across a network. Complete distributions make sense for workstations and for development environments.

8.1.5 Installing Multiple X Releases

Next, you should consider whether you want more than one release of the MIT X11 installed at one time. This would come in useful if you intend to test an X application under more than one X release.

---

* *comp.windows.x* also has an e-mail address for those who cannot get news, *xpert@expo.lcs.mit.edu.*

For example, you might want to have Sun OpenWindows, MIT R4, and MIT R5 distributions residing on your platform at the same time: you could do this so you can test clients under each environment. Each distribution can have its own directory hierarchy.

As a example of this, OpenWindows could be installed under */usr/openwin*, MIT X11R4 under */usr/X11R4*, and MIT X11R5 under */usr/X11R5*:

Contents	OpenWindows	X11R4	X11R5
Binaries	*/usr/openwin/bin*	*/usr/X11R4/bin*	*/usr/X11R5/bin*
Libraries	*/usr/openwin/lib*	*/usr/X11R4/lib*	*/usr/X11R5/lib*
Headers	*/usr/openwin/include*	*/usr/X11R4/include/X11*	*/usr/X11R5/include/X11*

Another possibility is that you can run a server from one MIT release with the client distribution from another. You might do this if you are installing a new version of X that doesn't supply a server for your workstation console: you can continue to use the vendor supplied server with updated clients until an updated server is available for your display hardware.

Mixing clients with a server from a different release may have unexpected results. For example, newer X servers have the SHAPE extension, which allows windows to be shapes other than rectangular. If you run the *oclock* client under a server without this extension, it would appear as a square instead of a circle, as shown in Figure 8-1.

Figure 8-1. oclock without the SHAPE extension

With the SHAPE extension, *oclock* appears as it should, as shown in Figure 8-2.

Figure 8-2. oclock with the SHAPE extension

8.2 Source Preparation

You can obtain the source code to X from any of the sites listed in Appendix F. The directory structure may vary slightly, but at the top of the source directory should be the *mit/* and *contrib/* directories. The contents of the *mit/* directory are usually referred to as the *core* distribution. The core software is supported by MIT and is usually included in every X distribution. The *contrib/* area is composed of "contributed" software that is not directly supported by MIT. If you have a problem with *contrib* software, you would typically complain directly to the author of the specific package, instead of to the X Consortium.

Over time, programs are promoted from *contrib* to *core* status if they gain MIT support, or demoted from *core* to *contrib* if they become obsolete (as *uwm* was). It is unusual to compile the entire *contrib* distribution; the typical practice is to compile and install the entire *core* distribution and then selectively compile just the sections you want from *contrib*. If you are using a common platform, you will likely be able to survive with only the *core* software.

When you have obtained the source, there are a few things to do before you can install X:

- Figure out if you have enough disk space.

- Figure out to what extent your platform is supported.

- Make sure your platform is up to date with OS patches.

- Apply all the patches to the X distribution.

- Create a link tree (optional).

8.2.1 Do You Have Enough Disk Space?

One of the first problems that many run into is the amount of disk space consumed by the source code. On top of that, additional disk space is needed to compile and install the source code.

Description	Size (in Mbytes)
R5 *core* source	79
R5 *contrib* source	135
Building R5 *core*	approx. 50-120
Building R5 *contrib*	300+
Installing R5 *core*	25-60
Installing R5 *contrib*	150+

The amount of space required for compiling the *core* distribution varies considerably from operating system to operating system. The type of processor (e.g., CISC or RISC), debugging options and shared libraries will all affect the size of the installation. Read Section 8.4.1 for some ideas on how to reduce the amount of disk space required for compilation and installation.

8.2.2　Is Your Platform Supported?

Before you go anywhere, find out if your platform is one of those supported by the X11 release that you want to build. As suggested in Section 8.1.3, look at the *RELNOTES.TXT* file in the *mit/* directory. If your operating system and platform are listed, you are very likely to be able to produce a working version with very little work. The supported platforms are listed in the section entitled "3. Building the Release":

```
...
The core distribution (code under the mit directory) has been built and
tested at MIT on the following systems:

AIX 3.1.5, on IBM RS/6000
AT&T Unix System V Release 4 V2, on AT&T WGS6386
A/UX 2.0.1
HP-UX 7.0, on HP9000/s300
IRIX 4.0
...
```

If you are unsure of what type of platform and operating system you are running, use one of the following methods to figure it out:

- Check the packaging of the OS distribution software for release and version information.

- The *uname* command is available on most systems. For example:

  ```
  % uname -a
  SunOS ruby 4.1 2 sun4
  ```

  This indicates that the host *ruby* is a *Sun4* running *SunOS 4.1*.

  ```
  % uname -a
  A/UX quartz 2.0.1 SVR2 mc68030
  ```

  The host *quartz* is a Macintosh running *AUX 2.0.1*.

  ```
  % uname -a
  IRIX pebble 4.0.1 11150233 IP6
  ```

  The host *pebble* is a Silicon Graphics running *IRIX 4.0.1*.

- The */etc/motd* file is sometimes helpful:

  ```
  % cat /etc/motd
  SunOS Release 4.1.2 (RUBY) #1: Fri May 29 10:55:44 EDT 1992
  ```

  You may also extract the OS name from the kernel using the *strings* command:

  ```
  % strings /vmunix | grep SunOS
  SunOS Release 4.1.2 (RUBY) #1: Fri May 29 10:55:44 EDT 1992
  ```

- The *arch* or *mach* commands are available on some systems to tell you the architecture of the host:

  ```
  % mach
  sparc
  % arch
  sun4
  ```

- Ask someone who knows.

The next question is, does an X server exist for your display hardware? Check the release notes for the supported displays on your platform. The section entitled "Structure of the MIT sources" contains a list of supported servers:

```
...
DECstation 2100/3100 monochrome and color displays DECstation 5000 CX
and MX displays IBM RS/6000 skyway adapter Macintosh monochrome and
color displays MIPS monochrome and color displays
...
```

You need to find out what sort of display hardware you have, and then find out whether it is supported for your platform. If you don't know what type of display is installed on your system, some operating systems provide a command that might help. For example, SunOS has the *dmesg* command, which reports system diagnostics. Among these diagnostics is a line reporting what sort of display hardware was installed at boot time.

```
% /etc/dmesg
...
cgthree0 at SBus slot 2 0x0 pri 7
...
```

cgthree0 is a color frame buffer. As the boot messages may get lost with time, you could also reboot the system and watch it during the auto-config phase where it looks for each attached device.

The manual pages for the X server should contain descriptions of supported graphics hardware.* They are located in subdirectories of the server source code. A quick way to find them is:

```
% find mit/server -name '*.man' -print
mit/server/ddx/macII/XmacII.man
mit/server/ddx/sun/constype.man
mit/server/ddx/sun/Xsun.man
mit/server/ddx/sun/kbd_mode.man
mit/server/ddx/dec/qvss/Xqvss.man
mit/server/ddx/dec/qdss/Xqdss.man
mit/server/ddx/dec/ws/Xdec.man
mit/server/ddx/mips/Xmips.man
mit/server/ddx/x386/X386.man
...
```

The manual page for *Xsun* lists the *cgthree* as a supported display:

```
/dev/cgthree0
        This color display is available on both the  Sun386i
        and SPARCstation 1 platforms.
```

You may also find some information in *README* files in the server source directory:

```
% find mit/server -name README -print
mit/server/ddx/ibm/README
mit/server/ddx/macII/README
mit/server/ddx/sun/README
mit/server/ddx/omron/README
```

---

*If you have the MIT documentation, hardcopy of the server manpages are included in it. They are also in present in the document *mit/hardcopy/man/man.PS.Z*.

```
mit/server/ddx/cfb/README
mit/server/ddx/x386/README
mit/server/ddx/x386/cfb.banked/README
```

The *cgthree* is mentioned in *mit/server/ddx/sun/README*:

```
    ...
Sun/2 bw2 cg2/3/5
Sun/3 bw2 cg2/3/4/5
SPARCstation cg3/6
    ...
```

From this information, you can determine that the Sun server supports the *cgthree* frame buffer that you have installed on your system.

If your platform is supported and a server exists for your display hardware, then you're home free.

8.2.3 Applying OS Patches

You should make sure your OS has the latest patches, as the MIT X distribution may rely on a patch being in place in order for it to work properly. This is especially true for security and compiler patches, as X relies on *setuid* programs and also tends to expose weaknesses in compilers during the build process.

The mechanism for obtaining OS patches varies depending on the vendor, but it usually involves a support contract or calling for technical support. Some vendors make their OS patches available on the Internet or from mail servers.

8.2.4 Applying X Patches

Before continuing with the build, you should verify that you're using the latest version of the MIT source and have all official MIT "fixes," or patches, applied. Some patches may affect installation or close security holes, so it's always a good idea to install the latest patch.

If you obtained the sources from a reputable location and they appear to be unmodified, try looking at the file *mit/bug-report*. There should be a line resembling:

```
R5, patch-level-0
```

"patch-level-0" indicates that no official patches have yet been applied. The patch-level number is incremented as each patch (or "fix") is applied.

You should go back to wherever you obtained the MIT source for the available patches. If you got the source from *export.lcs.mit.edu*, the patches are in the */pub/R5/fixes* directory. The contents of this directory are:

```
fix-01      fix-05      fix-09      fix-13      sunGX.uu
fix-02      fix-06      fix-10      fix-14
fix-03      fix-07      fix-11      fix-15
fix-04      fix-08      fix-12      fix-16
```

There are 16 patches available for R5 at the time of this writing.*

The fixes are small enough to be sent through mail and are available through a mail archive server. See Section A.3 for information on getting a patch through the mail.

Patches are applied using the *patch* program. If *patch* isn't already installed on your system, the source for this program is available in the *mit/util/patch* directory.

The top of each patch file describes how to use the *patch* program to install the patch, for example:

```
Release 5 Public Patch #1
MIT X Consortium

This patch comes in two parts: this file, and the file "sunGX.uu".
(If you obtained this patch via the xstuff mail daemon, and you
do not have "sunGX.uu", get it with the request "send fixes
sunGX.uu".)

To apply this patch:

cd to the top of the source tree (to the directory containing the
"mit" and "contrib" subdirectories) and do:
 patch -p -s < ThisFile
Patch will work silently unless an error occurs. You will likely
get two warning messages, which can be ignored:
 mkdir: mit: File exists
 mkdir: mit/hardcopy: File exists
If you want to watch patch do its thing, leave out the "-s"
argument to patch.

Next, from the same top-level directory do:
uudecode sunGX.uu
rm -f mit/server/ddx/sun/sunGX.o.dist
uncompress mit/server/ddx/sun/sunGX.o.dist
    . . .
```

This example assumes you created a directory for patches called *fixes* in the *mit/* directory. Apply the first patch (*fix-01*) simply by following directions:

```
% ls mit/fixes
fix-01      fix-05      fix-09      fix-13      sunGX.uu
fix-02      fix-06      fix-10      fix-14
fix-03      fix-07      fix-11      fix-15
fix-04      fix-08      fix-12      fix-16
% patch -p -s < mit/fixes/fix-01
mkdir: mit: File exists
mkdir: mit/hardcopy: File exists
% uudecode mit/fixes/sunGX.uu
% rm -f mit/server/ddx/sun/sunGX.o.dist
% uncompress mit/server/ddx/sun/sunGX.o.dist
```

(As mentioned in the instructions, the *mkdir* errors can be ignored.)

---

*The *sunGX.uu* file is a replacement object file for the Sun GX graphics accelerator. The *.uu* extension indicates that it is a binary file that has been converted to ASCII text by the *uuencode* program. This makes it possible to send a binary file through the mail. When the *sunGX.uu* file has been copied to your system, run the *uudecode* program on it to recreate the binary file.

Make sure you follow the directions and pay careful attention to the ordering of the patches. When you have exhausted all the available patches, the "patch-level" number will be incremented to the number of the last patch.

If you get an error message such as:

```
reversed (or previously applied) patch detected!  Assume -R? [y]
```

then abort the *patch* program, as it is likely that you are applying the patches in the wrong order or are applying the same patch twice.

Patches to *contrib* software are applied in a fashion similar to the *core* patches, but they are organized by specific packages. If you obtain them from the host *export.lcs.mit.edu*, they are in the directory */pub/R5/contrib-fixes*.

8.2.5 Creating a Link Tree (Optional)

One method of managing the X source distribution is to create a "link tree" of the MIT source code. The directory structure is the same as the original MIT distribution, but the files in the directories are symbolic links back to the original files. If the X distribution is built within the link tree, the object files and libraries will reside in the copy, not in the original. Using link trees makes it possible to build any number of different sets of binaries from one set of source code files. This makes it very easy to maintain a group of binaries for different platforms. It also conserves disk space, as the symbolic links will take up less space than a copy of the source files. If you are going to build the distribution only once, however, you may not want to use a link tree, since it complicates the directory structure and uses up disk space when creating links.

Link trees may be the only way to effectively use read-only copies of the X source, such as those mounted from a CD/ROM.

For example, the source area could look like:

```
% ls -F
mit/            rs_aix31/       sun3_411/
pmax_ul42/      sgi_40/         sun4_411/
```

The *rs_aix31*, *sun3_411*, *pmax_ul42*, *sgi_40*, and *sun4_411* directories* are link trees that are linked back to the *mit* directory. MIT supplies a shell script called *lndir* that creates the tree for you. You can find *lndir* in the source distribution as *mit/util/scripts/lndir.sh*.

---

*The example directory names are borrowed from AFS. They are intended to describe a platform and the version of the operating system. For example, *sun4_411* indicates a Sun4 running SunOS 4.1.1.

To build a link tree:

1. Install the *lndir* program:

   ```
   # cp mit/util/scripts/lndir.sh /usr/local/bin/lndir
   # rehash
   ```

2. Create a directory for the tree to reside in:

   ```
   # mkdir sun4_411
   ```

3. *cd* into the new directory:

   ```
   # cd sun4_411
   ```

4. Run the *lndir* program, supplying the relative path of the original source tree:

   ```
   # lndir ../mit
   config:
   extensions:
   include:
   PEX:
   lib:
   xinput:
     ...
   ```

When *lndir* finishes, you will be left with a usable copy of the X source tree.

8.3 Simplest Case Build

If you have confirmed that you have adequate disk space, have applied all the available patches, and are working on a supported platform, then you may be able to install the X *core* software quickly and painlessly.

This example uses the Sun4 running SunOS 4.1.1, as it is one of the most trouble-free builds. If you want to build X using all default settings, change directories to the top of the distribution (usually *mit/*) and type:

```
% make World >& world.log
```

If you would like to monitor the progress of the build, use the *tail* program on the log file:

```
% tail -f world.log
```

The build will probably take several hours on even the fastest machines.

When the *make* is complete, check for errors; any build problems should be reported in the file *world.log*.* Examine the file for the messages "not made because of" or "Error." You can the *grep* program to search for the ":", as it is commonly present in error messages:

```
% grep ":" world.log
Sun Jun  7 23:12:09 PDT 1992
```

---

*Be careful to search the entire file for errors, as it may still have the message "Full build of Release 5 of the X Window System complete." at the end even if there were problems with the build. This is because the *make World* target invokes *make* with the *–k* option, telling it to ignore non-fatal errors.

```
make: Fatal error: Command failed for target `subdirMakefiles'
make: Fatal error: Command failed for target `Makefiles'
make: Fatal error: Command failed for target `World'
make: Fatal error: Command failed for target `World'
```

If there are no errors, the next step is to install the distribution. In this example, we use the default installation pathnames—see Section 8.5.1.2 for information on how to change the default pathnames.

If you want to install X as an unprivileged user, you will need write permission to */usr/lib*, */usr/bin*, */usr/include*, */usr/man/man3*, and */usr/man/mann*. It is probably easier to install X as **root**, instead of touching up permissions after the installation is completed. (The permissions for the installed files are very important to the security of the X distribution.)

Become the superuser:

```
% su
Password:
```

Install the distribution:*

```
# make install >& install.log
```

Install the manual pages (if desired):

```
# make install.man >& man.log
```

If there are no errors at this point, X should be installed and usable. Any remaining administration work would involve customizing the installed files for your site. For example, you may want to configure the X Display Manager. If so, see Chapter 3 for more information.

8.4 Host Problems

There are some problems that can disturb even the default X build. These problems have more to do with the host configuration than with the X installation itself; that is, problems with disk space, shared libraries, or NFS.

8.4.1 Disk Space

There are several stages in the build process that can consume large amounts of disk space.

Optimization options

        The *–O* flag to the C compiler turns on *optimization* and can generate very large temporary files. These files are usually written to */tmp*.

---

*Note that the *install* process will write to the source area in some cases. One example of this occurs when installing the *xterm* binary for the Sun platform, as the binary is re-linked to overcome a security problem with Sun shared libraries.

Debugging options

> The −*g* flag to the compiler tells it to include information in the object files to be used by a debugger. This can increase the size of the executable to five or more times the size of an object compiled without the −*g* flag, depending on the compiler used.

Library creation

> The *ar* command builds libraries and may generate large temporary files, usually written to */tmp*. The `HasLargeTmp` configuration flag controls the location of the temporary file when the library for PEX (the PHIGS Extension to X) is created. If `HasLargeTmp` is set to YES, the */tmp* directory is used; if set to NO, *ar* will use the current directory to store the temporary file. You can also choose not to build the PEX library by setting the `BuildPex` flag to NO—see Section 8.5.1 on build flags).

Since most of the temporary files are stored in the */tmp* directory, you need to have anywhere from 10 to 20 megabytes free in */tmp*. If this is not possible, most compilers and archivers allow alternate directories to be specified. To find out how to redefine which directory to use for temporary files on your system, see the manual pages for the C preprocessor (usually named *cpp*), the C compiler (usually *cc*), the *ranlib* command, and the *ar* command.*

8.4.1.1 Changing the tmp Directory Using TMPDIR (Ultrix and HP-UX)

On some systems, the *ar* command checks if the environment variable TMPDIR is set. If so, *ar* uses the specified directory as an alternate location for temporary files. You might set TMPDIR if you ran out of disk space. For example, if the *make* produces the following errors:

```
ar rul libphigs.a archive/ar*.o c_binding/cb*.o cp/cp*.o cp/psl.o
css/
css*.o error/
er*.o input/sin*.o pex/pex*.o util/ut*.o ws/ws*.o ws_type/wstx*.o
ranlib libphigs.a
/usr/bin/ranlib: 13832 Memory fault - core dumped*** Error code 139
*** Error code 1
Stop.
*** Error code 1
Stop.
*** Error code 1
Stop.
```

The *ranlib* program has run out of disk space and has died. You can set TMPDIR and start the build process again:

```
% setenv TMPDIR .
```

This tells *ar* to create temporary files in the directory from which the *ar* command is invoked, instead of in */tmp*.

---

*On some systems, the *ranlib* command will be just a shell script that calls *ar* or it will not be present at all. This would be true for systems such as the SGI Iris, DecStation, and MIPS machines which use the MIPS compiler suite.

8.4.1.2 Changing the tmp Directory Using -temp (SunOS)

On some systems, the C compiler accepts the *–temp=* flag to specify an alternate directory for temporary compiler files. The optimizing pass of the compiler will sometimes create large files, causing an error such as:

```
compiler(iropt) error: write_irfile: No space left on device
*** Error code 1
Stop.
*** Error code 1
Stop.
*** Error code 1
Stop.
```

Call *cc* with the *–temp=* flag to redefine where temporary files are placed:

```
% cc -O -temp=/mondo -c foo.c
```

If you want this flag to be used when building the entire X distribution, it will have to be added to the platform configuration file (e.g., *sun.cf*) for it to show up in every Makefile. See Section 8.5.2 for an example of configuring your platform configuration file to use the *–temp=* flag.

8.4.2 Shared Library Installation (SunOS)

Under SunOS, the location of shared libraries is stored in a cache file called */etc/ld.so.cache*. The cache file needs to be rebuilt whenever a shared library is added to the system. The X distribution adds several shared libraries, and most clients cannot run until the cache is updated. Clients will report an error message such as:

```
ld.so: libX11.so.5: not found
```

Running the *ldconfig* command (as **root**) should fix this:

```
# ldconfig
```

(Rebooting the system would also work, since *ldconfig* is run from */etc/rc.local* at boot time.)

If the X binaries are intended to be NFS-mounted and executed on diskless workstations, you need to repeat the process on each of the remote machines. Since each host has its own private */etc/ld.so.cache* file, the *ldconfig* command has to be run on each of the diskless workstations. To simplify this process, you can use the *rdist* program, or even use a simple shell script. The following is an example using the C shell:

```
# foreach I (host1 host2 host3 host4)
? rsh $I ldconfig
? end
```

(This example depends on each of the remote workstations having the fileserver listed in */.rhosts*)

8.4.3 NFS Installation

You may choose to install X on a filesystem that is NFS-mounted from another host. You'll have problems installing X if the NFS-mounted filesystem does not allow **root** access over the NFS link. For security reasons, it's a bad idea to allow remote **root** users to write to your filesystem, but you can add **root** access temporarily to allow you to build X.

For **root** to be able to write to an NFS-mounted partition, you need an entry for the local system in the */etc/exports* file on the remote system.* For example, to give temporary **root** permission for the */usr* directory to the host named *rock*, you could change the following line in */etc/exports*:

```
/usr -access=rock
```

to:

```
/usr -root=rock,access=rock
```

On systems with the newer version of NFS, run the *exportfs* command to make this take effect:

```
rubble# exportfs -v /usr
re-exported /usr
```

Back on the local host, the installation can proceed from this point as if it was taking place on a local filesystem. Build X on *rock*:

```
% make world >& world.log
    . . .
```

When the installation is complete, the entry in */etc/exports* should be changed back to what it was and then re-exported with the *exportfs* command:

```
rubble# exportfs -v /usr
re-exported /usr
```

8.4.3.1 NFS Installation Without Root Access

An alternative to giving temporary NFS **root** access to the remote directory is to install the distribution as an unprivileged user and change the ownership of the files later. The problem with this approach is that it opens the system to attack during the installation, so it should be avoided if possible.

For this example, the ownership of the target directories is changed just long enough for the installation to take place. The permissions are then touched up as **root**. As in the previous example, the host that has the compiled X source on it is named *rock* and the host that NFS-mounts the *rock* partition is named *rubble*.

---

*If you have an older version of NFS, the */etc/exports* entries are simply the filesystem names followed by the hosts which have access. Changes to the file will have an immediate effect. This is in contrast to the current system, which uses the *exportfs* command to notify the system of changes in the */etc/exports* file and supplies different levels of permissions.

1. Become the superuser on *rubble*:

   ```
   rubble% su
   Password:
   ```

2. Create any directories you need that do not exist:

   ```
   rubble# mkdir /usr/bin/X11 /usr/lib/X11 /usr/include/X11
   ```

3. Change ownership of the top level installation directories to your user ID (*eap*, in this example). *Note that someone breaking into your account would also be able modify the system areas while they are writable by you.*

   ```
   rubble# chown eap /usr/bin/X11 /usr/lib/X11 /usr/include/X11 \
   /usr/lib /usr/man/man3 /usr/man/mann
   ```

4. Now complete the installation under your own account on *rock*. Install the distribution from the NFS-mounted partition:

   ```
   rock% make install >& install.log
   ```

   Install the manpages if you want them:

   ```
   rock% make install.man >& man.log
   ```

5. Back on *rubble*, change the ownership back to **root** and group **wheel**:*

   ```
   rubble# chown -R root.wheel /usr/bin/X11 /usr/lib/X11 \
   /usr/include/X11 /usr/man/man3 /usr/man/mann
   ```

   The *–R* flag recursively *chown*s all files in subdirectories. If the *chown* command on your system does not support the *–R* option, you could use the *find* command instead:

   ```
   rubble# find /usr/bin/X11 /usr/lib/X11 -exec chown root.wheel {} \;
   rubble# find /usr/include/X11 -exec chown root.wheel {} \;
   rubble# find /usr/man/man3 /usr/man/mann -exec chown root.wheel {} \;
   ```

6. Change ownership for only the top-level directory of */usr/lib*, as this maintains ownership information on the many non-X11 files within this directory:

   ```
   rubble# chown root /usr/lib
   ```

7. Now fix permissions for the *xterm* and *xload* clients.

   ```
   rubble# chmod 4755 /usr/bin/X11/xterm
   rubble# chgrp kmem /usr/bin/X11/xload
   rubble# chmod 2755 /usr/bin/X11/xload
   ```

   (*xterm* needs to be installed *setuid* **root**. *xload* needs to be *setgid* group **kmem**, as */dev/kmem* is readable only by the **kmem** group.)

---

*If your version of *chown* does not support the *user.group* syntax, use *chown* for the user and *chgrp* for the group.

Under SunOS, you will also need to rebuild the shared library cache, as described in Section 8.4.2:

```
rubble# ldconfig
```

8.4.3.2 Installation Over the Network (rdist)

A software distribution mechanism such as *rdist* may also be used to install X, but it will require at least one complete installation to be in place before it can be distributed to other hosts. To use *rdist*, a "master" copy is created on one host, and then *rdist* is used to duplicate it on other hosts.

rdist commands can be supplied on the command line or in a command file called a *Distfile*. A sample *Distfile* might look like this:

```
HOSTS = ( rubble )
FILES = ( /usr/lib/lib*X* /usr/lib/libphigs.a /usr/bin/X11
          /usr/lib/X11 /usr/include/X11 /usr/man/mann /usr/man/man3)

${FILES} -> ${HOSTS}
 install ;
 notify root@rubble ;
```

This *Distfile* copies an X distribution over to a host named *rubble*. The *notify* keyword sends mail describing what files have been installed. This is handy if you run the command regularly to keep the X distribution updated.

The *Distfile* can executed with the following command line:

```
source# rdist -f Distfile
updating rubble
```

For a network of Sun workstations, you can also use the *special* command within the *Distfile* to run the *ldconfig* command on the remote host whenever a new shared library is copied over:

```
special /usr/lib/lib*X*.so.* /usr/etc/ldconfig ;
```

See the manual page for *rdist* for more information.

8.4.4 Installing the termcap or terminfo Definition for xterm

The *xterm* program works best with the *xterm* terminal definition supplied in the *mit/clients/xterm* directory. If *xterm* does not work properly, or is missing altogether, you may need to install the terminal definition. For example, the following is an error caused by a missing description for *xterm* when you log in and your *.login* script tries to set the terminal type using *tset*:

```
% telnet crufty
Trying 140.186.64.3 ...
Connected to crufty.ora.com.
Escape character is '^]'.

login: eap
```

```
Password:

TERM=(xterm)
Type xterm unknown
TERM=(unknown)
```

You might also get error messages when you try using your favorite editor:

```
% vi foo
xterm: Unknown terminal type
I don't know what kind of terminal you are on - all I have is 'xterm'.
[Using open mode]
"foo" [Read only] 3564 lines, 133099 characters

:q!
% emacs foo
emacs: Terminal type xterm is not defined.
```

You could use *vt102* as a temporary value until you are able to install the *xterm* entry.

```
% setenv TERM vt102
```

The terminal definition for systems using **termcap** can be installed simply by inserting the contents of the file called *mit/clients/xterm/termcap* into the */etc/termcap* file on your system. It's a good idea to insert the **termcap** definition before any other definitions, since *xterm* is likely to be used frequently.

The **terminfo** definition can be installed by using the **terminfo** compiler, *tic*. For example:

```
# tic mit/clients/xterm/terminfo
```

(Note that you must be **root** for this to succeed.)

The **terminfo** definition is placed in */usr/lib/terminfo/x/xterm*.

See the Nutshell Handbook *termcap and terminfo* (O'Reilly & Associates, 1991) for more information on the **termcap** and **terminfo** terminal databases.

8.5 Simple Configuration

If you are not satisfied with the default configuration, you can change some simple configuration parameters, as described in this section. These parameters need to be configured before the build is begun.

The files used to configure the X compilation and installation reside in the directory *mit/config*. The syntax within these files should look familiar if you have used the C preprocessor (*cpp*) before. If you are not familiar with C preprocessor syntax, you should still be able to do the right thing by looking at other examples within the configuration files. Section 8.7 gives some more background on *imake* syntax; for most configurations, you can probably figure it out on your own.

You need to modify two files that will affect the build process: *site.def*, which defines parameters for your particular site, and a platform-specific file (e.g., *sun.cf*) which defines parameters for your particular platform.

A list of systems and their corresponding *.cf* files can be found in the *mit*/*RELNOTES.TXT* file, under the section "3.2.1 The vendor.cf file." Find the appropriate ***platform**.cf* file from this table:

```
    ...
AIX ibm.cf
AOS ibm.cf
AT&T Unix SVR4.2 att.cf
A/UX macII.cf
BSD bsd.cf
ConvexOS convex.cf
DG/UX DGUX.cf
    ...
```

Before you modify any of these files, make a backup copy. (You should probably choose some extension other than *.bak* or *.orig*, as these extensions have special significance to other programs.)

```
% cd mit/config
% cp sun.cf sun.cf.keep
% cp site.def site.def.keep
```

You could also use a revision control system, such as RCS or SCCS.

You may also have to give yourself write permission to the files:

```
% chmod u+w sun.cf site.def
```

8.5.1 Configuration Parameters

There are many configuration parameters that you can modify. Only a subset of those available are described here, as there are many special-purpose flags. The complete list is in *mit*/*config*/*README*.

8.5.1.1 site.def

The *site.def* file defines configuration parameters to be used for your entire site. Your site may include more than one type of platform or operating system; the *site.def* file is consulted regardless of the platform type, whereas the ***platform**.cf* file is looked at only when building on a particular platform.

An unmodified *site.def* looks like this:

```
#ifdef BeforeVendorCF

/* #define HasGcc YES */

#endif /* BeforeVendorCF */

#ifdef AfterVendorCF

/*
#ifdef ProjectRoot
#undef ProjectRoot
#endif
```

```
#define ProjectRoot /usr/X11R5
*/

#endif /* AfterVendorCF */
```

There are two sections to the *site.def* file. The first is delimited by the *BeforeVendorCF* conditional and the second by *AfterVendorCF*. As you might guess, the first section contains any flags that should be set before the ***platform**.cf* file is read, and the second section has flags that should be set afterwards.

(Note that the section containing the `ProjectRoot` flag is commented out with the `/*` and `*/` characters. The `ProjectRoot` flag is discussed in Section 8.5.1.2.)

A modified *site.def* might look something like this:

```
#ifdef BeforeVendorCF

/* #define HasGcc YES */

#endif /* BeforeVendorCF */

#ifdef AfterVendorCF

/*
#ifdef ProjectRoot
#undef ProjectRoot
#endif
#define ProjectRoot /usr/X11R5
*/
#define InstallXdmConfig YES
#define InstallXinitConfig YES
#define InstallFSConfig YES
#define StripInstalledPrograms YES
#define HasXdmAuth YES
#define ExpandManNames YES

#endif /* AfterVendorCF */
```

(You should consult the version of *config/README* that comes with your release, as many of the flags are release-specific.)

You might want to modify one or more of the following flags:

`InstallXdmConfig`
> By default, the configuration files for the *xdm* program are not installed. By setting `InstallXdmConfig` to YES, the *xdm* configuration files are installed in */usr/lib/X11/xdm/*.
>
> *Warning:* If you have files in */usr/lib/X11/xdm/* that you have already configured, copy them to a safe place before starting the installation. Enabling this flag will overwrite files that you may have customized.

`InstallXinitConfig`
> By default, the configuration files for the *xinit* program are not installed. By setting `InstallXinitConfig` to YES, they will be copied to */usr/lib/X11/xinit/*. These files are used by the *startx* front end to *xinit*.
>
> (The same warning for `InstallXdmConfig` applies here as well.)

InstallFSConfig

 The font server configuration files are not installed unless this flag is set to YES.

StripInstalledPrograms

 Setting this flag to YES will strip binaries as they are installed. The usual reason for doing this is to save disk space: removing the symbol table from the binary will reduce its size. It will be difficult to debug any run-time problem if the programs are stripped, but this is not a concern to most X users.

HasXdmAuth

 This flag indicates that the XDMCP library should include DES code. DES, or Data Encryption Standard, is an encryption scheme used in the authorization process. There are restrictions on exporting DES outside the United States. This flag must be on if you want to use the XDM-AUTHORIZATION-1 method of server access control. See Section 4.3 for more information.

ExpandManNames

 Some operating systems have restrictions on filename length. To deal with this problem, the manual pages for X library functions have their names shortened to 14 characters. If your operating system does not have this problem, the manual page filename can be expanded to its full name (for example, *XTranWCo.3* is expanded to *XTranslateCoordinates.3*).

HasLargeTmp

 This flag indicates that you have enough disk space in */tmp* for the *ar* command to create its temporary file. Setting this parameter to NO instructs *ar* to use the current directory.

InstallLibManPages

 There are two sections of manpages: client manpages and library function manpages. If this flag is set to NO, it prevents the library manual pages from being installed with the *make install.man* command. This flag is set to YES by default. You might set it to NO if no one at your site intends to program in X and if disk space is low. (The library manpages consume approximately 2 megabytes of disk space.)

8.5.1.2 The ProjectRoot Flag

The ProjectRoot flag defines the "root" directory for the build. It is not used in the example *site.def* file, but can be easily enabled by removing the C comments surrounding this section:

```
#ifdef ProjectRoot
#undef ProjectRoot
#endif
#define ProjectRoot /usr/X11R5
```

If ProjectRoot is already defined, it is first undefined. (The reason for this test is that some of the ***platform**.cf* files define ProjectRoot by default. The C preprocessor will complain if a flag is defined twice.)

The typical use of this flag is to install X in a non-standard location. You might do this for one of the following reasons:

- You may need to have more than one release installed at one time. You could have X11R3 under */usr/X11R3*, X11R4 under */usr/X11R4*, and X11R5 under */usr/X11R5*. This may be useful for migrating an application from one release to another. As it is much easier to install R5 in "non-standard" location than previous releases, you may wish keep a pre-R5 release in the default location and move R5.

- The release of X that you are installing does not include a server and you wish to leave the current X installation undisturbed. An example of this would be the SGI Indigo, as no R5 server exists for this platform, but the R5 libraries and clients are useful.

The directory specified in `ProjectRoot` becomes the root of the new installation, with the normal directories underneath it. If it is set to */usr/X11R5*, this would be:

New Name	Default Name	Contents
/usr/X11R5/bin	*/usr/bin/X11*	Binaries
/usr/X11R5/lib	*/usr/lib*	Libraries
/usr/X11R5/lib/X11	*/usr/lib/X11*	Fonts and support files
/usr/X11R5/include/X11	*/usr/include/X11*	Header files

8.5.1.3 The Platform Configuration File (platform.cf)

The platform-specific configuration file contains information specific to a certain platform or type of machine. It changes the default behavior of *imake*, as *imake* will make assumptions unless told otherwise.* An example ***platform**.cf* file is *sun.cf* for Sun platforms, or *sgi.cf* for Silicon Graphics platforms.

There may be other subtypes within the platform. For example, Sun3, Sun4, and Sun386i machines are all described within the *sun.cf* file. A file of this type should be all you need to add when porting the X distribution to a new platform (other than new server code!).

Even though the platform has been narrowed down to a specific machine, there are still variables that could affect the installation process. These are:

- **Operating system version.** There are flags to describe the release of the OS you are running. You must change these flags if you are trying to building a version other than the one described in the MIT-supplied release notes.

  ```
  #define OSName          SunOS 4.1.2
  #define OSMajorVersion  4
  #define OSMinorVersion  1
  ```

---

*The *imake* process would happily construct an Imakefile using a generic system. In fact, if you ever see that the *generic.cf* has been used by *imake*, something has gone wrong.

Any "features" specific to a release can be handled with conditional statements:

```
#if OSMajorVersion < 4 || (OSMajorVersion == 4 && OSMinorVersion < 1)
#define BootstrapCFlags    -DNOSTDHDRS
#define StandardDefines    -DNOSTDHDRS
#endif
```

- **Operating system-specific features.** There may be common software features missing on your vendor's release. Flags are provided to indicate their presence or absence:

```
  ...
#define HasVoidSignalReturn            NO
#define SetTtyGroup                    YES
#define UnalignedReferencesAllowed     NO
#define HasBsearch                     NO
  ...
```

- **Build options.** There are defaults for building the distribution on the optimal platform (or the one they had handy at MIT).

```
#define XsunServer       YES      /* has color and mono support */
#define XsunMonoServer   YES      /* monochrome only */
```

- **Hardware options.** You may have different graphics hardware or a floating-point chip that requires special treatment. In this example, the Sun3 (mc68000) processor has the mc68881 floating-point chip, but the Sun compiler does not use it by default.

```
#ifdef mc68000
#define DefaultCCOptions -f68881 -pipe
#else
#define DefaultCCOptions -pipe
#endif
```

The *–f68881* flag is meaningless on the *sun4* platform, requiring the test for a *sun3* (mc68000) platform.

You may wish to change the following flags in the ***platform**.cf* file:

OSName   This is full name of the operating system release. For example:

> SunOS 4.1.1

OSMajorVersion

> The "major" version number for the OS release (the number in front of the decimal). The version flags should reflect the current system, as they will be tested for later on in the ***platform**.cf* file. For example:

```
#if OSMinorVersion >= 1
#define HasBsearch                 YES
#else
#define HasBsearch                 NO
#endif
```

OSMinorVersion

> The "minor" version number.

`OSTeenyVersion`

A more precise version number for patch releases of the OS.

`BuildServer`

This flag controls whether the server should be built along with the rest of the X distribution. It is set to YES if the server exists; if a server doesn't exist for your platform, it is set to NO. You can also set it to NO if you don't want to build a server for some reason—for example, for the IBM RS/6000, the MIT server runs only on the *Skyway* display adaptor. If you do not have this particular board, you should set the `BuildServer` flag to NO.

Server Options

Look for any server specific options. This could include monochrome and color versions, as in:

```
#define XmfbpmaxServer NO
#define XcfbpmaxServer YES
```

8.5.2 Configuration Example 1

For this example, a Sun with limited available space in */tmp* is being used. The *–temp=* flag is needed to specify an alternate directory for the temporary files from the compiler. See Section 8.4.1.2 for more information on the *–temp=* flag.

The *–temp=* flag needs to be supplied on every *cc* command line used in the X build. This means that it needs to make it into every *Makefile* used in the X distribution. You can accomplish this by editing the `DefaultCCOptions` parameter in the *sun.cf* file. (Being a very system-specific flag, this parameter is specified in the **platform**.*cf* file, not in the *site.def* file.) The *README* file in the *mit/config/* directory describes all of the configuration parameters, including `DefaultCCOptions`:

```
DefaultCCOptions                default special C compiler options
```

In *sun.cf*, `DefaultCCOptions` is currently specified with the following lines:

```
#ifdef mc68000
#define DefaultCCOptions -f68881 -pipe
#else
#define DefaultCCOptions -pipe
#endif
```

(The test for *mc68000* is to add the flag for the *mc68881* floating-point chip, available only on the *sun3* platform.)

If you enough space in the area where you are building X, set the *–temp=* flag to the current directory ("."). The C compiler will then use whatever directory it is invoked in for temporary files:

```
#ifdef mc68000
#define DefaultCCOptions -f68881 -pipe -temp=.
#else
#define DefaultCCOptions -pipe -temp=.
#endif
```

8.5.3 Configuration Example 2

In this example, the *ibm.cf* file is modified to overcome a permissions problem in AIX 3.1 on the *RS/6000* platform. The problem arises when the *make install* command is issued. The *chown* program is executable only by **root**.* If you want to install X as an unprivileged user, this will cause the */usr/ucb/install* program to fail with the following error:

```
/usr/ucb/install: /bin/chown: cannot execute
```

The section of interest in the unmodified *ibm.cf* is the one specific to the *RS/6000*. (AIX runs on several different platforms, including the *PS/2*, *RT*, and *370* systems.) The section we want is surrounded by the test for RsArchitecture:

```
...
#ifdef RsArchitecture
...
#define OPERATING_SYSTEM AIX
#define InstallCmd /usr/ucb/install
#include <ibmLib.rules>
#else
...
```

Redefine the InstallCmd parameter to the *install.sh* shell script that comes with the R5 release in the *mit/util/scripts* directory (the variable SCRIPTSRC is set to this).

```
#ifdef RsArchitecture
...
#define OPERATING_SYSTEM AIX
#define InstallCmd sh $(SCRIPTSRC)/install.sh
#include <ibmLib.rules>
#else
```

Since attempting to run the */bin/chown* command will result in an error, the program run by the *install.sh* script should be redefined to something harmless. All the program definitions are at the top of the *install.sh* script:

```
# put in absolute paths if you don't have them in your path; or
#use env. vars.

mvprog="${MVPROG:-mv}"
cpprog="${CPPROG:-cp}"
chmodprog="${CHMODPROG:-chmod}"
chownprog="${CHOWNPROG:-chown}"
chgrpprog="${CHGRPPROG:-chgrp}"
stripprog="${STRIPPROG:-strip}"
rmprog="${RMPROG:-rm}"
```

You can just reset the CHOWNPROG environment variable to the */bin/true* script, since all it does is return a good exit status.

```
% setenv CHOWNPROG /bin/true
```

---

* *chown* returns an error if run by an unprivileged user on other systems, but on AIX 3.1 the executable has permissions -r-x------, so that it can't be executed by others even long enough to get an error message.

The *install.sh* program should then work when running *make install* as an unprivileged user:

```
% make install >& install.log
```

Since *chown* hasn't been run on any files, you will have to *chown* them later as **root**. See Section 8.4.3.1 for more information on touching up permissions after X is installed.

8.5.4 Configuration Example 3

If you are planning to add new fonts after installation, you may want to create a "local" directory that is always looked for by the X server. If this local directory is built into the X server, users will not have to manually modify the font path on the command line or in their start-up files.

To find the correct flag, take a look at the *config/README* file:

```
DefaultFontPath            default server font path
```

To find the current value, search the *config/Project.tmpl* file:

```
#define DefaultFontPath $(FONTDIR)/misc/,$(FONTDIR)/Speedo/,\
$(FONTDIR)/75dpi/,$(FONTDIR)/100dpi/
```

To override this definition, put your own version in *config/site.def*:

```
#define DefaultFontPath $(FONTDIR)/local,$(FONTDIR)/misc/,\
$(FONTDIR)/Speedo/,$(FONTDIR)/75dpi/,$(FONTDIR)/100dpi/
```

The X server will not start if one of the directories in the default font path is missing a *fonts.dir* file. The server will fail with the following error:

```
failed to set default font path '/usr/lib/X11/fonts/local,/usr/lib/X11/fo
nts/misc/,/usr/lib/X11/fonts/Speedo/,/usr/lib/X11/fonts/75dpi/,/usr/lib/X
11/fonts/100dpi/'
Fatal server error:
could not open default font 'fixed'
```

To prevent this, copy in a least one font into the font directory and run *mkfontdir*.

```
# mkdir /usr/lib/X11/fonts/local
# cd /usr/lib/X11/fonts/local
# cp ~eap/home/xtrek.pcf .
# mkfontdir
```

8.5.5 Configuration Example 4

It's a good idea to keep vendor-supplied software separate from "local" software, such as the MIT distribution. This will make software upgrades easier, as you are much less likely to overwrite local changes if they are confined to a discrete area.

The X distribution is already installed in discrete areas, but the manpages are generally installed directly into */usr/man*. You may want to install the manpages in */usr/local/man* instead. Most *man* commands will permit an alternate directory to be specified for searching by setting the MANPATH environment variable:

```
% setenv MANPATH /usr/man:/usr/local/man
```

The *man* command will then search each directory in the order they appear in the MANPATH.

By default, MIT X11 will install program manpages in */usr/man/mann* and library manpages in */usr/man/man3*. These values are defined in *config/Project.tmpl*. In this example, the suffix for client manpages is changed from "n" to "1", and the "root" of the man directory structure is changed from */usr/man* to */usr/local/man*. These should be specified in the *config/site.def* file:

```
#define ManSuffix 1
#define ManDirectoryRoot /usr/local/man
```

Program manpages will now go in */usr/local/man/man1*. Library manpages will go in */usr/local/man/man3*, where they are installed by default.

8.5.6 Configuration Example 5

If you know you will not be needing certain features of the distribution, you can suppress their compilation using Boolean flags. The names for most of these flags start with the string "Build":

```
% grep Build config/README | grep boolean
        BuildFontServer      boolean for building font server
        BuildFonts           boolean for building pcf fonts
        BuildPex             boolean for building all PEX-related code
        BuildPexClients      boolean for buildiing PEX clients/demos
        BuildPexExt          boolean for building PEX extension
        BuildServer          boolean for building X server
        BuildXInputExt       boolean for building X Input extension
        BuildXInputLib       boolean for building X Input library
```

These can be turned on or off in the *config/site.def* file:

```
#define BuildPex NO
#define BuildXInputExt NO
#define BuildXInputLib NO
```

First check the *config/platform.cf* file to see if their default value is changed for your specific platform. Modifying these values can save a lot of compilation time and disk space if you decide that you don't need to build a specific feature.

8.5.7 Other Build Flags

There are a number of compile-time flags that are not clearly documented in the release notes. They may be in a *Imakefile* or buried in the source code.

8.5.7.1 xterm Build Flags

mit/clients/xterm/Imakefile contains the following comment:

```
/*
 * add -DWTMP and -DLASTLOG if you want them; make sure that bcopy can
 * handle overlapping copies before using it.
 */
```

You may want to enable these flags if you want users who log into the system using *xterm* to be recorded in the *wtmp* file. They will then appear when the *last* command is used. Change the following line in *mit/clients/xterm/Imakefile* from:

```
MISC_DEFINES = /* -DALLOWLOGFILEEXEC */
```

to:

```
MISC_DEFINES = /* -DALLOWLOGFILEEXEC */ -DWTMP -DLASTLOG
```

8.6 Building Programs After X Is Installed

If you have people at your site who are going to be programming with X, you should supply them with the proper tools to do this. This usually means installing the libraries, header files, and configuration files in a public area in the same manner as other programming environments. Even if you choose non-standard locations for the X distribution, the *imake* program provides tools programmers can use without worrying about the location of the installed software.

Appendix B shows how to compile an X program after X is already installed.

8.6.1 xmkmf

The *xmkmf* program is a shell script front end to the *imake* program, supplied in X11R4 and X11R5. (See Section 8.7 for more information on *imake* itself.) It can be run in any directory than contains an Imakefile. This could be within a subdirectory of the X distribution source code or a program outside of it:

```
% xmkmf
mv Makefile Makefile.bak
imake -DUseInstalled -I/usr/lib/X11/config
```

It first makes a backup copy of any existing Makefile, as it will create a new one with the same name. It then invokes *imake* with the UseInstalled flag, which tells *imake* that the X distribution is installed and that it should use the header files and libraries on the system instead of expecting ones to be present in the X source tree. For example, in *config/Project.tmpl*:

```
#ifdef UseInstalled
#define PhigsInclude -I$(INCDIR)
#else
```

```
#define PhigsInclude -I$(BUILDINCDIR)
#endif
```

This sequence means "use the system include file area if `UseInstalled` is defined, otherwise use the *include* files in the source code for PHIGS."

If you set `ProjectRoot` before the build, *xmkmf* will use the new root directory. For example, if you set `ProjectRoot` in *site.def* before installation:

```
#ifdef ProjectRoot
#undef ProjectRoot
#endif
#define ProjectRoot /usr/X11R5
```

Running *xmkmf* would produce:

```
% xmkmf
mv Makefile Makefile.bak
imake -DUseInstalled -I/usr/X11R5/lib/X11/config
```

xmkmf uses the *–I* flag to tell *cpp* where to look for *include* files. The *include* files in this case are the *imake* configuration files. The default location for installing these files is */usr/lib/X11/config*. If you have your own private set of configuration files, you can invoke *imake* with a different *include* directory:

```
% imake -DUseInstalled -I/home/eap/myconfig
```

In R5, *xmkmf* also takes an *–a* flag, which executes the normal *make* targets automatically:

```
% xmkmf -a
mv Makefile Makefile.bak
imake -DUseInstalled -I/usr/lib/X11/config
make Makefiles
make includes
make depend
```

The `Makefiles` target will recursively build any Makefiles that may be present in subdirectories. The *includes* and *depend* targets are used to build a list of dependencies that are appended to the Makefile. These will force recompilation of the target if something related to the program changes elsewhere.

8.6.2 Include Files

Include or "header" files should be found automatically by the preprocessor, as they are stored in standard system directories, such as */usr/include*. Note that MIT supplied header files will have the *X11* directory already prepended to the name of the include file:

```
...
#include <X11/Shell.h>
...
```

or even a subdirectory within *X11*:

```
...
#include <X11/Xaw/Box.h>
...
```

cpp will interpret the complete path, for example, as */usr/include/X11/Xaw/Box.h*. If you wish to bury the *include* files in another subdirectory, you will still need to have the last directory named *X11*, as in */usr/X11R5/include/X11*. *cpp* would then be invoked with *−I/usr/X11R5/include*. You could also cheat and create a symbolic link from *X11* to the *include* file directory:

```
# ln -s X11 .
```

This would keep *cpp* happy when it looks for the files. It is often desirable to keep the MIT headers separate from the system headers, as this will keep them from being damaged during OS upgrades.

8.6.3 Libraries

The X libraries will usually be installed in */usr/lib*, but there are several reasons to install them in an alternate location. In any case, the Makefiles generated by *imake* should do the right thing if you configured the X distribution this way. Alternate library locations can be specified with the *−L* option. If you have `ProjectRoot` set to */usr/X11R5*, the X libraries will be in */usr/X11R5/lib*.

8.7 More About imake

This section describes the configuration process in more detail and may help if you encountered a problem with your X build.

imake is a project management tool that is used for building the X Window System from source code. This section describes *imake* in the context of building X11, but *imake* can be used for any large project that is going to be compiled on more than one type of platform. In particular, it is the tool of choice for public domain X programs that are distributed in source form. See Appendix B for more information on compiling public domain software.

imake uses a combination of *make* and the C preprocessor (*cpp*). A basic understanding of each is required to intelligently configure the X build process.

8.7.1 The make Program

The *make* program is the default UNIX tool for maintaining source code. It uses a configuration file called *Makefile* to describe each component of the source distribution, how each should be compiled, and how individual files relate to one another. It saves time and effort by automating common programming tasks. For example, if a header file has been modified, any program that uses it is recompiled, ensuring that everything is up to date.*

---

*See the Nutshell Handbook *Managing Projects with make* (O'Reilly & Associates, 1991) for more information on the *make* program.

The X11 distribution has been ported to many different platforms, with each one requiring its own particular flags and libraries to compile programs. For example, the Sun C compiler may require one set of flags:

```
cc -c -O -pic
```

While the MIPS C compiler needs a different set:

```
cc -O -prototypes -float -cckr  -Wf,-XNh2000
```

The usual way to handle this is to put all known options in a Makefile, and rely on the person compiling the program to figure out what options or flags should be enabled.

For example, a well-commented Makefile might read something like the following:

```
        ...
# Define the other compilation flags.
# Add -DBSD4_2 for 4.2bsd systems.
# Add -DSYSV for System V.
# Add -DSYSV -D__SVR3 for SCO ODT, ISC Unix 2.2 or before,
#   or any System III Unix, or System V release 3-or-older Unix.
# Add -DSVR4 (not -DSYSV) for System V release 4.
# XCFLAGS can be set from the command line.
CFLAGS=-O $(XCFLAGS)
        ...
```

This approach works fine for simple programs, but *make* is insufficient for maintaining the large number of libraries and clients that make up the X distribution. The X11 *core* distribution alone has several hundred Makefiles, and editing each one of these Makefiles by hand would be absurd.

Some large packages, such as TeX, use *make*'s ability to recursively invoke itself in subdirectories. *make* flags are passed down the directory structure by specifying the flag on the command line, with each Makefile inheriting the flag's value from the previous invocation of make. This is shown in Figure 8-3.

This approach works for flags, but complicated *make* commands must still be edited by hand in each Makefile.

Thus enters *imake*. The main function of *imake* is to "automatically" generate any number of Makefiles from one set of configuration files. It may help to call the *imake* program a "text filter," as all it really does is take a set of text files as input and create a text file as output. As input, *imake* uses a set of files in a configuration directory (such as */usr/lib/X11/config*) and a file in the current directory called *Imakefile*. As output, *imake* generates a Makefile.

8.7.2 The C Preprocessor

imake relies on the C preprocessor (usually named *cpp*). *cpp* provides a macro facility and conditional expressions. If you know how the C preprocessor works, then you have a good chance of understanding of how *imake* uses *cpp* syntax.

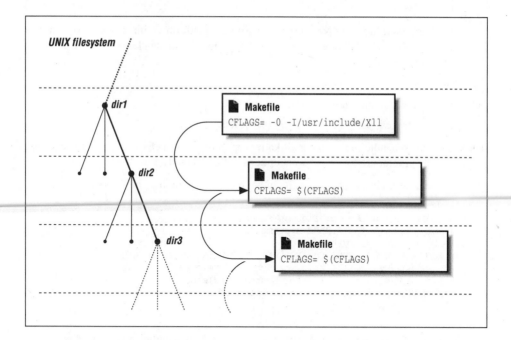

Figure 8-3. Recursive make

For a simple example of *cpp* syntax, examine the following lines:

```
#ifdef BSD
#define CCOPTS -DBSD
#endif /* BSD */
```

The `#ifdef` line, coupled with the `#endif` line, is an example of a *conditional*. These lines say that if the BSD variable is defined, then set the CCOPTS variable to "-DBSD." Similarly, you can use `#ifndef` to set up a negative conditional. For example:

```
...
#ifndef CppSedMagic
#define CppSedMagic sed -e '/^#  *[0-9][0-9]*  *.*$$/d' \
              -e '/^XCOMM$$/s//#/' \
              -e '/^XCOMM[^a-zA-Z0-9_]/s/^XCOMM/#/'
#endif /* CppSedMagic */
  ...
```

The lines between the `#ifndef` and `#endif` are executed only if the specified variable (CppSedMagic) is *not* currently defined. These lines say that if the CppSedMagic variable is not defined, then define CppSedMagic as instructed.

The second example also shows an example of a *macro*. Any subsequent occurrence of CppSedMagic is replaced by the multi-line *sed* expression.

This construction of defining a macro only if it isn't already defined is quite common: *cpp* will complain if you try to redefine something that is already defined.

8.7.3 Imake Syntax

cpp does not do anything except process text files: it cannot invoke other programs. *make* can actually do work, but it lacks the ability to test the value of a variable, making it inflexible. What *imake* does is combine the best features of *cpp* and *make*. The real value of *imake* is that it allows easy creation of Makefiles under changing conditions.

The syntax used by *imake* is based on syntax used by both *cpp* and *make*. When *cpp* and *make* syntax are inconsistent with one another (or when different versions of *cpp* are inconsistent with each other), *imake* needs to become the arbiter. This is most apparent when it comes to interpreting comments, defining multi-line macros, concatenating macros, and dealing with tabs.

8.7.3.1 Comments in imake

The *make* program expects comments to be preceded by the "#" character. The problem is that "#" indicates the start of a preprocessor directive (a *cpp* command) to *cpp*.

For example, if you had the following *make*-style comment in a file called *testfile*:

```
# All rights reserved.
```

If you run this file through the *cpp* program, you'll get an error message:

```
% /lib/cpp < testfile
# 1 ""
1: undefined control
```

cpp complains that it does not recognize whatever followed "#" as a valid *cpp* command.*

You may see C-language style comments in *imake* configuration files. For example:

```
/*
 * Concat - concatenates two strings.
 */
```

The "/**/" construction will work fine, but beware that the comment will be removed by the *cpp* program and never seen again. The comment will not appear in any *imake*-generated Makefiles. If you want your comments to appear in any Makefiles, you'll have to use an alternate comment mechanism:

- One way to protect the *make* comment from *cpp* is to put a "null" C-style comment in front of it:

  ```
  /**/# All rights reserved.
  ```

  cpp strips out the /**/ comments and passes the rest of the line to the Makefile untouched:

  ```
  % /lib/cpp < testfile
  # 1 ""
  # All rights reserved.
  ```

---

*Even worse, if the first string following the "#" *is* a valid *cpp* command (such as #if or #define), *cpp* will interpret it and generate a useless Makefile.

The *make* comment now survives its pass through *cpp*.

Now that ANSI C preprocessors are now becoming common, this can no longer be relied upon, as ANSI C will try to interpret even though it has a C comment in front of it.

- In R5, a *cpp*-proof comment prefix XCOMM is provided as a convenience. If you put the string XCOMM in front of comment text, *imake* will do the right thing with it. For example:

```
XCOMM All rights reserved.
```

Will generate into the resulting Makefile:

```
# All rights reserved.
```

8.7.3.2 Multi-line Macros (@@)

Some of the *cpp* macros used in the *imake* configuration files are quite complex and may expand into multi-line *make* commands later on. The default behavior of *cpp* is to collapse everything within a macro definition (anything following a #define) into a single line. To protect the macro's line breaks from *cpp*, the "@@" syntax is used. The *imake* program will replace all of the "@@" sequences with the newline character, preserving the structure of the *make* command.

For example, the following multi-line macro appears in an *imake* configuration file:

```
#ifndef InstallNonExec
#define   InstallNonExec(file,dest)                          @@\
install:: file                                      @@\
      $(INSTALL) -c $(INSTDATFLAGS) file $(DESTDIR)dest
#endif /* InstallNonExec */
```

If this is used in an Imakefile:

```
InstallNonExec(system.twmrc,$(TWMDIR))
```

It would be expanded later on into:

```
install:: system.twmrc
        $(INSTALL) -c $(INSTDATFLAGS) system.twmrc $(DESTDIR)$(TWMDIR)
```

This is a valid multi-line *make* command.

If the "@@" marker was not used, it would be squashed into a single line by *cpp*:

```
install:: system.twmrc $(INSTALL) -c $(INSTDATFLAGS) system.twmrc $(DESTD
IR)$(TWMDIR)
```

This will cause strange errors from *make*:

```
% make install
make: Warning: Infinite loop: Target `install' depends on itself
make: Fatal error: Don't know how to make target `-c'
```

8.7.3.3 Concatenating Macros

A common trick is to use the null comments "/**/" to concatenate macros or strings within *cpp*. For example, if you had a file called *testfile* containing the following:

```
#define MYTOPDIR /usr/
#define XLIBDIR lib/X11/
#define FONTDIR fonts/
```

You may want to concatenate these strings into one. If you try concatenating them directly, such as:

```
MYTOPDIRXLIBDIRFONTDIR
```

cpp will respond by trying to expand the entire string. Since the string is not defined, it will return the string itself, which is hardly what you want.

```
% cpp testfile
# 1 "testfile"


MYTOPDIRXLIBDIRFONTDIR
```

You can get around this with some versions of *cpp* by separating each component with null comments. The comments prevent the components from being interpreted as a single string. For example:

```
MYTOPDIR/**/XLIBDIR/**/FONTDIR
```

With the comments inserted, passing *testfile* through some versions of *cpp* yields:

```
% cpp testfile
# 1 "testfile"


/usr/lib/X11/fonts/
```

This works great. But the problem with this trick is that ANSI C preprocessors have a different and incompatible syntax for concatenation. Under an ANSI C preprocessor, the preceding example fails to concatenate. The null comments are expanded into white space, which is disastrous in this example:

```
% acpp testfile
# 1 "testfile"


/usr/  lib/X11/  fonts/
```

ANSI C uses the "##" sequence for concatenation. For example:

```
MYTOPDIR##XLIBDIR##FONTDIR
```

Running this through an ANSI C preprocessor yields the correct value:

```
% acpp testfile
# 1 "testfile"


/usr/lib/X11/fonts/
```

To concatenate macros within *imake*, *imake* provides the *Concat* and *Concat3* macros which do the right thing depending on what type of preprocessor you use. In this case, since we have 3 arguments, we use *Concat3*:

```
Concat3(MYTOPDIR,XLIBDIR,FONTDIR)
```

8.7.3.4 Dealing with Tabs

In some versions of *cpp*, tabs are converted to space characters. The *make* program, meanwhile, requires tab characters to precede the commands in a make rule. So if a version of *cpp* that converts tabs to spaces is used on a Makefile, *make* will bomb out with an error such as:

```
% make
make: Fatal error in reader: Makefile, line nn: Unexpected end of line seen
```

The *imake* program therefore tries to intelligently place the tab characters back in the Makefile after being processed by *cpp*. If the version of *cpp* that comes with your system is unsuitable for building the X distribution, the *contrib* area provides a replacement in *contrib/util/cpp*.

8.7.4 imake Configuration Files

imake uses a series of configuration files when creating Makefiles for a particular package. First, it uses a series of system-wide *imake* configuration files, found in the directory */usr/lib/X11/config*. In addition, *imake* looks for a file named *Imakefile* in the directory it is being invoked in, which defines parameters specific to that particular package.

This discussion will be much easier to follow if you have these files online and available to browse through while reading. If you have the X distribution source code available, look in the directory *mit/config*. If the distribution is already installed, look in the directory */usr/lib/X11/config*.

This looks very complex—it is. However, you should be relieved to know that any changes you make are confined to one file (unless you need to do something more complex, such as add support for a new platform).

The filenames indicate the function of the file in a general manner. Files ending in *.tmpl* are *template* files. They are like templates in that they provide a structure that is "generic" and later customized to a specific result. Files ending in *.cf* are configuration files, used to configure *imake* for a specific platform. Files ending in *.rules* contain *make* rules that describe how *make* should build programs and what files depend on the others.

One convention to keep in mind while browsing the files is that *cpp* macros are mixed-case (for example, `InstallAppDefaults`), and *make* flags are uppercase (for example, `INSTKMEMFLAGS`).

8.7.4.1 A Quick Tour of Files Used by imake

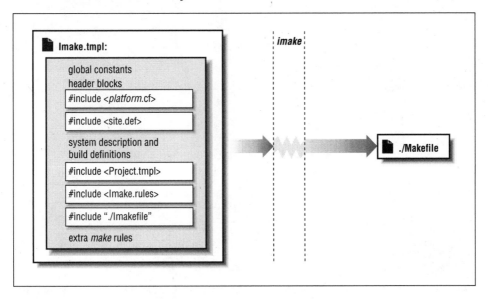

Figure 8-4. Files processed by imake

The following is a vastly simplified outline of the files used by *imake*, in the order in which they are used. Figure 8-4 demonstrates the use of these files.

- *Imake.tmpl* is fed to *cpp* and it uses the *#include* mechanism to incorporate the other files. It provides default values and a template for the generated Makefile.

- *platform*.cf overrides the default values and configures *imake* for a specific platform. (An example of a *platform*.cf file might be *sun.cf* or *ibm.cf*.)

- *site.def* provides another place to override default values, but on a site-wide basis, which could include more than one platform.

- *Project.tmpl* is where *imake* is configured for building X11, the "project" in this case. Other *imake* files should be generic, isolating the X11-specific information to this file.

- *Imake.rules* contains generic rules for generating components of any build, such as libraries and executables.

- *Imakefile* is the per-directory file that controls the operation of *imake* in the current directory.

There are certain platforms that require lots of platform-specific rules (they are usually for building shared libraries). To isolate these cases, there are separate *.rules* and *.tmpl* files that are included when a build is performed for the platform. For example, the files *ibmLib.rules* and *ibmLib.tmpl* are used by *imake* on the *ibm* platform.

8.7.5 Using imake to Build X11

You rarely ever need to run the *imake* program directly. It is usually run by the Makefile at the top level of the X11 source tree when the *make* command is used.

The usual thing to do when building X is to type:

```
% make World
```

If this fails with an error message such as:

```
...
*** Error code 1
make: Fatal error: Command failed for target `subdirMakefiles'
Current working directory /eap/X11R5/src/sun4_412
*** Error code 1
make: Fatal error: Command failed for target `Makefiles'
Current working directory /eap/X11R5/src/sun4_412
*** Error code 1
make: Fatal error: Command failed for target `World'
Current working directory /eap/X11R5/src/sun4_412
*** Error code 1
make: Fatal error: Command failed for target `World'
```

You will have to figure out what went wrong and correct it. After you have done this, you may be able to save some time by using a target other than *World*. A *target* is a specific task within a Makefile. The top-level Makefile has several targets:

Makefiles   This target creates a Makefile in any subdirectory that contains an Imakefile. You should run this anytime you change a configuration option.

clean   This target "cleans" or removes all the object files and libraries from the source tree. You should use this if you fail miserably and want to start over again.

includes   This target creates symbolic links from the current directory to where the *include* files are stored in the source tree. It should be used before the *depend* target.

depend   This target generates dependency information for *make*. A program called *makedepend* is invoked, which searches all the source files for *#include* statements and builds a list that is appended to the Makefile. For example:

```
...
Tekproc.o: /usr/include/fcntl.h /usr/include/sys/fcntlcom.h
Tekproc.o: /usr/include/sys/stat.h /usr/include/unistd.h
Tekproc.o: /usr/include/sys/time.h /usr/include/sys/time.h
Tekproc.o: ../../../X11/Xatom.h ../../../X11/cursorfont.h
Tekproc.o: ../../../X11/StringDefs.h ../../../X11/Shell.h
Tekproc.o: ../../../X11/Xmu/CharSet.h /usr/include/stdio.h
...
```

This should be run every time a Makefile is rebuilt.

World   This is the primary target for building the distribution. It runs *make* with the following targets: *Makefiles*, *clean*, *include*, *depend* and then with just with the *–k* option. (Keep in mind that *–k* tells *make* to keep running even if there are errors in the build process.) You probably only need to run this the first time you try to build on a new platform, as it will delete any previous effort to build the distribution.

Everything   This is similar to *World*, but it will only rebuild files that are out of date according the to the *make* rules. You should use this if you change any of the configuration files, as it will rebuild all the Makefiles. This is also smart to run after applying a patch, as the patch may modify something in the configuration area.

install   This target installs binaries, libraries, include files, and support files. The target will be affected by flags such as `InstallAppDefFiles`, `InstallFSConfig`, and `InstallXdmConfig`.

install.man   This target installs the manual pages. Flags such as `ExpandManNames` and `InstallLibManPages` will affect this target.

As you can see in the examples below, targets end in a double colon (::). By using the double colon, *make* allows the target to appear more than once in the Makefile. For example, there are two *install* targets in the following Makefile:

```
    ...
install:: $(PROGNAME).ad
    @if [ -d $(DESTDIR)$(XAPPLOADDIR) ]; then set +x; \
    else (set -x; $(MKDIRHIER) $(DESTDIR)$(XAPPLOADDIR)); fi
    ...
install::
    @case '${MFLAGS}' in *[ik]*) set +e;; esac; \
    for i in $(SUBDIRS) ;\
    do \
    ...
```

Both will be executed when a *make install* is performed.

A handy option to *make* is the *-n* option. The *–n* option shows all of the expected *make* output without actually executing the commands, so you can see where files are going to be installed before you actually install them:

```
% make -n install
install -c    xrn /usr/bin/X11
install -c -m 0444 XRn.ad /usr/lib/X11/app-defaults/XRn
echo "install in . done"
```

The *–n* option can avoid unpleasant surprises, such as accidentally overwriting something previously installed.

If you manage to destroy the top level Makefile (*mit/Makefile*), you can recover:

```
% cp Makefile.ini Makefile
```

This gives you a Makefile that can "bootstrap" the build from this point on.

8.8 Porting Hints

Here are some techniques that may be helpful when trying to build the distribution on platforms that are slightly different from the ones described in the MIT release notes.

8.8.1 Undefined Symbols or Functions

You will occasionally get errors when compiling or linking X programs. This is more likely to happen on platforms that are not listed in the release notes, but there will be times when errors occur on the supported platforms. This is especially likely to happen if your platform is slightly newer or older than the one described in the release notes; it is not unusual for vendors to change the location of header files between operating system releases, or to delete support for old devices in new releases. For example, the file *pmioctl.h* was in the directory */usr/include/machine/* in Ultrix 3.1, but moved to */usr/include/io/tc/* in Ultrix 4.0. The fix is often trivial, though, so don't give up in despair.

8.8.1.1 Missing Header Files

If the compiler dies with an "undefined symbol" or "no declaration" error when compiling C source code, try searching the system header files for the missing symbol:

```
% find /usr/include -type -f -exec grep symbol /dev/null '{}' ';'
... any matches will appear here ...
```

(We *grep* through */dev/null* to trick *grep* into reporting the name of the file that contained the symbol.)

If you find the symbol in a new location, edit the #include line to reflect the new location.

8.8.1.2 Missing Function Definitions

If the loader dies with an "undefined symbol" error when linking a binary:

```
ld: Undefined symbol
   _XtUnmanageChild
   _XtOpenDisplay
   _XtCreateApplicationContext
   _XtDispatchEvent
   _XtParent
   _XtToolkitInitialize
   ...
```

You can make an informed guess that the missing library is the X Toolkit (called with "-lXt"), as the function names start with "Xt". If the corresponding library is not obvious, try searching the system libraries for the symbol. The *nm* program can be used to list all the symbols present in a library or object file. The output of *nm* is very system-specific, but under SunOS it might produce something like the following:

```
% nm /usr/lib/libc.a
ftime.o:
         U .div
00000000 T _ftime
         U _gettimeofday

nice.o:
         U _errno
         U _getpriority
00000000 T _nice
   ...
```

The output displays all symbols that are used in the library, with a "U" if the symbol is only referenced, and a "T" if the symbol is defined.

To quickly find the library containing the symbol, automate the search process. For example, if the loader complained that the symbol "dlopen" is undefined, you could search all libraries in */usr/lib* with the following *csh* script:

```
% foreach I (/usr/lib/lib*)
? echo $I
? nm $I | grep dlopen
? end
```

As output, you'll get the names of the listed libraries with any matching lines in between:

```
   ...
/usr/lib/libcurses_p.a
/usr/lib/libdbm.a
/usr/lib/libdl.so.1.0
00000020 T _dlopen
/usr/lib/libf77plot.a
/usr/lib/libg.a
/usr/lib/libkvm.a
   ...
```

In some versions of *nm*, there may be options that simplify the search. The SunOS *nm* has the −*o* option for printing the library name and the −*g* option for printing only "global" symbols:

```
% nm -og /usr/lib/lib* | grep dlopen
nm: /usr/lib/lib.b: bad format
/usr/lib/libdl.so.1.0:00000020 T _dlopen
nm: /usr/lib/libm.il: bad format
```

In this example the script has found the "dlopen" symbol defined in the library */usr/lib/libdl.so.1.0*.

Once the new library is found, you can add it to the Imakefile for that directory, or you can add it system-wide in the ***platform**.cf* file. If the function is needed for the entire build, it's preferable to enter it into a system-wide file so that all future Makefiles generated by *imake* or *xmkmf* will automatically have the library included.

8.8.2 Searching for Preprocessor Symbols

An important feature of *cpp* is that it can tell other programs what type of platform it is being executed on. *cpp* provides pre-defined symbols indicating the platform, operating system, byte order, processor type, and type of C compiler. Some of these symbols are shown in the following table.

Table 8-1. cpp Symbols

Symbol Type	Examples
Architecture	mc68k, i386, i8086, iAPX286, sparc
OS	unix, DGUX, M_XENIX, UTS, ultrix, venix, xenix
Byte Order	MIPSEB, MIPSEL
Type	sun3, sun4, sun386, ns16000, ns32000, mips
Compiler	_POSIX_SOURCE, ANSI, __STDC__, _ANSI_C_SOURCE, _NO_PROTO

imake uses these symbols to automatically determine what type of platform it is being run on.* So one of the first tasks of porting X to a new platform is to find a unique preprocessor symbol so that *imake* can determine the type of platform. On some systems the BOOTSTRAPCFLAGS flag will have to be used for this function, but it's worth checking first. The following are hints about where to check:

1. The manual pages for the preprocessor and the compiler are the first places you should check. Beware that the names of the compiler programs vary. For example, the C compiler on the IBM RS/6000 is called *xlc*. There may be several different versions of the compiler available, each with its own behavior. It is not unusual to have an ANSI C and "K&R" C compiler on the same system. There may be more than one version of *cpp* as well—for example, IRIX has both *cpp* and *acpp*. Not surprisingly, some vendors do not list all the predefined flags and you will have to hunt for them.

2. See if the compiler or preprocessor has a "verbose" flag, usually *–v* or *–verbose*. This flag shows which flags are being passed to the preprocessor (where they are interpreted):

    ```
    % cc -v -E foo.c > /dev/null
    /lib/cpp -undef -Dunix -Dsun -Dsparc foo.c
    ```

    From this, you can determine that the flags unix, sun, and sparc are defined by the preprocessor. The *–E* flag means "run the preprocessor only," and the output of the preprocessor is discarded into */dev/null*.

---

*Some systems have no unique preprocessor symbols, requiring you to tell *imake* the type of platform when it is first invoked.

3. If the previous methods fail, it may require a low-tech approach. In most cases, this means the *strings* program. The *strings* program reports all printable strings in a binary file:

```
% strings /lib/cpp
  ...
too many -I options, ignoring %s
cpp internal bug alert, readinit(argv0), argv0=NULL
%s.init
unix
m68k
_SYSV_SOURCE
_BSD_SOURCE
_AUX_SOURCE
/usr/include
/usr/include
%s: %s
  ...
```

Experience would tell you that the strings clustered around `unix` are likely suspects for preprocessor symbols. You can test them by running them through the preprocessor and checking to see if they are defined. First, enter into a file the symbols you wish to test:

```
% cat > foo.c
unix
m68k
_SYSV_SOURCE
_BSD_SOURCE
_AUX_SOURCE
/usr/include
```

Then run the preprocessor on them:

```
% cc -E foo.c
# 1 "foo.c"
1
1
1
1
1
/usr/include
```

Any symbol that evaluated to "1" is being defined by the preprocessor. The "/usr/include" is unchanged, showing that it does not mean anything special to the compiler. (The line starting with the "#" character is a line number inserted by the preprocessor showing its position in the C source file.)

Beware that symbols may not be unique to a platform and BOOTSTRAPCFLAGS may have to be specified after all. For example, both Sequent and Encore define ns32000 on their machines. You would have to specify a unique symbol on the command line for the initial *make*:

```
% make World BOOTSTRAPCFLAGS="-Dumax"
```

The symbols can be added to the file *mit/config/imakemdep.h*. Look at the top of the file for directions on how to define new symbols:

```
/*
 * Step 1:  imake_ccflags
 *     Define any special flags that will be needed to get imake.c to compile.
 *     These will be passed to the compile along with the contents of the
 *     make variable BOOTSTRAPCFLAGS.
 */
```

Follow the steps described in the file to add information specific to the new platform.

8.9 Related Documentation

You should read the Release Notes before doing anything. The text version is *mit/REL-NOTES.TXT* and the PostScript version is *mit/RELNOTES.PS*.

There are several documents that explain *imake* in more detail. They include:

- The *imake* manual page (*mit/config/imake.man*).

- "Configuration Management in the X Window System," by Jim Fulton. In the source distribution, you can find this in the file *mit/doc/config/usenixws/paper.ms*.

- "The X User: Demystifying Imake," by Paul Davey, published in *The X Resource, Issue 2*, O'Reilly & Associates, Inc., Spring 1992.

- "Using Imake to Configure the X Window System," by Paul Dubois. Available via anonymous *ftp* from *ftp.primate.wisc.edu* in the directory *pub/imake-stuff*.

The flags used in the configuration process are listed in *mit/config/README*.

Documentation for porting the X server is contained in the *mit/doc/Server* and *mit/hardcopy/Server* directories.

NFS administration is described in *Managing NFS and NIS*, by Hal Stern (O'Reilly & Associates, 1991).

The *make* program is described in *Managing Projects with make*, by Andrew Oram and Steve Talbott (O'Reilly & Associates, 1991).

"The X Administrator: Building X11r5 in Limited Disk Space," by Adrian Nye, published in *The X Resource, Issue 0*, O'Reilly & Associates, Inc., Fall 1991.

A

Useful Things to Know

This appendix covers "miscellaneous" topics that either didn't fit cleanly into any other chapter, or fit into so many that we found ourselves repeating ourselves all the time.

In This Appendix:

A
Useful Things to Know

As we wrote this book, we found that there were a lot of odds-and-ends that didn't fit into any chapters but were too important to leave out. This appendix was devised as a "catch-all" for miscellaneous information.

A.1 The comp.windows.x Newsgroup

comp.windows.x is a Usenet newsgroup dedicated to the X Window System. You can use it to reach thousands of X programmers and users. You would normally use a *newsreader* such as *rn*, *vn*, *xrn*, or *readnews* to read the group. If you do not have Usenet access at your site, you can still reach the newsgroup through e-mail. To request that you be added to the list, send a polite message to *xpert-request@expo.lcs.mit.edu*. To send mail to the entire list, use *xpert@expo.lcs.mit.edu*.

In addition to *comp.windows.x*, there are also newsgroups for *comp.windows.x.motif*, *comp.windows.x.intrinsics*, *comp.windows.x.apps*, and *comp.windows.openlook*. Each of these newsgroups maintains a Frequently Asked Questions list, or FAQ, which contain a wealth of information on X. *comp.windows.x.announce* is a newsgroup dedicated to announcements about X, for example, announcements of new patches being released.

For more information on Usenet, see *Managing UUCP and Usenet* by Tim O'Reilly and Grace Todino (O'Reilly & Associates, Inc., 1992), *Using UUCP and Usenet* by Grace Todino and Dale Dougherty (O'Reilly & Associates, Inc., 1991), and *The Whole Internet User's Guide & Catalog* by Ed Krol (O'Reilly & Associates, Inc., 1992).

A.2 How to ftp a File

If you've never anonymous *ftp*'d a file before, a good file to start with is the *comp.windows.x* FAQ from *export.lcs.mit.edu*.

The first thing you do is connect to the site.

```
lmui@opal% ftp export.lcs.mit.edu
Connected to export.lcs.mit.edu
220 export.lcs.mit.edu FTP server (NEWS-OS Release 4.1C) ready.
Name (export.lcs.mit.edu:lmui):
```

By default, the *ftpd* assumes that you have an account on the remote machine, so if you press RETURN it will try to log you in under that name. Since you probably don't have an account on this machine, you don't want to press RETURN, but instead type in the name **anonymous**.

```
Name (export.lcs.mit.edu:lmui): anonymous
331 Guest login ok, send ident as password.
Password:
```

For your password, type in your e-mail address. (If you don't enter your e-mail address it may still let you in, but it's "good manners" to identify yourself properly when using someone else's machine.) *Don't type your real password here!!!*

```
Password: lmui@ora.com
230 Guest login ok, access restrictions apply.
ftp>
```

You are now logged in. (Note that although I typed my e-mail address at the Password prompt, it wouldn't actually be shown).

From here, there is a small set of commands you can run. Do a *help* at the ftp> prompt to see a list of commands. For browsing directories, use the commands *cd* and *ls*. The *dir* command is also commonly available for long listings.

In this example, we want the FAQ from the *contrib* directory. So first *cd* to that directory and then do a *dir* to make sure that the file is there:

```
ftp> cd contrib
250 CWD command successful.
ftp> dir *FAQ*
200 PORT command successful.
150 Opening data connection for /bin/ls (ascii mode) (0 bytes).
-rw-r--r--  1 ftp       ftp        213297 Aug  3 12:09 FAQ
-rw-r--r--  1 ftp       ftp         35742 Aug  5 17:10 FAQ-Xt
-rw-r--r--  1 ftp       ftp         16985 Aug  5 17:10 FAQ-Xt.Z
-rw-r--r--  1 ftp       ftp         97671 Aug  3 12:09 FAQ.Z
-rw-r--r--  1 ftp       ftp        169388 Jul 20 05:46 Motif-FAQ
226 Transfer complete.
remote: *FAQ*
311 bytes received in 0.062 seconds (4.9 Kbytes/s)
ftp>
```

(This *ftp* server understood my asterisks as wildcards, but not all do.) You probably want to get the compressed FAQ since it will transfer much faster. Turn on "binary" mode for binary transfer and use the *get* command to get the file:

```
ftp> binary
200 Type set to I.
ftp> get FAQ.Z
200 PORT command successful.
150 Opening BINARY mode data connection for FAQ.Z (84245 bytes).
226 Transfer complete.
local: FAQ.Z remote: FAQ.Z
84730 bytes received in 16.87 seconds (4.91 Kbytes/s)
ftp>
```

The file should now be in whatever directory you ran *ftp* from. Note that if you had another file in this directory called *FAQ.Z*, it would be overwritten even if you had the *csh* **noclobber** variable set.

For getting multiple files, use the *mget* command. (Use the *prompt* command first to toggle being asked to confirm each file transfer.)

If you are done with your *ftp* session, use the *quit* command to exit *ftp*.

```
ftp> quit
221 Goodbye.
lmui@opal%
```

A.2.1 Getting Files Using ftpmail

ftpmail is a mail server available to anyone who can send and receive electronic mail to and from Internet sites. This includes most workstations that have an *e-mail* connection to the outside world, and CompuServe users. You do not need to be directly on the Internet to use *ftpmail*.

Send mail to the *ftpmail* server, **ftpmail@decwrl.dec.com**. There are a set of commands that the server understands; to get a complete *help* file, send a message with no subject and the single word "help" in the body.

The following is an example mail session that will get you the *comp.windows.x* FAQ.

```
lmui@ruby 145% mail ftpmail@decwrl.dec.com
Subject:
reply lmui@ora.com
connect export.lcs.mit.edu
chdir /contrib
binary
uuencode
get FAQ.Z
quit
lmui@ruby 146%
```

The *reply* line is specified to ensure that the correct return address is used. Without this line, *ftpmail* will mail the file to whatever return address is in your mail header, which may be wrong.

The *connect* line is required to tell *ftpmail* what host to connect to. In this case, we set it to *export.lcs.mit.edu*. By default, *ftpmail* logs in as **anonymous**; you could actually supply a user name and password here if you had an account on the machine in question.

From here on, we ask to *chdir* to the */contrib* directory, set up *binary* transfer, *uuencode* file transfers, *get* the *FAQ.Z* file, and *quit*. A signature at the end of the message is acceptable as long as it appears after "*quit.*" The *ftpmail* daemon quickly replies with a message confirming that your request is in the queue, and telling you how many requests are in front of yours and how your message will be executed.

When the job finally goes through, all retrieved files will be split into 60KB chunks and mailed to you. In addition, you'll receive a message transcribing the activity.

```
lmui@ruby 120% mail
Mail version SMI 4.0 Wed Oct 23 10:38:28 PDT 1991  Type ? for help.
"/usr/spool/mail/lmui": 10 messages
    ...
   6 nobody@Pa.dec.com  Wed Aug 26 21:24  822/50654 part 001 of FAQ.Z (/contr
   7 nobody@Pa.dec.com  Wed Aug 26 21:24  821/50633 part 002 of FAQ.Z (/contr
   8 nobody@Pa.dec.com  Wed Aug 26 21:24  573/35113 part 003 of FAQ.Z (/contr
   9 nobody@Pa.dec.com  Wed Aug 26 21:25   43/1466  results of ftpmail reques
    ...
&
```

Save the files together and exit mail:

```
& save 6 7 8 FAQfile
"FAQfile" [New file] 2216/136400
& q
Held 7 messages in /usr/spool/mail/lmui
```

Now, remove the mail headers. The file should start with the word "`begin`," and end with the word "`end`", with lines of gibberish in between:

```
begin 644 ftpmail.uu
M'YV03LK<F7-&SILZ<.;H#`F'F31LX+NZ4/IC41<7%W2C%X0%W<.Z4D'D-'
MP90Z88.24LG<4-H2%'U!`$<!U6@9@<5-;.>A"&A\ ((+,,$#61%(P)G-??ii
    ...
MU3$U`4@'7PJJJ[B'I'o3W\'9"\X"(@)("\M'M%%$,:#.%:I'T'J2**'B'L:PUm&\'9m\'9
5`PT2=0$G'"-D!%'E%>Q(1@)G@2
`
end
```

Next, *uudecode* the file as shown in Section A.4.

```
lmui@ruby 125% uudecode FAQfile
```

uudecode creates a file called *ftpmail.uu* with permissions 644:

```
lmui@ruby 126% ls -l ftp*
-rw-r--r--  1 lmui        97671 Aug 27 10:20 ftpmail.uu
```

Since we requested a compressed file, we need to uncompress it before we can continue. Rename *ftpmail.uu* to *FAQ.Z* and uncompress it:

```
lmui@ruby 141% mv ftpmail.uu FAQ.Z
lmui@ruby 142% uncompress FAQ.Z
lmui@ruby 143% ls FAQ
FAQ
```

Now browse through the FAQ file at leisure.

A.2.2 BITFTP

BITFTP is a mail server for BITNET users. Send it electronic mail messages requesting files, and it sends you back the files by electronic mail. BITFTP currently serves only users who send it mail from nodes that are directly on BITNET. BITFTP is a public service of Princeton University.

To use BITFTP, send mail containing your *ftp* commands to BITFTP@PUCC. For a complete help file, send HELP as the message body. The following is the message body you should send to BITFTP:

```
FTP  export.lcs.mit.edu  NETDATA
USER  anonymous
PASS  include here your Internet email address, NOT your BITNET address
CD  /contrib
BINARY
GET FAQ.Z
QUIT
```

Questions about BITFTP can be directed to MAINT@PUCC on BITNET.

A.3 The xstuff Mail Archive Server

If you cannot use *ftp* to get to a site, there may be a *mail archive server* that can help you. A mail archive server is program that accepts commands via e-mail. It can be used to send you files that it has stored in its archive, or just to tell you what it has available.

MIT runs a mail archive server called *xstuff* that contains all the patches for MIT R5 and various other files. The first thing you should do is send mail to *xstuff@expo.lcs.mit.edu* and type "help" in the subject line. It will respond (after a while) with a full description of how to use the program:

```
Subject: How to use the Xstuff server
From: Xstuff service <xstuff@expo.lcs.mit.edu>
In-Reply-To: message from eap@ora.com (eric pearce)
To: eap@ora.com (eric pearce)
Status: R

This message comes to you from the xstuff server, xstuff@expo.lcs.mit.edu.
It received a message from you asking for help.

The xstuff server is a mail-response program. That means that you mail
it a request, and it mails back the response.

The xstuff server is a very dumb program. It does not have much error
checking. If you don't send it the commands that it understands,
it will just answer "I don't understand you".
   ...
```

As an example, if you sent mail with the subject line "send fixes 1", it will respond with "fix-1":

```
From: Xstuff service <xstuff@expo.lcs.mit.edu>
Subject:  fixes/1
In-Reply-To: Request from eap@ora.com (eric pearce) dated Tue Aug 25
13:00:01 EDT 1992
To: eap@ora.com (eric pearce)

                    Release 5 Public Patch #1
                       MIT X Consortium

This patch comes in two parts: this file, and the file "sunGX.uu".
 ...
```

The mail message can then be applied to the *patch* program to patch the X11 source distribution. See Section 8.2.4 for a description of applying X11 patches.

Try using the subject "index" to get a listing of available files.

A.4 Unpacking Files

The extension on the end of the file usually indicates what programs should be used for unpacking a file.

For *.Z* files:

```
% uncompress filename.Z
```

For *.tar.Z* files:

```
% zcat filename.tar.Z | tar xpvf -
```

For files that look like this (might have *.uu* extension):

```
begin 444 mit/server/ddx/sun/sunGX.o.dist.Z
M'YVO 08$.   0!5T!0F@*@@ 0D$#8!@RI( H(85.XWX!PW<"%!5X!D! J, 0
 ...
```

Run *uudecode*:

```
% uudecode filename
```

This will create the file *mit/server/ddx/sun/sunGX.o.dist.Z*.

A.5 Making a Filesystem Available via NFS

For a host to be able to mount a remote filesystem, it will have to have an entry in the /etc/exports file on the remote system. The format of this file has changed as NFS has gained new functionality. The "old" style of entry in /etc/exports is simply the name of the filesystem and list of hosts that can mount it:

```
/usr/lib/X11/fonts    ncd1 ncd2 ncd3 ncd4
```

The file is consulted every time a request is made to mount a filesystem.

The "new" style of entry has a different syntax with many more options. For example, the above example would be written as:

```
/usr/lib/X11/fonts    -access=ncd1:ncd2:ncd3:ncd4
```

Under "newer" NFS, you have to execute the *exportfs* command after the /etc/exports file is edited in order for the changes to take effect:

```
% exportfs -v /usr/lib/X11/fonts
exported /usr/lib/X11/fonts
```

To remove access to a filesystem, edit the file and run the *exportfs* command with the *–u* option:

```
% exportfs -v -u /usr/lib/X11/fonts
unexported /usr/lib/X11/fonts
```

For more information, see *Managing NFS and NIS* by Hal Stern (O'Reilly & Associates, 1991).

A.6 How to Add a Host

A common administration task is to add a new host name to the /etc/hosts file, the Network Information Service (NIS), or the Domain Name Service (DNS). The procedure for each of these is described here, but they will not be adequate for more complicated configurations. NIS is described in detail in *Managing NIS and NFS* by Hal Stern (O'Reilly & Associates, 1991). DNS is described in *DNS and BIND* by Paul Albitz and Cricket Liu (O'Reilly & Associates, 1992). All these examples assume a pre-existing, working configuration.

A.6.1 Adding a Host to /etc/hosts

If you are not using NIS or DNS, the new host can be added directly to the file /etc/hosts, with the IP address followed by the hostname and any aliases that the host is going to be known by:

```
140.186.65.13 ncd4.ora.com ncd4
```

A.6.2 Adding a Host Using NIS

If you are using NIS (previously known as Yellow Pages), you first have to determine which host is the NIS master. This is usually the hostname returned by the *ypwhich* command:

```
% ypwhich
ruby
```

(This not always the case, as NIS slave servers will also respond.)

Once you have located the master, add the new host entry to its */etc/hosts* file as shown above, and remake the NIS map:

```
# vi /etc/hosts
add hostname
# cd /var/yp
# make
updated hosts

pushed hosts
```

You should test the map to make sure it has the new entry (in some cases, it may take a while to propagate the new map to all hosts within an NIS domain):

```
% ypmatch ruby hosts
140.186.65.13   ncd4.ora.com ncd4
```

If there is a problem, you will get the error:

```
Can't match key ncd4 in map hosts.byname.  Reason: no such key in map.
```

A.6.3 Adding a Host Using DNS

For networks using DNS, you need to edit the configuration files for the name daemon *named*. *named* looks at a boot file at startup, usually */etc/named.boot*. On our name server, this file contains the lines:

```
directory /var/named

; type     domain                     source host/file          backup file
primary    ora.com                        ora.zone
primary    65.186.140.in-addr.arpa        ora.revzone
```

The */var/named* directory is where the configuration files live. The file */var/named/ora.zone* is the primary configuration file for the *ora.com* domain—this is the file that tells *named* how to convert hostnames to the proper IP address. The file */var/named/ora.revzone* contains the reverse entries—i.e., it tells *named* how to convert IP addresses to the proper hostnames within *ora.com*. Note that your site will undoubtedly use different pathnames.

To add ncd4 as address 140.186.65.13, we enter into */var/named/ora.zone*:

```
ncd4          IN     A       140.186.65.13
              IN     HINFO   NCD-16 2.2.0
```

(The HINFO line contains host information—in this case, the version of the X server.)

Then enter into */var/named/ora.revzone*:

```
13              IN      PTR     ncd4.ora.com.
```

Using the PTR keyword, this means that host 13 in the *ora.com* domain (140.186.65) resolves to hostname *ncd4.ora.com*.

Next, send a SIGHUP to the *named* daemon. This will force *named* to reread */etc/named.boot* and reload the database. Most systems maintain a file in */etc* called *named.pid* that contains the process ID of *named*.

```
# kill -HUP `cat /etc/named.pid`
```

If your system doesn't maintain the process ID of *named*, it's easy enough to run *ps* and learn it yourself.

```
# ps agx | grep named
   88 ?  S    24:48 in.named
 5239 q6 S     0:00 grep named
# kill -HUP 88
```

Test the new entry with *nslookup*. To verify the hostname to IP address mapping:

```
% nslookup ncd4
Server:  localhost
Address:  127.0.0.1

Name:    ncd4.ora.com
Address:  140.186.65.13
```

If there is a problem, it will fail with:

```
*** localhost can't find ncd4: Non-existent domain
```

To verify the IP address to hostname mapping, set the query type to "pointer", reverse the address and append the *in-addr.arpa* domain:

```
% nslookup -q=ptr 13.65.186.140.in-addr.arpa
Server:  localhost
Address:  127.0.0.1

141.65.186.140.in-addr.arpa     name = ncd4.ora.com
```

If there is a problem, it will fail with:

```
*** localhost can't find 13.65.186.140.in-addr.arpa: Non-existent domain
```

A.7 Adding an Ethernet Address

When you want to boot an X terminal or diskless workstation off a server machine, you will usually have to add its Ethernet address to the *ethers* database. Add the entry to the */etc/ethers* file:

```
00:00:a7:10:11:bf        ncd4
```

The letters within the hex number should be in lowercase.

If you run NIS, you will also have to remake the *ethers* map on the NIS master:

```
# cd /var/yp
# make
updated ethers

pushed hosts
```

A.8 Printing Documentation in the MIT X Distribution

If you have a PostScript printer, you can print out the MIT documentation in *mit/hardcopy/*. Any file with the *.PS* extension should print on BSD-based UNIX machines with:

```
% lpr filename.PS
```

or (on System-V based machines):

```
$ lp filename.PS
```

Any filename with a *.Z* extension is compressed. You should uncompress it before trying to print it:

```
% uncompress filename.PS.Z
% lpr filename.PS
```

or:

```
% zcat filename.PS.Z | lpr
```

If you do not have PostScript or if you just want to look at the document on your screen, you should use the files in the *mit/doc/* directory.

If the file has *.ms* extension, this indicates that it uses the *ms* macro package for *nroff* and *troff*:

```
% nroff -ms mit/doc/Xmu/Xmu.ms | more
```

If the file has a *.man* extension, it is meant to be installed so it can be used with the *man* command, but you can view it independently with:

```
% nroff -man mit/clients/xterm/xterm.man | more
```

If the file has a *.tbl* extension, run it through the *tbl* preprocessor and then through *col* after passing it through *nroff*:

```
% tbl mit/doc/Server/gdz.tbl.ms | nroff -ms | col | more
```

A.9 Converting a Number Into Hexadecimal and Back

Sometimes you will have to convert a number from decimal to hex. The *bc* program is handy for this. Make sure all letters in the hex numbers are in uppercase.

To convert the IP address `140.186.65.13` into hex, run *bc*:

```
% bc
```

Set the output base to 16 (hex):

```
obase=16
```

Type in the numbers to be converted, separated by a semi-colon (`;`):

```
140;186;65;13
8C
BA
41
D
```

Type ""^D"" to exit *bc*.

To use the hexadecimal value as a filename (for example, for an X terminal's remote configuration file), it would be:

```
8CBA410D
```

To convert from hex to decimal, use the same procedure, but set the *input* base to 16 (the output will default to base 10):

```
% bc
ibase=16
8C;BA;41;D
140
186
65
13
^D
```

A.10 Configuring a Sun as an X terminal

One way to breathe new life into your old Sun3 hardware is to reconfigure them as X terminals. A used Sun 3/50 is cheaper than most X terminals, and you get a 19" display, a nice keyboard, an optical mouse and the ability to run the latest R5 server.

The usual way to do this is to strip down the kernel and run just the X server. A more powerful host on the network can run *xdm* and manage the 3/50 as if it were an X terminal.

The procedure for the X terminal conversion has been packaged and is available via anonymous *ftp* from several sites, the main one being *ftp.ctr.columbia.edu*. Check the directory */pub/Xkernel* for the latest version.

There is no reason why you could not do this with other hardware. The 3/50 is singled out only because it is considered to be underpowered by today's standards.

A.11 Using More than One Frame Buffer Under SunOS

The MIT X server for the Sun platform can support more than one frame buffer at a time. It is possible to have two separate monitors on the same host or to use separate frame buffers within the same monitor. The *cgfour* frame buffer has an 8 bit color device and 1 bit monochrome device. The *Xsun* X server will not use both unless you modify the default workstation configuration.

1. Become **root** and change directories to */dev*:

   ```
   % su
   # cd /dev
   ```

2. Remove the default monochrome device:

   ```
   # rm /dev/bwtwo0
   ```

3. Create the new monochrome device:

   ```
   # MAKEDEV bwtwo1
   ```

4. Make sure the kernel contains the *bwtwo1* device and it is not commented-out. For example, on a Sun 3/60 with a kernel named "HARRY":

   ```
   # grep bwtwo1 /usr/sys/sun3/conf/HARRY
   device      bwtwo1 at obmem 7 csr 0xff300000 priority 4# 3/60
   device      bwtwo1 at obmem 7 csr 0xff400000# 3/60
   ```

   If the device is missing, add it to the kernel config file and build a new kernel.

If this procedure works, you should be able to toggle back and forth between the frame buffers just by moving the mouse pointer to the edge of the display.

Some systems can support more than one physical monitor. The Sun color IPC comes with a monochrome frame buffer built onto the CPU board and a *cgthree* card in one of the Sbus slots. If you connect a monochrome monitor to a CPU and a color monitor to the *cgthree* device, you can run the X server on both. Moving the mouse pointer to edge of the screen will move it onto the adjacent monitor.

B

Compiling Public Domain Software

Public domain software for X is available all over the Internet, but you may not think you have the right programming skills, or no one ever explicitly told you what to do. This appendix is a tutorial on how to find and compile public domain software.

In This Appendix:

B

Compiling Public Domain Software

You've probably seen this sort of talk over the newsgroups: "Does anyone know where I can get xtetris?" "Is there an ftp site for xpostit?" You know that one of the best things about X is that there's all this great public domain software available, but you're not sure how to go about getting it. Either you don't know how to *ftp* the sources, or you don't know how to use *imake* or *make*, or you aren't much of a C programmer so the whole idea of dealing with the source just scares you.

Well, the good news is that for most source distributions, you don't need to know very much about *make* or *imake*, and you don't really need to know much about programming in C—mostly all you need to know is how to follow directions. This appendix gives you some idea of how to compile sources without knowing a lot about what you're doing. If you've been installing X from source or if you're a competent (and confident) C programmer in your own right, then you already know all the material in this appendix and it isn't for you. But if you're one of these people who's Scared of the Source, then this appendix may help.

Don't expect to learn much about *make* or *imake* in this appendix, just enough to get through some of the simpler builds. If you're interested only in how to compile the X11 sources themselves, see Chapter 8. But if you already have X11 installed and you just want to install new software, read on.

B.1 Finding the Sources

There are a lot of ways to find out about a program. You might see a reference to it on a newsgroup, or you might see it running on someone else's machine, or you might have read about it in this book. Let's suppose you saw a posting on the net about the *xrolodex* client:

```
From:  hrp@world.std.com
Newsgroups:  comp.windows.x.apps
Subject:  xrolodex
  ....

Hey,

Has anyone seen the new xrolodex app?  How is it related to
xrolo?

     -Ross
```

When you read this message, you are intrigued by the possibilities of a rolodex program, and you wonder whether it's available at no cost.

B.1.1 Using an Archie Server

The first thing to try is to use an *Archie* server. Archie is a robust database of anonymous *ftp* sites and their contents. If you have Internet access, the most direct way to gain access to *archie* is to *telnet* directly to one of the Archie servers. Current Archie servers are listed in Table B-1.

Table B-1. Archie Servers as of January 3, 1992

Site	IP Address	Location
archie.mcgill.ca	132.206.2.3	McGill University, Montreal, Canada
archie.sura.net	128.167.254.179	SURAnet, College Park, Maryland, USA
archie.ans.net	147.225.1.2	ANS, New York, USA
archie.unl.edu	129.93.1.14	Lincoln, Nebraska, USA
archie.rutgers.edu	128.6.18.15	Piscataway, New Jersey, USA
archie.funet.fi	128.214.6.100	FUnet, Helsinki, Finland
archie.au	139.130.4.6	Deakin University, Geelong, Australia
archie.doc.ic.ac.uk	146.169.11.3	Imperial College, London, UK
cs.huji.ac.il	132.65.6.5	Hebrew University, Jerusalem, Israel

In our case, since Archie was written by the Archive Group at McGill University, it seemed fitting to use the one at McGill. In reality, you should use the server closest to you, since the McGill machine is generally overloaded with requests.

You should generally use a front-end Archie client program to access an Archie server, such as *archie* or *xarchie* (we show how to build *xarchie* later in this chapter, in Section B.2). But you can also connect to Archie directly using *telnet*.

```
lmui@opal% telnet archie.mcgill.ca
Trying 132.206.2.3 ...
Connected to quiche.cs.McGill.CA.
Escape character is '^]'.


SunOS UNIX (quiche.CS.McGill.CA)

login:
```

Log on as **archie**. (There is no password.)

```
login: archie
  ARCHIE: The McGill School of Computer Science Archive Server [2 Apr 1992]
    ...
  Use the 'servers' command to list all archie servers.

  A limit of 10 concurrent telnet sessions has been put on archie.mcgill.ca.
```

```
     Alternative access through the standalone clients available via
     anonymous ftp to this machine. See README file in ~archie/clients.

     ** 'help' for help
     ** corrections/additions to archie-admin@archie.mcgill.ca
     ** bug reports, comments etc. to archie-l@archie.mcgill.ca
     ======================================================================
     archie>
```

For a full listing of commands, type *help*.

As an example of how to use *archie* to find a program called *xrolodex*, type:

```
     archie> prog xrolodex
```

The first thing Archie does is find how many matches to *xrolodex* there are in the database. It keeps you updated on how many matches it's found so far, and how far it's gotten in its search.

```
     # matches / % database searched:    1 / 78%
```

When it is 100% through the database, the list of sites that have *xrolodex* will stream to your terminal. For the purposes of this example, we have deliberately chosen a recently-announced program that has not made it to many sites yet (at least, not at the time of this example). If we had searched for something like *xpostit*, many screenfuls of output would have been reported.

```
     archie> prog xrolodex
     # matches / % database searched: 4 / 100%
     Host think.com    (131.239.2.1)
     Last updated 05:54 25 Feb 1992

         Location: /think
            FILE      rw-rw-r--      53208  Dec  4  1990    xrolodex.shar.Z
     Host citi.umich.edu    (141.211.128.16)
     Last updated 16:05  9 Apr 1992

         Location: /afs/alw.nih.gov/dcrt/brunetti/Oldfiles
            DIRECTORY rwxrwxrwx      2048  Apr  1 10:16    xrolodex
         Location: /afs/alw.nih.gov/dcrt/brunetti
            DIRECTORY rwxrwxrwx      2048  Apr  1 10:16    xrolodex
     Host plaza.aarnet.edu.au    (139.130.4.6)
     Last updated 05:54 27 Apr 1992

         Location: /X11/contrib
            FILE       r--r--r--     103267 Apr 24 02:28   xrolodex.tar.Z

     archie>
```

In this example, the pattern used for the *prog* command is assumed to be an exact match to the name of the program we want. You can specify different ways of searching using the *set search* command. For example:

```
     archie> set search sub
     archie> prog rolo
```

will force a search of all items in the database with "rolo" as a substring.

Rather than using *telnet* to directly contact an Archie server, there are programs available to automate the search. See Section B.2 for information on obtaining and compiling *xarchie*, which provides an X11 interface to accessing an Archie server.

If you don't have Internet access at all, you can use the e-mail interface by sending mail to **archie@***host*, where *host* is one of the machines listed in Table B-1. See *The Whole Internet User's Guide & Catalog* by Ed Krol (O'Reilly & Associates, 1992) for more information.

B.1.2 Get the FAQ

Archie is a great way to find sources. However, if you have access to the *comp.windows.x* FAQ (Frequently Asked Questions) list, looking through the FAQ might actually be easier.

The FAQ is a great wealth of information that is posted at the beginning of each month to the newsgroup *comp.windows.x*. It is updated frequently, so if you have absolutely any question about X, the first place you should look is in the FAQ.

As far as sources are concerned, some public domain sources are placed on several anonymous *ftp* sites, but not all are updated when new versions or bug fixes are announced. If the *comp.windows.x* FAQ list tells you where to get sources, it's likely to tell you the most reliable site.

If you don't have a FAQ handy, either post to one of the *comp.windows.x* newsgroups for someone to send it to you, or *ftp* it yourself as described in Section A.2. You can also get it from **mail-server@pit-manager.mit.edu**. Or if you can wait a little, look for it on *comp.windows.x*—the FAQ is promptly re-posted at the beginning of every month, as are the FAQs for *comp.windows.x.motif* and *comp.windows.openlook*.

(If you don't have access to Usenet, you can get on a mailing list called **xpert**. To get on that mailing list, send mail to **xpert-request@expo.lcs.mit.edu**.)

At this writing, there are 145 questions answered in the FAQ, definitely worth the bandwidth to get it. If you find it useful, also look for the FAQs for OSF/Motif and for OPEN LOOK.

B.1.3 The Usual Suspects

You can find a description of other ways to find sources on the machine *rtfm.mit.edu*, in the directory */pub/usenet/news.answers*. A list of *ftp* sites can be found in the *ftp-list* directory, and the file *finding-sources* gives some more information on how to find what you want.

If neither the FAQ nor Archie mentions what you want, and you have Internet access, try a few of the usual suspects—such as *export.lcs.mit.edu* (where you'd also find the X11 sources themselves) in the */contrib* directory, or *ftp.uu.net* in the */comp.windows.x* directory.

(While you're at *export* or *uunet*, you might want to browse around a bit. There's a lot of good stuff available, you just need to know about it.)

If all else fails, try sending a polite post to *comp.windows.x* asking if this program is public domain and, if so, would anyone be kind enough to help you get it.

B.2 An Example: xarchie

If you're interested in trying out a lot of public domain software, it's a good idea to get *xarchie* to help you find things. For that reason, we use *xarchie* for our first example.

We are running SunOS 4.1.x under MIT X11R5, and *xarchie 1.3* builds cleanly for us. If you have trouble building *xarchie* on your platform, look for *xarchie 2.0*, which should be available by the time this book goes to press. Among other things, the new version of *xarchie* has a cleaner *Imakefile*, solving some build issues on OpenWindows and on SGI machines.

B.2.1 Getting the xarchie Sources

xarchie isn't listed in the FAQ, but we know via an earlier Archie query (which we spared you in this appendix) that it can be found on hundreds of archives. One of those archives is *export.lcs.mit.edu*. We *ftp* to *export*, log in as **anonymous**, and go directly to the *contrib/* directory.

```
lmui@opal% ftp export.lcs.mit.edu
Connected to export.lcs.mit.edu.
220 export.lcs.mit.edu FTP server (NEWS-OS Release 4.1C) ready.
Name (export.lcs.mit.edu:lmui): anonymous
331 Guest login ok, send ident as password.
Password:
230 Guest login ok, access restrictions apply.
ftp> cd contrib
250 CWD command successful.
ftp>
```

There, we look for anything resembling the name "archie." Not all *ftp* servers accept wildcards, but this one does.

```
ftp> ls *rchie*
200 PORT command successful.
150 Opening data connection for /bin/ls (ascii mode) (0 bytes).
xarchie-1.3.tar.Z
226 Transfer complete.
remote: *rchie*
19 bytes received in 0.015 seconds (1.2 Kbytes/s)
ftp>
```

The compressed tar file *xarchie-1.3.tar.Z* seems to be what we want. We set ourselves up for binary transfer, get the file, and then quit out of *ftp*.

```
ftp> bin
200 Type set to I.
ftp> get xarchie-1.3.tar.Z
200 PORT command successful.
150 Opening data connection for xarchie-1.3.tar.Z (binary mode)
(179119 bytes).
226 Transfer complete.
local: xarchie-1.3.tar.Z remote: xarchie-1.3.tar.Z
179119 bytes received in 46 seconds (3.8 Kbytes/s)
```

```
ftp> quit
221 Goodbye.
lmui@opal%
```

B.2.2 Untarring the Sources

Once we have the file on our system, it's a good idea to see what it contains before we untar
it. Use the *zcat* command to uncompress the file to standard output and pipe that to *tar tf –* to
see what files the tar archive contains.

```
lmui@opal% zcat x* | tar tf -
Ad2c/Imakefile
Ad2c/Makefile
Ad2c/README
Ad2c/ad2c.man
Ad2c/ad2c.script
EzMenu/EzME.c
EzMenu/EzME.h
EzMenu/EzMEP.h
EzMenu/EzMenu.c
EzMenu/EzMenu.h
EzMenu/EzMenuP.h
EzMenu/Imakefile
EzMenu/Makefile
EzMenu/README
EzMenu/ezMenu.man
Imakefile
MANIFEST
      ...
```

Since we don't want to clutter the current directory with all these files, create a new *xarchie*
subdirectory and move the compressed tar file into that directory.

```
lmui@opal% mkdir xarchie
lmui@opal% mv xarchie-1.3.tar.Z xarchie/
```

Change directory to the *xarchie* directory and then untar the file for real. Use the *p* option to
tar so you retain permissions. When it is done, list the contents of the directory.

```
lmui@opal% cd xarchie
lmui@opal% zcat *.Z | tar xfp -
lmui@opal% ls -aF
./                  classnames.c        pprot.h
../                 classnames.h        procquery.c
Ad2c/               confirm.c           procquery.h
EzMenu/             confirm.h           ptalloc.c
Imakefile           copyright.h         rdgram.h
MANIFEST            db.c                regex.c
Makefile            db.h                regex.h
README              dialog.c            settings.c
README.FILES        dialog.h            settings.h
README.PROSP        dirsend.c           stcopy.c
TODO                ftp.c               support.c
Xarchie.ad          ftp.h               types.c
Xarchie.ad.h        get_pauth.c         types.h
```

```
actions.c          get_vdir.c          udp.c
actions.h          patchlevel.h        vl_comp.c
alert.c            pauthent.h          vlalloc.c
alert.h            pcompat.h           xarchie-1.3.tar.Z
appres.h           perrmesg.c          xarchie.c
aquery.c           perrno.h            xarchie.h
archie.h           pfs.h               xarchie.man
atalloc.c          pmachine.h
lmui@opal%
```

Now we've come to the First Cardinal Rule of compiling sources: when there's a README, read it.

```
lmui@opal% more README
              README for Xarchie - X11 browser interface to Archie

              George Ferguson, ferguson@cs.rochester.edu

                     Last Change: 12 Nov 1991

DISCLAIMER:

       This is release 1.3 of xarchie -- an X browser interface to
       the Archie Internet information system.

       This software is provided as is with no warranty expressed or
       implied. I hope you find it useful, but I won't be held responsible
       for any damage that may occur from reading, compiling, installing,
       using, or even thinking about it.
              ...
```

Further down in the README are the instructions on how to actually install the program.

```
INSTALLATION:

       1. Edit the Imakefile to reflect any changes for your site. These
          include setting BINDIR, LIBDIR, and MANDIR if needed, and
          checking CDEBUGFLAGS if debugging or optimization is desired.

          If your system doesn't have re_comp() and re_exec(), then you
          need to uncomment the appropriate section in the Imakefile to
          include those routines.

          Compiling this program requires the "ad2c" program. You should
          have received a copy of ad2c with this distribution, in the
          subdirectory "Ad2c". You should set the AD2C variable as
          required. Actually, ad2c is only required if you change Xarchie.ad
          and want the new defaults compiled in as fallback resources.  If
          you don't have ad2c, you probably want to remove the line that
          adds Xarchie.ad.h to the "clean" target.

          You may want to change defaults in Xarchie.ad; consult the manpage
          for details, and see above about ad2c.
```

This brings us to Cardinal Rule Number 2: follow directions.

B.2.3 Editing the Imakefile

You may not feel up to editing an Imakefile, but we recommend that you give it a try regardless. The *xarchie Imakefile* is somewhat non-standard, but it is straightforward and well-documented, so it's a good place to start becoming familiar with *imake*. We'll build a more standard program, *xkeycaps*, later in this appendix.

If you don't know what *imake* is, it's basically a utility to create Makefiles based on system dependencies. It actually makes a lot of sense—if you're building a lot of applications for a lot of different machines, you end up editing your *Makefile* a lot according to each different machine, and then you have to edit the *Makefile* of the next application according to the same dependencies, and it seems as if you keep duplicating your edits. *imake* lets you set up system dependencies in an independent place, in a file called *Imake.tmpl*, usually kept in */usr/lib/X11/config*. For more information on *imake* syntax, see Section 8.7.

If you just read the *Imakefile* carefully, you'll get the idea of the sorts of things you might change.

```
#
# Imakefile for xarchie : X11 Browser interface to Archie
#
# George Ferguson, ferguson@cs.rochester.edu, 12 Sep 1991.
#

# Where do you want this stuff? Uncomment and adjust these to change the
# destinations of "make install" and "make install.man" if the defaults
# are not satisfactory.
#BINDIR = bin
#LIBDIR = lib
#MANDIR = man/man1
##undef ManSuffix
##define ManSuffix 1
```

BINDIR is the target directory where the *xarchie* program will eventually be installed. If you prefer that *xarchie* be installed in */usr/local/bin*, this is where you'd specify it. Otherwise, the program will be installed in whatever directory *imake* has been configured for on your system. On our system, the default is */usr/bin/X11*.

LIBDIR is your X library directory. On our system, the default is */usr/lib/X11*. MANDIR is where the manual pages go. On our system, the default is */usr/man*.

In all three cases, we are satisfied with the default values and leave them unchanged. Continue with the *Imakefile*:

```
# Where is the app-defaults to C converter?
# Only needed if you change the app-defaults file Xarchie.ad and want the
# changes compiled into the program. If you don't have ad2c you should
# remove the extra clean target for Xarchie.ad.h below. If you lose
# Xarchie.ad.h and can't remake it, create it to be an empty file. Of course
# then you'll have to use the resource file at run time.
# If your ad2c came from this xarchie distribution, then use the following
# target, otherwise change it to reflect where you put ad2c.
AD2C = Ad2c/ad2c.script

# Where is the EzMenu widget package?
# You should have received a copy of the EzMenu package with this
```

```
# xarchie distribution.
EZMENUDIR = EzMenu
EZMENULIB = ezMenu$(TARGET_MACH)
```

Since both the *ad2c* and *EzMenu* packages were included in the tar file, we don't have to do anything here.

```
# How excited are you about debugging? This can be -g, -O, or nothing.
CDEBUGFLAGS = -g

# To enable Prospero tracing (controlled by the -debug option), uncomment
# this
#PDEBUG = -DDEBUG

# Does your system have re_comp() and re_exec(), or regcmp() and regex()
# [in the case of A/UX]? If not, uncomment the following definitions.
#REGEXC = regex.c
#REGEXO = regex.o

###################################################################
# Nothing to change below here...
```

We don't care about debugging, we don't know what Prospero tracing is, and we've determined that we have the *re_comp()* and *re_exec()* functions by using the *man* command on them.

We thus declare ourselves to have finished editing the *Imakefile*.

As for editing the application defaults: the file *Xarchie.ad* is the systemwide resource file for the *xarchie* application. It's worth it to take a minute to make sure it's set up the way you want it.

```
!
! Xarchie.ad : Application defaults for the X11 browser interface to Archie
!
! George Ferguson, ferguson@cs.rochester.edu, 12 Nov 1991.
!

!    -    -    -    -    -    -    -    -
! Non-widget resources

Xarchie.archieHost:      archie.sura.net

! Possible values are: exact, substr, subcase, or regexp
Xarchie.searchType:      exact
```

This is when you'd change the name of the archie host to the one closest to you. For example, you might change it to the one at Rutgers:

```
Xarchie.archieHost:      archie.rutgers.edu
```

B.2.4 Compiling the Source

Once the *Imakefile* is set up, compiling is usually a matter of just executing a few commands and hoping it works. From the *README*:

```
2. Execute
            % xmkmf
   to create the Makefile.
```

If you're running X11R4 or later, your X distribution comes with a command called *xmkmf*, which stands for "X Make Makefile." *xmkmf* is a shell script (usually kept in */usr/bin/X11*) that is designed to run *imake* to create Makefiles for third-party X11 software distributions. See Section 8.6.1 for more information on *xmkmf*.

If a software distribution comes with a proper Imakefile, if your X distribution is set up properly, and if you're generally a lucky person, you can simply run *xmkmf* and your Makefile(s) are all set.

```
lmui@opal% xmkmf
mv Makefile Makefile.bak
imake -DUseInstalled -I/usr/lib/X11/config
lmui@opal%
```

You now have a new *Makefile*. (Although a *Makefile* was supplied with the distribution for sites that may not have *imake*, it's always better to use one generated by *imake*.)

3. Execute
```
% make Makefiles
```
to run xmkmf in the Ad2c and EzMenu subdirectories. Alternately, run it (or imake) in each subdirectory by hand.

4. Execute
```
% make depend
```
to add the dependencies to the Makefile. This is necessary to ensure that Xarchie.ad.h is created when needed.
IMPORTANT: Ignore the error message from makedepend if Xarchie.ad.h is not found; it will be created automatically.

Once again, follow directions.

```
lmui@opal% make Makefiles
making Makefiles in ./Ad2c...
rm -f Ad2c/Makefile.bak
+ mv Ad2c/Makefile Ad2c/Makefile.bak
cd Ad2c; imake -DUseInstalled -I/usr/lib/X11/config  -DTOPDIR=../.  -DCURD
IR=./Ad2c; \
make  Makefiles
making Makefiles in ./EzMenu...
rm -f EzMenu/Makefile.bak
+ mv EzMenu/Makefile EzMenu/Makefile.bak
cd EzMenu; imake -DUseInstalled -I/usr/lib/X11/config  -DTOPDIR=../.  -DCU
RDIR=./EzMenu; \
make  Makefiles
lmui@opal% make depend
makedepend  -s "# DO NOT DELETE" -- -I. -IEzMenu        -DARCHIE
-DXARCHIE -- aquery.c atalloc.c dirsend.c get_pauth.c get_vdir.c
permmesg.c ptalloc.c stcopy.c support.c vl_comp.c vlalloc.c xarchie.c
db.c actions.c types.c classnames.c procquery.c settings.c  ftp.c
alert.c confirm.c dialog.c
```

(In R5, *xmkmf –a* will take combine steps 2-4 of this example.)

Now you're ready for the moment of truth:

5. Make the package using
```
% make
```
or install it directly with
```
% make install install.man
```

Note that this will also "make install" in Ad2c and EzMenu by
default. Since you may want to install xarchie without installing
these other things, you can instead do
        % make install.xarchie
to install xarchie, its resource file, and its manpage only.

We don't recommend installing things until you know what you're installing and where it's
going to go. So *make* the program separately:

```
lmui@opal% make
making all in ./Ad2c...
ad2c is up to date
making all in ./EzMenu...
cc -g   -I/usr/staff/include        -target sun4 -c  EzMenu.c
cc -g   -I/usr/staff/include        -target sun4 -c  EzME.c
rm -f libezMenu-sparc.a
ar cq libezMenu-sparc.a EzMenu.o EzME.o
ranlib libezMenu-sparc.a
cc -g -pipe -I. -IEzMenu -DARCHIE -DXARCHIE -target sun4 -c aquery.c
cc -g -pipe -I. -IEzMenu -DARCHIE -DXARCHIE -target sun4 -c atalloc.c
cc -g -pipe -I. -IEzMenu -DARCHIE -DXARCHIE -target sun4 -c dirsend.c
cc -g -pipe -I. -IEzMenu -DARCHIE -DXARCHIE -target sun4 -c get_pauth.c
cc -g -pipe -I. -IEzMenu -DARCHIE -DXARCHIE -target sun4 -c get_vdir.c
cc -g -pipe -I. -IEzMenu -DARCHIE -DXARCHIE -target sun4 -c perrmesg.c
cc -g -pipe -I. -IEzMenu -DARCHIE -DXARCHIE -target sun4 -c ptalloc.c
cc -g -pipe -I. -IEzMenu -DARCHIE -DXARCHIE -target sun4 -c stcopy.c
cc -g -pipe -I. -IEzMenu -DARCHIE -DXARCHIE -target sun4 -c support.c
cc -g -pipe -I. -IEzMenu -DARCHIE -DXARCHIE -target sun4 -c vl_comp.c
cc -g -pipe -I. -IEzMenu -DARCHIE -DXARCHIE -target sun4 -c vlalloc.c
cc -g -pipe -I. -IEzMenu -DARCHIE -DXARCHIE -target sun4 -c xarchie.c
cc -g -pipe -I. -IEzMenu -DARCHIE -DXARCHIE -target sun4 -c db.c
cc -g -pipe -I. -IEzMenu -DARCHIE -DXARCHIE -target sun4 -c actions.c
cc -g -pipe -I. -IEzMenu -DARCHIE -DXARCHIE -target sun4 -c types.c
cc -g -pipe -I. -IEzMenu -DARCHIE -DXARCHIE -target sun4 -c classnames.c
cc -g -pipe -I. -IEzMenu -DARCHIE -DXARCHIE -target sun4 -c procquery.c
cc -g -pipe -I. -IEzMenu -DARCHIE -DXARCHIE -target sun4 -c settings.c
cc -g -pipe -I. -IEzMenu -DARCHIE -DXARCHIE -target sun4 -c ftp.c
cc -g -pipe -I. -IEzMenu -DARCHIE -DXARCHIE -target sun4 -c alert.c
cc -g -pipe -I. -IEzMenu -DARCHIE -DXARCHIE -target sun4 -c confirm.c
cc -g -pipe -I. -IEzMenu -DARCHIE -DXARCHIE -target sun4 -c dialog.c
(cd EzMenu; echo "making all in ./EzMenu..."; \
make  'CDEBUGFLAGS=-g' all);
making all in ./EzMenu...
rm -f xarchie
cc -o xarchie aquery.o atalloc.o dirsend.o get_pauth.o get_vdir.o
perrmesg.o ptalloc.o stcopy.o support.o vl_comp.o vlalloc.o xarchie.o
db.o actions.o types.o classnames.o procquery.o settings.o  ftp.o
alert.o confirm.o dialog.o  -g -pipe  -LEzMenu -lezMenu-sparc -lXaw
-lXmu -lXt -lXext -lX11
lmui@opal%
```

And now, believe it or not, the *xarchie* program is done.*

```
lmui@opal% ls -F xarchie
xarchie*
```

---

*If you get a compilation error, it's probably because of missing header files or function definitions. See Section
8.8.1 for more information on what to do in this situation.

We like to try out a program before we install it and its application defaults. Copy the *Xarchie.ad* file to *Xarchie*, and set your XAPPLRESDIR environment variable to the current directory so that the application will find the resource file. Or just set your XENVIRONMENT environment variable to *Xarchie.ad*. Then start up the application.

```
lmui@opal% setenv XENVIRONMENT Xarchie.ad
lmui@opal% ./xarchie &
```

You should see something like the window shown in Figure B-1.

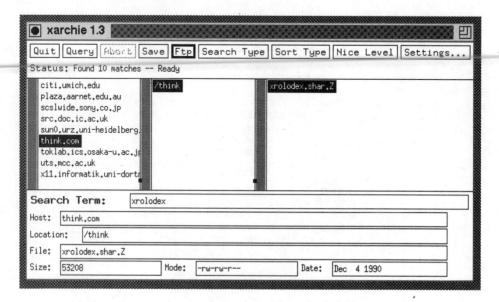

Figure B-1. xarchie window

In the example figure, you see that once *xarchie* has located the utility you want, you can automatically *ftp* it by selecting a site and pressing the `ftp` button.

Play with *xarchie* a bit. When you're happy with it, install it. Before you do that, it's a good idea to do *make –n install* first to see where *make* intends to install the *xarchie* program. (The *–n* option to *make* says not to actually execute these commands but just tell you what it would do. It's a good idea since you should never trust that you won't end up blowing away some system files.)

We're choosing to install the *xarchie* program, manpage, and application defaults only—we aren't installing the other packages that came with *xarchie*. (The *xarchie* build is unusual in that it installs the manual page as it installs the application itself. Most builds usually require you to run a separate *make install.man* to install the manual page for the application.)

```
lmui@opal% make -n install.xarchie
(cd EzMenu; echo "making all in ./EzMenu..."; \
make -n 'CDEBUGFLAGS=-g' all);
making all in ./EzMenu...
rm -f xarchie
```

```
cc -o xarchie aquery.o atalloc.o dirsend.o get_pauth.o get_vdir.o
perrmesg.o ptalloc.o stcopy.o support.o vl_comp.o vlalloc.o xarchie.o
db.o actions.o types.o classnames.o procquery.o settings.o  ftp.o
alert.o confirm.o dialog.o  -g -pipe  -LEzMenu -lezMenu-sparc -lXaw
-lXmu -lXt -lXext -lX11
install -c -s xarchie /usr/bin/X11
install -c -m 0444 Xarchie.ad /usr/lib/X11/app-defaults/Xarchie
install -c -m 0444 xarchie.man /usr/man/mann/xarchie.1
```

If you're satisfied with these locations, run the installation for real. (You may have to become **root** now.)

```
lmui@opal% su
Password:
opal# make install
making all in ./EzMenu...
rm -f xarchie
cc -o xarchie aquery.o atalloc.o dirsend.o get_pauth.o get_vdir.o
perrmesg.o ptalloc.o stcopy.o support.o vl_comp.o vlalloc.o xarchie.o
db.o actions.o types.o classnames.o procquery.o settings.o  ftp.o
alert.o confirm.o dialog.o  -g -pipe  -LEzMenu -lezMenu-sparc -lXaw
-lXmu -lXt -lXext -lX11
install -c -s xarchie /usr/bin/X11
install -c -m 0444 Xarchie.ad /usr/lib/X11/app-defaults/Xarchie
install -c -m 0444 xarchie.man /usr/man/mann/xarchie.1
```

And now it's just a matter of running *rehash* and starting the *xarchie* application.

```
lmui@opal% rehash
lmui@opal% xarchie &
```

Note that, for this example, you didn't need to know any C programming, you just needed to use some basic common sense. Not all compilations work this easily, but many do.

B.3 Using Patches

A *patch* to a program is exactly what it sounds like: a fix to build on the current sources. As an example, in the following example we have the *xwebster* sources from *export.lcs.mit.edu*, which we will unpack and untar.

```
lmui@opal% zcat xwebster.tar.Z | tar xfp -
lmui@opal% cd xwebster
lmui@opal% ls -F
Imakefile       controlpanel.c  user_prefs.h     xwebster.c xwebster.xbm
Makefile        display_def.c   wordlist.c       xwebster.h
Xwebster.ad     patches/        xwebster.README  xwebster.man
```

(The *xwebster* program is a client program depending on access to a licensed Webster server. Unless you have access to such a server, you will not be able to use this program. It also requires a compiled Xw library, which many vendors don't include—you'll have to build it yourself.)

Note the *patches/* subdirectory: within that directory you find three patch files:

```
lmui@opal% ls patches
patch-00        patch-01        patch-02
```

All patches should be applied in order.

The *patch* program is available in the *mit/util/patch* directory in the X11 source distribution. The best way to recognize a *patch* file is by lines starting with asterisks (*), dashes (-), hash signs (#), plus signs (+), and exclamation points (!). When you look at the file *patches/patch-00*, you'll see that it reads:

```
Replied: Wed, 28 Feb 90 16:04:12 PST
      ...
Received: by church.csri.toronto.edu id 1012; Tue, 20 Feb 90 02:20:02
EST
From: Mark Moraes <moraes@csri.toronto.edu>
To: mayer@hplnpm.hpl.hp.com
Subject: R4 xwebster fix
Cc: moraes@csri.toronto.edu
Message-Id: <90Feb20.022002est.1012@church.csri.toronto.edu>
Date:   Tue, 20 Feb 90 02:19:47 EST

xrdb doesn't seem to like comments in defaults files starting with #.
(Possibly a bug in Hence this fix.  I also fixed the Xw widgets to
stop Xt whining every time xwebster tries to change the titlebar.  (see
fixes on expo) (It doesn't matter when Xwebster.ad is installed in
LIBDIR/app-defaults, but since I test the program by xrdb'ing the
app-defaults file and then running the program, it didn't work then)

*** #Xwebster.ad~       Mon Feb 19 23:57:14 1990
--- Xwebster.ad Mon Feb 19 23:57:14 1990
**************
*** 1,3 ****
--- 1,4 ----
+ /*
    ###########################################################################
##
    #
    # File:          Xwebster
**************
*** 31,36 ****
--- 32,38 ----
    ##
    ## this is the help display that comes up initially when you run Xwebster.
    ##
      ...
```

To apply the *patch* file, do:

```
lmui@opal% patch < patches/patch-00
Hmm... Looks like a new-style context diff to me...
The text leading up to this was:
--------------------------
|*** #Xwebster.ad~       Mon Feb 19 23:57:14 1990
|--- Xwebster.ad        Mon Feb 19 23:57:14 1990
--------------------------
Patching file Xwebster.ad using Plan A...
Hunk #1 succeeded at 1.
```

```
Hunk #2 succeeded at 32.
Hunk #3 succeeded at 57.
Hunk #4 succeeded at 71.
Hunk #5 succeeded at 105.
Hunk #6 succeeded at 116.
Hunk #7 succeeded at 131.
Hunk #8 succeeded at 166.
Hunk #9 succeeded at 173.
Hunk #10 succeeded at 199.
Hunk #11 succeeded at 259.
Hunk #12 succeeded at 271.
Hunk #13 succeeded at 287.
Hunk #14 succeeded at 319.
Hunk #15 succeeded at 332.
Hunk #16 succeeded at 342.
Hunk #17 succeeded at 372.
Hunk #18 succeeded at 386.
Hunk #19 succeeded at 411.
done
```

(The message starting with "Hmm   . . . " is the *patch* program's polite way of telling you what it thinks it's doing.)

The second patch (*patches/patch-01*) resembles the first in form:

```
Return-Path: root@gauss.llnl.gov
       . . .
Received: from localhost.ARPA by gauss.llnl.gov (4.0/1.15)
        id AA00823; Tue, 3 Apr 90 13:11:46 PDT
Message-Id: <9004032011.AA00823@gauss.llnl.gov>
From: casey@gauss.llnl.gov (Casey Leedom)
To: mayer@hplms2.hpl.hp.com (Niels P. Mayer)
Subject: Small fixes to X.V11R4/contrib/clients/xwebster/Imakefile
Date: Tue, 03 Apr 90 13:11:45 -0700
Sender: root@gauss.llnl.gov

*** Imakefile-dist     Mon Mar  6 03:41:36 1989
--- Imakefile   Wed Mar 28 11:00:54 1990
**************
*** 1,37 ****
  #
  # This assumes that the HP Xwidget sources patched for r3 have been placed
! # in $(TOP)/lib/Xw.
  #
! XWLIB        = $(TOP)/lib/Xw/libXw.a
     . . .
```

Apply this patch in a similar fashion:

```
lmui@opal% patch < patches/patch-01
Hmm... Looks like a new-style context diff to me...
The text leading up to this was:
--------------------------
|*** Imakefile-dist     Mon Mar  6 03:41:36 1989
|--- Imakefile   Wed Mar 28 11:00:54 1990
--------------------------
Patching file Imakefile using Plan A...
Hunk #1 succeeded at 1.
done
```

The third patch file looks different.

```
From sam@blanche.ICS.UCI.EDU Wed Jun 28 15:13:32 1989
To: mayer@hplabs.hp.COM
Subject: New xwebster features
Reply-To: Sam Horrocks <sam@ics.UCI.EDU>
Date: Wed, 28 Jun 89 15:08:45 -0700
Message-Id: <12090.615074925@blanche.ics.uci.edu>
From: Sam Horrocks <sam@blanche.ICS.UCI.EDU>

I've added a couple of new features to xwebster and I'm sending you the
patches. I've added a button to do spelling of the word (alternate spellings
appear in the upper window) and I've added a toggle to put xwebster into
thesaurus mode.  Here are the diffs:

: Remove anything above this line.
: This is a shar archieve.  Extract with sh, not csh.
: The rest of this file will extract:
: xwebster.diffs
echo extracting - xwebster.diffs
sed 's/^X//' > xwebster.diffs << '/*EOF'
X*** /tmp/,RCSt1a11790   Wed Jun 28 14:27:31 1989
X--- xwebster.man        Wed Jun 28 14:22:32 1989
    ...
```

This file is a *shar* file. Edit out the mail header and extract the patch file with *sh* or (prefer-ably) use the *unshar* command. (If you use *unshar*, you don't have to edit out the mail header.) Do *not* unpack the *shar* file as **root**.

```
lmui@opal% unshar patches/patch-02
unshar:  Sending header to patch-02.hdr.
unshar:  Doing patches/patch-02:
extracting - xwebster.diffs
```

The resulting *xwebster.diffs* file contains:

```
*** /tmp/,RCSt1a11790    Wed Jun 28 14:27:31 1989
--- xwebster.man         Wed Jun 28 14:22:32 1989
***************
*** 50,55 ****
--- 50,65 ----
  attempt to complete the word. If the word can be completed, the new word
  is placed in the TextEdit widget; otherwise, the program beeps and
  displays a message indicating that the word is ambiguous.
+ .PP
+ Typing \fB'.'\fP or mousing \fB[Spell]\fP causes the program to look up
+ alternate ways to spell what you just typed.  The list of spellings will
+ be displayed in the browser panel.
    ...
```

Run the *patch* command to complete the patches:

```
lmui@opal% patch < xwebster.diffs
Hmm...  Looks like a new-style context diff to me...
The text leading up to this was:
--------------------------
|*** /tmp/,RCSt1a11790   Wed Jun 28 14:27:31 1989
|--- xwebster.man        Wed Jun 28 14:22:32 1989
--------------------------
Patching file xwebster.man using Plan A...
```

```
Hunk #1 succeeded at 50.
Hmm...  The next patch looks like a new-style context diff to me...
The text leading up to this was:
--------------------------
|*** /tmp/,RCSt1a11804  Wed Jun 28 14:29:00 1989
|--- Xwebster.ad        Wed Jun 28 14:22:26 1989
--------------------------
Patching file Xwebster.ad using Plan A...
Hunk #1 succeeded at 48 (offset 2 lines).
Hunk #2 succeeded at 307 with fuzz 1 (offset 28 lines).
Hunk #3 succeeded at 297 (offset 4 lines).
Hunk #4 failed at 368.
Hunk #5 succeeded at 454 (offset 49 lines).
1 out of 5 hunks failed--saving rejects to Xwebster.ad.rej
Hmm...  The next patch looks like a new-style context diff to me...
The text leading up to this was:
--------------------------
|*** /tmp/,RCSt1a11812  Wed Jun 28 14:30:18 1989
|--- controlpanel.c     Wed Jun 28 14:22:27 1989
--------------------------
Patching file controlpanel.c using Plan A...
Hunk #1 succeeded at 40.
Hunk #2 succeeded at 47.
Hunk #3 succeeded at 209.
Hunk #4 succeeded at 270.
Hunk #5 succeeded at 330.
Hunk #6 succeeded at 374.
Hunk #7 succeeded at 402.
Hunk #8 succeeded at 426.
Hunk #9 succeeded at 483.
Hunk #10 succeeded at 502.
Hunk #11 succeeded at 520.
Hmm...  The next patch looks like a new-style context diff to me...
The text leading up to this was:
--------------------------
|*** /tmp/,RCSt1a11826  Wed Jun 28 14:32:56 1989
|--- xwebster.c Wed Jun 28 14:22:31 1989
--------------------------
Patching file xwebster.c using Plan A...
Hunk #1 succeeded at 266.
Hunk #2 succeeded at 275.
done
```

The error you may want to pay attention to is the one that failed, at line 368 in the *Xweb-ster.ad* file. The *patch* program is nice enough to tell you what failed and to save the rejected patch in a file called *Xwebster.ad.rej*. (You can use the *–s* option to *patch* to suppress comments and report failures only.) You can examine that file and see if you can reconstruct what it intends to do, but that's beyond the scope of this exercise.

When you are satisfied that all patches are applied, you can complete the build:

```
lmui@opal% xmkmf
mv Makefile Makefile.bak
imake -DUseInstalled -I/usr/lib/X11/config
lmui@opal% make depend
makedepend  -s "# DO NOT DELETE" -- -I/work/lmui/src/Xw
-DAPPDEFAULTSDIR=
display_def.c wordlist.c xwebster.c
```

```
lmui@opal% make
cc -O -pipe -I/work/lmui/src/Xw -DAPPDEFAULTSDIR=
-target sun4 -c controlpanel.c
cc -O -pipe -I/work/lmui/src/Xw -DAPPDEFAULTSDIR=
-target sun4 -c display_def.c
cc -O -pipe -I/work/lmui/src/Xw -DAPPDEFAULTSDIR=
-target sun4 -c xwebster.c
rm -f xwebster
cc -o xwebster controlpanel.o display_def.o wordlist.o xwebster.o -O
-pipe  /work/lmui/src/Xw/Xw/libXw.a -lXt -lXext -lX11
lmui@opal%
```

Once the you have edited the application defaults to reflect the location of the Webster server, you can install the *xwebster* program system-wide by executing *make install* and (optionally) *make install.man* as root. Then read the manual page to learn how to run the program and enjoy.

B.4 Another Example: xkeycaps

Before we end this appendix, let's show a more "standard" compilation. For this we choose *xkeycaps*, a public domain program that's useful as a front end for the *xmodmap* program. *xkeycaps* can be taken from *export.lcs.mit.edu*:

```
lmui@ruby 35% ftp export.lcs.mit.edu
Connected to export.lcs.mit.edu.
220 export.lcs.mit.edu FTP server (NEWS-OS Release 4.1C) ready.
Name (export.lcs.mit.edu:lmui): anonymous
331 Guest login ok, send ident as password.
Password:
230 Guest login ok, access restrictions apply.
ftp> cd contrib
250 CWD command successful.
ftp> ls *keycaps*
200 PORT command successful.
150 Opening data connection for /bin/ls (ascii mode) (0 bytes).
xkeycaps.tar.Z
226 Transfer complete.
remote: *keycaps*
16 bytes received in 0.014 seconds (1.2 Kbytes/s)
ftp> bin
200 Type set to I.
ftp> get xkeycaps.tar.Z
200 PORT command successful.
150 Opening data connection for xkeycaps.tar.Z (binary mode) (121687 bytes).
226 Transfer complete.
local: xkeycaps.tar.Z remote: xkeycaps.tar.Z
121687 bytes received in 31 seconds (3.9 Kbytes/s)
ftp> quit
221 Goodbye.
lmui@ruby 36%
```

Now that we have it, unpack the compressed *tar* file, take a look at the resulting directory contents. Once again, since there's a *README*, read it.

```
lmui@ruby 36% zcat xkeycaps.tar.Z | tar xpf -
lmui@ruby 37% ls -a
./                  info.c              kbd-ncd-vt220.h
../                 kbd-atari-tt.h      kbd-sco-110.h
Imakefile           kbd-dec-1k201.h     kbd-sgi-iris.h
KbdWidget.c         kbd-dec-1k401.h     kbd-sony-nws.h
KbdWidget.h         kbd-dell.h          kbd-sun-type2.h
KbdWidgetP.h        kbd-explorer.h      kbd-sun-type3.h
KeyWidget.c         kbd-hp-700x.h       kbd-sun-type4.h
KeyWidget.h         kbd-hp-720.h        kbd-sun-type4ow.h
KeyWidgetP.h        kbd-hp-pc.h         sunOS.c
README              kbd-ibm-rs6k.h      version.h
actions.c           kbd-ncd-n101.h      vroot.h
all-kbds.h          kbd-ncd-n102.h      xkeycaps.c
commands.c          kbd-ncd-n102fr.h    xkeycaps.h
defaults.h          kbd-ncd-n102n.h     xkeycaps.man
defining.txt        kbd-ncd-n102sf.h    xkeycaps.tar.Z
guess.c             kbd-ncd-n108.h
hierarchy.txt       kbd-ncd-n97.h
lmui@ruby 38% more README
```

xkeycaps is a graphical front-end to xmodmap. It opens a window that looks
like a keyboard; moving the mouse over a key shows what KeySyms and Modifier
bits that key generates. Clicking on a key simulates KeyPress/KeyRelease
events on the window of your choice. It is possible to change the KeySyms
and Modifiers generated by a key through a mouse-based interface. This
program can also write an input file for xmodmap to recreate your changes
in future sessions. See the manpage for more details.

xkeycaps currently knows about the following types of keyboards:

    Sun type2 (MIT layout)   Silicon Graphics Iris/Indigo
    Sun type3 (MIT layout)   Sony NWS 1250
      ...

The *README* introduces the program, but doesn't include any build instructions. Look at the
Imakefile:

```
/**/# Imakefile file for xkeycaps, Copyright (c) 1991, 1992 Jamie Zawinski.

/*
 *  To specify a different default keyboard (for when the vendor display
 *  string isn't recognized) do something like this:
 *
 *    KBD_DEFINES = -DDEFAULT_KBD_NAME="\"Sun3\""
 *
 *  to make there not be a default (meaning the keyboard must be specified
 *  if the vendor display string isn't recognized) you can do
 *
 *    KBD_DEFINES = -DDEFAULT_KBD_NAME=0
 *
 *  If you don't have the file X11/DECkeysym.h (which comes with the MIT
 *  distribution) then add -DNO_DEC_KEYSYMS to DEFINES.
 *
 *  If you get a link error about _XInitKeysymDB being undefined, then add
 *  -DNO_XInitKeysymDB to DEFINES.  In this case, you might also want to
 *  add -DKEYSYMDB=/some/file/XKeysymDB to DEFINES, to tell XKeyCaps where
 *  the vendor-specific keysym database file resides.  Otherwise, you will
 *  have to set the $XKEYSYMDB environment variable before running this
 *  program, or else it won't let you select from the set of vendor keysyms.
```

```
*
* Folks running R4 or older don't get to select from the set of vendor
* keysyms anyway.  If anyone comes up with a workaround to this, please
* let me know.
*
* If you have XTrap, add the line
*
*  #define HAVE_XTRAP
*
* The XTrap support isn't quite finished yet.
*/

/* #define HAVE_XTRAP */
   ...
```

This *Imakefile* is somewhat more "standard" than the *xarchie Imakefile*, since it concentrates on variables that affect the behavior of the application itself. We alter the *Imakefile* to make the default keyboard N101, which is what most users at our site have. To do so, we add the following line towards the top of the *Imakefile*:

```
KBD_DEFINES = -DDEFAULT_KBD_NAME="\"N101\""
```

We poke around in */usr/include/X11* and determine that we have *DECkeysym.h* installed. Since we've never heard of *XTrap*, we assume we don't have it. We now try to build the program, heeding the *Imakefile* warning that we might have a link error. In R5, *xmkmf −a* will create the *Makefile* and also run *make Makefiles*, *make includes* and *make depend*.

```
lmui@ruby 46% xmkmf -a
mv Makefile Makefile.bak
imake -DUseInstalled -I/usr/lib/X11/config
make Makefiles
make includes
make depend
makedepend  -s "# DO NOT DELETE" -- -DDEFAULT_KBD_NAME="\"N101\""   -- \
xkeycaps.c KbdWidget.c KeyWidget.c info.c actions.c  commands.c guess.c
sunOS.c
lmui@ruby 48%make
cc -O -pipe   -DDEFAULT_KBD_NAME="\"N101\""   -target sun4 -c xkeycaps.c
cc -O -pipe   -DDEFAULT_KBD_NAME="\"N101\""   -target sun4 -c KbdWidget.c
cc -O -pipe   -DDEFAULT_KBD_NAME="\"N101\""   -target sun4 -c KeyWidget.c
cc -O -pipe   -DDEFAULT_KBD_NAME="\"N101\""   -target sun4 -c info.c
cc -O -pipe   -DDEFAULT_KBD_NAME="\"N101\""   -target sun4 -c actions.c
cc -O -pipe   -DDEFAULT_KBD_NAME="\"N101\""   -target sun4 -c commands.c
cc -O -pipe   -DDEFAULT_KBD_NAME="\"N101\""   -target sun4 -c guess.c
cc -O -pipe   -DDEFAULT_KBD_NAME="\"N101\""   -target sun4 -c sunOS.c
rm -f xkeycaps
cc -o xkeycaps xkeycaps.o KbdWidget.o KeyWidget.o info.o actions.o
commands.o guess.o sunOS.o -O -pipe  -lXaw -lXt  -lXext  -lXmu -lXext -lX11
```

xkeycaps built without a hitch. Since there's no *app-defaults* file, we can try it out without having to concern ourselves with resource definitions:

```
lmui@ruby 51% xkeycaps
xkeycaps: a keyboard type was not specified, and the vendor ID string,
"Acme X Servers, Tucson, AZ"
 is not recognized.  We will guess that you are using a keyboard of
 type "N101." If this is incorrect, please supply the -keyboard
 option with one of the following names:
```

```
Sun2        - Sun type2 (MIT layout)
Sun3        - Sun type3 (MIT layout)
Sun4        - Sun type4 (MIT layout)
Sun4ow      - Sun type4 (OpenWindows layout)
N97         - Network Computing Devices N97
N101        - Network Computing Devices N101
N102        - Network Computing Devices N102
N102SF      - Network Computing Devices N102 (Swedish/Finnish layout)
N102N       - Network Computing Devices N102 (Norwegian layout)
N102F       - Network Computing Devices N102 (French layout)
N108        - Network Computing Devices N108
NCD220      - Network Computing Devices vt220
LK201       - Digital Equipment Corporation LK201
LK401       - Digital Equipment Corporation LK401
RS6k        - Inferior But Marketable RS/6000
SCO110      - Santa Cruz Operation 110
HP700X      - Hewlett Packard 700X
HP720       - Hewlett-Packard 720
HPPC        - Hewlett-Packard PC
TT          - Atari TT
NWS         - Sony NWS 1250
DELL        - DELL PC
SGI         - Silicon Graphics
Explorer    - Texas Instruments Explorer
```

As the default, we get the N101 keyboard:

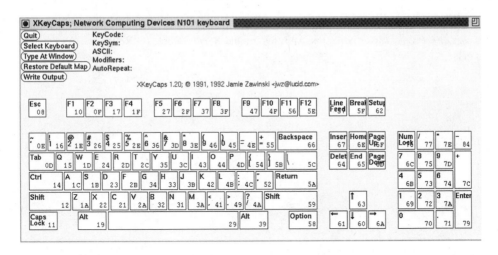

Figure B-2. xkeycaps window

When you decide to install *xkeycaps*, run both *make install* and *make install.man* as **root**. As before, it's a good idea to check what's going to be installed before you actually do it, using the *–n* option to *make*:

```
lmui@ruby 82% make -n install install.man
if [ -d /usr/bin/X11 ]; then set +x; \
else (set -x; /bin/sh /usr/bin/X11/mkdirhier /usr/bin/X11); fi
```

```
install -c -s  xkeycaps /usr/bin/X11
echo "install in . done"
if [ -d /usr/man/mann ]; then set +x; \
else (set -x; /bin/sh /usr/bin/X11/mkdirhier /usr/man/mann); fi
install -c -m 0444 xkeycaps.man /usr/man/mann/xkeycaps.n
echo "install.man in . done"
```

If this is fine with you, go ahead and install the program:

```
lmui@ruby 83% su
Password:
# make install install.man
install -c -s  xkeycaps /usr/bin/X11
install in . done
install -c -m 0444 xkeycaps.man /usr/man/mann/xkeycaps.n
install.man in . done
#
```

B.5 Related Documentation

imake is discussed in more detail in Section 8.7.

For more information on *xmkmf*, see its manual page and Section 8.6.1 of this book.

The Whole Internet User's Guide & Catalog by Ed Krol (O'Reilly & Associates, 1992).

Managing Projects with make, by Andy Oram and Steve Talbott (O'Reilly and Associates, 1991).

C

X on Non-UNIX Platforms

X runs on all types of hardware, on all sorts of operating systems. Both clients and servers run on IBM-compatible PCs running DOS, as well as Macintosh computers. Full X distributions are available for NeXT machines, but the servers have to negotiate with the NeXTstep interface. This chapter briefly describes the X products available on those platforms.

In This Appendix:

C
X on Non-UNIX Platforms

This book concentrates on X as it runs on UNIX systems. But X is OS-independent. Our office equipment consists mostly of UNIX systems and X terminals, but we also have Macintosh computers, PCs, and NeXT machines. X runs on all of them.

- We have one PC user who runs an X server on top of his Microsoft Windows environment. He runs PC applications locally, but also displays X windows alongside his MS-Windows windows. He runs project management software on the PC, while he writes and debugs UNIX programs and reads his mail using X applications.

- We have a diehard Macintosh user who runs an X server on top of his Macintosh operating system. He works primarily with Macintosh programs but occasionally needs to edit *troff* files on a UNIX system and preview them with an X-based previewer.

- We have a NeXT user who runs a full X distribution on top of the NeXTstep environment. She uses the NeXT environment for its newsreader, dictionary, and mailer, while she uses the X environment for compiling and testing X programs.

Each of these users has the advantage of keeping his or her favorite user environment, while also maintaining the same connectivity that co-workers have with workstations or X terminals.

Convenience is not the only advantage to running X on other operating systems. Probably the most significant advantage is price. Offices can upgrade to X without having to invest in new hardware. X server software might cost anywhere from $200 to $500, as opposed to $1000 for a low-end X terminal. As for disadvantages ... X servers running on PCs and Macs are noticeably slow compared to X terminals, sometimes painfully slow. PC monitors are generally smaller than X terminal monitors and the resolution is much worse. And the low-cost advantage isn't always valid, since a PC has to meet many requirements before an X server can run with reasonable performance.

Currently, the PC and Macintosh users at our office run only X servers, relying on a UNIX host to run clients for them to display. However, X clients and libraries have recently been ported to the PC platform (notably with Quarterdeck's Desqview/X product), and Macintosh X clients are also available. This gives us the ability also do it the other way around—that is, to display display both PC and Macintosh programs on X terminals. The potential is immense. X allows the sort of interconnectivity between operating systems that was previously limited largely to file sharing and remote logins.

Since there are so many products out there, this appendix only covers generalities about X running on other platforms. For more information, look for the monthly posting on *comp.windows.x* on X servers for PCs, Macs and Amigas. This document is also kept on *export.lcs.mit.edu* in the file */contrib/XServers-NonUNIX.txt.Z*.

C.1 X on DOS-based PCs

Most X software available on PCs running DOS is server software. There are two types of PC X servers on the market: those that run on top of DOS directly, and those that run on top of Microsoft Windows.

The X servers that run on top of DOS replace the entire desktop, and returning to DOS usually requires exiting (or suspending) X. The X servers that run on top of Windows, on the other hand, provide an integrated environment with access to both X and Microsoft Windows applications simultaneously. Some Windows-based X servers also let you cut-and-paste between the X environment and the Windows environment.

If the PC will be used primarily for running X—that is, as an economical X terminal—then the DOS-based X servers are probably sufficient for your needs. If the PC will frequently be used to run Windows applications as well, however, Windows-based X servers give you the best of both worlds.

Desqview/X by Quarterdeck Office Systems provides the first distribution of both X clients and servers for PCs running MS/DOS. Desqview/X runs on top of Quarterdeck's Desqview multi-tasking GUI, integrating DOS applications, MS-Windows applications, and X applications. You can use Desqview/X to remotely execute PC applications as X clients and display them on any connected X server.

C.1.1 Requirements for PC X Servers

We mentioned that PCs have to meet serveral requirements before they can run X servers. In general, before you can run a PC X server, you have to meet the following requirements:

Processor The PC should have a 80386 or '486 CPU processor. (Some vendors also support '286 machines, but no one recommends it.)

Monitor The PC needs an enhanced video display. Most vendors require either a VGA or Super VGA display. Some vendors also support EGA and 8514 graphics. Note that what the PC world calls a "high resolution" monitor still has lower resolution than a low-resolution X terminal.

Mouse The PC must have a two-button or three-button mouse.

Memory The PC must have 640K bytes of base memory, plus either 1.4 megabytes of usable extended memory for DOS-based X servers, or 2 megabytes of memory for Windows-based X servers.

Disk Space The PC must have a hard disk with at least 3 megabytes of free disk space (sometimes up to 5 if you want all the fonts installed).

Networking The PC needs to have TCP/IP installed. Some vendors supply TCP/IP packaged with the X server, but most of those that do charge extra for it. Furthermore, beware that not all implementations of TCP/IP are equal—if you have other applications on your PC that require TCP/IP, you may find that a vendor's proprietary version does not work properly with them. Networking packages supported by most vendors are FTP Software's PC/TCP, Excelan's LAN WorkPlace Network Software for PC DOS TCP/IP Transport System, and Sun Microsystem's PC-NFS. (Other frequently supported TCP/IP packages are Beame & Whiteside and WIN/TCP.)

Ethernet Card

The PC requires an Ethernet card supported by the selected TCP/IP package. Not all Ethernet cards are equal, but most TCP/IP vendors support 3COM, DEC DEPCA, Intel PC586, Ungermann-Bass NIC, Western Digital, and the XIRCOM Pocket Ethernet Adapter.

Be aware of these requirements before you invest in PC X servers for your site. It may turn out that it's cheaper to buy an X terminal.

C.1.2 Installing and Configuring PC X Servers

Installing and configuring the actual PC X servers themselves is generally a breeze. Most packages are designed to be installed with one command, prompting for information as you go along. The procedure varies from manufacturer to manufacturer, but you usually need to supply the following in order to complete installation:

- Type of VGA monitor

- Resolution of VGA monitor

- Type of TCP/IP package (Note that if the one you have isn't listed as an option, you're out of luck.)

- Name and IP address of PC. (You may have to give it the pathname of your hosts file on the PC.)

- Name and IP address of the name server

- An access control list (if applicable). (Some products provide their own host-based security by allowing only the listed hosts to connect to the server.)

In addition, you can choose the following preferences:

- Virtual screen, for X servers that support it. This means that the X server will pretend that your screen is larger than it is, with a portion of the "virtual" screen hidden but accessible by moving the mouse to that area. This is useful if you are running any applications requiring a full-page display on a standard sized monitor.

- Session startup with XDMCP (for those that support it) or with remote execution. We strongly recommend using XDMCP. See Section 3.3 for information on setting up *xdm*.

Most manufacturers will happily provide technical support if you have problems. We strongly advise calling the manufacturer if you have problems getting a PC X server to work. Manufacturers are the ones who is most likely to be aware of incompatibilities between their product and other software you have installed on your PC.

As far as the network is concerned, if you can *ftp* or *telnet* to the host machine from the PC using the software that came with your TCP/IP package, you don't have to do any other configuring from the PC end for the X connection to work. On the host end, you need to enter the PC's IP address into the network configuration, as you would for an X terminal; see Section A.6 for more information.

Windows-based X servers may require some special network configuration before they will run properly. The way this is done is heavily dependent on your vendor's implementation, but it may involve changes in both the Windows configuration file *win.ini* and in *autoexec.bat*.

C.1.3 Problems Particular to PC X Servers

The following are problems that we've encountered with PC X servers:

- Most PC X servers give you 4 bits per pixel for color displays. This confuses many X programs. See Section 7.1.1.3 for more information.

- If you use remote execution to start your X session instead of *xdm*, you might have a special problem with *xrdb*. Most PC X servers reset the server when the last X client has terminated. This is fine, except that it puts you in a Catch-22 situation with *xrdb*: you want *xrdb* to run and complete executing before you run any other clients (since you need to have those resources loaded), but then the server resets, losing all the resources you just loaded!

  There are many solutions to this problem if you don't want to just use *xdm*. Probably the easiest solution is to use the *–retain* option to *xrdb*. Another is to use *rexec* to run a script rather than individual X clients. A third option is to start up a "dummy" client to keep running while *xrdb* does its stuff, preferably one whose defaults you don't mind.

- Some PC TCP/IP products limit the number of connections allowed. For example, FTP Software's PC/TCP limits the PC to four TCP/IP connections, which isn't enough for any decent X session. You have to see your TCP/IP vendor's documentation for information on how to increase this default. For PC/TCP, the solution is to start up the kernel program in *autoexec.bat* using the *–t* option to specify the number of connections to allow. For example, for our 3COM 3c501 Ethernet card, the command was:

  ```
  3c501 /t 8
  ```

  This increased the number of TCP/IP connections to eight.

C.2 X on Macintosh Computers

Full X distributions are available on Macintosh computers that run UNIX as well as the Macintosh OS. Two UNIX products for the Macintosh are System-V based A/UX by Apple Computer, and BSD-based MachTen from Tenon Intersystems.

If you don't have a full UNIX distribution, you can still run an X server, or set up the Macintosh to run an X client. There are currently two X server products for the Macintosh: MacX and eXodus. MacX is a Macintosh X server that is available from Apple Computer (it is also bundled with their System V-based UNIX operating system, A/UX, as of version 2.0.1). eXodus is a Macintosh X server distributed by White Pine Software.

There are also currently two X client products for the Macintosh: Planet X and Xgator. Planet X is distributed by InterCon Systems and Xgator is distributed by Cayman Systems. The advantage of a Macintosh X client is that you can run Macintosh programs on your X terminal. Unfortunately, only one user can access the same Macintosh at a time, so the Macintosh becomes disabled while the X client is running, and no other X users can start up the client software while someone else is using it.

Macintosh-based X servers and clients alike require either a direct Ethernet connection or a LocalTalk connection to a LocalTalk/IP gateway such as Cayman's GatorBox. The Communications Toolbox must also be installed (standard with System 7), with the MacTCP tool installed and configured properly.* (eXodus works with DECnet as well as TCP/IP.)

C.2.1 Macintosh-based X Servers

Both X servers for the Macintosh, MacX and eXodus, can run either "rootless" or "rooted." By "rootless," we mean that X clients open directly on the Macintosh desktop, intermixed with other Macintosh windows. The Macintosh OS acts as a window manager for both X and Macintosh windows. By "rooted", we mean that a typical X root window is active, either enclosed entirely within a Macintosh window, or available through a pull-down menu. An X window manager can be used in a rooted window (such as *twm*, *mwm* or *olwm*).

Some X programs may have problems with a rootless environment; to run those programs, use rooted screens only. MacX defines 4 screens: screen 0 is rootless monochrome, screen 1 is rooted monochrome, screen 2 is rootless color, and screen 3 is rooted color. eXodus allows you to define up to 6 screens as either rooted or rootless.

One of the most obvious problems with using a Macintosh as an X server is that the Macintosh mouse only has one button. MacX uses the left-arrow and right-arrow keys to act as the second and third mouse button (respectively). eXodus provides a little more flexibility for configuring mouse behavior. In addition, there are third-party mice for Macintosh computers that have two or three buttons.

---

*SLIP has also recently become available for the Macintosh.

(Users of OPEN LOOK programs can use the *props* utility to change the behavior of the SELECT mouse button so that it brings up menus instead of selecting the default item when pressed on a menu button. This is a good tip for all 1- and 2- button mouse users. Mac users who also run *olwm* might also want to use *props* to turn off "pointer jumping," by which *olwm* and *olvwm* move the mouse pointer automatically to follow scrollbars and pop-up notices.)

You can get upgrades to MacX from *aux.support.apple.com*, in the */aux.patches/supported/MacX* directory. You are encouraged to retrieve the MacX upgrades only if you already have a legal license for MacX. (Only the server is redistributed on the *ftp* site, which is useless without the fonts or a font conversion utility anyway.)

If you use either MacroMaker or QuickKeys on your Mac, it is strongly recommended that you disable it. MacroMaker and QuickKeys translate keystrokes, conflicting with the X server.

C.2.2 MacTCP and the Communications Toolbox

To run Macintosh X products, you generally need to have MacTCP running. MacTCP was developed by Apple, and is distributed by several third-party vendors. It is also bundled with MacX.

MacTCP runs under the Communications Toolbox. The following tips are important to note when installing MacTCP:

1. You *must* install the Communications Toolbox correctly. Under System 7, the Communications Toolbox is already installed as part of the base OS distribution. If you need to install the Communications Toolbox for a Macintosh that is not running System 7, however, you can't simply create a Communications folder under your System folder and copy the *MacTCP* tool in there. You must run the installation utility that is bundled with the Communications Toolbox.

   If you don't install the Communications Toolbox correctly, you'll never get a message that tells you it's improperly installed. Instead, you'll get an error message such as "No Communications Tools Installed," which misleadingly implies that the Toolbox is installed correctly but MacTCP isn't.

2. You need to copy the *MacTCP* tool to the new Communications folder within the system folder, and copy the *MacTCP* and *AdminTCP* files to the System folder (under System 7, these files reside in the Control Panels folder). We strongly recommend that you do *not* copy these files from another Macintosh, but take them directly from the distribution floppies. If you do copy them from another Mac, make sure *not* to take the *MacTCP Preferences* file.

3. Configure MacTCP using the *AdminTCP* control panel document. (*AdminTCP* is identical to *MacTCP*, except that you can use *AdminTCP* to lock the configuration after it is properly configured.) Here is where you specify things like your IP address, subnet mask, name server, etc.

4. Reboot and try running a MacTCP program.

5. Once you have confirmed that MacTCP is properly configured, put a lock on it and throw the *AdminTCP* file in the trash.

A possible conflict with MacTCP is that if you are also running NCSA Telnet, you need to be sure that you are running the version that is MacTCP-compatible. That means that you need to install the version of NCSA Telnet entitled something like *Telnet 2.4 – MacTCP*. If you don't do this, then after running an application that uses MacTCP, you won't be able to run NCSA Telnet again until you reboot.

Notes on configuring MacTCP are available on *sumex-aim.stanford.edu* in the file */info-mac/report/mac-tcp-info.txt*.

C.3 X on NeXT Computers

The NeXT machine does not technically belong in a chapter about non-UNIX machines, since it is based on UNIX. The NeXT machine also has built-in Ethernet and TCP/IP, so a lot of the issues for running X on PCs and Macs don't apply to the NeXT. However, we discuss them here because NeXT X distributions are a different breed from other UNIX distributions, since they have to deal with the NeXTstep interface.

A public domain R4 X distribution for the NeXT called XNeXT is available through anonymous *ftp* from *cunixf.cc.columbia.edu*. (Although an R5 server is currently available for the NeXTstation Turbo, it is not yet available for other NeXT machines.)

There are also three commercial products for the NeXT. These are co-Xist by Pencom Software, Cub'X by Cub'X Systemes (distributed in the U.S. by Interactive Technology), and eXodus from White Pine Software. Cub'X and co-Xist are full X distributions including servers, clients, and libraries, with OSF/Motif clients and libraries also available. eXodus is just a server with a select group of clients.

All three commercial implementations meld X with the NeXTstep interface much in the way Macintosh and Windows-based X servers do, in a "rootless" mode. XNeXT, on the other hand, supplants the NeXTstep interface and requires you to "hot-key" to switch between the two modes.

Regardless of what X server you choose to run on the NeXT, you should make sure that the second mouse button is enabled in NeXTstep (through the Preferences application), or it won't be available to the X server.

D

Resources and Keysym Mappings

Resources and keysym mappings are topics that the administrator needs to be familiar with in order to configure applications and set up user environments. This appendix gives some background material on both of those topics.

In This Appendix:

D
Resources and Keysym Mappings

Two important pieces to the X puzzle are resources and keysym mappings. Although these two issues are unrelated, they both come into play when administrators have to debug user environments or configure applications system-wide. This appendix gives some background material on both of those topics.

Resources are covered in detail in Volume Three, *X Window System User's Guide*, by Valerie Quercia and Tim O'Reilly (O'Reilly & Associates, 1990). Some of the material in this chapter repeats what you'll find there, but we also give some useful tips and advanced information for administrators. Even if you are familiar with how to use resources, you may want to scan this appendix.

D.1 Using Resources

Resources are tricky to deal with, but understanding how they work is extremely important for X administration. They are used for configuring not only everyday clients like *xterm* and *xclock*, but also special clients such as window managers and the X Display Manager (*xdm*). Resource syntax is used even by some X terminal vendors for configuring the X server remotely. For these reasons, we think it's worth it to cover resource definition in depth.

D.1.1 Resource Definition Syntax

The syntax for defining resources can be quite complex, requiring some familiarity with widget hierarchies. For our purposes, however, it will suffice to know that the syntax for a simple resource follows the form:

```
name*variable:value
```

For example:

```
xterm*background:cadetblue
xterm*foreground:deeppink
```

specifies that the client named *xterm* should use a background color of cadet blue and a foreground color of deep pink. Similarly, you can specify a specific font with:

```
xterm*font:-schumacher-clean-bold-r-normal--16-160-75-75-c-80-iso8859-1
```

If you want the client named *xbiff* always to appear in a certain spot, you can have:

```
xbiff*geometry:+750+900
```

Resource definitions can be commented out by preceding them with exclamation points (!), and definitions can span multiple lines by using a backslash (\) to suppress newlines. Note that if a resource cannot be properly interpreted—for example, if you forget the colon between the variable name and the value—no error message is generated, but the entry is simply ignored.

There are additional syntax rules if you are loading your resources directly into the server with *xrdb*, since *xrdb* runs the file through the C pre-processor (*cpp*) as well. See Section D.1.3 for more information.

D.1.1.1 Loose and Tight Bindings

The asterisk (*) between the name of the client and the variable to be specified means that these definitions are using *loose bindings*, which are recommended for general use. The true name for a resource, using *tight bindings*, might be something much more complicated, delimited with periods between each field, such as:

```
Xwebster.panel.display_scroller.display.alignment: Left
```

but in most situations, you can shorten this to:

```
Xwebster*alignment:  Left
```

(One notable exception we make to this rule is with the XTerm*VT100.geometry resource definition. This is because whereas the VT100 widget for *xterm* uses the size of a character for the window geometry, other widgets within *xterm* use pixels. If you specified 90x40 as the window size for all *xterm* widgets, *xterm* menus would appear unusually small.)

A full explanation of the syntax of resource variables and their precedence can be found in *The X Window System Users Guide*. For now, just know that when you use the asterisk in a resource name, you may be matching several fields at once.

As you would expect, if you omit the client name and simply start the resource definition with an asterisk, then all clients inherit that resource definition. That is, should you define a global resource as:

```
*geometry:+0+0
```

then all clients would appear at coordinates (0,0) by default.

However, the asterisk does not work like the shell wildcard it resembles. You cannot use it as a general-purpose wildcard in resource definitions. The asterisk can't be used to match partial names of fields, but only as a replacement for complete fields in the resource name. That is, if you want both *xterm* and *xtetris* to appear with yellow backgrounds, you cannot simply write:

```
xt*background:yellow
```

This resource definition would not affect *xterm* or *xtetris*; it would affect only a client with the name *xt*. The reason for this is simple: you wouldn't want loosely-bound resources set for the *xcal* calendar program, for example, to affect the behavior of the *xcalc* calculator program as well.

A resource can be overridden by a more specific resource—for example, if you set the following resources:

```
xterm*background:      blue
xterm.VT100.background: red
```

and then open a standard *xterm* window with the *VT100* widget, the second declaration is more specific than the first and the window background will appear in red. However, note that any other *xterm* widgets, such as *mainMenu*, will appear with a blue background.

In R5, the question mark (?) character is introduced in resource names. A question mark in a resource name represents exactly one field in a loose binding. Loose bindings using question marks are considered to be more specific than bindings using only asterisks. Bindings with question marks will therefore take precedence over other loose bindings.

D.1.1.2 The –name Command-line Option

An X toolkit option that has an important effect on which resources a client uses is the *–name* option, which effectively changes the name of the client. By changing the name of the client, it changes the name of the resources it accepts as well.

The possibilities available with the *–name* option are best illustrated by example. A user might want to have *xterm* windows from a host called *sapphire* with a blue border, but windows from host *ruby* with a red border. There are multiple ways of doing this, but one way might be to define the following resources to be accessed by all *xterm* clients:

```
xterm-sapphire*BorderColor:    blue
xterm-ruby*BorderColor:        red
```

and then start up the windows with *–name* options, to give the window from machine *ruby* the name *xterm-ruby* and the window from the machine *sapphire* the name *xterm-sapphire*.

```
% xterm -name xterm-ruby &
% xterm -name xterm-sapphire &
```

Although the *–name* option for the *xterm* client changes the string in the titlebar as well, it should not be confused with the *–title* option, which changes the string in the titlebar but does not change the name of the client itself.

D.1.1.3 xterm Versus XTerm

Although we'd like to avoid all the complexities of how resources are named, there is one detail that we can't escape. Sometimes the name `xterm` is used in resource names, and sometimes `XTerm` is used. Although this usage seems arbitrary, it isn't at all, and the two terms should not be confused.

The name of your window is usually the name of the client; that is, if you just run *xterm*, the window that comes up will have the name `xterm`. As described above, however, you can use the *–name* toolkit option to change the name of the window. For example, if you are running a console window (started with the *–C* option to *xterm*), you might want to name that window

"CONSOLE." Similarly, if you are running a window with a particularly large geometry, you might want to name it "bigxterm." You can start the clients with the *–name* option shown above:

```
% xterm -name CONSOLE
% xterm -name bigxterm
```

and then use these names in resource specifications, such as:

```
CONSOLE*font:        fixed
bigxterm*geometry:   140x60
```

Resources written with the name CONSOLE will apply only to windows with the name *CONSOLE*, and resources with then name bigxterm will apply only to windows with the name *bigxterm*. However, although the *bigxterm* and *CONSOLE* windows have different names, they can both be considered instances of a larger class, called XTerm. All windows begun with the *xterm* client belong to the class XTerm, and any resources written for the name XTerm will apply to all *xterm* windows, whether their name is *CONSOLE*, *bigxterm*, *goofy*, *dumbo*, or just plain *xterm*. Note also that they would apply to the *xterm-ruby* and *xterm-sapphire* windows shown in the previous example. The following resource definitions:

```
XTerm*scrollbar:true
XTerm*font:-schumacher-clean-bold-r-normal--16-160-75-75-c-80-iso8859-1
```

would apply to both the *CONSOLE* and *bigxterm* windows, with one caveat: since the font for *CONSOLE* is explicitly redefined to "fixed" as shown earlier, it will ignore the XTerm*font definition, because when all else is equal (i.e., the bindings are the same), instance specifications override class specifications.

Learning the Class and Instance Names

Knowing the class name for a given client is important in order to set client-specific resources. The manual page should also tell you the class name; but another way to learn the class name for a given window that is currently displayed is to use the *xprop* client, which among other things lists a WM_CLASS category. In that category, the first name listed is the name of the particular window, and the second name is the name of the class. For example:

```
% xprop -name bigxterm
   ...
WM_CLASS(STRING) = "bigxterm", "XTerm"
   ...
```

twm users can also use the f.identify function to learn the class name for a window. See the *twm* manpage for more information.

This is only one example of instances and classes. Within the application itself, classes are used to group together several properties. For example, the *xterm* client considers the color of the text, the pointer color, and the text cursor color to all be instances of the same class, called Foreground. The following resource:

```
xterm*foreground:    red
```

only changes the color of the text. But the resource:

```
xterm*Foreground:    red
```

changes the color of the text, the pointer, and the text cursor all to the same color. This is equivalent to:

```
xterm*foreground:    red
xterm*pointerColor:  red
xterm*cursorColor:   red
```

D.1.2 Where Resources Are Defined

For each client application, there are dozens of available resources, and any number of ways to specify them. The behavior you want may depend on what host the client is running on or what X server is used, or just on your personal preferences. For that reason, a client's resources can be set at the system level, at the server level, and at the user level. Therein lies the problem: since there are so many ways resources can be defined, tracing their definitions can be a frustrating task.

Upon startup, clients build the resource database. The resource manager searches for resource variable definitions in multiple places and then passes those variable definitions back to the client program. The resource manager typically searches in the following places for resources, with later definitions overriding earlier ones:

1. System-wide application defaults, in */usr/lib/X11/app-defaults/* directory. The name of the file used for application-specific defaults is the name of the client class, not the client itself. For example, */usr/lib/X11/app-defaults/XTerm* contains application defaults for the *xterm* client. Note that the *app-defaults* resources are read only by clients that run on that particular host, regardless of where they display.

2. User-specific per-application defaults, usually in a user's home directory. For example, *$HOME/XTerm* on a given host is read by all *xterm* clients started on that host by a particular user. If your home directory is shared among multiple hosts, therefore, that single *XTerm* file can specify resources used by all *xterm* clients on each of those host machines.

3. Host-specific defaults (not specific to an application), usually in a user's home directory. For example, *$HOME/.Xdefaults-sapphire* is read by all clients running on the machine *sapphire*. This means, for example, that even if your home directory is shared among multiple hosts, you can have *xterm* windows appear in one font on one machine, in another font on another machine, and in reverse video on a third machine—simply by having multiple *.Xdefaults-**hostname*** files in your home directory. The name of the file used for system-specific defaults can be redefined with the XENVIRONMENT environment variable; for example, if you were to set XENVIRONMENT to *My.resources*, the resource manager would look in that file instead.

4. Resources loaded directly into the server (into the *resource database*) with the *xrdb* client. This means that you can have all *xterm* clients from any host use the same foreground, background, fonts, etc., without having to maintain *$HOME/.Xdefaults-**hostname*** files for each machine, or multiple *$HOME/XTerm* files if your home directory is not

shared among multiple hosts. In general, the preferred way of specifying a reasonable number of resources for a user is to use *xrdb*.

The *xrdb* client is typically run in the user's startup script, e.g., *.xsession* or *.xinitrc*, to load a resource file (any filename can be used, but common names are *.Xresources* and *.Xdefaults*). An administrator can also set up a default resource file for all users, to be read by *xrdb* in the systemwide startup script (for sessions started with *xdm*, this would be */usr/lib/X11/xdm/Xsession*). Note that resources loaded into the resource database are still read only at client startup: a change will affect only subsequent clients, not clients already running.

5. If no resources are loaded directly into the server (i.e., if *xrdb* has not been run), defaults are read from a file called *.Xdefaults*, usually in the user's home directory. Note that this means that clients run from different hosts may use different resources if your home directory is not shared among machines.

6. Resources loaded directly on the command line, using the *–xrm* option.

In the list above, we say that some default files are "usually" read from a user's home directory. The directory in which you keep your application defaults is assumed to be your home directory. The XAPPLRESDIR environment variable comes into play here—if you set XAPPLRESDIR to *$HOME/Xstuff*, the resource manager will look under that directory for client-specific resource files (such as *XTerm*). Other environment variables that affect where resources are read from are XFILESEARCHPATH and XUSERFILESEARCHPATH.

Seeing Where Resources are Read (SunOS, Solaris, SVR4)

To see what resource files are read on client startup, try using the *trace* command on a SunOS machine, or the *truss* command on a Solaris 2.0 or SVR4 machine. For example:

```
lmui@ruby% trace xterm >& /tmp/xterm.trace
```

Then examine the resulting file:

```
gethostname ("", 1002) = 0
open ("/home/lmui/.Xdefaults-ruby", 0, 017777777) = -1 ENOENT (No such
file or directory)
access ("/home/lmui/XTerm", 04) = -1 ENOENT (No such file or directory)
access ("/usr/lib/X11/app-defaults/XTerm", 04) = 0
stat ("/usr/lib/X11/app-defaults/XTerm", 0xf7ffed90) = 0
open ("/usr/lib/X11/app-defaults/XTerm", 0, 036734323664) = 4
stat ("/usr/lib/X11/app-defaults/XTerm", 0xf7fff200) = 0
read (4, "*SimpleMenu*BackingStore: NotUse".., 2800) = 2800
close (4) = 0
```

In the example, note that the user had resources loaded into the server, so *$HOME/.Xdefaults* was not opened. The only resource file in its path that it found and opened was the system-wide *app-defaults/XTerm* file.

D.1.3 Advantages of xrdb

Using *xrdb* to load your resources directly into the X server is the preferred way of allocating resources. Using *xrdb* helps to make things more consistent—clients run from a host on which you have a different home directory (thus different *$HOME/.Xdefaults* files) are guaranteed to use the same resources if all your resources are kept directly in the server.

One of the most powerful things about *xrdb* is that it gives you special flexibility since it runs the resource file through a C pre-processor (*cpp* by default). Using *cpp* means that you can have #ifdef and #include commands in your resource files, and that you can use the *–D* and *–U* options to define and undefine symbols.

For example, you can call *xrdb* with the *–D* option to set defaults according to the current hostname:

```
xrdb -D`hostname` -merge $HOME/.Xdefaults
```

This allows us to set up our *Xdefaults* file with different defaults for different hosts. (On a system that doesn't have the *hostname* command, you might use *uname –n*.) For example, your *Xdefaults* file might contain:

```
! ruby windows with red borders
#ifdef ruby
XTerm*bordercolor:red
#endif /*ruby*/

! sapphire windows with blue borders
#ifdef sapphire
XTerm*bordercolor:blue
#endif /*sapphire*/
```

You can also do some fancy stuff with setting colors or fonts "consistently." For example, if you like to use fonts in the same family, you might do:

```
#define SMALL -schumacher-clean-medium-r-normal--10-100-75-75-c-80-iso8859-1
#define BIG -schumacher-clean-medium-r-normal--16-160-75-75-c-80-iso8859-1
    ...
smallxterm*Font:    SMALL
Xconsole*Font:  SMALL
bigxterm*Font:  BIG
```

Under R5, *xrdb* becomes much more powerful since it now pre-defines several useful symbols, such as COLOR.

```
#ifdef COLOR
xterm*background:    yellow
#else
xterm*background:    white
#endif
```

Other useful symbols are PLANES, HEIGHT, WIDTH, SERVERHOST, and CLIENTHOST.

A common mistake in defining resources is to try to comment out lines using an initial hash sign (#) instead of an exclamation point (!). If you then run the resource file through *xrdb*, you'll get the error message "Unknown preprocessor directive" or "undefined control."*

There are two ways to load resources using *xrdb*:

xrdb –load filename

> The resources listed in the specified file replace all resources already loaded into the server. All previous resources are erased. This is the default behavior of *xrdb*.

xrdb –merge filename

> The resources listed in the specified file are merged into the list of resources already loaded into the server. New resource definitions with names matching previous definitions will take precedence, but any resources that are not redefined are retained.

The *–query* option to *xrdb* shows you all resources currently set for your server.

D.1.4 Translation Tables

An important type of resource for many applications is a *translation*, with which keystokes and mouse buttons can be defined within an application. (Note that this is distinct from redefining keystrokes and button presses at the server level, which is controlled by the *xmodmap* client, described in Section D.2.) You can also use a translation table to change the action a client performs when a particular event is reported.

Translations are best described by demonstrating their use in a common application. A client that defines a lot of translations is *xcalc*. The *xcalc* window generally resembles the window shown in Figure D-1.

Each of the buttons shown in the *xcalc* window is defined using a translation table. The *app-defaults/XCalc* file defines the fourth row of keys on the standard *xcalc* keypad with the lines:

```
XCalc.ti.button16.Label:PI
XCalc.ti.button16.Translations:#override<Btn1Up>:pi()unset()
XCalc.ti.button17.Label:x!
XCalc.ti.button17.Translations:#override<Btn1Up>:factorial()unset()
XCalc.ti.button18.Label:       (
XCalc.ti.button18.Translations:#override<Btn1Up>:leftParen()unset()
XCalc.ti.button19.Label:       )
XCalc.ti.button19.Translations:#override<Btn1Up>:rightParen()unset()
XCalc.ti.button20.Label:       /
XCalc.ti.button20.Translations:#override<Btn1Up>:divide()unset()
```

---

*Some X applications edit resource files, often removing comment lines. If you use such an application, you might want to fake a comment using resource syntax:

```
Comment.line1:   This is a comment
```

This takes advantage of the fact that invalid resources are simply ignored by applications.

Figure D-1. xcalc window

Each button is given its label (e.g., PI for the first button), followed by the event translation when it is pressed. In the case of the 16th button, the internal function *pi()* is called, presumably returning the value of π. (Since the foreground and background colors are reversed on the button when it is initially pressed, the Athena Command widget action *unset()* is then called, returning the button colors to the default.) For the 20th button, "/" is the label, and pressing it calls the *divide()* function. Clearly a user could easily redefine the behavior of each button on the *xcalc* keypad by switching the translations in their own resource files. (Be sure to switch the labels too, though!)

Also in the *XCalc* application defaults file is a full translation table for interpreting keystrokes within the *xcalc* window:

```
XCalc.ti.bevel.screen.LCD.Translations:#replace\n\
            Ctrl<Key>c:quit()\n\
            Ctrl<Key>h:clear()\n\
            None<Key>0:digit(0)\n\
            None<Key>1:digit(1)\n\
                ...
            <Key>KP_0:digit(0)\n\
            <Key>KP_1:digit(1)\n\
                ...
            <Key>KP_9:digit(9)\n\
                ...
            <Key>KP_Divide:divide()\n\
                ...
            <Key>.:decimal()\n\
            <Key>+:add()\n\
            <Key>-:subtract()\n\
            <Key>*:multiply()\n\
            <Key>/:divide()\n\
            <Key>(:leftParen()\n\
            <Key>):rightParen()\n\
            <Key>!:factorial()\n\
```

```
        . . .
    <Key>p:pi()\n\
        . . .
    <Btn1Down>,<Btn1Up>:toggle()selection()\n
```

These definitions allow you to type a "1" on the keyboard (either on the keypad or on the main part of the keyboard) rather than clicking the correct button in the *xcalc* window. They also allow keyboard shortcuts to many of the functions. You can access the `divide()` function by pressing a slash on either keyboard or keypad. You can get the value of π by pressing a "p," and get the factorial of a number by pressing an exclamation mark. As you could expect, this translation table can also be redefined at the user level.

Beware that translations are very specific about their syntax. A single space after one of the trailing backslashes will cause the resource manager to ignore all subsequent translations, with no error message reported.

For full information on the syntax for event translation resources, see the *X Window System User's Guide*. For now, administrators should just be aware that translation tables are potentially another tool in customizing a client for a user.

D.2 Defining Keys and Button Presses With xmodmap

An important piece to the X puzzle is filled by the *xmodmap* client. When the user performs any action—such as typing a key or moving the mouse—the server sends a packet of information to the client called an *event*. These events are then translated into actions by the client. You can use the *xmodmap* client to effectively change the event that is reported to the client.

Keysym mappings are mappings of keyboard events at the server level, before the event is sent to the client. Keysyms are the symbols used for each key on the keyboard.

The X server maintains a *keymap table* which contains a listing of keys on the keyboard and how they should be interpreted. A client gets the keymap table from the server upon client startup. In most cases, the keymap table is used to interpret keys literally—when you press the letter "a," a key code is sent to the client which corresponds to the letter "a" in the keymap table.

You can use the *xmodmap* client to reassign key codes within the keymap table. *xmodmap* can therefore be used to redefine how a key is interpreted by the client. You probably wouldn't want to translate the alphanumeric keys on the keyboard, but you may want to translate others. For example, you might want to change the BackSpace key to a Delete:

    % xmodmap -e "keysym BackSpace = Delete"

Another example is if you mistakingly hit the CAPS LOCK key a bit too often, you can disable it completely. Some people might disable CAPS LOCK the low-tech way (by just removing the key from the keyboard!), but you can also render it harmless with the command:

    % xmodmap -e "keysym Caps_Lock = "

effectively disabling the CAPS LOCK key entirely. Note that the symbol is now gone and can't be redefined without using the hardware key code.

If you are a DVORAK typist, you can use *xmodmap* to translate every key on the keyboard so your QWERTY keyboard behaves like a DVORAK keyboard.

If it ever seems that keystrokes are not working correctly, you can check current keysym settings by running *xmodmap* with the *–pk* argument. Use the *xev* client if you need to determine exactly what keycode a key generates on your display. There is also a public domain client called *xkeycaps* that can be used to display the keysyms for selected keyboards, as shown in Section B.4.

You can use *xmodmap* to add or remove keysyms, or even to redefine the keycode associated with that keysym. You can also use it to redefine the mouse buttons, using the `pointer` keyword. For example, to have the second and third mouse buttons switch places, you can enter:

```
lmui@opal % xmodmap -e "pointer = 1 3 2"
```

If you have a large number of keys to remap, you can put the commands in a file that is read when your X session starts. For example, you create a file called *.Xmodmap*:

```
! my .Xmodmap file
remove Lock = Caps_Lock
remove Control = Control_L
keysym Control_L = Caps_Lock
keysym Caps_Lock = Control_L
add Lock = Caps_Lock
add Control = Control_L
   ...
```

These commands effective reverse your Control and CAPS LOCK keys. (Control and CAPS LOCK are "switched" on PC and Macintosh keyboards, which can be exceedingly frustrating.) This file can then be read automatically in a X startup script:

```
   ...
xset b 10 100 10
xrdb $HOME/.Xdefaults
xmodmap $HOME/.Xmodmap
twm &
   ...
```

One danger of using *xmodmap* is that anything set with *xmodmap* might remain in effect after you have logged out. This isn't a problem if you use the same X server every day, but beware that if you use a co-worker's X terminal in his absence, he may come back complaining that you broke his CAPS LOCK key. This might happen if you use *xdm*, since the server is not restarted after every X session. On some X terminals, you can fix this problem by toggling "retain X settings" on the X terminal setup menu.

The *xkeycaps* client, available on *export.lcs.mit.edu*, is a front-end to *xmodmap*. *xkeycaps* has the default keysym mappings for several different types of keyboards. If your keyboard is supported by *xkeycaps*, you can use it to reset your keysym mappings to its defaults. Beware that if your keyboard is not identical to the one *xkeycaps* thinks you have, you will quickly regret having done this.

D.2.1 Using xev to Learn Keysym Mappings

The *xev* client is essential for debugging keysym mappings. When you start up *xev*, a small "event window" appears. All events that take place within that window are shown on standard output. This means screenfuls of output, but it also means that when you type a key, you can immediately trace the resulting event. For example, if you need to know what keysym is sent when you type the Delete key on the keyboard, just run *xev* and type the Delete key in the event window. Typical output might be:

```
KeyPress event, serial 13, synthetic NO, window 0x800001,
  root 0x8006d, subw 0x800002, time 1762968270, (50,36),
  root:(190,176), state 0x0, keycode 27 (keysym 0xffff, Delete),
same_screen YES,
  XLookupString gives 1 characters: "^?"

KeyRelease event, serial 15, synthetic NO, window 0x800001,
  root 0x8006d, subw 0x800002, time 1762968336, (50,36),
root:(190,176),
  state 0x0, keycode 27 (keysym 0xffff, Delete), same_screen YES,
  XLookupString gives 1 characters: "^?"
```

This tells you that the Delete key (keycode 27), interpreted as keysym 0xffff, which is Delete and character ^?. If you do an *xmodmap –pk*, you should see a line resembling:

```
27    0xffff (Delete)
```

If you redefine the Delete key as the Backspace key and do the same exercise (run *xev* and press the Delete key), you should see something like:

```
% xmodmap -e "keysym Delete = BackSpace"
% xev
    ...
KeyPress event, serial 13, synthetic NO, window 0x800001,
  root 0x8006d, subw 0x800002, time 1763440073, (44,39),
root:(240,235),
  state 0x0, keycode 27 (keysym 0xff08, BackSpace), same_screen
YES,
  XLookupString gives 1 characters: "^H"

KeyRelease event, serial 15, synthetic NO, window 0x800001,
  root 0x8006d, subw 0x800002, time 1763440139, (44,39),
root:(240,235),
  state 0x0, keycode 27 (keysym 0xff08, BackSpace), same_screen
YES,
  XLookupString gives 1 characters: "^H"
```

This tells you that now the Delete key (still keycode 27) is being interpreted as hexadecimal 0xff08, keysym BackSpace, and generates character "^H." *xmodmap –pk* should show you:

```
27    0xff08 (BackSpace)
```

D.3 Related Documentation

The following X manual pages may be of interest: *xrdb*, *xmodmap*, *xcalc*, *xcalc*, *xprop*, *xev*, and *twm*.

For more information, see *X Window System User's Guide*, by Valerie Quercia and Tim O'Reilly (O'Reilly & Associates, 1990).

"Making Better Use of Resources," by Paul Davey, published in *The X Resource, Issue 3*, O'Reilly & Associates, Inc., Summer 1992.

E

The Components of X Products

This appendix lists the contents of various X distributions.

In This Appendix:

E
The Components of X Products

This appendix provides an overview of some of the X products that are currently available. We summarize various vendors' implementations, and discuss features that may help you to identify them. The following implementations are covered:

- MIT Release 5
- OSF/Motif GUI
- Sun OpenWindows
- DECWindows
- AIXWindows
- Silicon Graphics

We also include a listing of some of the libraries that you may need in compiling software.

Some of these implementations may overlap and may contain components of several other systems. For example, the Motif Toolkit is included in most current vendor-supplied installations. Several vendors also offer applications that can switch back and forth between OSF/Motif and OPEN LOOK "modes."

With a complete distribution, X software is installed in the following directories.

Table E-1. X Distribution Directories

File	Description
/usr/bin/X11/	X executables, including clients, demos, and the X server.
/usr/lib/X11/	Server-specific software, including fonts, color databases, and configuration files.
/usr/lib/	X programming libraries.
/usr/include/X11/	X header files and bitmaps.
/usr/man/	X manpages.
$HOME/	User-specific startup and resource files.

Keep in mind that your pathnames may differ, but the directories *bin*, *lib*, and *include* should exist in some form.

The names of libraries vary depending on the system—SunOS shared libraries have a *.so.version* or *.sa.version* extension, while Silicon Graphics shared libraries have a _s_ extension. A _p_ extension usually means that the library has been "profiled" for performance analysis. An extension such as _G0_ indicates it was built with a specific compiler option.

The following information should help you determine what type of installation you currently have and what you would like to install.

E.1 MIT X11 Release 5

To the user, Release 5 looks very similar to Release 4. Most of the new features (such as the font server, PEX, and the Xcms color system) are more visible to the X programmer and to the administrator than they are to the user. As in R4, the *include* files for toolkits and related files are grouped into subdirectories. (In previous MIT releases and some vendor implementations, the *include* files were in one directory.)

Table E-2. MIT X11R5 Files

File	Description
/usr/bin/X11/X	A link to a server executable. The server name usually starts with a capital X. For example, *Xsun*, *Xcfbpmax*, and *Xsgi* are the names for X servers. The X server will be present in complete installations.
/usr/bin/X11/twm	Tab window manager. This is the default window manager in MIT R4 and R5.
/usr/bin/X11/fs	The font server program.
/usr/lib/X11/PEX/	A directory of files used by PEX, the 3-D extension to X11. This directory is new to R5.
/usr/lib/X11/XKeysymDB	A list of keysyms. This should be installed on any system using OSF/Motif clients and MIT R5 (A different version of this will file comes with MIT R5). Most Motif clients will fail to work properly without this file.
/usr/lib/X11/XErrorDB	A mapping of X error codes to error messages.
/usr/lib/X11/app-defaults/	A directory of system-wide default resources for clients.
/usr/lib/X11/config/	A directory of configuration files copied from the source build area. These configuration files are used by *imake* when building X programs after the X distribution is installed.
/usr/lib/X11/fonts/	A directory of fonts for the X server. If a local X server is not present (i.e., if it is a client-only installation), this directory may be unnecessary. The font server could also read fonts from this directory over the network for a remote server.
/usr/lib/X11/fs/	A directory of font server configuration files.

File	Description
/usr/lib/X11/xdm/	A directory of files required by the *xdm* client.
*/usr/lib/X11/rgb/ or rgb.**	Files that contain the RGB database for color names.
/usr/lib/libX11.a	The main library of X functions (Xlib).
/usr/lib/libXaw.a	The Athena Widget library.
/usr/lib/libXmu.a	The miscellaneous functions library.
/usr/lib/libXt.a	The X Toolkit functions library.
/usr/lib/liboldX.a	The backward compatibility library.
/usr/lib/libXdmcp.a	The XDMCP library (R4 and R5).
*/usr/lib/lib*X*.a*	Other X libraries (release-dependent).
/usr/include/X11/	A directory of include files for compiling X programs.
/usr/include/X11/bitmaps/	A directory of bitmaps for random X programs.
$HOME/.Xdefaults	User-specific resources for X clients.
$HOME/.Xresources	User-specific resources for X resources.
$HOME/.twmrc	The user-specific startup file for the *twm* window manager.
$HOME/.xinitrc	The user-specific startup file for starting the X server using *xinit*.
$HOME/.xsession	The user-specific startup file for starting the X server using *xdm*.

E.2 OSF/Motif

If you administer any systems that run OSF/Motif with X, the files shown in Table E-3 should be present. Of the files listed, *XKeysymDB* is an important one that is often forgotten with some Motif installations. This file maps the official OSF names for keysyms—most Motif programs will complain and generate numerous error messages if they cannot find this file when they start up. *XKeysymDB* is included in the MIT R5 release.

The names of the OSF/Motif libraries may be slightly different on your system, depending on the release of X11. Early releases of Motif (1.0.A) came with their own version of the X toolkit library. Most people named this *libXtm.a*, *libMXt.a*, or something similar to avoid confusion with the standard MIT *libXt.a*. If you are compiling a Motif program on one of these systems, the Motif specific X Toolkit library needs to be linked with:

```
% cc -o motifthing motifthing.c -lXm -lXtm -lX11
```

The location of the Motif *include* files may also vary depending on the implementation. The default location provided by OSF places them in */usr/include*, but they may be in */usr/include/X11* instead. You may want them under */usr/include/X11* in order to keep all X11 files in one place. If so, the alternate location has to be specified with the *–I* flag to *cc*:

```
% cc -c -I/usr/include/X11 motifthing.c
```

Motif programs include the header files with the Motif subdirectory prepended:

```
#include <Xm/Xm.h>
```

The complete pathname of this file becomes */usr/include/X11/Xm/Xm.h*.

Table E-3. Motif Files (Motif 1.1.x)

File	Description
/usr/bin/X11/mwm	The Motif Window Manager.
/usr/bin/X11/uil	The UIL (User Interface Language) compiler.
/usr/bin/X11/mre	The Motif Resource Editor (this is officially a "demo," but it is potentially quite useful—only present in version 1.x).
/usr/lib/libMrm.a	The Motif resource manager library.
/usr/lib/libXm.a	The Motif toolkit library.
/usr/lib/libUil.a	The Motif UIL library.
/usr/lib/X11/XKeysymDB	A database of special OSF keysyms for Motif applications.
/usr/lib/X11/app-defaults/Mwm	System-wide default resources for *mwm*.
/usr/lib/X11/system.mwmrc	The default startup file for *mwm*.
/usr/lib/X11/uid/	A directory of compiled UIL files for clients.
/usr/include/Xm/	A directory of Motif toolkit *include* files.
/usr/include/Mrm/	A directory of Motif resource manager *include* files.
/usr/include/uil/	A directory of Motif UIL *include* files.
$HOME/.mwmrc	The user-specific startup file for *mwm*.

E.3 Sun OpenWindows

The OPEN LOOK GUI is currently packaged as part of the OpenWindows environment on Sun systems. OpenWindows is laid out differently from the MIT X installation: all software is installed under */usr/openwin*, as listed in Table E-4.

Table E-4. OpenWindows Files (Sun4, SunOS 4.1.1)

File	Description
bin/openwin	The server start-up script.
bin/	A combination of X, OpenWindows, and NeWS clients.
demo/	A combination of X, OpenWindows, and NeWS demo programs (including a demo *xterm*).
etc/	Configuration information for NeWS.
include/	Header files for X and OpenWindows.

X Window System Administrator's Guide

File	Description
lib/	Server-specific software for OpenWindows.
man/	Man pages for X and OpenWindows. (You may have to do "*setenv MAN-PATH /usr/man:/usr/openwin/man*" for the *man* command to find them.)

Table E-5 summarizes the more important OPEN LOOK files.

Table E-5. OPEN LOOK Files

File	Description
/usr/openwin/bin/xnews	The OpenWindows server.
/usr/openwin/bin/olwm	The OPEN LOOK Window Manager.
/usr/openwin/bin/props	The resource editor (similar to Motif's *mre*).
/usr/openwin/lib/lib*	Programming libraries for OPEN LOOK functions.
/usr/openwin/lib/openwin-*	System-wide default files.
$HOME/.openwin-*	Per-user default files.

E.4 DECWindows

DECWindows is moving towards a Motif-like environment, but is still different in many ways. Most of it should be quite familiar to someone used to a MIT distribution. The MIT-derived X11 is available as an unsupported subset that can co-exist with the DECWindows environment.

Table E-6. DECWindows Files (DecStation, Ultrix 4.2)

Files	Description
/usr/bin/Xws	The DECwindows server.
/usr/bin/dxwm	The DECwindows window manager.
/usr/bin/dxsession	The DECwindows session manager.
/usr/bin/Xprompter	The login window tool (similar to *xdm*).
/usr/bin/dxuil	The DECwindows User Interface Language compiler.
/usr/lib/X11/uid/	A directory of compiled UIL files.
/usr/include/X11/	A directory of both of DECwindows and MIT header files.
/usr/include/mit/X11/	A directory of vanilla MIT header files.
/usr/lib/libXext.a	The DECwindows version of *libXext*.
/usr/lib/libXext-mit.a	The vanilla MIT *libXext*.

E.5 AIXWindows

AIXWindows is quite different than the MIT distribution and it may take some work to get it to look like the MIT environment. The names and options of standard clients have been changed from what you are used to, and the layout of the software is quite different than other vendors' implementations. The current version of AIX, 3.2, is also missing some clients you would expect when using an MIT distribution. The layout of libraries and *include* files is relatively standard.

Table E-7. AIXWindows Files (RS/6000, AIX 3.2)

Files	Description
/usr/bin/X11/X	The AIXWindows server.
/usr/bin/X11/mwm	The Motif window manager.
/usr/bin/X11/xdt	The AIXWindows desktop.
/usr/bin/X11/aixterm	The AIXWindows version of *xterm*.
/usr/bin/info	The InfoExplorer hypertext X documentation browser.
/usr/include/X11/*.h	AIXWindows header files.
/usr/include/Xm/*.h */usr/include/Mrm/*.h* */usr/include/uil/*.h*	Motif 1.x header files.
/usr/lib/lib*.a	Standard X11 R4 and Motif 1.x libraries.
/usr/lib/X11/	Standard X11 R4 *lib* files.
/usr/lpp/info/X11fonts/	A directory of fonts for the InfoExplorer utility.

E.6 Silicon Graphics

SGI has had a decent NeWS implementation for several years, working together with the SGI Graphics Library system (GL). X functionality was added over time in a piecemeal fashion. With the release of IRIX 4.0, X11 is an integral part of the server, and works well along with GL and NeWS. The clients are based on OSF/Motif, which comes with the OS.

Table E-8. Graphics X11 Files (Indigo, IRIX 4.0)

Files	Description
/usr/bin/X11/Xsgi	A combined *X11/GL/NeWS* server.
/usr/bin/X11/4Dwm	A mwm-like window manager.
/usr/bin/X11/toolchest	A "desktop" manager client.
/usr/lib/X11/	A directory of X11 R4 "lib" files.

Files	Description
/usr/include/X11/	A directory of both X11 R4 and Motif 1.1 header files.
/usr/lib/lib*	X11 R4 and Motif 1.1 libraries.

E.7 A Guide to X11 Libraries

When compiling software, you may suddenly discover that it requires a library you've never heard of. In your X11 adventures, you may see references to the following libraries.

Library	Description
libX11.a	Xlib
libXaw.a	Athena widget set
libXext.a	Extensions to Xlib
libXt.a	Toolkit
libXau.a	Authorization
libXdmcp.a	XDMCP
libXinput.a	Input methods
libXmu.a	Misc Utilities
liboldX.a	Backwards compatibility library for X10
libphigs.a	R5 phigs
libXm.a	Motif widgets
libUil.a	Motif user interface language
libMrm.a	Motif resource manager
libXtm.a libMXt.a	Names for libXt when Motif (1.0.A) required its own version
libMu.a	MIT Motif utilities library (sometimes found in software from MIT Athena project)
libXw.a	HP Widgets in R3 and R4 contrib

F

Getting X11

This appendix lists where you can get the sources and patches to both Release 4 and Release 5 of X11.

In This Appendix:

F
Getting X11

The information in this chapter is taken from the *comp.windows.x* Frequently Asked Questions List. We provide it here for your convenience, but we encourage you to get the latest version of the FAQ (as described in Section A.2) for more updated information.

F.1 Where Can I Get X11R5?

Information about MIT's distribution of the sources on 6250bpi and QIC-24 tape and its distribution of hardcopy of the documents is available from Software Center, Technology Licensing Office, Massachusetts Institute of Technology, 28 Carleton Street, Room E32-300, Cambridge MA 02142-1324, phone: 617-258-8330.

You will need about 100Mb of disk space to hold all of Core and 140MB to hold the Contrib software donated by individuals and companies.

PLEASE use a site that is close to you in the network.

Note that the RELEASE notes are generally available separately in the same directory; the notes list changes from previous versions of X and offer a guide to the distribution.

Table F-1. North America Anonymous ftp

State	Name	Directory	Address
California	*gatekeeper.dec.com*	*pub/X11/R5*	16.1.0.2
California	*soda.berkeley.edu*	*pub/X11R5*	128.32.131.179
Indiana	*mordred.cs.purdue.edu*	*pub/X11/R5*	128.10.2.2
Maryland	*ftp.brl.mil* (good for MILNET sites)	*pub/X11R5*	128.63.16.158
Massachusetts	*crl.dec.com*	*pub/X11/R5*	192.58.206.2
Massachusetts	*export.lcs.mit.edu* (*crl.dec.com* is better)	*pub/R5*	18.24.0.12
Michigan	*merit.edu*	*pub/X11R5*	35.1.1.42
Missouri	*wuarchive.wustl.edu*	*packages/X11R5*	128.252.135.4
Montana	*ftp.cs.montana.edu*	*pub/X.V11R5*	192.31.215.202
New Mexico	*pprg.eece.unm.edu*	*pub/dist/X11R5*	129.24.24.10
New York	*azure.acsu.buffalo.edu*	*pub/X11R5*	128.205.7.6

Table F-1. North America Anonymous ftp (continued)

State	Name	Directory	Address
North Carolina	*cs.duke.edu*	*dist/sources/X11R5*	128.109.140.1
Ohio	*ftp.cis.ohio-state.edu*	*pub/X.V11R5*	128.146.8.52
Ontario	*ftp.cs.utoronto.ca*	*pub/X11R5*	128.100.1.105
Washington DC	*x11r5-a.uu.net*	*X/R5*	192.48.96.12
Washington DC	*x11r5-b.uu.net*	*X/R5*	137.39.1.12

Table F-2. Europe/Middle East/Australia Anonymous ftp

Country	Name	Directory	IP Address
Australia	*munnari.oz.au*	*X.V11/R5*	128.250.1.21
Denmark	*freja.diku.dk*	*pub/X11R5*	129.142.96.1
United Kingdom	*src.doc.ic.ac.uk*	*graphics/X.V11R5*	146.169.3.7
	hpb.mcc.ac.uk	*pub/X11r5*	130.88.200.7
Finland	*nic.funet.fi*	*pub/X11/R5*	128.214.6.100
France	*nuri.inria.fr*	*X/X11R5*	128.93.1.26
Germany	*ftp.germany.eu.net*	*pub/X11/X11R5*	192.76.144.129
Israel	*cs.huji.ac.il*	*pub/X11R5*	132.65.6.5
Italy	*ghost.sm.dsi.unimi.it*	*pub/X11R5*	149.132.2.1
Netherlands	*archive.eu.net*	*windows/X/R5*	192.16.202.1
Norway	*ugle.unit.no*	*pub/X11R5*	129.241.1.97
Norway	*nac.no*	*pub/X11R5*	129.240.2.40
Switzerland	*nic.switch.ch*	*software/X11R5*	130.59.1.40

Table F-3. Japan Anonymous ftp

Region	Name	Directory	IP Address
Kanagawa	*sh.wide.ad.jp*	*X11R5*	133.4.11.11
Kwansai	*ftp.ics.osaka-u.ac.jp*	*X11R5*	133.1.12.30
Kyushu	*wnoc-fuk.wide.ad.jp*	*X11R5*	133.4.14.3
TISN	*utsun.s.u-tokyo.ac.jp*	*X11R5*	133.11.11.11
Tokyo	*kerr.iwanami.co.jp*	*X11R5*	133.235.128.1
Tokyo	*scslwide.sony.co.jp*	*pub/X11R5*	133.138.199.1

Table F-4. UUCP

Name	Comment	Directory
uunet	for UUNET customers	*~/X/R5*
decwrl	existing neighbors only	*~/pub/X11/R5*
osu-cis	(not online until early September)	*~/X.V11R5*
WJanon	(host: watjo.swp.wj.com)	*~/X/X11R5/*
	Modem: Telebit TB2500 (PEP, V.32, etc)	
	Systems or L.sys suggested/approximate	
	entry:	
	WJanon Any ACU 19200	
	1-408-435-0240 "" \ login: WJanon	
utai	existing neighbors only	*~/ftp/pub/X11R5*
hp4nl	Netherlands only	*~uucp/pub/windows/X/R5*

Table F-5. Other File Transfer Methods

Method	Region	Comments
NFS	Missouri	*wuarchive.wustl.edu*
		/archive/packages/X11R5
		128.252.135.4
		mount point: */archive*
AFS	Pennsylvania	*/afs/grand.central.org/pub/X11R5*
NIFTP	United Kingdom	*uk.ac.ic.doc.src*
(hhcp, cpf, fcp, ...)		<X.V11R5>
		00000510200001
		user "guest"
anon FTAM	United Kingdom	000005102000 (Janet)
		X.V11R5
		146.169.3.7 (Internet)
		204334504108 (IXI)
ACSNet	Australia	*munnari.oz* (fetchfile)
		X.V11/R5
		Please fetch only one file at a time, after check-
		ing that a copy is not available at a closer site.

[9/2/91; updated for contrib 10/91]

Anyone in Europe can get a copy of the MIT X.V11R5 distribution, including the core and contributed software and all official patches, free of charge. The only requirement is to agree to return the tapes, or equivalent new tapes. Only QIC and TK format cartridges can be provided. Contact: Jamie Watson, Adasoft AG, Nesslerenweg 104, 3084 Wabern, Switzerland. Tel: +41 31 961.35.70 or +41 62 61.41.21; Fax: +41 62 61.41.30; jw@adasoft.ch.

UK sites can obtain X11 through the UKUUG Software Distribution Service, from the Department of Computing, Imperial College, London, in several tape formats. You may also obtain the source via Janet (and therefore PSS) using Niftp (Host: uk.ac.ic.doc.src Name: guest Password: your_email_address). Queries should be directed to Lee McLoughlin, 071-589-5111#5037, or to info-server@doc.ic.ac.uk or ukuug-soft@uk.ac.ic.doc (send a Subject line of "wanted". Also offered are copies of comp.sources.x, the export.lcs.mit.edu contrib and doc areas and most other announced freely distributable packages.

X11R5 and X11R4 source along with X11R5 contrib code, prebuilt X binaries for major platforms, and source code examples from O'Reilly's books is available on an ISO-9660-format CD-ROM from O'Reilly & Associates. [as of 3/92].

X11R5 source is available on ISO-9660-format CD-ROM for members of the Japan Unix Society from Hiroaki Obata, obata@jrd.dec.com.

X11R5 source along with GNU source, the comp.sources.x archives, and SPARC binaries is available on an ISO-9660-format CD-ROM from PDQ Software, 510-947-5996 (or Robert A. Bruce, rab@sprite.Berkeley.EDU).

X11R5 source is available from Automata Design Associates, +1 215-646-4894.

Various users' groups (e.g., SUG) offer X sources cheaply, typically on CD-ROM.

Source for the Andrew User Interface System 5.1 and binaries for common systems are available on CD-ROM. Information: info-andrew-requests@andrew.cmu.edu, 412-268-6710, fax 412-621-8081.

Binaries for X11R5, with shared libX11 and libXmu, for A/UX 2.0.1 are now available from wuarchive.wustl.edu:/archive/systems/aux/X11R5. Patches for X11R5 compiled with gcc (but not shared libraries) are also available. [John L. Coolidge (coolidge@cs.uiuc.edu, 10/91)]

Binaries by Rich Kaul (kaul@ee.eng.ohio-state.edu) for the Sun386i running SunOS 4.0.2 are available on dsinc.dsi.com (please only after-hours USA EST).

Binaries for the Sun386i are available from compaq.com (131.168.249.254) in pub/sun-386i/sources and from vernam.cs.uwm.edu (129.89.9.117).

A binary tree for the Next by Douglas Scott (doug@foxtrot.ccmrc.ucsb.edu) is on foxtrot.ccmrc.ucsb.edu; it is missing the server, though.

Binaries for the Sun386i are in vernam.cs.uwm.edu:/sun386i.

Binaries for the HP-PA are on hpcvaaz.cv.hp.com (15.255.72.15).

Also, Binaries are available from Unipalm (+44 954 211797, xtech@unipalm.co.uk), probably for the Sun platforms.

F.2 Where Can I Get Patches to X11R5?

The release of new public patches by the MIT X Consortium is announced in the comp.windows.x.announce newsgroup.

Patches themselves are available via ftp from export and from other sites from which X11 is available. They are now also distributed through the newsgroup comp.sources.x. Some source re-sellers may be including patches in their source distributions of X11.

People without ftp access can use the xstuff mail server. It now has 17 patches for X11R5 [8/92]. Send to xstuff@expo.lcs.mit.edu the Subject line:

```
send fixes #
```

where # is the name of the patch and is usually just the number of the patch.

Here are a few complications:

1. Fix 5 is in four parts; you need to request "5a", "5b", "5c" and "5d" separately

2. The file sunGX.uu, which was part of an earlier patch, was re-released with patch 7

3. Fix 8 is in two parts: "8a" and "8b"

4. Fix 13 is in three parts: "13a", "13b", and "13c"

5. Fix 16 is in two parts: "16a" and "16b"

F.3 Where Can I Get X11R4?

Integrated Computer Solutions, Inc., ships X11R4 on half-inch, quarter-inch, and TK50 formats. Call 617-621-0060 for ordering information.

The Free Software Foundation (617-876-3296) sells X11R4 on half-inch tapes and on QIC-24 cartridges.

Yaser Doleh (doleh@math-cs.kent.EDU; P.O. Box 1301, Kent, OH 44240) is making X11R4 available on HP format tapes, 16 track, and Sun cartridges. [2/90]

European sites can obtain a free X11R4 distribution from Jamie Watson, who may be reached at chx400!pan!jw or jw@pan.uu.ch. [10/90]

Non Standard Logics (+33 (1) 43 36 77 50; requests@nsl.fr) makes source available.

IXI Limited (+44 223 462 131) is selling X11R4 source on quarter-inch cartridge formats and on 5.25" and 3.5" floppy, with other formats available on request. [IXI, 2/90]

Virtual Technologies (703-430-9247) provides the entire X11R4 compressed source release on a single QIC-24 quarter-inch cartridge and also on 1.2 meg or 1.44 meg floppies upon request. [Conor Cahill (cpcahil@virtech.uu.net) 2/90]

Young Minds (714-335-1350) makes the R4 and GNU distributions available on a full-text-indexed CD-ROM.

[Note that some distributions are media-only and do not include docs.]

X11R4 is ftp-able from export.lcs.mit.edu; these sites are preferable, and are more direct:

Location	Name	Address	Directory
(1) West USA	*gatekeeper.dec.com*	16.1.0.2	*pub/X11/R4*
Central USA	*mordred.cs.purdue.edu*	128.10.2.2	*pub/X11/R4*
(2) Central USA	*giza.cis.ohio-state.edu*	128.146.8.61	*pub/X.V11R4*
Southeast USA	*uunet.uu.net*	192.48.96.2	*X/R4*
(3) Northeast USA	*crl.dec.com*	192.58.206.2	*pub/X11/R4*
(4) UK Janet	*src.doc.ic.ac.uk*	129.31.81.36	*X.V11R4*
UK niftp	*uk.ac.ic.doc.src*	<XV11R4>	
(5) Australia	*munnari.oz.au*	128.250.1.21	*X.V11R4*

The giza.cis.ohio-state.edu site, in particular, is known to have much of the contrib stuff that can be found on export.

The release is available to DEC Easynet sites as CRL::"/pub/X11/R4".

Sites in Australia may contact this address: ftp.Adelaide.EDU.AU [129.127.40.3] and check the directory pub/X/R4. The machine shadows export and archives comp.sources.x. (Mark Prior, mrp@ucs.adelaide.edu.au, 5/90)

Note: a much more complete list is distributed regularly by Dan Heller (argv@sun.com) as part of the introductory postings to comp.sources.x.

A set of X11R4 binaries built by Tom Roell (roell@informatik.tu-muenchen.de) for the 386/ix will available from export.lcs.mit.edu in /contrib and in /pub/i386/X11R4 from 131.159.8.35 in Europe. Stephen Hite (shite@sinkhole.unf.edu) can also distribute to folks without ftp facilities via disks sent SASE; contact him for USmail and shipping details. [12/90] In addition, the binaries are available via uucp from szebra [1-408-739-1520, TB+ (PEP); ogin:nuucp sword:nuucp] in /usr2/xbbs/bbs/x. In addition, the source is on zok in /usr-X/i386.R4server/. [2/91] In addition, if you are in the U.S., the latest SVR4 binary (April 15), patches, and fonts are available on piggy.ucsb.edu (128.111.72.50) in the directory /pub/X386, same filenames as above. (Please use after 6pm Pacific, as these are large files.) [5/91]

A set of HP 9000/800 binaries is available on hpcvaaz.cv.hp.com (15.255.72.15) as ~ftp/pub/MitX11R4/libs.x800.Z. [2/91]

A set of X11R4 binaries for the NeXT 2.x have been made available by Howie Kaye on cunixf.cc.columbia.edu

A set of binaries by John Coolidge (coolidge@cs.uiuc.edu) for the Mac running A/UX 2.0 is available from wuarchive.wustl.edu in the file (/archive/systems/aux/X11R4/Xupdate2.tar .Z). Also in X11R4/diffs is a set of patches for making X11R4 with shared libraries with mkshlib.

A complete distribution of SCO X11R4 binaries by Baruch Cochavy (blue@techunix.techn-ion.ac.il) can be found on uunet. The server is Roell's X386 1.1b, compiled for ET4000 based SVGA boards.

G

Error Messages

This appendix lists error messages that you might get when running X clients. We not only list errors from X programs but also UNIX errors that you often encounter when running or compiling X programs.

In This Appendix:

G
Error Messages

This appendix lists error messages that you might get when running X clients. This appendix is broken up into the following categories:

X Errors	Errors that you may get from X clients.
UNIX Errors	Errors that you may get when running X clients, but which reflect problems more closely associated with UNIX.
Compilation Errors	Errors that you may get when compiling programs under UNIX.

G.1 X Errors

Can't Open display

or

Unable to open display

There is a problem with the DISPLAY variable or with the display specified using the *–display* option. The DISPLAY variable may not be set properly, or the specified host may be unknown. The host may also not have access to the specified display. Correct the setting of the DISPLAY variable, or extend server access as appropriate using either *xhost* or *xauth*. See Section 2.3.1 for more information on setting the DISPLAY variable, or Chapter 4 for information on server access control.

(This particular error is actually generated by the application, so it may not be worded exactly like this. "Can't open display" is the wording generated by Xt-based applications.)

Unknown preprocessor directive

or

n: **undefined control**

You might get this error from *xrdb* if you used the "#" character to comment out a line in a resource file. For a resource file, replace the "#" with a "!", or use a dummy resource entry. See Section D.1.3 for more information.

X Error of failed request: BadValue (integer parameter out of range for operation)
  Major opcode of failed request: 51 (X_SetFontPath)
  Minor opcode of failed request: 0
  Resource id in failed request: 0x4
  Serial number of failed request: 4
  Current serial number in output stream: 6

Error from the *xset* client when you try to add a new element to the font path. This could be because of any of the following problems:

- The new font directory doesn't exist or it not readable by the server. This could be a filesystem permissions problem or an NFS access problem.

- The *fonts.dir* file could be missing or damaged.

- If you try to add a font server to the font path, the font server could have died or may not be running on the specified port number.

See Section 5.1.4 for more information.

---

failed to set default font path '/usr/lib/X11/fonts/misc/,/usr/lib/X11/fonts/Speedo/,
/usr/lib/X11/fonts/75dpi/,/usr/lib/X11/fonts/100dpi/'
Fatal server error:
could not open default font 'fixed'

You may get this error when starting the X server. One or more of the default font directories is missing, unreadable or has something wrong with the *fonts.dir* file. Check that each of those directories is readable. You might also get this error if a font server is part of the font path and is not currently running. You can override the default font path using the *–fp* option to the X server command; see Section 5.1.4 for more information.

Warning: Cannot convert string " ... " to type FontStruct

You cannot access the specified font, either because it doesn't exist or because the server does not have read access to it. See Section 5.1.4 for more information.

Warning: Color name ... is not defined in server database

You have specified a color to an application that is not defined. Either the color name was misspelt, or it was not properly installed for the server. See Chapter 6 for more information.

X Toolkit Warning: Cannot allocate colormap entry for White
X Toolkit Warning: Cannot allocate colormap entry for Black
X Toolkit Warning: Cannot allocate colormap entry for white
X Toolkit Warning: Cannot allocate colormap entry for black

Your color database is corrupted. You need to recreate the color database; see Section 6.1.3 for more information.

Xlib: connection to "*hostname*:0.0" refused by server
Xlib: Client is not authorized to connect to server
Error: Can't Open display

The client does not have permission to connect to the specified server. Either host-based or user-based access control is in effect. You need to add the host to the *xhost* list for that server, or you need to copy the code to your *.Xauthority* file on this host using *xauth*, or (if you are using SUN-DES-1 security) you need to be added to the *xhost* list on the server. See Chapter 4 for more information.

Warning: Widget class *nnn* version mismatch (recompilation needed):
widget 11004 vs. intrinsics 11003.

You are probably mixing MIT clients with Sun OpenWindows libraries or vice versa. You should specify the right libraries for the client:

```
% (setenv LD_LIBRARY_PATH /usr/openwin/lib; OW-client)
% (setenv LD_LIBRARY_PATH /usr/lib; MIT-client)
```

Fatal server bug! no screens found.

You might get this error when starting a Sun X server, where you can use the *–dev* option to specify a different device (such as *–dev /dev/cgfour0 –dev /dev/bwtwo1*). A device listed with the *–dev* option is incorrect, or the device may be missing from */dev*.

mwm: Invalid accelerator specification on line *n* of specification string
mwm: Invalid accelerator specification on line *m* of configuration file

The Motif Window Manager *mwm* uses function keys which your server does not have defined. You should define the function key using *xmodmap*, or alter your *.mwmrc* to use a different key.

unknown keysym osfDown ...

Motif-based applications (such as *mwm*) require the proper installation of the file */usr/lib/X11/XKeysymDB*. This file comes with most Motif distributions and is also present in X11R5.

Binding Unix socket: No such file or directory
Fatal server error:
Cannot establish unix listening socket

You may get this error when starting the X server on a workstation display. The server will try to create the socket in */tmp/.X11-unix/*. If the */tmp* directory is not writable, the X server will fail.

XIO: fatal IO error 32 ...
The connection was probably broken by a ...

Older X Toolkit clients don't handle orderly shutdown well. Modern window managers use the ICCCM to terminate a client; older versions of clients will complain when they are killed by the window manager, instead of going away quietly like they are supposed to.

G.2 UNIX Errors

Permission denied.

You may get this error if you're running an X client from a remote host. This is a *rsh* error, not an X error: the local host needs to be in the remote host's *hosts.equiv*, or in the user's *.rhosts* file. See Section 2.3.4 for more information.

hostname: *hostname*: **No such file or directory**
or
hostname: *hostname*: **cannot open**

You may get this error if you're running an X client from a remote host. You are probably trying to use *rsh*, but are running the *restricted* shell instead of the *remote* shell. You should change your path to get the right one. See Section 2.3.4.1 for more information.

stty: Operation not supported on socket

You may get this error if you're running an X client from a remote host. If you are using *rsh*, the *.cshrc* file on the remote host probably has an interactive command in it (such as *stty*).

Type xterm unknown
or
emacs: Terminal type xterm is not defined.
or
xterm: Unknown terminal type
I don't know what kind of terminal you are on - all I have is 'xterm'.

The *xterm* entry is missing from the **termcap** or **terminfo** database. You need to install the entry; see Section 8.4.4 for more information.

Not login shell.

You might get this error in an *xterm* window when you try to run *logout* instead of *exit* to close the window. *xterm* does not open login shells by default. To start *xterm* as a login shell, use the *–ls* option to *xterm*, or set the `xterm*loginShell` resource to `true`. To exit a shell that isn't a login shell, use *exit* instead of *logout*.

There are stopped jobs

You are trying to exit a shell without properly exiting or killing all jobs started in that shell. You should properly quit the jobs before exiting the shell—use the *jobs* command for a list of your stopped jobs.

command: Command not found.

You may get this error if the requested command isn't in your search path, or if it doesn't exist. Make sure the command is installed and make sure its path is in your search path.

command:Permission denied.

You may get this error if the command is in your search path but you don't have execute permission for it.

Host is unreachable
no network route is known to that host

You may get this error when there is a routing problem—the gateway is probably down or misconfigured.

Connection timed out

You tried to connect to a host that is currently down or otherwise unreachable.

ld.so: libX11.so.4: not found

You might get this message if you are running SunOS. Either the shared library cache is out of date, the shared library is missing, or the shared library is not in your LD_LIBRARY_PATH. You should either set the LD_LIBRARY_PATH environment variable to the appropriate value, run *ldconfig* to update the library cache, or install the missing library. See Section 8.4.2 for more information.

No more processes

Your host has reached its process limit. You should increase the number of processes that the host can handle at once; see Section 7.7.1 for more information.

Sorry, pid ... was killed due to lack of swap space

Your host has run out of swap space. You should increase the amount swap space on your host; see Section 7.7.3 for more information.

G.3 Compilation Errors

---

reversed (or previously applied) patch detected! Assume -R [y]

You might get this error when running the *patch* program. You should abort *patch*, since you are probably applying the patches in the wrong order.

---

ld: /lib/libX11.a: warning: table of contents for archive is out of date; rerun ranlib(1)

You might get this error when compiling sources. The modification date on the library file is different than the stored time stamp in the library—probably from copying the library from another location. Run *ranlib –t* on the libraries.

---

make: Fatal error in reader: Makefile, line *n*: **Unexpected end of line seen**

Some *cpp* programs convert tabs to spaces. Tabs are required by *make*. If you get this error, you might have to install another version of *cpp*; see Section 8.7.3.4 for more information.

Unknown preprocessor directive
  or
n: **undefined control**

You might get this error from *imake* or *xmkmf* if a line is commented in your *Imakefile* using a hash sign (#) instead of using the XCOMM command. See Section 8.7.3.1 for more information.

---

ld: Undefined symbol

You are trying to compile a program which uses a library that is missing. See Section 8.8.1.2 for more information.

---

filename: *n*: **Can't find include file ...**

You are trying to compile a program which includes a header file that is missing. See Section 8.8.1.1 for more information.

Index

::(double colon), in Makefiles, 225
: (colon), in resource definitions, 281
! (exclamation point), in resource definitions, 282
   in resource files, 287
   in Xaccess file, 56
(hash sign), 219
   in resource definitions, 287
   in RGB specification, 145
   used to comment out lines, 315
% (percent sign), in Xaccess file, 59
* (asterisk), and specifying fonts, 108
   in resource definitions, 281-283
   in Xaccess file, 56-57
/**/ (null comment), 219
? (question mark), in resource definitions, 283
@@ (imake syntax), 220
\ (backslash), in resource definitions, 282

A

access control
   server, 73-93;
     host-based (see host-based access control), ;
     reasons for, 73;
     user-based (see user-based access control), ;
     X terminals, 83, 175;
     xauth vs. xhost, 82-83
   xdm, 47
.ad files, (see application defaults)
additional style, font name field, 102

Adobe fonts, 101
   converting to F3, 113
   converting to X11/NeWS format, 126
AIX, 188
   chown command, 211
   installing font server on, 133
   installing xdm on, 70
AIXWindows, 8, 187
   components of, 302
   fonts; example, 121-122
   InfoExplorer client, 117
aliases
   for fonts, 108-109, 114;
     DECWindows, 119;
     OpenWindows, 124
   for hostnames, 138
   for RGB color, 145
   for Xcms color, 149
alternate-servers (font server), 129, 134
anonymous ftp, (see ftp command)
AnswerBook, 186
app-defaults directory, (see application defaults)
Apple Macintosh computers, Communications Toolbox, 275-277
   MacTCP, 275-277
   UNIX and, 275
   X clients and, 271, 275
   X servers and, 271, 275
application defaults, 258, 285
ar command, 199, 207
arch command, 192
Archie, 248-250
   help command, 249
   mail server, 250
   prog command, 249
   servers, 248

Archie (cont'd)
  set search command, 249
  xarchie client, 251-259
archie command, 248
arp command, 169
arp tables, 169
Athena widgets, 7
autologout feature, 26
average width, font name field, 102

B

background color, 281
  specifying, 23, 144
background processes, 26
backing store, 161-162
Backspace character, mapping to Delete, 290
bc command, 81, 146, 243
BDF format, 111, 125, 129
  converting DECWindows fonts to, 120
  converting SNF to, 112
  converting to PCF, 112, 138
  converting to SNF, 112, 114
  converting to X11/NeWS formats, 112
  getting from font server, 112, 136
  getting from X server, 112
.bdf files, 111
bdftohds command, 171
bdftopcf command, 112
bdftosnf command, 112, 125, 170
  –t option, 114
Berkeley Internet Name Domain, (see DNS)
–bg option, 144, 23
big endian, 111, 170
binaries, stripping, 207
BIND, (see DNS)
BITFTP, 237
bitmap, fonts, 110
Bitmap Distribution Format, (see BDF format)
BITNET, 237
bits per pixel, 159
Bitstream fonts, 101
bldfamily command, 107, 126
boot files, AIX, 70, 133
  IRIX, 70, 132-133

SunOS, 69, 131
System V, 132-133
Ultrix, 70
booting, X terminals, 167-168
BOOTP, 163, 165-166
  X terminals and, 164
bootpd daemon, 165
  errors, 169
Bootstrap Protocol, (see BOOTP)
BOOTSTRAPCFLAGS, 228
broadcast address, 168, 173
broadcast queries, 55-57
  and subnet, 173
  X terminals and, 173
bug reports, 194
build errors, memory fault, 199
build flags, 205-210
  BuildServer, 210
  DefaultCCOptions, 210-211
  DefaultFontPath, 117, 212
  ExpandManNames, 207
  HasLargeTmp, 199, 207
  HasSecureRPC, 86
  HasXdmAuth, 84, 207
  InstallCmd, 211
  InstallFSConfig, 128, 207
  InstallLibManPages, 207
  InstallXdmConfig, 206
  InstallXinitConfig, 206
  ProjectRoot, 207-208
  StripInstalledPrograms, 207
building X, 185-230
  configuration flags, 205-210
  disk space, 191, 198-200
  fixes, 186
  from MIT sources, 185-186
  from source code, 188-189
  issues, 185-190
  link trees, 196-197
  NFS-mounted systems, 201-203
  patches, 194-196
  preparation, 191-197
  trouble-free example, 197-198
  with imake, 216-225
  (see also installing X.)
BuildServer build flag, 210
byte order, 111, 170

C

C compiler, (see cc)
C preprocessor, (see cpp)
.ca100 files, 153
cache-size (font server), 128
CAPS LOCK key, 159
  disabling, 290
  switching with Control, 291
cat, Bill, 73
catalogue (font server), 129, 136
catalogue-list (font server), 129,
  136
cc, debugging, 199
  –E flag, 228
  –g flag, 199
  –O flag, 198
  optimization, 198
  –temp= flag, 200
  –v flag, 228
.cf files, 222
character cell fonts, 102-103
character set, font name field, 102
chkconfig command, 133
chkey command, 86-87
  error messages, 93
chmod command, 97
chooser client, 53, 55, 57-59
  indirect queries and, 57
  resources, 57, 60
  uses for, 59
chown command, 96
  AIX, 211
  –R flag, 202
  recursive, 202
chroot command, 167, 171
CIE, 147
class names, 283-284
clean, make target, 224
client-limit (font server), 129, 135
client-only distribution, 189
clients, 3, 13
  application defaults, 285
  chooser, 55, 57-59
  cm, 118;
    font problems, 123-125
  command-line options, 20-23;
    –bg, 23;
    –display, 27-29, 36;
    –fg, 23;
    –fn, 20, 103;
    –geometry, 20-22;
    –iconic, 26;

    –name, 283-284;
    –rv, 23;
    –server (for font server cli-
     ents), 134;
    –xrm, 286
  crtca, 153
  customizing, 20
  DOS-based, 272
  dxcalendar, 117
  fsinfo, 134
  fslsfonts, 135
  getbdf, 112
  InfoExplorer, 117, 121
  Macintosh computers and, 271,
   275
  mre, 145-146
  props, 145-146
  public domain, 247-268;
    compiling, 255-268;
    patching, 259-264
  remote; setting DISPLAY for,
   36;
    starting, 34-36
  resize, 31-33
  resources, 6
  running locally on X terminals,
   161
  xarchie, 248, 251-259
  xcalc, 14
  xclock, 14, 16
  xcmsdb, 152-153
  xcoloredit, 145-146
  xcolors, 144
  xconsole, 26, 62
  xdpyinfo, 158
  xdvi, 115
  xev, 291-293
  xfd, 103, 108, 115
  xfontsel, 20, 104
  xhost, 28, 35-36, 74-77, 93;
    SUN-DES-1 and, 85, 88-90
  xinit, 81-82
  xkeycaps, 264-268, 291
  xloadimage, 96
  xlsfonts, 20, 103, 108
  xmessage, 33
  xmodmap, 264, 290-293
  xpostit, 14, 249
  xrdb, 24-25, 60-61, 64, 285,
   287-288
  xrolodex, 247
  xrsh, 79
  xsccd, 153

commands (cont'd)
  mkfontdir, 107, 114, 116, 139;
    fonts.scale, 107
  newkey, 86-87
  nm, 226
  nroff, 242
  nslookup, 241
  openwin, 37
  patch, 195, 238
  perl, 81
  pstat, 180
  ranlib, 199
  rexec, 173
  rgb, 146
  rlogin, 34
  rsh, 35-36, 79, 81
  screendump, 96
  screenload, 96
  setenv, 27-28, 30, 134, 149,
    151, 164, 199, 204, 211, 213,
    317
  showrgb, 23, 144
  snftobdf, 112
  startx, 37-38
  strings, 192, 229
  swapon, 180-181
  tail, 197
  tar, 238, 252
  tbl, 242
  telnet, 164, 248
  trace, 286
  truss, 286
  tset, 31
  uname, 192
  uncompress, 238, 242
  unshar, 262
  uudecode, 195, 236, 238
  uuencode, 195, 238
  wait, 26
  X, 16, 38, 53
  xauth, 36, 79-83, 93;
    SUN-DES-1 and, 89;
    using with xinit, 81-82
  xinit, 16, 25, 37-38
  xmkmf, 214-215, 256, 266
  xrsh, 36, 79
  ypbind, 87
  ypmatch, 85-86, 240
  ypwhich, 86, 240
  zcat, 238, 242, 252
comments, ! (exclamation point),
  282
  # (hash sign), 128, 219

/**/ (null comment), 219
  in font server configuration file,
    128
  in imake files, 219
  in resource definitions, 282, 287
  in Xservers file, 55
  XCOMM, 220
commercial clients, FrameMaker,
  65, 159
  zmail, 33
Communications Toolbox (Macintosh computers), 276-277
Compat.list file, 109, 126
compiling sources, 255-268
  porting hints, 226-230
compress command, 112
compressed files, 236, 238, 242
  fonts and, 107, 112-113
CompuServe, 235
comp.windows.x, 157, 187, 189,
  233, 250
  FAQ, 234-237, 250
config file (font server), 128-130,
  139
configuration files, app-defaults
    files, 258
  .cshrc, 29-30, 33-34, 36
  /etc/hosts.equiv, 81;
    Secure RPC and, 86, 90
  /etc/syslog.conf, 169
  /etc/Xn.hosts, 74-75, 82
  for font server, 128-131
  imake, 222
  .login, 33-34
  on remote system, 35-36
  .profile, 29-30, 36
  .rhosts, 35, 81;
    Secure RPC and, 86, 90
  shell environment, 27-36
  startup script, 25-26
  syslog, 169
  system.twmrc, 18
  twm, 15, 18-19
  .twmrc, 15, 19
  user environment, 14
  X session, 14
  X terminals, 161, 175-178
  .Xdefaults, 286-287
  .Xdefaults-hostname, 285
  xdm, 46-66;
    installing, 206;
    rereading, 52, 55, 59, 67-68;
    Xaccess, 55-59, 164, 174;

error messages (cont'd)

I

IBM Token Ring, 162
ibm.cf, 211
–iconic option, 26
iconifying windows, 19
#ifdef command (cpp), 218
#ifndef command (cpp), 218
imake, 216-225, 254, 256
   additional documentation for, 230
   .cf files, 222
   comments in, 219
   Concat macro, 222
   Concat3 macro, 222
   concatenating macros, 221-222
   configuration files, 222-223
   flags; BuildServer, 210, 212;
     DefaultCCOptions, 210-211;
     ExpandManNames, 207;
     HasLargeTmp, 199, 207;
     HasXdmAuth, 207;
     InstallCmd, 211;
     InstallFSConfig, 207;
     InstallLibManPages, 207;
     InstallXdmConfig, 206;
     InstallXinitConfig, 206;
     ProjectRoot, 198, 207-208;
     StripInstalledPrograms, 207
   function of, 217
   multi-line macros in, 220
   .rules files, 222
   syntax, 219-222
   .tmpl files, 222
   UseInstalled flag, 215
   XCOMM command, 220
   xmkmf, 214
Imakefile, 214
   editing, 254-255
Imake.rules, 223
Imake.tmpl, 223, 254
include files, (see header files)
includes, make target, 215, 224
indirect queries, 55, 57-59
   chooser client and, 57
   X terminals and, 173
inetd daemon, 88, 167
   errors, 169
   rereading inetd.conf, 88
   SIGHUP and, 88, 168
InfoExplorer client, 117
   fonts, 121
init program, 44

install, make target, 198, 225
InstallCmd build flag, 211
InstallFSConfig build flag, 128, 207
installing X, 8, 185-230
   DES code, 207
   disk space, 191, 198-200
   from MIT sources, 185-186
   in alternate location, 207
   link trees, 196-197
   manpages, 207
   NFS-mounted systems, 201-203
   preparation, 191-197
   unprivileged, 201-203
   using rdist, 203
   vendor-supplied, 185-187
   (see also building X.)
InstallLibManPages build flag, 207
install.man, make target, 198, 225
install.sh, 211
InstallXdmConfig build flag, 206
InstallXinitConfig build flag, 206
instance names, 283-284
Inter-Client Communication Conventions, 7
Interprocess Communication, (see IPC)
IP addresses, 168-169, 242
   adding to hosts database, 239-240
   converting hostnames to, 240
   finding with nslookup, 241
   getting with BOOTP, 165-166
   getting with RARP, 165
   in display name, 28
   name server and, 169
   X terminals and, 164
   xhost and, 76
IPC, 97
   connecting via, 28
IRIX, 185, 187
   fonts, 111
   installing font server on, 132-133
   installing xdm on, 70
ISO (International Standards Organization), 102

About the Authors

Linda Mui started working for O'Reilly & Associates in 1986. She was first hired as a production assistant, later became an apprentice system administrator, and is now a writer. Her first writing job was for *termcap and terminfo*, which she co-authored with John Strang and Tim O'Reilly. She also wrote *Pick BASIC*, on programming applications for Pick systems. In between writing jobs, Linda works on *troff* macros and tools for the O'Reilly & Associates production staff.

Linda was raised in the Bronx, New York and now lives in Cambridge, Massachusetts. Lately she has been trying to improve herself by learning how to swim, play billiards, and accessorize.

Eric Pearce is an author and technical resource for O'Reilly & Associates. In addition to co-authoring this book, he is also responsible for developing CD-ROM companion disks for books produced by O'Reilly & Associates. Eric's interests include promoting public domain software, Internet connectivity, and network services.

Before coming to work for O'Reilly & Associates, Eric worked as a systems programmer for Boston University, which he also attended as a student. His favorite activities include bicycling, snowboarding, rock climbing, and dangerous sports.

BOOKS *from*

O'Reilly & Associates, Inc.

FALL / WINTER 1995-96

"For programmers and people who like to understand the full gory detail of how things work, I must recommend the O'Reilly series of X books."

—Peter Collinson, *SunExpert*

The X Window System in a Nutshell

Edited by Ellie Cutler, Daniel Gilly & Tim O'Reilly
2nd Edition April 1992
424 pages, ISBN 1-56592-017-1

Indispensable companion to the X Window System series. Experienced X programmers can use this single-volume desktop companion for most common questions, keeping the full series of manuals for detailed reference. This book has been updated to cover R5, but is still useful for R4.

"If you have a notebook computer and write X code while backpacking the Pennine Way or flying the Atlantic, this is the one for you!"
— *Sun UK User*

X User Tools

By Linda Mui & Valerie Quercia
1st Edition November 1994
856 pages, ISBN 1-56592-019-8

X User Tools provides for X users what *UNIX Power Tools* provides for UNIX users: hundreds of tips, tricks, scripts, techniques, and programs—plus a CD-ROM—to make the X Window System more enjoyable, more powerful, and easier to use. This browser's book emphasizes useful programs culled from the network, offers tips for configuring individual and systemwide environments, and incudes a CD-ROM of source files for all—and binary files for some—of the programs.

FOR INFORMATION: **800-998-9938**, 707-829-0515; **INFO@ORA.COM**; **HTTP://WWW.ORA.COM/**

The X Window System Series

When it comes to X, think of these books as the ultimate owner's manuals. Because of its power and flexibility, X is also extremely complex. We help you sort through that complexity with books that show you, step-by-step, how to use, program, and administer the X Window System.

Programmer's Supplement for Release 6

Edited by Adrian Nye
1st Edition September 1995
452 pages, ISBN 1-56592-089-9

This book is for programmers who are familiar with Release 5 of the X Window System and who want to know how to use the new features of Release 6. Intended as an update for owners of Volumes 1, 2, 4, and 5 of the X Window System series, it provides complete tutorial and reference information to all new Xlib and Xt toolkit functions.

The book includes:

- An overview of the R6 changes as they affect application programming

- Preparing applications for Session Management

- New Xt features, including session management, signal handling, and C++ support

- Creating multithreaded X applications

- Using transformed (rotated, scaled, or obliqued) fonts

- Internationalizing X applications

- An introduction to the X Image extension

- Reference pages for all new Xlib and Xt functions

Together with Volumes 2 and 5, owners of the *Programmer's Supplement for Release 6* have a complete set of reference pages for the current X Consortium standards for Xlib and Xt.

The X Companion CD for R6

By O'Reilly & Associates
1st Edition January 1995
(Includes CD-ROM plus 126-page guide)
ISBN 1-56592-084-8

Our new X11 R6 CD-ROM, a companion to our *X Window System Administrator's Guide* (Volume 8 of the X Window series), is a helpful resource for system administrators and programmers alike.

The CD-ROM contains:

- Precompiled binaries for X11, Release 6 (X11 R6) for the following platforms: Sun4, Solaris, HP-UX on the HP700, DEC Alpha, DEC ULTRIX, and IBM RS6000

- X11 R6 source code from the 'core' and 'contrib' directories

- X11 R5 source code from the 'core' directory

- Examples from O'Reilly and Associates X Window System series books and *The X Resource* journal

The package includes a 126-page book describing the contents of the CD-ROM, how to install the R6 binaries, and how to build X11 for other platforms. The book also contains the X Consortium release notes for Release 6.

X Protocol Reference Manual

Edited by Adrian Nye
4th Edition January 1995
458 pages, ISBN 1-56592-083-X

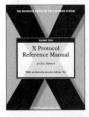

This manual describes the X Network Protocol, which underlies all software for Version 11 of the X Window System. It not only provides a practical demonstration of what is involved in a client session, but also an extensive set of reference pages for each protocol request and event. Reference pages, alphabetized for easy access, include encoding of requests and replies. The fourth edition of *X Protocol Reference Manual* includes protocol clarifications of X11 Release 6 and can be used with any release of X. Note: This edition does not contain the Inter-Client Communication Conventions Manual (ICCCM) or the X Logical Font Description Convention (XLFD). This material will be included in an upcoming O'Reilly book.

Xlib Programming Manual

By Adrian Nye
3rd Edition July 1992
824 pages, ISBN 1-56592-002-3

A complete programming guide to the X library (Xlib), the lowest level of programming interface to X. Covers X11 Release 5. Includes introductions to internationalization, device-independent color, font service, and scalable fonts.

Xlib Reference Manual

By Adrian Nye
3rd Edition June 1992
1138 pages, ISBN 1-56592-006-6

Complete reference guide to the X library (Xlib), the lowest level of programming interface to X. Covers X11 R4 and R5.

X Window System User's Guide

Standard Edition
By Valerie Quercia & Tim O'Reilly
4th Edition May 1993
836 pages, ISBN 1-56592-014-7

Orients the new user to window system concepts and provides detailed tutorials for many client programs, including the *xterm* terminal emulator and window managers. Later chapters explain how to customize the X environment. This popular manual is available in two editions, one for users of the MIT software, one for users of Motif. Revised for X11 Release 5.

X Window System User's Guide

Motif Edition
By Valerie Quercia & Tim O'Reilly
2nd Edition January 1993
956 pages, ISBN 1-56592-015-5

Highlights the Motif window manager and graphical interface, including new features such as tear-off menus and drag-and-drop. Revised for Motif 1.2 and X11 Release 5.

X Toolkit Intrinsics Programming Manual

Standard Edition
By Adrian Nye & Tim O'Reilly
3rd Edition April 1993
567 pages, ISBN 1-56592-003-1

A complete guide to programming with Xt Intrinsics, the library of C language routines that facilitates the design of user interfaces with reusable components called widgets. Available in two editions. The *Standard Edition* uses Athena widgets in examples; the *Motif Edition* uses Motif widgets.

X Toolkit Intrinsics Programming Manual

Motif Edition
By Adrian Nye & Tim O'Reilly
2nd Edition August 1992
674 pages, ISBN 1-56592-013-9

The *Motif Edition* of Volume 4 uses the Motif 1.2 widget set in examples and covers X11 Release 5.

X Toolkit Intrinsics Reference Manual

Edited by David Flanagan
3rd Edition April 1992
916 pages, ISBN 1-56592-007-4

Complete programmer's reference for the X Toolkit, providing reference pages for each of the Xt functions, as well as the widget classes defined by Xt and the Athena widgets. This third edition has been reorganized and expanded for X11 Release 5.

Motif Programming Manual

By Dan Heller, Paula Ferguson & David Brennan
2nd Edition February 1994
1016 pages, ISBN 1-56592-016-3

A source for complete, accurate, and insightful guidance on Motif application programming. In addition to information on Motif, the book is full of tips about programming in general and about user-interface design. It includes material on using UIL, drag-and-drop, and tear-off menus and covers Motif Release 1.2 (while remaining usable with Motif 1.1). Complements Volume 6B, *Motif Reference Manual*.

Motif Reference Manual

By Paula Ferguson & David Brennan
1st Edition June 1993
920 pages, ISBN 1-56592-038-4

A complete programmer's reference for the Motif toolkit. This book provides reference pages for the Motif functions and macros, the Motif and Xt widget classes, the Mrm functions, the Motif clients, and the UIL file format, data types, and functions. The reference material has been expanded from the appendices of the first edition of Volume 6 and covers Motif 1.2. This manual is a companion to Volume 6A, *Motif Programming Manual*.

Volume 6C: Motif Tools

By David Flanagan
1st Edition August 1994
1024 pages (CD-ROM included), ISBN 1-56592-044-9

Motif Tools and the Xmt programming library that accompanies it on CD-ROM offer resources that will empower Motif programmers and dramatically speed up application development with the X Toolkit and Motif.

While the book is a complete programmer's guide and reference manual for the Xmt library, it is not just a dry volume about programming mechanics; it also describes a holistic philosophy of development of a complete application, from first conception, through design and implementation, and on to the finishing stylistic touches.

The author writes: "The need for a convenience toolkit is something that not enough programmers and managers realize; Motif is too often viewed as a complete GUI development package, when in fact it was designed only to provide a standard base level of functionality. My aim was to put programmer ease-of-use first and create a library that really simplifies GUI development."

X Window System Administrator's Guide

By Linda Mui & Eric Pearce
1st Edition October 1992
372 pages, ISBN 0-937175-83-8

This book is the first and only book devoted to the issues of system administration for X and X-based networks, written not just for UNIX system administrators, but for anyone faced with the job of administering X (including those running X on stand-alone workstations). Note: The CD that used to be offered with this book is now sold separately, (*The X Companion CD for R6*), allowing system administrators to purchase the book and the CD-ROM in quantities they choose.

"For...those system administrators wanting to set up X11 for the first time, this is the book for you. As an easy-to-use guide covering X administration, it doesn't get bogged down in too much detail.... This is not a book for bedtime reading or to generate an all-consuming interest in X windows, but a thoroughly good text to help you over the first hurdle or two." —*Sun UK User*

Volume 9: X Window Programming Extensions

Edited by Adrian Nye
1st Edition January 1996 (est.)
500 pages (est.), ISBN 1-56592-133-X

X Window Programming Extensions contains complete tutorial and reference documentation for several X Consortium standard extensions and conventions and utility libraries. Many of these are new in Release 6 or have been standardized since Release 6.

These extensions have become common in commercial X servers, providing opportunities for programmers to include powerful features in their applications. For example, the Shape extension lets programmers use round or arbitrarily shaped windows, instead of just rectangles.

X Window Programming Extensions covers the Session Manager, InterClient Exchange (ICE), Xmu (miscellaneous utilities), and XPM (pixmap file) libraries, as well as ICCCM (interclient communication conventions) and XLFD (font naming) specifications. It also includes the following extensions: Shape (non-rectangular windows); Input (nonstandard input devices like spaceballs); Double-Buffering (animation); Synchronization (multimedia, games); X Test (event simulation, demos); Shared Memory (imaging performance); Record (capture events); and Image (imaging).

In short, *X Window Programming Extensions* is essential to complete the documentation set of any X programmer.

The X Resource Journal

The X Resource, *a quarterly working journal for X programmers, provides practical, timely information about the programming, administration, and use of the X Window System.* The X Resource *is the official publisher of the X Consortium Technical Conference Proceedings.*

"*The X Resource* is the only journal that I have ever come across which has a permanent place for every issue among the 'reference books in use' on my desk."

—*John Wexler,*
Computing Services, Edinburgh University

"I find the journal invaluable. It provides in-depth coverage of topics that are poorly documented elsewhere, or not documented at all."

—*Peter Nicklin,*
Vice President R&D, Version Technology

The X Resource: Issue 15

Edited by Paula Ferguson
Summer 1995
174 pages, ISBN 1-56592-140-2

Articles for Issue 15 include:
- The X User: XScript-Shell Programming with X, by Jan Newmarch
- Best of Netnews, edited by Marc Albert
- Simplifying GUI Construction by Embedded Scripting, by Lawrence A. Stabile
- X over the Web, by Daniel Dardailler
- A Korean Environment for the X Window System, by Jinsoo Yoon, Yanghee Yoon, Sunghun Park, and Kilnam Chon
- The X11 Testing Extension: Tutorial and Reference, by Martha Zimet

The X Resource: Issue 14

Edited by Paula Ferguson
Spring 1995
208 pages, ISBN 1-56592-122-4

Articles for Issue 14 include:
- WILLOW: The Washington Information Looker-Upper Layered Over Windows
- Tickling Fvwm: Extending Tk as an Fvwm Module
- The Knvas Widget: A 2D Graphics Framework
- Koalatalk: An ICE-based Lightweight Message Bus
- Hush: A C++ API for Tcl/Tk

The X Resource: Issue 13

Edited by Paula Ferguson
Winter 1995
308 pages, ISBN 1-56592-121-6

Articles for Issue 13, taken from the 9th Annual X Technical Conference, include:
- Help! There's a Spy in My Code
- Embedding of X Applications
- OpenDoc and Its Architecture
- A Pseudo-Root Extension: X Window System Nesting on a Budget
- Common Desktop Environment Architectural Overview
- The X Public Access Mechanism: Software Cooperation for Space Science and Beyond
- A Remote Access Protocol for the X Window System

The X Resource: Issue 12

Edited by Paula Ferguson
Fall 1994
222 pages, ISBN 1-56592-069-4

Articles for Issue 12 include:
- The XPM Format and Library: A Tutorial and Reference
- The Xmsg Library: An Application-Level Message-Reporting Facility
- Event-Free Structured Graphics in the X Environment
- An Object-oriented Approach to Motif 1.2 Drag and Drop
- The X Administrator: Configuration and Administration of a Scalable X-based UNIX Service

Issues 0 (Fall 1991) through 11(Summer 1994) are also available.
The last issue of the X Resource Journal will be Issue 16 (Winter 1996).

At Your Fingertips—

A COMPLETE GUIDE TO O'REILLY'S ONLINE SERVICES

O'Reilly & Associates offers extensive product and customer service information online. We invite you to come and explore our little neck-of-the-woods.

For product information and insight into new technologies, visit the O'Reilly Resource Center

Most comprehensive among our online offerings is the O'Reilly Resource Center. You'll find detailed information on all O'Reilly products, including titles, prices, tables of contents, indexes, author bios, software contents, and reviews. You can also view images of all our products. In addition, watch for informative articles that provide perspective on the technologies we write about. Interviews, excerpts, and bibliographies are also included.

After browsing online, it's easy to order, too, with GNN Direct or by sending email to **order@ora.com**. The O'Reilly Resource Center shows you how. Here's how to visit us online:

☞ *Via the World Wide Web*

If you are connected to the Internet, point your Web browser (e.g., **mosaic, netscape,** or **lynx**) to:

http://www.ora.com/

For the plaintext version, **telnet** to:
www.ora.com (login: **oraweb**)

☞ *Via Gopher*

If you have a Gopher program, our Gopher server has information in a menu format that some people prefer to the Web.

Connect your **gopher** to: **gopher.ora.com**
Or, point your Web browser to:
gopher://gopher.ora.com/

Or, you can **telnet** to: **gopher.ora.com**
(login: **gopher**)

A convenient way to stay informed: email mailing lists

An easy way to learn of the latest projects and products from O'Reilly & Associates is to subscribe to our mailing lists. We have email announcements and discussions on various topics, for example "ora-news," our electronic news service. Subscribers receive email as soon as the information breaks.

☞ *To join a mailing list:*

Send email to:
listproc@online.ora.com

Leave the message "subject" empty if possible.

If you know the name of the mailing list you want to subscribe to, put the following information on the first line of your message: **subscribe** "listname" "your name" **of** "your company."

For example: **subscribe ora-news Kris Webber of Fine Enterprises**

If you don't know the name of the mailing list, listproc will send you a listing of all the mailing lists. Put this word on the first line of the body: **lists**

To find out more about a particular list, send a message with this word as the first line of the body: **info** "listname"

For more information and help, send this message: **help**

For specific help, email to: **listmaster@online.ora.com**

The complete O'Reilly catalog is now available via email

You can now receive a text-only version of our complete catalog via email. It contains detailed information about all our products, so it's mighty big: over 200 kbytes, or 200,000 characters.

To get the whole catalog in one message, send an empty email message to: **catalog@online.ora.com**

If your email system can't handle large messages, you can get the catalog split into smaller messages. Send email to: **catalog-split@online.ora.com**

To receive a print catalog, send your snail mail address to: **catalog@ora.com**

Check out Web Review, our new publication on the Web

Web Review is our new magazine that offers fresh insights into the Web. The editorial mission of Web Review is to answer the question: How and where do you BEST spend your time online? Each issue contains reviews that look at the most interesting and creative sites on the Web. Visit us at **http://gnn.com/wr/**

Web Review is the product of the recently formed Songline Studios, a venture between O'Reilly and America Online.

Get the files you want with FTP

We have an archive of example files from our books, the covers of our books, and much more available by anonymous FTP.

ftp to:

ftp.ora.com (login: **anonymous** – use your email address as the password.)

Or, if you have a WWW browser, point it to:

ftp://ftp.ora.com/

FTPMAIL

The ftpmail service connects to O'Reilly's FTP server and sends the results (the files you want) by email. This service is for people who can't use FTP—but who can use email.

For help and examples, send an email message to:

ftpmail@online.ora.com

(In the message body, put the single word: **help**)

Helpful information is just an email message away

Many customer services are provided via email. Here are a few of the most popular and useful:

info@online.ora.com
For a list of O'Reilly's online customer services.

info@ora.com
For general questions and information.

bookquestions@ora.com
For technical questions, or corrections, concerning book contents.

order@ora.com
To order books online and for ordering questions.

catalog@online.ora.com
To receive an online copy of our catalog.

catalog@ora.com
To receive a free copy of *ora.com*, our combination magazine and catalog. Please include your snail mail address.

international@ora.com
Comments or questions about international ordering or distribution.

xresource@ora.com
To order or inquire about *The X Resource* journal.

proposals@ora.com
To submit book proposals.

info@gnn.com
To receive information about America Online's GNN (Global Network Navigator).™

O'Reilly & Associates, Inc.

103A Morris Street, Sebastopol, CA 95472
Inquiries: **707-829-0515, 800-998-9938**
Credit card orders: **800-889-8969** (Weekdays 6 A.M.- 5 P.M. PST)
FAX: **707-829-0104**

O'Reilly & Associates—
LISTING OF TITLES

INTERNET

CGI Scripting on the World Wide Web
(Winter '95-96 est.)
Connecting to the Internet:
An O'Reilly Buyer's Guide
Getting Connected (Winter '95-96 est.)
HTML Handbook (Winter '95-96 est.)
The Mosaic Handbook for
Microsoft Windows
The Mosaic Handbook for
the Macintosh
The Mosaic Handbook for
the X Window System
Smileys
The USENET Handbook
The Whole Internet User's
Guide & Catalog
The Whole Internet for Windows 95
Web Design for Designers
(Winter '95-96 est.)
The World Wide Web Journal
(Winter '95-96 est.)

SOFTWARE

Internet In A Box ™ Version 2.0
WebSite™ 1.1

WHAT YOU NEED TO KNOW SERIES

Using Email Effectively
Marketing on the Internet
(Winter '95-96 est.)
When You Can't Find Your
System Administrator

HEALTH, CAREER & BUSINESS

Building a Successful Software Business
The Computer User's Survival Guide
Dictionary of Computer Terms
(Winter '95-96 est.)
The Future Does Not Compute
Love Your Job!
TWI Day Calendar - 1996

USING UNIX

BASICS

Learning GNU Emacs
Learning the bash Shell
Learning the Korn Shell
Learning the UNIX Operating System
Learning the vi Editor
MH & xmh: Email for Users &
Programmers
SCO UNIX in a Nutshell
UNIX in a Nutshell: System V Edition
Using and Managing UUCP
(Winter '95-96 est.)
Using csh and tcsh

ADVANCED

Exploring Expect
The Frame Handbook
Learning Perl
Making TeX Work
Programming perl
Running Linux
Running Linux Companion CD-ROM
(Winter '95-96 est.)
sed & awk
UNIX Power Tools (with CD-ROM)

SYSTEM ADMINISTRATION

Building Internet Firewalls
Computer Crime:
A Crimefighter's Handbook
Computer Security Basics
DNS and BIND
Essential System Administration
Linux Network Administrator's Guide
Managing Internet Information Services
Managing NFS and NIS
Managing UUCP and Usenet
Networking Personal Computers
with TCP/IP
Practical UNIX and Internet Security
(Winter '95-96 est.)
PGP: Pretty Good Privacy
sendmail
System Performance Tuning
TCP/IP Network Administration
termcap & terminfo
Volume 8 : X Window System
Administrator's Guide
The X Companion CD for R6

PROGRAMMING

Applying RCS and SCCS
C++: The Core Language
Checking C Programs with lint
DCE Security Programming
Distributing Applications Across DCE
and Windows NT
Encyclopedia of Graphics File Formats
Guide to Writing DCE Applications
High Performance Computing
lex & yacc
Managing Projects with make
Microsoft RPC Programming Guide
Migrating to Fortran 90
Multi-Platform Code Management
ORACLE Performance Tuning
ORACLE PL/SQL Programming
Porting UNIX Software
POSIX Programmer's Guide
POSIX.4: Programming for
the Real World
Power Programming with RPC
Practical C Programming
Practical C++ Programming
Programming with curses
Programming with GNU Software
(Winter '95-96 est.)
Programming with Pthreads
(Winter '95-96 est.)
Software Portability with imake
Understanding and Using COFF
Understanding DCE
Understanding Japanese Information
Processing
UNIX Systems Programming for SVR4
(Winter '95-96 est.)
Using C on the UNIX System

BERKELEY 4.4 SOFTWARE DISTRIBUTION

4.4BSD System Manager's Manual
4.4BSD User's Reference Manual
4.4BSD User's Supplementary Docs.
4.4BSD Programmer's Reference Man.
4.4BSD Programmer's Supp. Docs.
4.4BSD-Lite CD Companion
4.4BSD-Lite CD Companion: Int. Ver.

X PROGRAMMING

THE X WINDOW SYSTEM

Volume 0: X Protocol Reference Manual
Volume 1: Xlib Programming Manual
Volume 2: Xlib Reference Manual
Volume 3: X Window System
User's Guide
Volume. 3M: X Window System
User's Guide, Motif Ed.
Volume. 4: X Toolkit Intrinsics
Programming Manual
Volume 4M: X Toolkit Intrinsics
Programming Manual, Motif Ed.
Volume 5: X Toolkit Intrinsics
Reference Manual
Volume 6A: Motif Programming Man.
Volume 6B: Motif Reference Manual
Volume 6C: Motif Tools
Volume 8 : X Window System
Administrator's Guide
PEXlib Programming Manual
PEXlib Reference Manual
PHIGS Programming Manual
PHIGS Reference Manual
Programmer's Supplement for Release 6
The X Companion CD for R6
X User Tools (with CD-ROM)
The X Window System in a Nutshell

THE X RESOURCE

*A QUARTERLY WORKING JOURNAL
FOR X PROGRAMMERS*

The X Resource: Issues 0 through 15

TRAVEL

Travelers' Tales France
Travelers' Tales Hong Kong (12/95 est.)
Travelers' Tales India
Travelers' Tales Mexico
Travelers' Tales Spain
Travelers' Tales Thailand
Travelers' Tales: A Woman's World

O'Reilly & Associates—
INTERNATIONAL DISTRIBUTORS

Customers outside North America can now order O'Reilly & Associates books through the following distributors. They offer our international customers faster order processing, more bookstores, increased representation at tradeshows worldwide, and the high-quality, responsive service our customers have come to expect.

EUROPE, MIDDLE EAST, AND AFRICA
(except Germany, Switzerland, and Austria)

INQUIRIES
International Thomson Publishing Europe
Berkshire House
168-173 High Holborn
London WC1V 7AA, United Kingdom
Telephone: 44-71-497-1422
Fax: 44-71-497-1426
Email: itpint@itps.co.uk

ORDERS
International Thomson Publishing Services, Ltd.
Cheriton House, North Way
Andover, Hampshire SP10 5BE, United Kingdom
Telephone: 44-264-342-832 (UK orders)
Telephone: 44-264-342-806 (outside UK)
Fax: 44-264-364418 (UK orders)
Fax: 44-264-342761 (outside UK)

GERMANY, SWITZERLAND, AND AUSTRIA

International Thomson Publishing GmbH
O'Reilly-International Thomson Verlag
Königswinterer Straße 418
53227 Bonn, Germany
Telephone: 49-228-97024 0
Fax: 49-228-441342
Email: anfragen@ora.de

ASIA *(except Japan)*
INQUIRIES
International Thomson Publishing Asia
221 Henderson Road
#08-03 Henderson Industrial Park
Singapore 0315
Telephone: 65-272-6496
Fax: 65-272-6498

ORDERS
Telephone: 65-268-7867
Fax: 65-268-6727

JAPAN
O'Reilly & Associates, Inc.
103A Morris Street
Sebastopol, CA 95472 U.S.A.
Telephone: 707-829-0515
Telephone: 800-998-9938 (U.S. & Canada)
Fax: 707-829-0104
Email: order@ora.com

AUSTRALIA
WoodsLane Pty. Ltd.
7/5 Vuko Place, Warriewood NSW 2102
P.O. Box 935, Mona Vale NSW 2103
Australia
Telephone: 02-970-5111
Fax: 02-970-5002
Email: woods@tmx.mhs.oz.au

NEW ZEALAND
WoodsLane New Zealand Ltd.
21 Cooks Street (P.O. Box 575)
Wanganui, New Zealand
Telephone: 64-6-347-6543
Fax: 64-6-345-4840
Email: woods@tmx.mhs.oz.au

THE AMERICAS
O'Reilly & Associates, Inc.
103A Morris Street
Sebastopol, CA 95472 U.S.A.
Telephone: 707-829-0515
Telephone: 800-998-9938 (U.S. & Canada)
Fax: 707-829-0104
Email: order@ora.com